RIVERSIDE COMMUNITY COLLEGE
1916

OPENINGS : ORIGINAL ESSAYS BY
DK 266.4 O64 1990
A10904801001

P9-ECT-139

[redacted]

Sponsored by

Port of Seattle

Edited by ROBERT ATWAN

and VALERI VINOKUROV

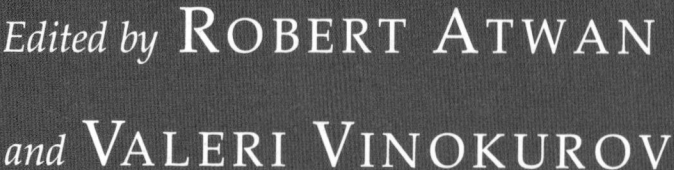

Russian Essays Translated by Dudley Hagen

OPENINGS

Original Essays by Contemporary Soviet and American Writers

UNIVERSITY OF WASHINGTON PRESS *Seattle & London*

Riverside Community College
Library
JUL '92
4800 Magnolia Avenue
Riverside, California 92506

Acknowledgments

The story of how this volume was conceived, developed, and produced would make an interesting book in itself. A unique and pioneering publishing project, it involved the creative talents and cooperative efforts of many individuals and groups from both the Soviet Union and the United States.

The idea of a jointly published United States-Soviet book examining the cultures of the two nations originated when the Arts Festival of the 1990 Seattle Goodwill Games was being planned. The co-chairs of the Arts Festival Committee, Paul Schell and Jane Williams, deserve credit for including the book as part of the festival. Ann Focke did the early work on the proposal. Jarlath Hume, head of the Seattle Organizing Committee responsible for the Arts Festival, established a relationship with the Soviet publisher, Fizkultura i Sport, coordinated the fundraising, and introduced Donald Ellegood of the University of Washington Press and Robert Atwan to their Soviet counterparts. Others from the Organizing Committee who offered invaluable assistance were the committee's president Bob Walsh; special projects coordinator Katya Garrow; and the administrative assistant for community relations Beth Horowitz. Layla Makhmutova Hagen was very helpful in organizing discussions between the American and Soviet writers and publishers in Moscow, Seattle, and New York City.

Special appreciation is extended to the families of Nan and Doug Little and Pam and Don Tufts, who hosted the Soviet editorial staff while they worked on the book in Seattle. Nina Alexandrovna Walsh facilitated the work in Seattle between the staffs of Fizkultura i Sport and the University of Washington Press.

The book was made possible through the assistance of the United States Information Agency, and we are appreciative of Raymond Harvey's coordination of the project. The Burlington Northern Foundation under the direction of Don North also provided support at a critical point. Jim Dwyer gave the project leadership.

Donald Ellegood and Robert Atwan would also like to thank several people who helped unofficially in various ways at different stages of the project: Annie Dillard, Joan Kerr, Cathy Young, Jane Bobko, Charles O'Neill, Gerald Freund, Beth Ann McCabe, Norm Langill, Leith Gaines, Guada Castro, Lorraine Jenson, and Helene Atwan. Mr. Atwan also received valuable assistance from the McLaughlin Library at Seton Hall University.

Publication of the book was made possible through generous support of the Port of Seattle, and we extend special thanks to its commissioners: Patricia Davis, president; Jack Block; Gary Grant; Paige Miller; Paul Schell; and Zeger van Asch van Wijck, executive director.

SPONSORED BY THE PORT OF SEATTLE

Introduction by Robert Atwan and English translations of Russian essays copyright © 1990 by the University of Washington Press
"In Search of a New American Past" copyright © 1990 by Geoffrey C. Ward
"The American Geographies" copyright © 1990 by Barry Lopez
"Art in America" copyright © 1990 by Eleanor Munro
"American Literary Culture: A Personal Perspective" copyright © 1990 by Joyce Carol Oates
"Technology in America" copyright © 1990 by Elting E. Morison
"House of Ruth, House of Robinson: Some Observations on Baseball, Biography, and the American Myth" copyright © 1990 by Gerald Early
"Living Souls" copyright © 1990 by Scott Russell Sanders

Edited by Valeri Shteinbakh, Julidta Tarver, and Gretchen Van Meter
Designed by Aleksandr Litvinenko and Veronica Seyd
Picture editing (USA) by Elizabeth Meryman and Laurie Platt Winfrey of Carousel Research, Inc., New York
Production supervision by Veronica Seyd
Jacket design by Audrey Meyer
Composition by University of Washington Department of Printing, Seattle
Preparation of camera copy by Corinna Campbell
Printing and binding by Toppan Printing Co., Tokyo, Japan

Published simultaneously in Russian by Fizkultura i Sport, Moscow

All rights reserved. No portion of this publication may be reproduced or transmitted in any form or by any means, electronic or mechanical, including photocopying, recording, or any information storage or retrieval system, without permission in writing from the publisher.

Library of Congress Cataloging-in-Publication Data

Openings : original essays by contemporary Soviet and American writers edited by Robert Atwan and Valeri Vinokurov; Russian essays translated by Dudley Hagen.
p. cm.
ISBN 0-295-96968-7
1. Soviet Union—Civilization—1917– 2. United States—Civilization—20th century. I. Atwan, Robert. II. Vinokurov, Valeri.
[DK266.4.064 1990]
947.08—dc20 89-49585
CIP

The paper used in this publication meets the minimum requirements of American National Standard for Information Sciences—Permanence of Paper for Printed Library Materials, ANSI Z39.48–1984.
∞

Title page photographs: *Seattle*, photograph by Will Landon; *Moscow*, photograph by Vassily Mishin.

Jacket illustration: Wassily Kandinski, *Improvisation*

Contents

Introduction

ROBERT ATWAN

When I was a boy growing up in Paterson, New Jersey, in the early 1950s, I took the Cold War quite literally. Night after night I'd go to bed dressed warmly and wearing thick wool socks. For who knew? I might suddenly be awakened in the middle of the night by Soviet troops—I vividly pictured their ruddy faces and furry earmuffed hats—ordering me out of bed and prodding me with rifle butts into a long forced march. I had seen movies where such things happened. At least I'd be prepared.

These nighttime fears were fueled by frequent daytime air raid drills. A siren would suddenly blast and—"Class, take cover!"—all of us sixth graders would crouch down on our knees and seek shelter beneath our desks. Another drill or the real thing? Hands clasped across my head, I waited for the explosion that would destroy my nation, my city, my school, my family, myself. I had seen the newsreels. I knew what rubble looked like.

No wonder at mass on that March morning in 1953, though I dutifully said a prayer for the soul of Joseph Stalin, I secretly rejoiced that he was finally gone. With a twelve-year-old's naivete I thought my Cold War would now be over.

These childhood memories all returned to me as I walked about Moscow in the exciting spring of 1988. For the first time in my life, despite all the thaws, detentes, and summit meetings, I thought that the awful tensions between our countries might be drawing to a close. Whoever was ultimately to blame for engineering the East-West crisis and its frightening arms race—whether American hard-liners or Kremlin hard-liners—four decades of tension had surely taken their toll on the spirits of both peoples. I realized that political mistrust and suspicion may linger for a long time, but as I rambled through Moscow wearing my medal of a butterfly with Soviet and American wings, I also began to realize (though this is an unpopular thing to say at a time when we look for political solutions to every problem) that in the long run culture is a more powerful force than politics. This may be why so many twentieth-century political leaders have shown such hostility to culture. When they hear the word, do they always want to pull out their revolvers?

I grew up reading translations of Russian writers in cheap editions, novels and short stories mostly. I was flunked out ("gigged" we called it) of college military training when, having skipped drill one cold morning, I was caught hiding in the back of a friend's car reading *Crime and Punishment*. I was so engrossed I didn't even see the officers coming. A year before that, in Catholic high school, I had angered our pastor when he found me at Good Friday services deep into *The Brothers Karamazov*. I had taken the black cover off a prayer book and used it to disguise my paperback Dostoevsky. I don't know what tipped off the priest; it must have been my profound religious concentration. These books and many others over the years introduced me to the Russian people, their personalities, their culture, their soul. Walking the avenues of Moscow, I felt curiously at home. At best, politics can make us allies; but culture—books, art, music, dance, games, sport—can make us friends.

Friendship is what this volume is about. When Donald Ellegood, the director of the University of Washington Press, and I went to Moscow for meetings with the publisher and editors of Fizkultura i Sport, our agenda was to work out the plans for a book commissioned by the Seattle Goodwill Games of 1990. *Openings*—one of the major undertakings of the Goodwill Arts Festival associated with the Seattle Games—represents a unique cultural endeavor. Though several excellent joint anthologies and specialized books of scholarship have by now appeared, this is the first time that Soviet and American publishers have cooperated so extensively to commission a book featuring original work by outstanding writers from each nation. I should add that, in its rich inclusion of fine art and photography, this may also be the most graphically ambitious of all U.S.–Soviet joint publications to date. At our meetings—both in Moscow and Seattle—we expressed our mutual hope that this book would open up a new intellectual dialogue between our countries.

Here is how the book works. We agreed in Moscow that we should cover seven main areas of culture and society—history, geography, the arts, literature, science, sport, and everyday life. We then invited writers to contribute essays on each of these topics. I should point out a few things. There were no ground rules other than topic and length requirements. Rather than list certain points each writer should cover, we decided to invite the writers to handle their topics—history, science, sport, and so on—however they saw fit. We cared less about uniformity than spontaneity; we wanted to see how some of the outstanding writers, journalists, and critics from our two countries currently assess their respective cultures. No contributor, I should add, knew how his or her topic was being handled by the other side.

Openings is therefore three books in one. And it can be read in three interesting ways: as a commentary by American writers on their present culture and society; as a separate commentary by Soviet writers on theirs; and, most significantly, as a series of parallel essays counterpointing the various ways Soviet and American writers view similar themes and topics. Though the writers worked without knowing how their foreign counterparts were proceeding, the essays nonetheless show many surprising juxtapositions. Both of us clearly share many of the same anxieties—we are worried about our endangered natural environments, the erosion of historical consciousness in our young people, the alienation of our ethnic populations, our uncontrolled technologies. Running beneath these parallel concerns we can see yet another theme, one that is harder to put a finger on but that is felt in the book's totality; our anxiety about the endurance of culture in a world of power. These fourteen essays, the entire 1990 Arts Festival in Seattle, and the overarching concept of the Goodwill Games are dedicated to the spirit of cultural exchange, to the grand opening of a new era of friendship and good will.

"You Russians and we Americans!" Walt Whitman once wrote. "Our countries so distant, so unlike at first glance—such a difference in social and political conditions . . . and yet in certain features, and vastest ones, so resembling each other." Whitman wrote those words over one hundred years ago and they seem as appropriate today as they did then. Perhaps even more so.

Introduction

VALERI VINOKUROV

I write these lines several months before the publication of *Openings,* but already I imagine the book in my hands. It is so right, so logical that this book should appear on the eve of the Goodwill Games—nominally a sporting event, but in essence going far beyond sport; an event of singular social, cultural, political, and human significance. If by *goodwill* we mean all that—and how could it be otherwise?—then the publication of these essays at this time must seem right and logical.

True, the road from *Openings'* conception to the book you now hold was not as smooth as it might seem. The idea was indeed simple: to invite Soviet and American authors to appear together in a single volume, thereby demonstrating mutual understanding and goodwill; to have them tell readers about their countries, their cultures, traditions, interests, and everyday life. But what shape should this take? What historical periods should be included? And what should the two groups of authors write about: the interrelations of our two cultures, or different periods and approaches in our relations, or the similarities and differences in our traditions and views over—let us say—two centuries? One road had to be chosen from numerous possibilities.

I remember the hours of conversation on this topic, including many people, especially the Soviet and American editors: Jarlath Hume, vice-president of the Goodwill Games Organizing Committee; Vassily Zhiltsov, director of the publishing house Fizkultura i Sport; and Donald Ellegood, director of the University of Washington Press. Everybody liked the idea right away, but it took a long time to find the single road we finally chose. By now, of course, it is impossible to reconstruct who first hit upon the precise formula.

In the end we decided to make self-examination the book's key idea—self-examination by society, but expressed in the perception of a particular theme by each author as an individual. How does today's society look at history, geography, art, literature, science, and sport? What is their place in the life of society? It was not by a sociological survey, I repeat, that we would seek the answers to these questions, but through the authors' individual perceptions. And then it was natural that the book's final, seventh chapter should look at the place that each of these six aspects of society occupies in the life of a single, more-or-less typical American and Soviet family. The answer to this last question was sought by an American author visiting with a Soviet family, and a Soviet visiting with an American family. And what they sought, of course, was not a sampling. Rather, they wanted genuine insight into a new reality. They wanted to understand, to serve as representatives for readers at home.

And now the book is in the hands of readers in America and Russia. It is not my intention to interpose as some sort of guide to what you will find here. There are a few things, however, that I think should be explained. First, the authors did not intend to write exhaustive accounts. Indeed, how could one essay take in the breadth and depth of the historical development, the scientific achievements, or the geographical diversity of a great country? What account could be given of art or sport, both so multifaceted and limitless? And so the authors chose what was closest to them, what they saw as most important or typical. They went looking for the living soul of a society. And I think that through the branches so carefully sketched by these authors, readers will be able to make out the sky unaided, especially since our readers' acquaintance with one another certainly will not begin with this book. We have known each other a long while, and rather well at that. In the past few years, moreover, we have come to know each other better and better as we come closer together.

The individual and distinctive approach is also apparent in the illustrations to each chapter. The American essay on literature, for example, is illustrated with portraits of contemporary authors, while its Soviet counterpart features mostly portraits of our greatest authors from the past. Perhaps, too, that makes a kind of sense. In the last few years—and this is a major point made by Aleksandr Mulyarchik in his literature essay—we Russians have begun to regard our literature as an integral whole, not to be divided by historical or geographical borders, by political views, or by where the writers lived. The photographs illustrating the American essay on sport should probably be interpreted along the same lines. The subject there is baseball, America's most characteristic sport, but for us something totally new—although it bears some likeness to our Russian *lapta*.

Reading through the essays by American and Soviet authors, I cannot help feeling that the Americans convey greater well-being, self-confidence, and social calm, whereas the Soviets seem more critical, often sorely dissatisfied and uneasy about society's future. Let us ask openly, however: Is there anything surprising about that? From time to time, don't we wonder why, in various spheres of production and the life of society, we are less well off than the Americans? And if our American colleagues have been silent about certain of their problems, might it not be because no one has ever kept them from speaking and writing about what is painful and bitter? It is only with the advent of *perestroika* and *glasnost*—words already needing no translation into English—that we have received the opportunity to speak out.

Let us also remember, by the way, that speaking or writing is not always the same as thinking. Among these Soviet authors, there is none who used to think otherwise than he or she does today. Our authors, perhaps, had no chance to say and write what they felt. They had to use whispers, shadings. This was not our fault, but our misfortune—a misfortune that has now, I believe, passed away from us forever.

The book is called *Openings*. To open is to discover, to disclose. In disclosing ourselves to ourselves, we also discover each other. Still, we do not want to claim to be first discoverers! That would be untrue. However impenetrable the iron curtains of different varieties seemed to the rulers and politicians, however low the mercury dropped in the Cold War, we always knew a good deal about America and Americans. And some of them, I feel sure, were not so ignorant about us. Think what we might about the rulers and politicians, in the nineteenth century—and even more so in the twentieth—our two great nations looked at each other with respect, interest, sympathy, and sometimes compassion, because we were able to distinguish the interests and character of ordinary people from those of the high and mighty. I am confident that, among the authors of this book, there is none who used to denigrate the other side because that was how the wind was blowing, and who has only now "seen the light" of *perestroika*. I mention this because I know many such among my fellow countrymen, just as I know many Americans I never trusted before, and do not now. I think of this book as an antidote to all the poison they have ever spread.

History

GEOFFREY C. WARD is the author of *Before the Trumpet: Young Franklin Roosevelt 1882–1905* and *A First-Class Temperament: The Emergence of Franklin Roosevelt*, which won the National Book Critics Circle Award in 1990. His most recent book is *The Civil War: An Illustrated History*. A former editor of *American Heritage* magazine, for which he writes a regular column on history and biography, "The Life and Times," he also writes documentary films for public television and contributes articles and reviews to many magazines. He is currently at work on two books about India, where he spent part of his boyhood, *Return Passage* and *Tiger-Wallahs*.

YURI NAGIBIN has written numerous stories, novellas, and books of literary criticism as well as several screenplays, including his memorable *The Chairman* and a film in progress on Rakhmaninov. A veteran of World War II, Nagibin titled his 1943 debut collection of stories *The Man from the Front. The Great Heart* and *Two Forces* followed. His novellas include *Happiness Hard Won; Pages from the Life of Trubnikov; Far from War; The Kingdom of Women; The Peak of Success; The Stern Man's Day; One to One;* and *Arise and Go.* Nagibin is an accomplished critic of the arts, and his essays appear frequently in periodicals. His books of literary criticism include *Thoughts on the Story, Literary Reflections,* and *Not Anothers' Craft. Time to Live* is a wide-ranging collection of essays on the arts and the history of Moscow and Russia.

In Search of a New American Past

Geoffrey C. Ward

Shortly after dawn one morning several years ago, my wife and I found ourselves being rowed along the Benares ghats by an elderly boatman. As we skirted that astonishing riverfront, coppery in the early light and lined with canted temples and decaying palaces and crowded with bathers cleansing themselves of sin, the old man asked me where I came from.

"Amr*ee*ka," I said, that being how it is most often pronounced in India.

"Ah," he smiled, "Link-own. Link-own."

I was puzzled. He clearly was, too. Didn't I know the name of the greatest man from my country?

He said it again, slowly this time. *"Ah-bram* Link-own."

I got it. Abraham Lincoln. We both smiled.

"Link-own and Mahatma Gandhi same," the boatman said, leaning into his oars. "Both great souls. Both very poor."

And so, as our boat moved slowly up the river and back again, the air around us filled with the sounds of bells and Sanskrit prayers and the rhythmic creaking of the oars, we talked of Abraham Lincoln. Of his lowly birth—in a mud-walled village, the boatman insisted (the sturdy logs of Thomas Lincoln's cabin would have seemed luxurious in his birthplace)—of his rise to prosperity and power, of the curious civilization that had somehow permitted a mere villager to climb so high, and of his freeing of the slaves.

How the boatman had ever learned of Lincoln in the teeming streets of his city, I do not know. But Lincoln's example clearly meant something important to this man, tied to the same waterfront his father and grandfather and their ancestors had worked since the earliest days of this oldest city on earth (or so he said), the same waterfront his own sons and their sons were already working.

Compared with India, of course, the United States is impossibly young. When my grandmother was a little girl, she was allowed to sit on the lap of Buffalo Bill. Buffalo Bill's grandfather fought in the American Revolution. That brief span encompasses all the U.S. history there is. Yet it is astonishing how little of it most Americans now seem to know.

This is not a new complaint. Moses Coit Tyler, who would soon become the very first professor of American history at an American college or university, lodged it succinctly more than a century ago: "Who shall explain the odd contradiction in our national habits of furiously boasting of American history, and steadily refusing to know anything about it?"

Students of my generation were expected to know *something* about it, though much of what we thought we knew was wrong, and most of it was superficial. The historian Bernard A. Weisberger has likened the American history taught to students of his generation and mine to a vast imaginary mural, "The Story of America," teeming with

Abraham Lincoln, 1858.

W. G. Read, *Teddy's Rough Riders.*

familiar events, all of them uplifting: The Pilgrims coming ashore, miraculously dryshod; barefoot patriots in the snow at Valley Forge; Old Ironsides and Lewis and Clark and the forty-niners; Lincoln at Gettysburg and Theodore Roosevelt at San Juan Hill; the driving of the golden spike; the Wright brothers' first flight; the Empire State Building.

We know now that the old history mural suffered from all the weaknesses of that art form: comic-book colors, overdrawn heroes and caricatured villains, exaggerated gestures and grotesque oversimplifications. It told an all-white, mostly male story of a country beset by few contradictions and with no doubts whatsoever about its virtues or its future.

But it did *tell* a story, traced an extraordinary adventure in which we all could feel we fit somewhere. That mural has been allowed to fade in recent years, and nothing has yet replaced it on the surface of our common consciousness. More than half of today's high school students now study no American history at all. (Still fewer study world history.) And it does not seem to make much difference if they do. A recent national sampling of seventeen-year-olds, most of whom were enrolled in history classes, found that a third did not know in what century Columbus sailed from Spain or when the Declaration of Independence was signed. Two-thirds did not know within fifty years when the Civil War or World War I were fought. Half did not recognize the names of Winston Churchill or Joseph Stalin.

What has happened?

No new nation was ever launched with more noisy confidence than ours. We saw ourselves as the fortunate heirs of all history everywhere, *the* nation of nations. "We Americans," wrote a youthful Herman Melville, "are the peculiar, chosen people—the Israel of our time; we bear the ark of the liberties of the world. . . . God has predestined, mankind expects, great things from our race; and great things we feel in our souls. The rest of the Nations must soon be in our rear. . . . Long enough have we been skeptics in regard to ourselves, and doubted whether, indeed, the political Messiah had come. But he has come in *us*."

The founders of the American republic were well schooled in the history of the republics of Greece and Rome, whose heirs they believed themselves to be: they had themselves depicted implausibly in togas, saw to it that their children learned Latin, and were chronically concerned that their fledgling republic not go the way of its distant predecessors. But a good many of their successors would find even that cautionary interest in classical history arcane and antiquarian. Ancient history did not matter in a wholly new world. Guaranteed a glorious future, we needed no past. "It is for the other nations to boast of what they have been," wrote James Paulding, "and like garrulous age, muse over the history of their youthful exploits that only renders decrepitude more conspicuous. Ours is the more animating sentiment of hope, looking forward with prophetic eye."

As Americans both looked and moved forward across the years, forging a nation out of thirteen sparsely settled coastal states, spreading across the continent, surviving a bloody Civil War that threatened to end the American experiment in self-government less than a century after it began, absorbing wave upon wave of immigrants from everywhere, shifting from pastoral isolation to industrial superpower, they were sustained always by the faith that unbroken progress was their destiny and the envy of other nations their due.

"All history," said Henry Ford in 1916, "is more or less bunk. We don't want tradition. We want to

Completing the transcontinental railway, Utah, 1869.

Jefferson Vail, *Monticello, Home of President Thomas Jefferson.*

live in the present and the only history worth a tinker's dam is the history we make today." The history Americans came to write and read reflected that boastful, unrelenting optimism: it was that proud, gaudy story which the history mural of my boyhood was meant to illustrate, and its message was further reinforced by a rich profusion of national symbols and monuments and landmarks—Plymouth Rock, the liberty bell, the stars and stripes, Gettysburg, Arlington—for which Americans developed a secular reverence that sometimes threatened to outstrip religious faith. Until just a few years ago all the sites associated with Lincoln's life in and around Springfield, Illinois, were still officially designated "shrines." We accomplish so much in so little time, in part *because* we believed that we were fated to accomplish no less.

Ours was a prolonged (and astonishingly productive) adolescence, but "maturity"—the polite word for weary middle age—was inevitably waiting for us up ahead. The idea of progress had blinked out early in Europe. It still shone brightly here during the early 1920s, but began steadily to fade, a victim of the Great Depression and of an appalling second war, with all the dangers and dislocations that followed in its wake.

We no longer believe in progress, let alone that history is its record. We began life as the only colonial people to have overthrown their European masters; now, most nations fit that definition, and we are no longer sure what unique role, if any, we are still meant to play in a harsh but interdependent world, upon whose very existence we can no longer confidently rely. The prenuclear past already seems impossibly distant, and it is hard to see how lessons learned in an age of musketry and canal boats and steam engines could possibly still pertain to us.

And so our schoolchildren take "social studies," not history. Past events, bleached of color and life, are set forth in pallid texts and are trundled out as

Thompson, Connecticut, in the 1890s.

object lessons in how society supposedly functions. Even professional historians shy away from trying to discern much pattern in the past; unable to agree on where American history is going—if indeed, it is going anywhere—they have abandoned narrative. They prefer, instead, to take pseudoscientific core samples, and then to quarrel over methods of analysis.

"Critical historians are more or less cannibals," Albert Bushnell Hart told his fellow historians three-quarters of a century ago. "They live by destroying each others' conclusions." That was too harsh then and is too harsh now. In a free society, history will always be an endless argument and revisionists can count only on being revised. Lively intramural debate among historians over the past thirty years has greatly enriched our understanding of our past, demolishing ancient myths, dramatically altering our understanding of episodes we once were sure we understood completely, belatedly restoring to something approaching their rightful place the blacks and women and Indians and other "minorities" who were virtually absent from the history I was taught in school.

But in the process, our sense of a comprehensible past has been dangerously, perhaps fatally, fragmented. Consider these titles from among the learned papers delivered at a recent convocation of the organization of American Historians: "Gender Differences and School Politics in Late Nineteenth-Century New York State"; "Interstate 95 and the Black Community in Miami"; "Key Pittman: Discontinuities in Role Performance";

Winslow Homer, *Snap the Whip*, 1872.

"Source, Home and Haven: The Meanings of Place at Laguna Pueblo, New Mexico"; "The Politics of Class: Urban Reform and Working-Class Mobility in Cleveland and Milwaukee, 1905 to 1912." Minute topics, microscopically examined, they suggest the obsessively meticulous notes made by the kind of perennial graduate student who never quite gets around to writing a thesis.

Too many of today's academic historians "are scared to death to suggest that life has a plot," the novelist and historian Shelby Foote once told an interviewer. "I'm not saying what they do has no validity; I am saying it has no art." And without art it is hard for the rest of us to stay interested.

It is not that history is too important to leave to historians; it is that too many historians have stopped trying to talk to the rest of us. Those of us interested in discerning a new and more satisfactory pattern in the American past are left more and more to seek it elsewhere, on our own.

During the 1930s, a number of small Massachusetts towns were flooded by a giant reservoir. The old cemeteries were moved to higher ground, but the towns themselves were left to drown. Years later an old man I knew, who had been born and raised in one of the towns, remembered taking a boat out onto the huge surface of the reservoir in the late afternoons. He would row around until he spotted the spire of his old church, its belfry far below the surface but still faintly visible in the slanting, shifting shafts of sunlight. It was comforting he said, to find it again, but sad that he could see so little of it. Looking for the scattered relics of our common past is a bit like that.

In the headlong pace at which we live our lives, if not our politics, ours remains a revolutionary country. We are restless, impatient, eager to get on with it, even when we are sometimes unclear what "it" is. "If God were suddenly to call the world to judgment," a South American visitor wrote in 1818, "He would surprise two-thirds of the American population on the road, like ants." That is now more true than ever. Few of us live where our parents did. I'm a stay-at-home compared with many of my friends, and I was born in Ohio, raised in Illinois, and during my forty-eight years have lived twice more in Illinois, twice abroad, once in Connecticut, three times in Massachusetts, and twice in New York State before moving to my current home in Manhattan.

We have always telescoped time. Most of our cities grew from muddy riverbank or forest clearing to cluster of cabins to market town to clotted metropolis in what seemed like no time at all to observers from the Old World. "Gain! Gain! Gain!" wrote an English immigrant in 1818, "is the beginning, the middle and the end, the alpha and omega of the founders of American towns." Gain is rarely very far from the minds of those who have been rebuilding them ever since. But they have been driven also by the booster's impulse to better and beautify, to show the world that the old home town is up-to-date.

One generation's idea of beauty and unity has always altered that of the next. Nineteenth-century Americans destroyed colonial buildings they thought impossibly plain and replaced them with ornate edifices that their descendants in turn tore down in favor of severe and "functional" buildings that many of us now find dreary and bloodless—and so tear down. And driving along our highways these days, with their interchangeable motels and malls and fast-food franchises, only the natural landscape remains what Ralph Waldo Emerson called it: "a poem in our eyes." Man-made America seems more and more doggedly prosaic.

Our sense of a shared past has inevitably suffered strain from all this change and homogenization, and history is among the things that most often seem to get lost in the move. The links between us and the places that once nurtured us are fading: No one but Thomas Jefferson could have conceived of Monticello; Lincoln could not have become Lincoln without the village of New Salem that gave him his start; the serenity of Springwood, Franklin Roosevelt's home high above the Hudson, perfectly mirrors the confidence with which he faced the world. But when Richard Nixon, on vacation in California during his presidency, set out to show his aides his own birthplace, he got lost. President George Bush has lived in twenty-four homes in twenty-one cities.

One autumn afternoon toward the end of his long life, my grandfather took me back to Thompson, the pretty Connecticut town where he had spent his boyhood. Thompson is a rare exception to the restive American rule—or it was twenty years ago—a New England village largely unaltered since the nineteenth century. When we parked beside the common, the once-familiar sights loosed a flood of small-scale memories. Two widely separated trees, thick-trunked now, but saplings when my grandfather was a boy, reminded him of the town drunk, who somehow managed to stumble into both of them one night on his way home from the Vernon Stiles tavern and then bellowed out his bafflement at the forest that had unaccountably grown up since he had last passed by.

My grandfather could recall most of the people who had once lived in the handsome old houses that surrounded us—Mr. Dike, the Congregational deacon, who liked to say he was "amphibious" because he could play golf with either hand; Mr. Lewis, a widower who lived with his unmarried daughter and an older female relative and was barred by them from smoking anywhere except the cellar; grey-bearded Mr. Bebee, who had served in the Civil War and was therefore always deferred to as "Major," even by the town's wealthiest citizen, a railroad magnate whom Abraham Lincoln's son Robert sometimes visited during the summer.

We found the big federal-style farmhouse in which my grandfather had lived during the 1880s and nineties; the Congregational church up whose steeple he and a friend had crept before dawn to ring the bell and wake the town one especially memorable Fourth of July; even the cleft boulder in which he and his classmates had left one another secret messages on the way to and from their one-room school.

My grandfather had a good afternoon at Thompson, I think, until he noticed that something was missing. During all his boyhood years, a tiny Greek Revival bank, built of brick in the time of Andrew Jackson and painted white, had stood a few doors away from his house. He had played hide-and-seek around its four Doric columns, packed snowballs on its narrow porch, and been encouraged to deposit in its vault each week the small change his uncle gave him for collecting eggs and cleaning out the chicken house, and, far less frequently, the big silver dollars a showy uncle gave him when he came to town to shoot pheasant.

Now, the old bank was gone, an overgrown and empty lot the only sign that it had ever existed. Not a brick remained. Had there been a fire? Had the old building simply been allowed to collapse? No one then still living in Thompson had known my grandfather, and the New England reticence he had learned while living there kept him from asking strangers about changes in the town he still considered his. He left Thompson considerably distressed and never went back again.

Later that year, I happened to visit Old Sturbridge Village, the "nearly full-scale model of a typical small community of South-Central New England about the year 1830" that has been lovingly assembled just seventeen miles from Thompson. It was a snowy day, and I had some difficulty getting around—the verisimilitude of Old Sturbridge properly extends to its unpaved paths—but there, its classic pediment edged with white, stood my grandfather's bank, miraculously intact.

My grandfather was pleased that evening when I called him from my motel, glad to hear that a new use had been found for the old building, that it had not been razed, after all. But he was wistful, too, that the handsome little building that meant so much to him, had been stripped of its authentic human associations, crated up, and brought here to serve as an antiseptic sampling of its time.

Old Sturbridge is in many ways a marvelously evocative place, perhaps the finest of the historical re-creations now scattered across the country. Even the chickens that scratch around the working farm have been back-bred to scrawny authenticity, and it is easy, strolling in and out of its parsonage and smithy, its barns and cooper's shop and working gristmill, to believe for a moment that you are actually inhabiting the real, hand-hewn country of our ancestors.

But the illusion never lasts long. A vapor trail in the cold autumn sky above the trees or the arrival of a troop of distinctly contemporary schoolchildren can destroy it in an instant. And there is a more subtle flaw. Real nineteenth-century New Englanders exhibited qualities beyond the skill, ingenuity, and thrift that Old Sturbridge celebrates so effectively. There were good qualities, like the stubborn independence and inbred suspicion of centralized power exemplified by the Town Meeting, but more dubious qualities, as well—prejudice and parochialism and quirks of individual personality that cannot be conveyed through anonymous antiques and artifacts, no matter how well chosen and carefully preserved, but without which the re-created past inevitably remains an impersonal museum.

The older America, like our own, was filled with troubling contradictions, hard truths, flawed human beings. Had there ever really been any residents of Old Sturbridge, and were we able actually to visit them, we would find the problems that faced them daily—wandering pigs, the reek of raw sewage and unwashed bodies, the frequent deaths of children—different problems from those that confront us today, but no less disturbing.

A good many history-minded Americans seem curiously unwilling to accept such facts. They prefer a warm, cozy past to the real thing; they like to see history as a sort of cheerful gift shop, its shelves stocked with colorful quilts and scented candles and nostalgia. The late writer Walter Karp traced that unwillingness to what he called the "San Andreas Fault in the American soul—the schism between our faith in technological progress and our . . . gnawing suspicion that the old rural republic was a finer, braver and freer place than the industrial America that now sustains us."

In Rome some years ago, I watched a busload of elderly American tourists slowly unload at the Forum—women mostly, with a ragged escort of surviving husbands. One man, wearing a blue baseball cap and green golf pants, stood and listened just long enough to hear the guide say that the ruins spread out before him were more than a thousand years old. He shook his head and started for the bus. "Certainly shows its age, doesn't it?" he said, as he climbed aboard, eager to get back to his hotel. "Why don't they fix the place up?"

That is a quintessentially American attitude. For Europeans, as the historian Daniel Boorstin has pointed out, "the past is the great storehouse of greatness and romance, which declines into the prosaic, insoluble problems of the present." It therefore, "becomes a patriotic act to leave the remains of that past in their surviving disarray." Our tradition is entirely different. Believing ourselves to represent history's climax, that the past was interesting only to the extent that it led to us, we dismissed most of its vestiges as embarrassing reminders of crude beginnings best forgotten.

We are settled enough now to have begun to think at least some of our own relics worth preserving, but we also ensure that they are spruced-up and made to seem perennially shiny and new, and that the history they convey is reassuring and easily assimilated by the families that eagerly file in from the parking lot. In the process, harsh realities routinely get smoothed away. Almost the first thing the National Park Service did when it took over Franklin Roosevelt's house after his death in 1945 was to remove the ramps without which he could not have moved from room to room in his wheelchair, thereby rendering his house off-limits to any visitor similarly afflicted. (The ramps have since been replaced.) Those who restore antebellum plantations in the South have only recently begun to pay attention to the slave cabins, without which the gracious lives lived in the Big House would hardly have been possible. The bright, glowing brickwork of the restored textile mills that sprawl along the Merrimack River at Manchester, New Hampshire, seems to deny the appalling conditions endured by those who once worked inside them. A re-created Indian village at the edge of the fine Plimoth Plantation restoration near the Pilgrims' landing site was abandoned after the understandably touchy Indians hired to people it proved less hospitable to newcomers than their ancestors had been.

When my children *were* children they grew weary of my obsession with the past, which in those days sometimes took the form of wanting to tour through every restored house and re-created village we happened to pass. They tagged along willingly enough at first. It was the over-eager guides who eventually got to them, dolled up in pristine period dress, waving a candle snuffer or an apple parer and cooing, "I'll bet you're too young to know what *this* is!" They usually did know—though they were far too polite ever to

President Franklin D. Roosevelt at Hyde park, 1941.

spoil the guide's surprise; it was just that, after a while, they no longer cared. Finally, they refused even to get out of the car. After a while, I did, too.

When my grandparents were children, they and their friends supplemented their history texts with dime novels about Buffalo Bill and other half-authentic heroes of the not-yet-Old West. In my boyhood, it was that most American art form, the movies, that put lurid flesh on the dry bones of dates and names and places we memorized in school. I imagine most Americans still learn most of what little history they know from watching one kind of screen or another. The Past that flickers there from time to time tells more about movie makers and television producers and their audiences than it does about the real lives lived by those it pretends to portray.

America itself was the Hero in a good many of the movies I loved as a boy, making itself up as it went along, thanks to all those cowboys and sodbusters, schoolmarms and gunfighters, town marshals and cavalry troopers—and even the Indians who so dependably charged into their guns. In *The Man Who Shot Liberty Valance,* a John Ford Western released in 1962, a persistent newspaperman discovers that the career of a prominent state politician (James Stewart) is built upon a lie: It had been not he, but John Wayne, who had rid the territory of the murderous bully who was all that had once stood between it, statehood, and civilization. At the end, Stewart nervously asks the newspaperman if he plans to print the truth, now that he knows it. "No sir!" says the editor. "This is the West, sir! When the legend becomes fact, print the legend."

It is the legend with which Hollywood has always felt most comfortable. There's always been more money to be made in confirming preconceptions than in setting the record straight. But profits are only part of it; I suspect most moviemakers have themselves believed the myths.

D. W. Griffith set the style. By 1930, he had fallen from Hollywood favor. Sound had replaced silence and the relentlessly sophisticated new magazine, *The New Yorker,* had pronounced him "automatically . . . out of our set" because he "has the corner on treacle . . . and trash." His most recent film, *Lady of the Pavements,* had failed to make money, and—still worse from his point of view—for the first time in his career, reviewers had paid less attention to him than they had to his leading lady, the maniacally energetic Lupé Velez, then in the midst of a much-publicized affair with Gary Cooper and known to the fan magazines as "Whoopee Lupé."

But in 1930, Griffith did manage to persuade United Artists to re-release his silent Civil War epic, *Birth of a Nation,* with a musical sound track. To manufacture a suitable air of high-mindedness for what was, after all, a cheap reissue of a seventeen-year-old silent, Griffith filmed a talking trailer. In it, a big-eyed boy and girl tiptoe into a firelit, book-lined room to eavesdrop on the Great Director and the actor Walter Huston, soon to appear as Lincoln in the film that would prove to be Griffith's next-to-last.

Both men wear dinner jackets, and a good deal is made of their lighting up cigars before they launch into what is billed as "an intimate conversation." Huston presents Griffith with a gift—a Confederate saber. Griffith, courtly and enormously tall, rises from his leather chair to receive it, gravely thanking his visitor as he turns the weapon over and over in his hands. His father had worn such a saber, he muses. Huston tells him how much he has always admired *Birth of a Nation.* Griffith smiles modestly. He had been destined to tell the story of the Civil War, he explains, because he had heard his father reminisce about it while, at the age of five, he crouched beneath the family dining table. The story he told in his film was "true," he tells Huston, "as true as that blade." And then he adds, "As Pontius Pilate said: 'What is Truth? What is the Truth?' "

As anyone who has seen *Birth of a Nation* knows, for Griffith, the Truth was an upside-down world of Reconstruction, where whites, not blacks, were the "victims of mob license"; where integrated courtrooms were "outrages" to be avenged; where members of the Ku Klux Klan, fearless in the face of ambush by cowardly freedmen, sought only a fair trial for black transgressors; and where the highest duty of former Confederates and Union men alike was to reunite in the interest of their shared "Aryan heritage," keeping freedmen from the polls until they could all be shipped off to Africa.

Part of the film's initial popularity was due, of course, to Griffith's skill as a filmmaker. Even in its blurry, reissued version, with its bigotry watered down and its sound track hoked-up with Stephen Foster melodies, *Birth of a Nation* retains some of its impact: the battle scenes bring Mathew Brady's photographs to life; set pieces such as the sur-

Charles M. Russell, *The Buffalo Hunt No. 39*, 1919.

render at Appomattox and the assassination of Lincoln are still eerily convincing. But audiences in 1915 were clearly responding to Griffith's familiar message as much as to his innovative use of the medium. His version of Reconstruction was the version in which most white Americans, North and South, already believed. Denunciations from liberal pulpits and picketing organized by the fledgling National Association for the Advancement of Colored People only boosted ticket sales. President Woodrow Wilson himself declared it "like writing history with Lightning . . . my only regret is that it is so terribly true." Anyone who has looked at scholarly texts of the time knows that the then-current historians' view of Reconstruction differed from Griffith's only in the virulence of its racism.

Nearly a quarter of a century after *Birth of a Nation*'s original release, when Hollywood revisited the Civil War era with *Gone With the Wind*, movie audiences were still receptive to old misconceptions: "There was a land of cavaliers and cotton fields, called the Old South," the film began, over a silhouetted parade of apparently contented slaves plodding home at sunset. "Here was the last ever to be seen of knights and their ladies fair, of master and slave. Look for it only in books, for it is no more than a dream remembered."

The star of that film, the British actress Vivien Leigh, nicely summed up Hollywood's traditional attitude toward history. As she stepped down from the airplane that had carried her from Hollywood to Atlanta for the premiere, a high school band struck up "Dixie," the jaunty anthem of the Confederacy. She smiled her most radiant smile. "Oh!" she said, clutching the arm of her lover, Laurence Olivier. "They're playing the song from our picture!"

Movies with historical themes date at least as fast as do those about contemporary life. Even with its raw bias, Griffith's version of the Civil War strikes today's audiences as curiously innocent—"life," as one of his florid titles has it, "in a quaintly way that is to be no more." *Gone With the Wind*'s rosy Old South could not now fool an Ole Miss sophomore, and John Ford's West, which I so eagerly inhabited on Saturday afternoons in the fifties, seems remote, predictable, and hopelessly romantic. How could I have ever been so caught up in it?

But the films of the sixties, too, in which our past was self-consciously *de*-romanticized and the old myths were all turned on their heads—*Little Big Man, Bonnie and Clyde, The Wild Bunch*—also already seem as antiquated, as out-of-date as the resolutely strident national mood they mirrored.

The films of my boyhood now survive only on the shelves of videocassette stores. Before long, our own brutal, blood-spattered renderings of the American past—*Platoon, The Untouchables, Full Metal Jacket,* and all the rest—will be shelved there, too, and I suspect they will strike the next generation of moviegoers as the earlier movies strike us—as the work of people who undeniably had talent, but who were also awfully naïve about their past.

The Upper West Side of Manhattan, where I now live, was settled around the turn-of-the-century by moderately well-to-do New Yorkers who had moved uptown to escape the immigrant tide then steadily spilling northward from the island's crowded tip. The buildings on my block attest to the old-world pretentions of their builders. They include miniature Italian palaces, French châteaus, and step-roofed Dutch dwellings, each meant initially to house a single family and its servants, some fitted out with wrought-iron hoists to haul up fuel and supplies from the horse-drawn wagons that have not plied my double-parked street for fifty years.

In those days, even apartment buildings meant to house less prosperous families were massive and richly embellished. Some had gardens and cobbled courtyards so that children would have a safe place to play and carriages could drive in to deliver tenants out of the rain. I live with my wife on the tenth floor of one of the more modest of these (our complex never had a courtyard). Built in 1906, it is no longer what it once was. The art-nouveau stained-glass windows in the lobby bulge alarmingly where their panes have not already been replaced by clear glass. The oldest tenants sigh for the Persian carpets that once warmed the badly chipped mosaic floor, in which the building's original pseudo-British name can still be read: "Rossleigh Court."

But my building was meant to last: the ceilings are twice as tall as I am; the walls are soundproof and nearly a foot thick; and at dusk, from the roof, the view of Central Park and the midtown skyline dazzles every out-of-towner to whom we show it. From up there, everything about New York seems settled, permanent.

Nothing could be further from the truth; things begin to change as soon you go downstairs.

Ours is a perpetually unfinished country. The idea that the United States is an experiment in self-government whose outcome is uncertain is at least as old as the more familiar, cocky bluster about manifest destiny and sacred mission—and every bit as American.

And we are a perpetually unfinished people. Most of us have no ancestral link with either the rural republic memorialized by Old Sturbridge or the wide-open spaces romanticized on screen. It is from the nearly fifty million immigrants who have chosen to start new lives here since 1789 that the overwhelming majority of us are descended, not from those who were here to receive them so uneasily. "What then is the American, this new man?" asked the French settler Michel Guillaume Jean de Crèvecoeur in 1782. There can never be a final, authoritative response to that famous question, because any accurate answer would have to include whoever happened to get here last.

Nowhere are those two central truths about America more vividly displayed than in the crowded streets of Manhattan. Nothing stays still. The residential block along which you strolled yesterday is a parking lot today and will be who knows what tomorrow. Much less of Dutch New York survives, the late historian Marshall Davidson pointed out, than survives of the Athens of Pericles. When the last living link with it—a gnarled pear tree planted by Governor Peter Stuyvesant in 1647 that stood at the northeast corner of Third Avenue and Thirteenth Street—was knocked over by an errant carriage shortly after the Civil War, no one minded much.

Anonymous, *Washing Gold, Calaveras, California,* 1853.

Turn left at my front door, and you enter Central Park, the long, 840-acre rectangle of lakes and lawns and glades that runs up the center of the island from 59th to 110th Streets and makes this teeming city livable. Begun in the 1850s, the park and its environs are filled with discarded history, old issues, and abandoned enthusiasms fossilized in bronze and marble. Streams of joggers puff past a stubby, brooding statue of Daniel Webster, oblivious of the words carved in its base that were once taught to every schoolchild: LIBERTY AND UNION, NOW AND FOREVER, ONE AND INSEPARABLE. Civil War General William Tecumseh Sherman sits astride his horse at the southeastern corner of the park, glaring still farther south toward the once-rebellious states he laid waste to ensure that Liberty and Union did survive together. An equestrian statue of Theodore Roosevelt, flanked by an African and an American Indian, in front of the sprawling Museum of Natural History, perfectly embodies the ambivalent nature of turn-of-the-century American imperialism: TR rides, his companions walk, but all stride forward together.

My apartment building figures in the background of one of the most familiar photographs of the Great Depression. It shows a cluster of temporary tar-paper shacks which the merciful city fathers had permitted the jobless to erect within the park. One hut bravely flies the American flag. The bare, stony ground where those shanties stood is planted now with grass. Young men play baseball there on weekends, and the shady paths around them are filled with families, black and Spanish mostly, for whom the park now provides a play-

Johann Mongels Culverhouse, *Skating Scene in Central Park at 59th Street*, 1865.

ground. A father shows his son how to fly a crimson kite. Playful dogs plunge in and out of a long line of theater-goers, who sunbathe while they wait to see an open-air production of Shakespeare. A string quartet of music students plays Mozart as white blossoms shiver down on them and their rapt audience. But it is impossible not to notice that, here and there, the city's homeless, fewer in number but no less desperate than the Depression-era squatters, must now make do with park benches.

Turn right at my front door, toward the bustle of Columbus and Amsterdam Avenues and Broadway, and you find that even now, with the first frontier long closed and the New Frontier dead for almost three decades, we are still busily inventing ourselves. You hear as much French and Spanish on my block as English. The old brownstones built by turn-of-the-century Americans fearful of newcomers from eastern and southern Europe have long since been divided into apartments and are now occupied by newcomers from Haiti and Puerto Rico, while young attorneys and apprentice stockbrokers consider themselves fortunate to find basement rooms once intended for Irish serving girls.

America still draws immigrants from everywhere, eager to make good and more-or-less willing to make themselves over to do so. They may or may not be aware of what earlier generations of Americans endured to assert and defend the rights we and they now enjoy. The long-ago sprinkling of patriot blood on Lexington Green must seem impossibly remote to a fresh arrival from, say, Vietnam or Cambodia, whose own memories encompass oceans of it. But they are nonetheless infused with the same yearning for personal freedom, the identical sense of infinite possibilities that Lincoln was willing to wage his war to preserve, that the Benares boatman felt from eight-thousand miles away.

In the Greek-owned coffee shop where my wife buys her morning cup of coffee on the way to work, the Bangladeshi immigrants behind the

Squatters' shacks in Central Park in the early 1930s.

counter shout "Amigo!" to a steady customer from Colombia. Yesterday, the woman ahead of me in line at the pizza stand asked the whereabouts of an especially genial Mexican waiter. She was told he had left—to open his own restaurant.

When I moved here nine years ago, the three Korean brothers who owned the nearest grocery store spoke only an eccentric smattering of English words. Their elderly mother, who spoke none, squatted out front much of the day, wearing traditional Korean dress and washing fruits and vegetables, much as she must have done in the marketplace in Seoul. The old woman is no longer there, but the store has doubled its size, and her sons wear New York Yankees caps and seem as encyclopedic about baseball statistics as were my boyhood friends.

Will the American experiment work? We will never know for sure, but based on the evidence everywhere around me, two things seem certain: we will continue to change, and we will remain the same.

We still yield to no other country on earth in the glassy-eyed fervor of our reflexive patriotism: Where else do presidential candidates campaign in flag factories? What other government but ours would issue four-color airmail forms emblazoned CELEBRATE AMERICA for us to send to startled friends abroad?

But we are also unmatched, I think, in our eagerness to uncover and confess our own sins, in our willingness to flagellate ourselves for faults that are, in fact, universally shared. Those shell-shocked veterans of the 1960s and '70s, whose understandable disillusionment with almost everything has caused them to conclude that the American story is not worth retelling, are simply wrong. In viewing our vices as unique, they are as blind as their forebears who believed our virtues to be ours alone.

C. W. Peale, *Thomas Jefferson*, 1791.

Americans have a notorious weakness for superlatives, but President John Adams was surely right when he called ours "a mighty Revolution." It was the first war ever fought in defense of the inalienable rights of all mankind; the first whose outcome could truly be said to matter to every man and woman on earth. It was the opening signal—distant now, but still distinctly heard—for two centuries of revolution, first in Europe, then in South America, Asia, Africa.

And there is more. It was the first revolution to declare that legitimate government must rest on the consent of the governed; the first to proclaim religious freedom; the first to seek to establish a society based on classless equality (save for the tragic exception of black slavery); the first to understand that even democratically elected officials with the best of intentions could be counted upon to lurch toward tyranny unless their powers were delimited and the inalienable rights of the individual were spelled out in a written Constitution and a Bill of Rights.

We have come a very long way in a very short time from that revolution, so far and so fast that it is hard to encompass it all. And we have often fallen short of the loftiest aspirations our revolutionary ancestors had for us. But for all our failings, the United States still provides a freer and more prosperous life for more people than any other nation. Our Constitution and Bill of Rights remain central to our lives and are still a talisman to those elsewhere who only dream of liberties we take for granted.

Even our most grievous sins—the refractory prejudice that sanctioned slavery and still hampers the slaves' descendants, our recalcitrant refusal to accept responsibility for the least fortunate among us, the smug ferocity with which we have sometimes adventured overseas—have been mitigated by the grandeur of those Americans who have struggled to efface them in the name of the nation's highest ideals.

It was foolish to revere our ancestors, as we once universally did. But it is just as foolish to patronize them, as so many of us now do. Knowing little about our forebears as individual men and women, lacking any real understanding of the world in which they lived, we too often think of them as having been somehow simpler, more innocent, than our presumably sophisticated selves. We forget that neither times nor people have ever been simple. They only seem that way because we know how at least some things turned out.

Seeing our forebears whole—as both bold and devious, brave and fearful, enlightened and ignorant, defeated and victorious—should reassure, not frighten us. To know them and what they did is to begin to know ourselves and to see what we might do.

Thomas Jefferson understood that. In his *Notes on the State of Virginia,* written in 1781, he urged that history be made the heart of the curriculum for secondary school students throughout his state: "History, by apprizing them of the past, will enable them to judge of the future; it will avail them of the experience of other times and other nations; it will qualify them as judges of the actions and designs of men; it will enable them to know ambition under every disguise it may issue and knowing it, to defeat its views."

Jefferson was writing then of classical history, of the lessons his fellow citizens might draw from the sad fate of the early republics, and he was writing at a time when his own five-year-old republic had precious little history of its own upon which to draw. But we have two crowded centuries of it behind us now, centuries during which ambition has issued forth under a host of home-grown disguises. If we hope to continue to unmask ambition and to judge correctly the actions and designs of men, we'd better begin again to apprize ourselves.

ЧЮДО·СТГО·ГЕѠРЬГИꙖ·ѠЗМИИ

Discovering Our Past

Yuri Nagibin

In the spring of 1988, Soviet newspapers announced that schools would not be holding final exams in history. Still another case of bankruptcy, this time in a highly important ideological endeavor: the historical education of our people. It was openly and unequivocally admitted that the history drummed into the heads of Soviet school children for years and years had been sheer falsification, that the knowledge they had been stuffed with was useless. "The hell with it and forget it," as Chapayev said in the Vasilyev brothers' film.

At first glance it would seem the decision affected only schoolchildren, who were no doubt delighted. (And how! One less tiresome exam to get through!) But it went much further. It was a revolutionary gesture, sweeping away more than half a century of misinforming the people about history, of substituting calculated lies, tailored to suit those in power, for what the nation had lived through over the centuries. Yes, we had long since returned to seeing history as an organ of national conceit, in the spirit of Lomonosov's rhetorical amplification of the facts.

It should be said that the falsification of history is no modern invention. Even the Chronicles, the main source for Russian history from the most ancient times to the middle of the sixteenth century, very early began "to serve not the purpose of moral instruction but the purposes of state policy," as historian Aleksandr Kizevetter noted:

> Starting with the end of the fifteenth century and the beginning of the sixteenth, no longer content with a biased account of contemporary events, [the Chronicles] begin to depict the past as well in a tendentious light. A series of unofficial legends was created to justify Moscow's political claims, the right of Moscow's sovereign to all Russia, to the Kievan legacy, and finally to the authority of the Byzantine emperors.

The tendentious pragmatism of the Chronicles found its way into the tales interpolated among them. And from there into the "full account of Russian history" written in Kiev, the so-called *Synopsis.* While the Kievan clergy were extolling, in the *Synopsis,* the spiritual role of their city in Russian history, the Moscow scribe Fyodor Griboyedov was writing for the tsar's behoof the first *History of the Tsars and Grand Princes of the Russian Land.* This was no work of genius, but nonetheless it set the direction that Russian historical thinking would long follow: seeing the history of Russia as an account of the tsars' reigns. Even here, in the distant past, bias and the falsification that goes hand in hand with it are clearly evident. The churchmen exaggerated the services of the church; the government men put everything down to the princes and tsars. Even before becoming a science, History wants to be the handmaiden of the powers that be.

Needless to say, history is not an exact science. Relying on facts recorded in the chronicles, in written records, in documents of all kinds, history depends as does no other science on the character of the investigator: on his good conscience, his

Saint George and the Dragon. Ancient Christian icon, Novgorod.

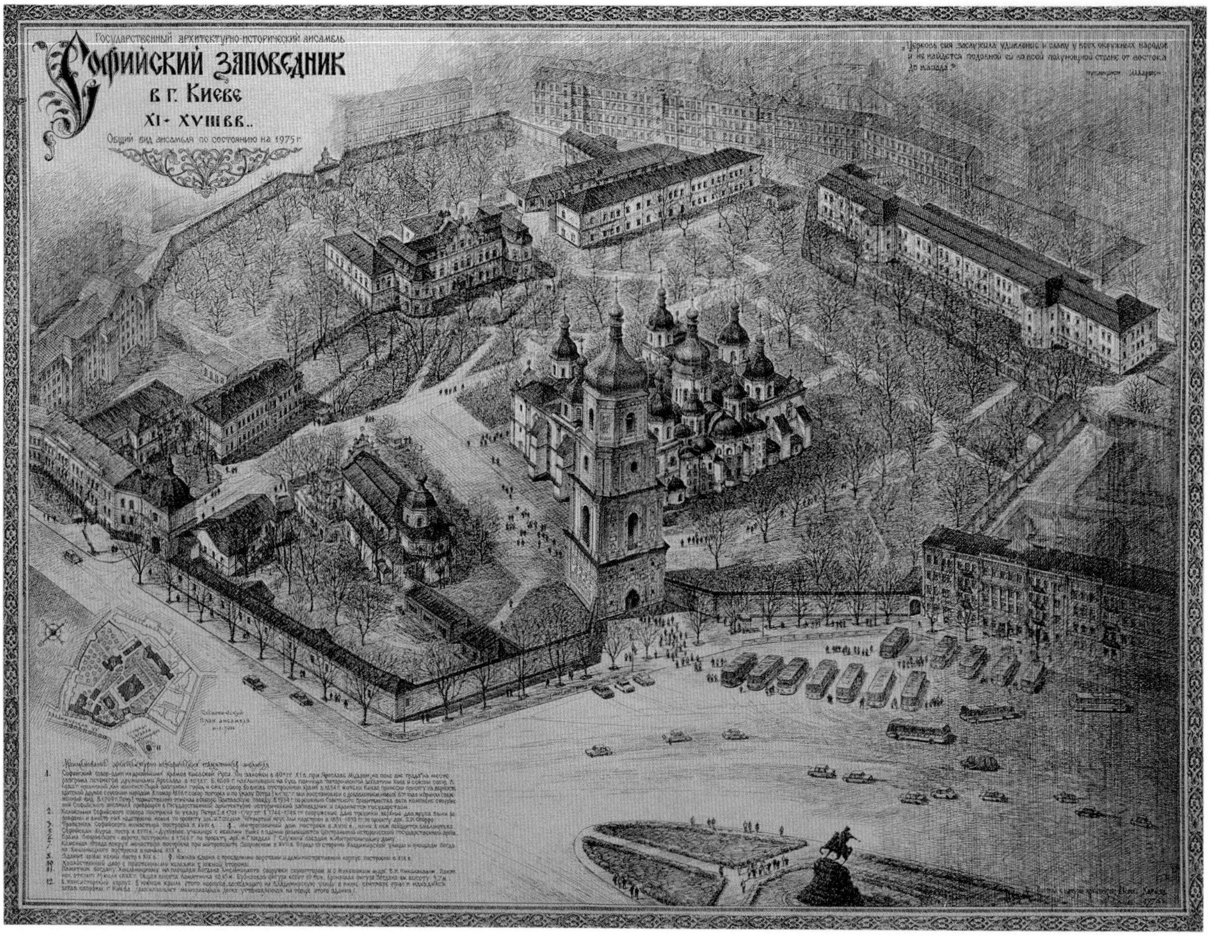

Kiev. Saint Sophia Cathedral (lithograph).

insight and diligence, his moral strength and freedom from servility, his readiness to stand up to the authorities—and on his convictions, too. Even the most honest and most noble of men, the hardest-working, the most responsible, and so forth and so on, if he professes monarchist views, will write history so that it serves the idea of monarchy. An example is Nikolai Karamzin's *History of the State of Russia*. Remember Pushkin on Karamzin:

> His *History,* all elegant simplicity,
> Proves to us, beyond all reasonable doubt,
> The necessity of autocracy
> And the sweet charm of the knout.

This should not be forgotten by those who take such boundless delight in the rather bizarre action of the journal *Moskva,* which is now reprinting Karamzin's work in its entirety. Unprecedented in Soviet journalism, this is a shrewd move to bolster flagging circulation. To my mind, *Moskva* is one of the three "thick" journals not only at odds with *perestroika* but openly hostile to it.

Can a historical work ever be unbiased? Probably it can, when it is history that forms the historian, and not the historian who twists history to suit himself. Examples would be Niebuhr, Mommsen, and to a certain degree our own Vasyly Klyuchevsky. In writing his *Course in Russian History,* Klyuchevsky did not bind the living flesh of history to a Procrustean bed, cutting off everything that did not fit his preconceived notions or cruelly stretching it. He studied, reached out to comprehend, approached every fact and document freely and critically, drew conclusions. His published course (unfortunately, he brought it only as far as Peter the Great) is a brilliant furthering of his predecessors' idea: history as the development of society. What is more, Klyuchevsky managed to avoid falling in with either the Westernizers or the Slavophiles. His work towers above that of Sergei Solovyov, the fruit of so many years' labor. Solovyov was a government man. In essence, albeit on a higher level than Karamzin, he traced the deeds of the tsars, getting bogged down in their endless disputes and intrigues. Aleksandr Kizevetter is right to say that "his general views, with certain brilliant exceptions, are attached to the material in a very superficial way."

I will not compare the merits and demerits of history courses prepared by Russian scholars. I will say only that Russia had much to expect from Nikolai Kostomarov, with his idea about the national characteristics of history. But he never wrote his summa. At the height of his powers he was dismissed from the universities, retreating, in part, to belles-lettres. Russian scholarship suffered a serious blow.

All in all, Russian historians before the Revolution were a tendentious lot, and their works were not a pure quest for the truth (the task the great Niebuhr set himself). Lomonosov thought history's task was "extolling the ancestors and morally edifying the descendants." Mikhail Shcher-

I. Repin, *The Death Scene.* Ivan the Terrible and his son Ivan, 16 November 1581.

batov looked for ways to use history: by discovering the connections between causes and effects, one would acquire "power over future times." I see nothing shameful in such utilitarianism. German scholars, however, categorically refused "to set practical goals for the study of history, maintaining that its only goal, as in any branch of scientific knowledge, must be to uncover the truth, independent of any national or partisan bias whatever." But was Niebuhr himself so godlike in his freedom from the fetters of society, estate, class, nationality, ideology, and (finally) personality as he sought the truth? "What is truth?" as Pilate asked when, forgoing his inner freedom, he sent to the torments of the cross one before whom he exclaimed, "Behold the man!"

What is noteworthy, though, is that Russian scholars, while professing one set of views or another, were not acting (the great majority of them) on direct orders from the authorities. Yes, among them were bombastic "singers of bygone times," government men, populists, Slavophiles, Westernizers, analysts. Anyone who wanted to know the history of Russia could find a source to slake *his* thirst, sufficient to his desires. And anyone who did not like to be led could form his own opinion, based on a variety of points of view and different investigative methods. Nobody imposed a single, obligatory vision, superior to all the rest only because that was how the tsar saw things. The gymnasium fed its pupils the worst and most primitive of all the courses, Ilovaysky's. But any youngster hungry for knowledge could take Klyuchevsky or Solovyov as a corrective to the official teachings. And then there were numerous works, remarkable for their forceful thinking, on individual historical problems: works by Shchapov, Buslayev, Semevsky, Pynin, Sergeyevich, Zabelin, Platonov, and others too numerous to recall.

Of course, autocratic Russia was not the best place for the daring play of free intellect. But the limitations of that time—its constraints, administrative actions, falsifications pleasing to the ruling class—all pale before what was made of historical science by an era which first announced that it marked the beginning of conscious human history.

If we are to speak of history as a science, it must be said to have ended with Mikhail N. Pokrovsky. An eminent figure in government and Party life, deputy commissar of education, and academician, Pokrovsky published his five-volume *Course in Russian History from Earliest Times* between 1910 and 1913. After the Revolution he put out the two-volume *Brief History of Russia*, which became the only manual for anyone studying history in our country. Pokrovsky examined economic and social factors in Russia's history, excluding almost totally whatever was personal. Reading this work, you get the feeling history does not need mankind to realize its potentialities. This extreme emphasis on society, cutting out the "heroes" of the past, was originally in keeping with the outlook of the masses, who had emerged for the first time into the forefront and wanted to turn the wheel of history with their own hands, not through the hands of celebrated representatives. Pokrovsky was in favor, and in 1919, the department at Moscow university was named after him. True, malicious wits said that according to Pokrovsky all historical events in Russia depended on the price of hemp.

His depersonalized history was found wanting by one prominent personality that began, at the end of the twenties, to shoot up above its comrades-in-arms, taking on more and more power until, aided by unprecedented terror, it became all-powerful.

Pokrovsky's history was driven out in disgrace, but no new one was written. Some pitiful textbooks, having nothing to do with history as a science, were put out for schools and other institutions of learning. In the thirties there began that incomparable falsification of history which continued until just recently, culminating in the present confusion.

Nobody set out to restore, in a theoretical way, the rights and significance of the individual in history. That happened, as it were, spontaneously. And it assumed grotesque forms.

Statue of Peter the Great, Leningrad.

Lenin in his Kremlin study with American lawyer Parley P. Christensen, 1921.

Stalin tried on various guises. Depending on who held sway over his imagination, on whom he wanted to resemble, one figure or another would emerge from the gloom of history to shine brightly. And there is nothing surprising in the Communist Stalin's eying a crown or two.

I once heard S. S. Geychenko, renowned curator of Pushkin's museum near the former Svyatogorsk Monastery, tell a remarkable story. Geychenko was the son of the tsar's superintendent of stables at Petergof. After graduating from the Museum Institute (this unusual school produced just one graduating class before it was closed), he was sent back home to be deputy director of the local museum. Petergof, with its unique fountains, splendid palace, and amusements of every sort, invented by Peter the Great non-genius, had been a summer residence of the tsars.

Once, in the midthirties, the museum's small staff received the disquieting news that Stalin was coming to have a look at the museum. The Leader arrived. Unhurriedly, as was his way, he made the tour of the tsar's chambers. Then he said he wanted to be left alone; he was fed up with the "explaining comrades." Everyone tiptoed out of the room, where the tsar's crown was kept under a glass case.

Quite some time passed before Geychenko got up the courage to glance into the hallway leading to the room where the symbol of autocracy reposed. The director of the museum crouched at the door, peering through the keyhole. The startled director was relieved to see it was Geychenko, with whom he was on friendly terms. He beckoned. Geychenko approached, put his eye to the keyhole, and beheld a singular performance.

Stalin was circling the crown, drawing nearer, then moving away. Sometimes he would look quickly around at the door, and the men peeking in would feel their hearts dive down into their heels. It was as if he could see them through the tiny opening. But of course that was impossible. The exalted visitor would again begin his circling. Then he stepped up to the crown and, slowly but resolutely, lifted away the glass case. Again he began to circle. The men squatting by the door felt their legs go numb, their backs turn to wood. But they could not tear themselves away. At last Stalin stood still. For half a minute or so he glared at the crown from under his brows. He reached out and took it off the stand. He held it for a long time at arm's length, then lifted it towards his head. The men watching breathlessly outside realized they were about to glimpse the future. Stalin almost put the crown on his head, but stopped short. He quickly replaced it, plopped the case down over it, and headed for the door. Geychenko and the director barely had time to get away.

As it turned out, they did not get away. Soon after, both were imprisoned. The director perished in a camp. Geychenko got the chance to redeem himself in the war. It cost him his left arm. For all his keen intelligence, Geychenko still cannot imagine who informed on them. In the depths of his soul, he is inclined to think Stalin saw them through the door.

Leaving the tsar's crown in peace, Stalin began trying on other guises. Aleksei Tolstoy, who had a keen nose for such things (the only match for him in this was Konstantin Simonov, who had far less literary talent), was first to understand that the ban had been lifted from the historical theme. He offered Stalin the role of Peter the Great. His novel delighted even Ivan Bunin, who was not delighted by much in literature. It stunned the Soviet public. And not only because of the talent it showed, its superb language, its wealth of sweeping and vivid pictures of the time, but because a Russian tsar was shown as a national hero and not a fool-despot-oppressor. A reforming tsar, a tsar who served the people, intelligent, stern when the good of the state demanded it, kind to his friends, a passionate lover (he would have been a good husband, but had no luck with family life), limitlessly hungry for learning and science, not fond of war but always ready to bare his sword if interloping neighbors forced him, just in all his actions, never overstepping the bounds in retribution, extravagant only in dispensing rewards, virtuous and noble, unerring in his knowledge of Russia's path and of everything that would profit her—such is the Peter who emerges from the novel—the ideal ruler and man.

The battleship *Aurora*, Leningrad. Her cannon signaled the attack on the Winter Palace, the start of the 1917 Revolution.

Peter was not like that, of course. Lenin said that our failings are a continuation of our virtues. This is entirely true of Peter. Hungry for everything new and exotic, he spread himself too thin, leaving many projects unfinished. His passion could turn into cruelty. For him the end justified the means, and human life was not worth a farthing. It is no metaphor when they say that St. Petersburg was built on bones. Pushkin defined this duality in Peter with the vision of an artist and the dispassion of a historian: "There is an astounding difference between the government institutions of

Peter the Great and his day-to-day orders. The former are the fruit of a broad mind, filled with good will and wisdom; the latter are *often cruel and arbitrary, as if written with the knout*. The former were for eternity, or at least for the future; the latter burst forth from an *impatient*, despotic lord of the manor."

It is no coincidence that the people nearest to Peter were wholly lacking in moral restraint. There was Prince-Caesar Romadanovsky, master sleuth and torturer. There was Peter's bosom friend, the illustrious Prince Menshikov, who helped him execute his most incredible schemes; a thief, bribe-taker, and extortioner, he completed his doglike service to the tsar by helping him on his way to a better world. Admiral Apraksin was a thief; Vice-Chancellor Shafirov, a thief and unscrupulous wheeler-dealer. Menshikov was also Peter's mentor in carousal and monstrous debauchery.

Aleksei Tolstoy knew all this. But then, he was not trying to paint a faithful portrait of Peter. He wanted Stalin to see himself in Peter, and Peter in himself. And Stalin took the bait, which indeed he himself may have set. It is doubtful that Tolstoy, however sharp-witted, would have undertaken such a thing without prompting—or at least a hint, something along the line that the time had come for a Russian tsar to become a hero in Soviet literature. Till then the history of the house of Romanov had been treated only in the satiric imagery of Saltykov-Shchedrin's *Fooltown*.

Stalin was pleased. No matter how you look at him, Peter is splendid. He drinks charmingly. The infamous buffoonery of his court is depicted as the witty, high-spirited gaiety of youth. (In fact, old men often played the most despicable parts.) Moreover, it was a slap in the face of the mossbacked boyars and reactionary clergy. He lops off the heads of the *streltsy* charmingly. Though not quite so charmingly as Alek Menshikov, coming to the rescue of that weak-kneed Swiss, Lefort, who could not become an executioner even to please his sovereign. So Menshikov did the lopping for two—for himself and for friend Franz. Peter is endlessly charming in that terrible story with his son. You really feel for him: the awful trouble the good man had chasing down, trapping, imprisoning, torturing, and destroying the prodigal son who would not believe in his cause! Literature is a dirty business when talent is not backed up with morality! Any crime can be excused, any abomination served up so as to seem upright and just.

Tolstoy's novel is spellbinding. Even Bunin's nose, which could smell out literary fakery as easily as fried chicken, failed to catch the author at his toadying.

From the pages of the novel, Peter stepped out onto the screen. The brilliance of one of Russia's best actors, Nikolai Simonov, made him even more charming. Nothing to carp at this time—it's not just the honor and glory we are shown. Here is Peter fleeing the battlefield in a sled. Here he is snatching a maiden from Menshikov. (Served him right, too. He had taken her from poor old Sheremetev.) Here he is beating a favorite for thievery. Quick with his blows, stern, terrible in wrath, but winsome, oh so winsome!

Too winsome, Stalin eventually decided. He lost the desire to be another Peter. Too magnanimous and, excepting justifiable outbursts of anger, too awfully pliable. Too ready to forgive, to back down. It was only with the *streltsy* that he really showed some mettle. Peter was too wan, too far from the ideal of the ruler as Stalin conceived it at the time of the great terror. But such an ideal was to be found elsewhere in Russian history: Ivan Vasilyevich, known as the Terrible.

One of the famous commentators on Russia—Alexandr Herzen, it seems—forewarned that the time would come when Ivan the Terrible and his butcher Tomila would be called our greatest humanists. That time came when Stalin had had enough of Peter's weakness and glimpsed himself in Ivan, and Ivan in himself. The literary embodiment of this fad was Aleksei Tolstoy's play *Ivan the Terrible* and his screenplay of the same title. The obscure Tomila, however, was replaced by the well-known Malyuta Skuratov-Belsky.

Let us talk first about the film, directed by Sergei Eisenstein. Casting predetermined the image of the redheaded, bloodthirsty Malyuta—he was played by the highly appealing Mikhail Zharov. It was he, by the way, who had played Alek Men-

Reviewing a parade, Red Square, 1936. *Left to right:* Molotov, Khrushchev, Stalin.

shikov in *Peter the First*. In essence, Malyuta was the same Menshikov, but transposed to the distant, boding past. The same touching devotion to his tsar, though not pretending to friendship. Stalin—phooey! Ivan, I mean!—could not stand namby-pamby. The same willingness to be ground into dust for the sake of the Fatherland, epitomized by the tsar. And if sometimes he scowled, that was from an excess of vigilance, from the incredible perspicacity with which he discerned a plot around every corner, the murky sediment of treason in every pair or eyes, an evil intent in every word and gesture. And the astute, seasoned viewer understood that the same plotters were eying Stalin from every shadow. Because only *he* was good, and everyone around him was bad. Because he was the country's only strength, and all the rest wanted to ruin it, sell it, destroy it. So all of them, without distinction, must be done away with. No danger of making a mistake here: every one of them was guilty of something. The boyars were conspirators; the military governors, traitors; the civil servants, bribe-mongers; the churchmen, vipers; the simple people, rogues and mutineers; the palace guard, a pack of curs only waiting to turn upon the one they were supposed to protect. All guilty, all criminals. Cut them down, torture them, put them to death, send them into exile. Show no mercy. There was no other way to save the visionary statesman exerting himself for the good of the Fatherland.

All of which went for Stalin, too. He too, like Ivan, destroyed not only his enemies, or even mostly his enemies, but mostly his friends, people devoted to him in spite of everything, because he seemed to them the embodiment of a great idea. He destroyed government and Party officials, old Bolsheviks, military leaders, scholars, doctors, the technical and creative intelligentsia, workers, peasants, and—with special gusto—Lenin's comrades-in-arms and people with a gift, since he knew in the depths of his soul he had none.

American and Soviet soldiers meet at the Elbe River, Germany, 1945.

Nikolai Cherkasov had never, in any role, been as good as he was as Ivan the Terrible. Even his dashing, heroic Aleksandr Nevsky paled by comparison. Sometimes he looked like an angel in his white garments, with his delicate (well-lighted) unearthly face. In a word, the spitting image of Comrade Stalin. Naturally, the Leader could hardly wait for part two, the apotheosis of the *Oprichnina* [the one-time imperial corps of bodyguards to Ivan IV (the Terrible)—ED.], whose counterpart he also held dear.

Cinema being a clumsy, time-consuming thing, the theaters were called into service. Plays about Ivan the Terrible were commissioned from three famous dramatists: Aleksei Tolstoy, Ilya Selvinsky, and Vladimir A. Solovyov. Not much was expected from Selvinsky. He was too much of a poet. (And so it turned out. He wrote with genius about the Livonian war, but it was so complicated, so elevated. Something more down-to-earth would have been better.) Solovyov could write verse too, but he was no poet. He was closer to the mark, and the play went well. As always, Tolstoy came out on top. His drama, in the Maly Theater, was the event of the season. Here the statesmanly greatness and spiritual beauty of Malyuta's sovereign were fully displayed. Malyuta himself came off looking a little more stern, since enemies were on the prowl. No time for smiles. With their sort around, you have to be on the lookout every minute. The rest of the *Oprichnina,* though, vied with one another in kindness and derring-do. Fedka Basmanov, the sly double-dealer, seemed a paladin of old, a shining, fearless knight. The obtuse, bloodstained Gryaznoy came off as a simple-minded, heroic oaf. But the intelligent and indispensable priest Sylvester was portrayed as the worst sort of villain, and the brave and gifted Kurbsky, as an envious turncoat.

In sum, talented dramatists, working on different periods of Ivan's reign, managed by their concerted efforts to justify and exalt the tsar's abhorrent personal life, his failures in war and statecraft, and the senseless terror that weakened Russia, depriving it of its best heads and sharpest swords, preparing the way for the Time of Troubles. Most important, they whitewashed the accursed *Oprichnina*. Russian history, sometimes inclined to find reasons of state not only in Ivan's early policies but also in his bloodthirsty later years, had up to then found very little good to say about it.

It should be noted that as falsifiers of history the dramatists were completely outdone by the novelist Valentin Kostylev, whose trilogy presents a truly cloying image of a humanitarian tsar, Russia's benefactor, defender of the common people, leading light in every endeavor, best friend of Old Russia's sportsmen (as if they were there) and of every sort of mummery—the theater, that is to say. Here, all joking aside, was the lynx eye of Stalin winking from under the sable band of Monomakh's hat.

The second part of Eisenstein's *Ivan the Terrible*, though, deeply disappointed the Leader. The great and tormented director's artistic conscience had awakened. Instead of the expected gilding of the *Oprichnina*, the conferring of law and order on the Russian state through the aid of limitless bloodshed, what emerged on the screen was the impenetrable night of Ivan's soul, a demonic *Oprichnina* like the winged powers of darkness, the whole nightmare of a time turned inside out. The film was banned, and the director did not long outlive its downfall.

But that was only an irritating detail. On the whole, the thing was done: the hearts and minds of the citizens were imprinted with the inspiring image of Tsar Ivan, the wise founder of the *Oprichnina*. For him everything was permitted, any repression, as long as it was for the good of the Fatherland. And the sovereign alone, answerable to no one, would decide what was for the good and what was not.

The historians seized upon the image the writers had whipped up and provided it with the necessary scholarly apparatus. Oddly enough, when it became possible to get rid of this travesty and go back to the real Ivan the Terrible, scholars were in no hurry to take a hard new look. Maybe they thought that a new cult would surely demand

The eternal flame at the Tomb of the Unknown Soldier, Moscow.

he be put back on his pedestal, so why rush? Until recently, you could run across very lenient assessments of the *Oprichnina* in scholarly works. It was wrong to murder, wreak mayhem, and plunder, of course. But what could you do with hot-blooded youngsters? And think how much they accomplished! The terror certainly wasn't a good thing, but it did strengthen the state. The Time of Troubles? Well, that's a bourgeois term, really. There wasn't any Time of Troubles, just some temporary difficulties. After Ivan, the grip on the reins loosened, and the *Oprichnina* was disbanded. Soon enough, though, the peasant Ivan Susanin, the merchant Kuzma Minin, and the nobleman Dmitri Pozharsky joined forces and set things right.

Incidentally, historical novels that showed gen-

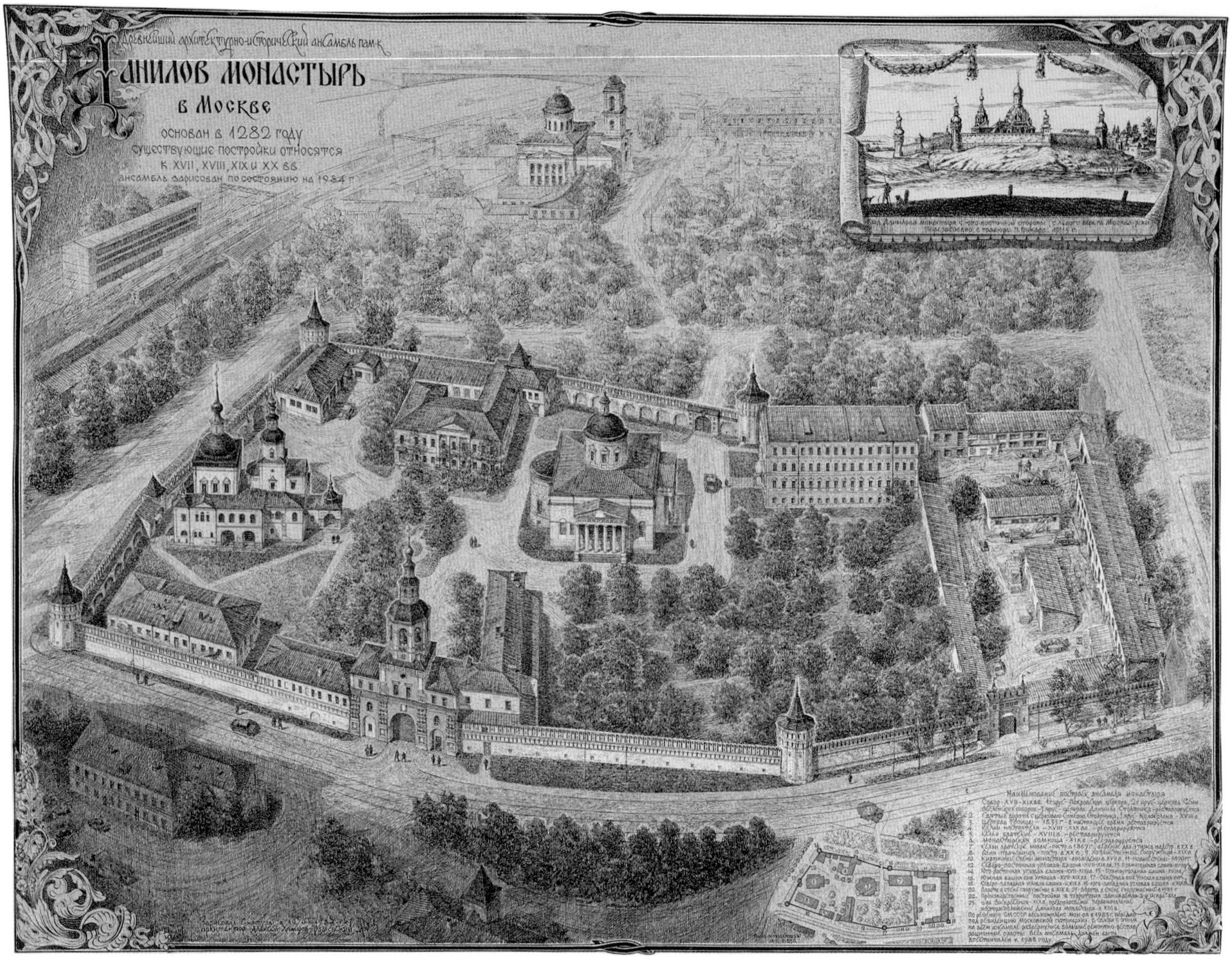

The Danilov Monastery, residence of the All-Russia Patriarch in Moscow (lithograph).

uine talent were appearing even at that time. The best of them, Zinovi Davydov's *The Newcomer from Goshcha,* went all but unnoticed by the official critics. Its subject is an escapade involving the first Pseudo-Dmitri. The main hero is a historical personage, Prince Khvorostinin, a noted writer of syllabic verse, a young man with a burning interest in science, the arts, and the great world beyond Russia's boundaries. And so he became a follower of the pretender Dmitri, a wind blowing into the backwaters of Russia from the West. The Dmitri portrayed here is not the traditional knavish figure. He is a lively, earnest, rather well-informed fellow who wants to bring Moscovy out of hibernation; a predecessor of people like Prince Vasili Golytsyn, the boyar Matveev, and Peter himself.

I do not know how close much of this comes to the historical truth, if indeed such a thing is known. What is certain, though, is that such a role—from monk to monarch—could not have been acted by a clown, a man of straw. I go along with Pushkin on this. When his Dmitri tells Marina Mnishek, "Enough. I am ashamed to abase myself before a proud woman of Poland," he is admirable and noble. Of course Davydov's novel, taking this view of things, could hardly suit the official taste, although it is rich in marvelous portraits of common people—patriots with no thought of personal gain, willing to sacrifice everything for the good of their country. It is a wonder the book ever appeared. They say Aleksandr Fadeyev, an important figure in Stalin's day, fell in love with it and helped it along.

Sergei Borodin wrote a fine novel about Dmitri

Donskoy, which was even awarded the Stalin Prize, second class. The big prize went to Vasili Yan's novels *Genghis Khan* and *Batu*—or maybe just one of them. It is too long ago for me to remember, and it makes no difference here. Yanchevetsky (Yan was a pseudonym) was a teacher, a modest fellow with no discernible literary gift. His bulky, rather gray novels were hardly more than chronicles of historical events, but he beat out the talented Borodin. Stalin himself decided who should get the prizes bearing his name, and in what degree. It was to be expected that he would prefer Yan's chronicles. Borodin paints an ironic picture of Mamay, but Yan's two conquerors are stupendous. They are monolithic, intelligent, decisive, and merciless. That was precisely what pleased Stalin. What impressed him was power unrestrained from within or without, crushing everything in its path. He himself, after all, was a Genghis Khan, a Batu, coming to a foreign land and laying it at his feet.

At the time, Stalin was not much concerned with patriotism—Borodin's strong suit. (It is scarcely to be felt in Yan's novels, which are largely written from the Tatar point of view.) Stalin had no use for Russian patriotism. It was only when the war began that he missed it and began to blow life back into the smoldering coals. In fact, it was only to the accompaniment of the roar of Hitler's tanks and the tramp of iron boot soles that the word "Russian" was revived. Konstantin Simonov, first to sense which way the wind blew, threw together a play called *Russian People*. What stunned everybody was its name, not the dreary story. Then the pomp of the old army was salvaged from the rubbish heap, and the glorious, if somewhat faded, old names were remembered: Suvorov, Kutuzov, Ushakov, Rumyantsev. Even Yermolov was brought back, although he had subdued mountain tribesmen, a thing considered reprehensible not long before.

Patriotism took hold of Stalin together with the terrible fright he had at the beginning of the war, when Hitler suddenly and treacherously broke the bonds of friendship, and with them the Molotov-Ribbentrop pact. He never got over that fright. He realized once and for all that when he was in trouble he had only the Russian people, with their boundless obedience, to rely on. From then on ideology, literature, and art came under the sway of "Le style russe" and of old-time Russian patriotism in the spirit of popular prints from World War I, with their hero Kuzma Kryuchkov. The myth of a hopelessly backward Russia, beaten by everybody, was replaced with the myth of an invincible Russia, which had beaten everybody, although it had never ever attacked anyone, had invented and discovered everything, and had always been ahead of the West. This model was to have a long life, even when it was not carried to such extremes as during the fight against "Cosmopolitanism" (the name give to the campaign of annihilation that gave expression to Stalin's zoological anti-Semitism). Ah yes—the national question. Stalin provided a few astonishing answers that greatly enriched Marxist-Leninist thought. First, the Jews were not a nation, since they did not have their own territory (and so it would be good to give them that territory, in faraway but quiet parts). Second, whole nations could be sent into exile, driven from the age-old land of their fathers, if they behaved badly.

It might seem strange that although my theme here is history, I keep thinking about literature. But there is nothing strange about it. The Russia of old, unlike that of today, had history and historians. But among them was no colossus, no Macaulay or Niebuhr. Still, Russia did have great historians: Pushkin and Lev Tolstoy. It was the same in philosophy: however remarkable Vladimir Solovyov and—uh—Chelpanov may be, they are not equal to Kant or Hegel. But Russia did have great philosophers: Dostoevsky and Tolstoy. Always and everywhere, it was literature that redeemed Russia. Our great religious thinkers were not Father Filaret and his brethren, but again Dostoevsky and Tolstoy, to whom we may add Nikolai Leskov.

Pushkin also wrote history in the narrow sense: the *History of the Pugachev Rebellion* and the materials prepared for a history of Peter the Great. It might seem that the latter contain nothing but facts, but facts chosen with such skill, set forth with such clarity! There is just no way to describe the hidden current of poetry pulsing under the laconic, businesslike prose. From time to time Pushkin allows himself some irony, thereby adding an extra dimension. Here are two juxtaposed phrases: "The death of Petr Petrovich, the tsarevich and heir apparent, finally broke the iron spirit of Peter." And then: "On the first of June, Peter was taken sick (from drinking)." What depths of meaning in that parenthetical "from drinking"! You were expecting it would be from grief. But no, nothing in Peter's iron spirit was broken by the death of the long-awaited heir, who could have been put on the throne, bypassing Aleksis. The death was a shock. But the tsar struck back, and that's what made him sick. Nothing to worry about. He would sleep it off, then drink some cold *kvas* with horseradish for his aching head, or some sour cabbage soup, and the tireless human machine would set to work again.

In reporting the death of Charles XII of Sweden, an implacable enemy of Peter and of Russia, who first defeated us and then was defeated by us but who never ceased to display undaunted courage and diabolical energy, Pushkin adds: "Peter wept for him." It is meant literally. Peter broke into tears when he learned that the warrior-king had perished in the trenches. This is proof of Peter's unusually broad nature. Yes, Charles was an enemy, but Peter had been impressed by his dynamism, strength of will, and rare courage. And Peter was grateful to him for the Swedes' having taught the Russians to fight battles and win them.

The senate and synod conferred on Peter the titles "Father of the Fatherland, All-Russian Emperor, Peter the Great." Pushkin adds, in italics: *Peter, not standing long on ceremony, accepted them.* Would Aleksei Tolstoy ever have permitted himself a remark like that? He was capable of something even sharper, but his behind-the-scenes patron would never have forgiven him. Pushkin shows Peter as cynical, lacking in decorum and, again, in restraint. For him, the unseemliness of these made-to-order honors was no stumbling block. But it does irk Pushkin: there is something servile in the officials, and yes, in Peter too, together concocting this piece of bad taste. A free man—a man of inner freedom—ought to have refused this doubtful honor.

Aleksei Tolstoy's patron would never have stood for mockery of that kind. An uneducated man, with no clear conception of anything, Stalin quite seriously dubbed himself Supreme High Commander, adding the title of Generalissimo, like Suvorov. He was the Leading Light of Science, the Greatest Strategist of all times and nations, a Great Innovator in linguistics. Actually a Trotskyite, he was called "the Lenin of today." Besides which he was the Leader of the Communist party, having destroyed its best members, the Father of the nationalities, and the best friend of Soviet sportsmen. The lickspittles of Peter's day vanish into insignificance alongside these achievements.

But back to our main theme. Pushkin's historical works show him as an important historian, but his literary works show him as a great one. The Pugachev of *The Captain's Daughter* surpasses the figure that emerges from the historical record. Using his artist's intuition, Pushkin divined more than he could with the narrow archival view. In the history, Pugachev is fierce; in the tale he is fierce, and dreadful, and horrifying, and touching, and human. Today, we know that Yemelyan Pugachev was just such a man, but in Pushkin's time the biased selection of documents in the archives portrayed him as a villain pure and simple. Once again, intuition had triumphed over pure scholarship. Pasternak said that only art is always on target.

War and Peace is on target too. Tolstoy's gift to us is not only aesthetic enjoyment but also a deep knowledge of one of the most important periods of Russian history. His magnificent novel is inspired with the same "hidden warmth of patriotism" that helped the Russian people overcome the invincible Napoleon. The wily Kutuzov correctly saw it as his task to let events take their natural course.

In the Soviet period, literature has remained the people's chief source of historical knowledge. Unfortunately, our art, even if through no fault of its own, has only rarely been on target. The brazen rewriting of history began in Stalin's day, and so it continued until just recently. And I do not mean the history of ancient times, but our own Soviet history, involving quite recent events, things we saw with our own eyes. It would have been impossible to get away with such a thing, of course, if our *sense* of history had not been damaged.

Back before the war, Stalin decided to put in order with his own hand the history of the Party, an important component of Soviet history. And so he wrote his *Short Course.* It was first published anonymously; afterwards, we were astounded to learn who had authored this masterpiece. Had anyone ever before written of himself as "great" and "wise," as a "genius"? Even the last of the Caesars, in their decadence, had not been so "objective" about themselves. Only when he was dying had Nero let slip: "What an artist dies with me!" But that isn't the main thing, of course: the main thing is that we received a history of the Party with everything turned on its head. History as it should have been, in the eyes of Comrade Stalin. It is pointless to examine his creation in detail. Let's just say that Stalin announced himself to be not only the greatest historian but also the greatest philosopher. The whole country, young and old, from the schoolboy Pioneer to the gray-haired Academician, settled down to study the fourth chapter, a naïve and dim-witted but, because of its clumsy writing, nonetheless opaque account of the principles of dialectical materialism.

Another example of bold-faced falsification: the three volumes of Leonid Brezhnev's memoirs, written not by him but by three different authors. And no one found it surprising that, although they did the writing, somebody else got the Lenin Prize. It was a bit of a shock, though, to find out that the decisive event of the war was not the Battle of Stalingrad, which had turned everything around, but the amphibious assault on the Little Land. That was where Colonel Brezhnev had headed the political department of a division. A gloomy joke was born: the Great Patriotic War, people said, was only a skirmish in the great battle for the Little Land.

They set things straight about the war. Four stars, four Heroes of the Soviet Union, shone on that portly chest. To these was added the Order of Victory, which went to our most eminent strategists for key battles. Bushy-Brows was not around long enough to make generalissimo—he bowed out as a plain marshal. But before the marshal left us orphaned, Leonid Ilyich, through his ghostwriter Anatoli Agranovsky, created a new masterpiece, *Rebirth.* It seemed we also owed the postwar renaissance to Brezhnev.

From the third volume we learned that it was Brezhnev, once again, who had given the country its virgin lands. And we had thought that opening them up had been Khrushchev's idea, and that P. K. Ponomarenko, secretary of the Kazakhstan Central Committee, had headed up the work. (Brezhnev had served under Ponomarenko as an obscure second secretary.) Well, it just wasn't so. It was Brezhnev, remaining in the shadows out of modesty, who had conceived the historic project and had seen it through. This last volume of the trilogy appeared when the hero had stopped doing anything at all but collecting foreign cars and muttering at the occasional ceremonial event. And this entire phantasmagoria was performed, as shamelessly as a striptease, before the eyes of a nation of 280 million.

Dozens, hundreds of ready pens set about rewriting the history of the war and the postwar renewal "according to Brezhnev." Stalin was not forgotten, of course—there was no getting along without him in telling the Big Lie. But where would he have been if Brezhnev had not decided the course of the war on the Little Land, or pulled the country out of its postwar devastation?

In *1984* Orwell describes an institution devoted to the day-by-day revision of the recent past. At the Ministry of Truth a large staff looks through old newspapers, cuts out all the things that from today's point of view are unsuitable, and replaces them with other, suitable things. And so it goes, endlessly, depending on what Big Brother needs today. Saddest of all, this is no caricature. It is how things were with us until just recently. A bitter truth sounded in Pasternak's words: "In the Soviet Union, there is no reality."

We have talked about the condition of the science of history (if indeed that term can be applied to voluntaristic exercises on a historical theme) under Stalin and Brezhnev, but we have somehow omitted the time of the Thaw. Khrushchev did a

Celebrating the millennium of Christianity in Russia.

The bell-ringer in Tolgosky Monastery.

great deal for the country. He exposed the personality cult; closed the camps; returned their good name to hundreds of thousands who had been falsely condemned; made quiet our terrible, watchful nights; removed the Iron Curtain; let in a breath of fresh air. Unfortunately, he also considered culture and the humanities to be of secondary importance, along with protecting the environment. Let's get communism built first, then we can think about culture, and nature, and all that intellectual stuff. Khrushchev was a keen-witted peasant. He had no time for the intelligentsia—that talkative, wearying, restless lot. He truly could not see what use they were, and that was finally his downfall. His decisions—hotheaded, contradictory, with no knowledge or analysis behind them—did nothing to improve industry or agriculture, or to raise the standard of living. They only spoiled Khrushchev's character. The country had barely got moving again, and now it was at another dead end. He was looking forward, not back—of what use was history to him? He really wanted to see the coming of communism in his lifetime; he had set 1984, the year Orwell wrote about, as the date. Khrushchev did not live to see communism. Neither have we, so far.

Under Stalin, little was heard about the Decembrists, and nothing at all about the revolutionary assassins of the People's Will. The ruthless and rather cowardly Georgian hated rebels, to say nothing of regicide—a bad example can be catching. Under Khrushchev the heroes of Senate Square were remembered, along with Nikolai Kibalchich, and Sofya Perovskaya, and many other half-forgotten historical figures.

In the years of stagnation, as we call the twenty years after Khrushchev, historical thought slumbered. Some dubious games continued to be played with history, though. Stalin was partly rehabilitated, primarily as a military leader, and Khrushchev, who had done so much good, was crossed out of Russian history altogether.

As always, literature marched in the vanguard of historical thought, which had almost died out. Ivan Stadnyuk, a bad but officially esteemed writer, sang paeans to Stalin as a military leader in his multivolume novel, *War.* Nothing can dim this bright image in the eyes of those who do not want to see the truth: not the destruction of brilliant men in the top military echelons; not the entrusting of the war's conduct to a plumber from Lugansk, a headless horseman, and a noncommissioned officer from the tsarist army (Voroshilov, Budyonny, and Timoshenko); not the floundering of the first months, which handed half of European Russia over to the Germans (the Leader just couldn't believe his friend Hitler had betrayed him).

Scholars followed the writers' lead. Military historians renewed their homage to Stalin. They had a strong trump card in the memoirs of Marshal Zhukov. It is only now, as the truth begins to surface, that we learn how they pressured the old man into bringing his recollections into accord with the "spirit of the time." Thus, the laughable phrase about how he (Zhukov!) needed to consult with the unknown political officer Brezhnev. Thus the heel-clicking before Stalin. In private con-

Monument to Vladimir I, who proclaimed Christianity in Russia, A.D. 988.

versation (but somehow it got into print), Marshal Rokossovsky used to say about Stalin, "Do you think we listened to that seminary dropout? We pretended to be following orders, but we did as we saw fit." That was the true picture.

Another notion hatched by writers, and taken up by scholars: Two-thirds of our country is in Asia, so Russia is Asian, not European. Peter had no business opening a window on Europe; there is nothing for us there. Nothing, true enough, for literary savages who have nothing to do with European culture. This theory never won official approval—it has remained latent. Criticism is leveled at Peter, but no one has said outright that Russia had no need of the reforms that diluted its individuality, its Asiatic character. Things haven't gone that far yet, and it looks like they won't.

In the years of stagnation it was Soviet history, beginning with the war, that was most actively falsified. There was no way, alas, that Brezhnev could be brought into the Revolution or the Civil War. As for Russian history, there seemed to be no need for it at all. The unwritten rule of that dreary time was: don't look forward; don't look back. Better keep your eyes on your feet, so you don't stumble.

From time to time, though, writers attempted to return history to objective truth. This happened both in the years of "voluntarism" (as they have dubbed the Khrushchev years, when the worn-out people did get some kind of breather) and in the years of "stagnation" (no objections to that term). A book about Ivan the Terrible cautiously but clearly asserted that he had not been the greatest humanitarian of his time, and that the *Oprichnina* had done more harm than good. A book on the Time of Troubles certified that there had indeed been such a time in Russian history, and that Ivan was mainly to blame for it.

The meekness here is rooted in Ivan's image having got fused inextricably with Stalin's image. The latter had to be handled with kid gloves. It had shown an amazing ability to rise from the dead. Having been laid to rest, seemingly forever, at the Twentieth and Twenty-First Party Congresses, it appeared anew, perhaps not in its earlier splendor but certainly imposing enough, in the years of stagnation. Even *glasnost,* which has told the whole (or nearly whole) truth about Stalin's bloody crimes, has not nailed the coffin shut. On the contrary, the voices have grown louder: "There was order under Stalin." Yes, the order of a torture chamber, a prison, a cemetery. Others keep repeating: "Under Stalin Magnitogorsk was built, and the Dnieper hydroelectric dam." Somehow it never occurs to them that other countries have built their Magnitogorsks and great dams, often even bigger and more powerful, without paying for them in rivers of blood. No need to go far for examples. Japan, defeated, deafened by the explosion of atom bombs, has today emerged as the world's industrial leader, and this stunning success has not cost a single murder.

It was Stalin himself who imposed on his countrymen this overblown idea of the marvels his industrialization program had accomplished. His people sought constantly to enlarge on the myth of a hopelessly backward Russia, a purely agricultural country with insignificant, embryonic industry. That was a lie; capitalism in Russia was fairly well developed before the October Revolution. The breadbasket of Europe (today we import grain from Argentina, Canada, and the United States) was steadily building its industrial might. Metallurgy was strong, and Russia's artillery was considered the best in the world, which says something about the state of the arms industry. Russian capitalism's engineering know-how was proven in the old Trans-Siberian Railway. The new one has never dreamed of such quality. Russia's economy was so strong that it could fight an enervating war with the Kaiser's Germany and come repeatedly to the rescue of its allies, at the cost of heavy casualties, without relying on their bread or their weapons.

During World War II we made extensive use of lend-lease. Weapons, ammunition, strategic raw materials, and foodstuffs were delivered from the United States. Spam was part of our officers' supplementary rations, and behind the lines it was Spam again, and powdered milk and eggs, which our grateful people called "Roosevelt eggs." At work places, clothing contributed by American citizens was periodically distributed. Our transport and freight planes were from Douglas Aircraft, and Jeeps went everywhere on land. These things have been half-forgotten somehow. They have a knack for throwing off our historical memory.

It is curious that Ivan the Terrible seems to have put a spell on the historians with his serpent's gaze—they have written most about him, and the years before and after. Books have been published about the War of 1812, the Crimean War, and the Decembrists. We have learned about the tragic figure of the unlucky Paul the First in a good book by Nathan Eydelman, published not too long ago. But for the time of Peter's merry daughter Elizabeth, or of Catherine the Great, we have only Valentin Pikul's swashbuckling novels. And some spots are utterly blank: the epoch of the first Romanovs, the stern days of the Empress Ann, the beginning of the reign of Aleksandr the First, the revolution of 1861 (the abolition of serfdom was a revolution, even if it was made at the top), the complicated reign of Aleksandr the Third. Broad segments of our population know practically nothing about these, or about the early days of Rus.

A while back, the academician Boris Rybakov published a weighty tome about our obscure Slavic past. Try to make out who these Slavs were, though, or where they came from, or what relation they had to the tribes of Rus, or what the Varangians had to do with any of this, and your brain will tie itself up in knots. Is there some kind of purpose behind this muddy verbiage? Is it to drive the Varangians out of our history? Or to show that Christianity only touched the surface of the pagan world of Rus? Or could I be mistaken?

People without historical memory, without an understanding of their past, are unfortunate people. Chekhov said, "To live in the present, the past must be redeemed. And for that, it must be known." Now the leaders heading up the revolutionary restructuring of our lives have armed themselves with that simple and indisputable truth. Cancelling the examinations in history was an eloquent gesture, indicating that falsification has come to an end. Our people's history will be returned to them. They will redeem the past and create a reality in place of the mirage.

Geography

BARRY LOPEZ has published several collections of short stories and is the author of *Arctic Dreams,* which won the National Book Award in 1986, and *Of Wolves and Men,* which won the John Burroughs Medal in 1979. He is a contributing editor of *Harper's* and *North American Review,* and a recipient of the Award in Literature from the American Academy and Institute of Arts and Letters. His most recent book is *Crossing Open Ground,* a collection of essays.

VIKTOR ASTAFYEV published his first novel, *The Snows Are Melting,* in the late 1950s. A veteran of World War II, his numerous novels and plays are often autobiographical. Astafyev's journalistic writings notably explore moral and ecological concerns and come to grips with the recent past. His novels include *The Crossing; Old Oak; Starfall; The Theft; Shepherd and Shepherdess; Queen Fish; Somewhere War Is Thundering;* and *A Sad Detective Story.* The novel *Last Greeting* and the story cycle *Blazings* are the fruits of some twenty years' work. Astafyev's dramas include *The Bird Cherries; Pardon Me;* and the screenplay *Thou Shalt Not Kill* (with E. Federovsky). *The Falling of a Leaf* is a collection of his stories and essays, and his selected journalistic writings appear in *Everything in Its Time.* Astafyev is currently working on a book entitled *The Seeing Shepherd.*

The American Geographies

Barry Lopez

It has become commonplace to observe that Americans know little of the geography of their country, that they are innocent of it as a landscape of rivers, mountains, and towns. They do not know, supposedly, the location of the Delaware Water Gap, the Olympic Mountains, or the Piedmont Plateau; and, the indictment continues, they have little conception of the way the individual components of this landscape are imperiled, from a human perspective, by modern farming practices or industrial pollution.

I do not know how true this is, but it is easy to believe that it is truer than most of us would wish. A recent Gallup Organization and National Geographic Society survey found Americans woefully ignorant of world geography. Three out of four couldn't locate the Persian Gulf. The implication was that we knew no more about our own homeland, and that this ignorance undermined the integrity of our political processes and the efficiency of our business enterprises.

As Americans, we profess a sincere and fierce love for the American landscape, for our rolling prairies, free-flowing rivers, and "purple mountains' majesty"; but it is hard to imagine, actually, where this particular landscape is. It is not just that a nostalgic landscape has passed away—Mark Twain's Mississippi is now dammed from Minnesota to Missouri and the prairies have all been sold and fenced. It is that it's always been a romantic's landscape. In the attenuated form in which it is presented on television today, in magazine articles and in calendar photographs, the essential wildness of the American landscape is reduced to attractive scenery. We look out on a familiar, memorized landscape that portends adventure and promises enrichment. There are no distracting people in it and few artifacts of human life. The animals are all beautiful, diligent, one might even say well-behaved. Nature's unruliness, the power of rivers and skies to intimidate, and any evidence of disastrous human land management practices are all but invisible. It is, in short, a magnificent garden, a colonial vision of paradise imposed on a real place that is, at best, only selectively known.

Sunrise, Nauset salt marsh, Cape Cod National Seashore, Massachusetts.

The real American landscape is a face of almost incomprehensible depth and complexity. If one were to sit for a few days, for example, among the ponderosa pine forests and black lava fields of the Cascade Mountains in western Oregon, inhaling the pines' sweet balm on an evening breeze from some point on the barren rock, and then were to step off to the Olympic Peninsula in Washington, to those rain forests with sphagnum moss floors soft as fleece underfoot and Douglas firs too big around for five people to hug, and then head south to walk the ephemeral creeks and sun-blistered playas of the Mojave Desert in southern California, one would be reeling under the sensations. The contrast is not only one of plants and soils, a different array, say, of brilliantly colored beetles. The shock to the senses comes from a different shape to the silence, a difference in the very quality of light, in the weight of the air. And this relatively short journey down the west coast would still leave the traveler with all that lay to the east to explore—the anomalous sand hills of Nebraska, the heat and frog voices of Okefenokee Swamp, the fetch of Chesapeake Bay, the hardwood copses and black bears of the Ozark Mountains.

No one of these places, of course, can be entirely fathomed, biologically or aesthetically. They are mysteries upon which we impose names. Enchantments. We tick the names off glibly but lovingly. We mean no disrespect. Our genuine desire, though we may be skeptical about the time it would take and uncertain of its practical value to us, is to actually know these places. As deeply ingrained in the American psyche as the desire to conquer and control the land is the desire to sojourn in it, to sail up and down Pamlico Sound, to paddle a canoe through Minnesota's boundary waters, to walk on the desert of the Great Salt Lake, to camp in the stony hardwood valleys of Vermont.

To do this well, to really come to an understanding of a specific American geography, requires not only time but a kind of local expertise, an intimacy with place few of us ever develop. There is no way around the former requirement: if you want to know, you must take the time. It is not in books. A specific geographical understanding, however, can be sought out and borrowed. It resides with men and women more or less sworn to a place, who abide there, who have a feel for the soil and history, for the turn of leaves and night sounds. Often they are glad to take the outlander in tow.

These local geniuses of American landscape, in my experience, are people in whom geography thrives. They are the antithesis of geographical ignorance. Rarely known outside their own communities, they often seem, at the first encounter, unremarkable and anonymous. They may not be able to recall the name of a particular wildflower—or they may have given it a name known only to them. They might have forgotten the precise circumstances of a local historical event. Or they can't say for certain when the last of the Canada geese passed through in the fall, or can't differentiate between two kinds of trout in the same creek. Like all of us, they have fallen prey to the fallacies of memory and are burdened with ignorance; but they are nearly flawless in the respect they bear these places they love. Their knowledge is intimate rather than encyclopedic, human but not necessarily scholarly. It rings with the concrete details of experience.

America, I believe, teems with such people. The paradox here, between a faulty grasp of geographic knowledge for which Americans are indicted and the intimate, apparently contradictory familiarity of a group of largely anonymous people, is not solely a matter of confused scale. (The local landscape is easier to know than a national landscape—and many local geographers, of course, are relatively ignorant of a national geography.) And it is not simply ironic. The paradox is dark. To be succinct: the politics and advertising that seek a national audience must project a national geography; to be broadly useful that geography must, inevitably, be generalized and it is often romantic. It is therefore frequently misleading and imprecise. The same holds true with the entertainment industry, but here the problem might be clearer. The same films, magazines, and television features that honor an imaginary American landscape also tout the worth of the anonymous men and women who interpret it. Their affinity for the land is lauded, their local allegiance admired. But the rigor of their local geographies, taken as a whole, contradicts a patriotic, national vision of unspoiled, untroubled land. These men and women are ultimately forgotten, along with the details of the landscapes they speak for, in the face of more pressing national matters. It is the chilling nature of modern society to find an ignorance of geography, local or national, as excusable as an ignorance of hand tools; and to find the commitment of people to their home places only momentarily entertaining. And finally naïve.

If one were to pass time among Basawara people in the Kalahari Desert, or with Kreen-Akrora in the Amazon Basin, or with Pitjantjatjara Aborigines in Australia, the most salient impression they

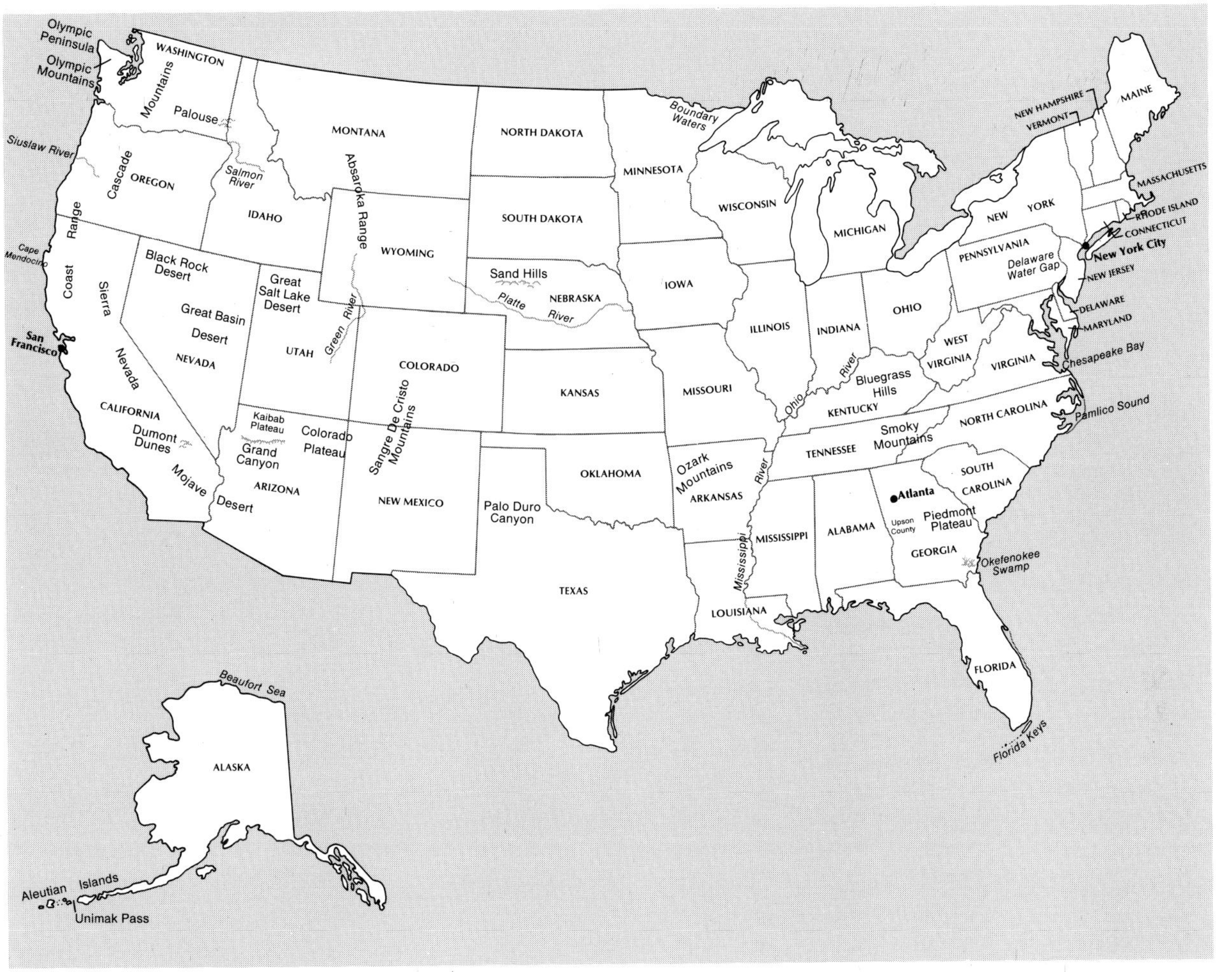

United States of America.

might leave is of an absolutely stunning knowledge of their local geography—geology, hydrology, biology, and weather. In short, the extensive particulars of their intercourse with it.

In 40,000 years of human history, it has only been in the last few hundred years or so that a people could afford to ignore their local geographies as completely as we do and still survive. Technological innovations from refrigerated trucks to artificial fertilizers, from sophisticated cost accounting to mass air transportation, have utterly changed concepts of seasons, distance, soil productivity, and the real cost of drawing sustenance from the land. It is now possible for a resident of Boston to bite into a fresh strawberry in the dead of winter; for someone in San Francisco to travel to Atlanta in a few hours with no worry of how formidable might be crossings of the Great Basin Desert or the Mississippi River; for an absentee farmer to gain a tax advantage from a farm that leaches poisons into its water table and on which crops are left to rot. The Pitjantjatjara might shake their heads in bewilderment and bemusement, not because they are primitive or ignorant people, not because they have no sense of irony or are incapable of marveling, but because they have not (many would say not yet) realized a world in which such manipulation of the land—surmounting the imperatives of distance it imposes, for example, or turning the large-scale destruction of forests and arable land into wealth—is desirable or plausible.

In the years I have traveled through America, in cars and on horseback, on foot and by raft, I have

David Muench photograph

Fern spread and hardwoods, Allegheny National Forest, Pennsylvania.

repeatedly been brought to a sudden state of awe by some gracile or savage movement of animal, some odd wrapping of a tree's foliage by the wind, an unimpeded run of dew-laden prairie stretching to a horizon flat as a coin where a pin dot sun pales the dawn sky pink. I know these things are beyond intellection, that they are the vivid edges of a world that includes but also transcends the human world. In memory, when I dwell on these things, I know that in a truly national literature there should be odes to the Triassic reds of the Colorado Plateau, to the sharp and ghostly light of the Florida Keys, to the aeolian soils of southern Minnesota and the Palouse in Washington, though the modern mind abjures the literary potential of such subjects. (If the sand and floodwater farmers of Arizona and New Mexico were to take the black loams of Louisiana in their hands they would be flabbergasted, and that is the beginning of literature.) I know there should be eloquent evocations of the cobbled beaches of Maine, the plutonic walls of the Sierra Nevada, the orange canyons of the Kaibab Plateau. I have no doubt, in fact, that there are. They are as numerous and diverse as the eyes and fingers that ponder the country—it is that only a handful of them are known. The great majority are to be found in drawers and boxes, in the letters and private journals of millions of workaday people who have regarded their encounters with the land as an engagement bordering on the

David Muench photograph

Pond cypress and pines, Okefenokee Swamp, Georgia.

spiritual, as being fundamentally linked to their state of health.

One cannot acknowledge the extent and the history of this kind of testimony without being forced to the realization that something strange, if not dangerous, is afoot. Year by year, the number of people with firsthand experience in the land dwindles. Rural populations continue to shift to the cities. The family farm is in a state of demise, and government and industry continue to apply pressure on the native peoples of North America to sever their ties with the land. In the wake of this loss of personal and local knowledge, the knowledge from which a real geography is derived, the knowledge on which a country must ultimately stand, has come something hard to define but I think sinister and unsettling—the packaging and marketing of land as a form of entertainment. An incipient industry, capitalizing on the nostalgia Americans feel for the imagined virgin landscapes of their fathers, and on a desire for adventure, now offers people a convenient though sometimes incomplete or even spurious geography as an inducement to purchase a unique experience. But the line between authentic experience and a superficial exposure to the elements of experience is blurred. And the real landscape, in all its complexity, is distorted even further in the public imagination. No longer innately mysterious and dignified, a ground from which experience grows, it becomes a curiously generic backdrop on which experience is imposed.

In theme parks the profound, subtle, and protracted experience of running a river is reduced to a loud, quick, safe equivalence, a pleasant distraction. People only able to venture into the countryside on annual vacations are, increasingly, schooled in the belief that wild land will, and should, provide thrills and exceptional scenery on a timely basis. If it does not, something is wrong, either with the land itself or possibly with the company outfitting the trip.

People in America, then, face a convoluted situation. The land itself, vast and differentiated, defies the notion of a national geography. If applied at all it must be applied lightly, and it must grow out of the concrete detail of local geographies. Yet Americans are daily presented with,

David Muench photograph

West prong, Little Pigeon River, Great Smokey Mountain National Park, Tennessee/North Carolina.

Mississippi River, Perrott State Park, Wisconsin.

David Muench photograph

and have become accustomed to talking about, a homogenized national geography, one that seems to operate independently of the land, a collection of objects rather than a continuous bolt of fabric. It appears in advertisements, as a background in movies, and in patriotic calendars. The suggestion is that there *can* be a national geography because the constituent parts are interchangeable and can be treated as commodities. In day-to-day affairs, in other words, one place serves as well as another to convey one's point. On reflection, this is an appalling condescension and a terrible imprecision, the very antithesis of knowledge. The idea that either the Green River in Utah or the Salmon River in Idaho will do, or that the valleys of Kentucky and West Virginia are virtually interchangeable, is not just misleading. For people still dependent on the soil for their sustenance, or for people whose memories tie them to those places, it betrays a numbing casualness, a utilitarian, expedient, and commercial frame of mind. It heralds a society in which it is no longer necessary for human beings to know where they live, except as those places are described and fixed by numbers. The truly difficult and lifelong task of discovering where one lives is finally disdained.

If a society forgets or no longer cares where it lives, then anyone with the political power and the will to do so can manipulate the landscape to conform to certain social ideals or nostalgic visions. People may hardly notice that anything has happened, or may assume that whatever happens—a mountain stripped of timber and eroding into its creeks—is for the common good. The more superficial a society's knowledge of the real dimensions of the land it occupies becomes, the more vulnerable the land is to exploitation, to manipulation for short-term gain. The land, virtually powerless before political and commercial entities, finds itself finally with no defenders. It finds itself bereft of intimates with indispensable, concrete knowledge. (Oddly, or perhaps not oddly, while American society continues to value local knowledge as a quaint part of its heritage, it continues to cut such people off from any real political power. This is as true for small farmers and illiterate cowboys as it is for American Indians, native Hawaiians, and Eskimos.)

The intense pressure of imagery in America, and the manipulation of images necessary to a society with specific goals, means the land will inevitably be treated like a commodity; and voices that tend to contradict the proffered image will, one way or another, be silenced or discredited by those in power. This is not new to America; the promulgation in America of a false or imposed geography has been the case from the beginning. All local geographies, as they were defined by hundreds of separate, independent native traditions, were denied in the beginning in favor of an imported and unifying vision of America's natural history. The country, the landscape itself, was eventually defined according to dictates of Progress like Manifest Destiny, and laws like the Homestead Act which reflected a poor understanding of the physical lay of the land.

When I was growing up in southern California, I formed the rudiments of a local geography—eucalyptus trees, February rains, Santa Ana winds. I lost much of it when my family moved to New York City, a move typical of the modern, peripatetic style of American life, responding to the exigencies of divorce and employment. As a boy I felt a hunger to know the American landscape that was extreme; when I was finally able to travel on my own, I did so. Eventually I visited most of the United States, living for brief periods of time in Arizona, Indiana, Alabama, Georgia, Wyoming, New Jersey, and Montana before settling twenty years ago in western Oregon.

The astonishing level of my ignorance confronted me everywhere I went. I knew early on that the country could not be held together in a few phrases, that its geography was magnificent and incomprehensible, that a man or a woman could devote a lifetime to its elucidation and still feel in the end that he had but sailed many thousands of miles over the surface of the ocean. So I came into the habit of traversing landscapes I wanted to know with local tutors and reading

Autumn reflection, Heyman Lake, Boundary Waters Canoe Area, Minnesota.

David Muench photograph

Toroweap East, Grand Canyon National Park, Arizona.

what had previously been written about, and in, those places. I came to value exceedingly novels and essays and works of nonfiction that connected human enterprise to real and specific places, and I grew to be mildly distrustful of work that occurred in no particular place, work so cerebral and detached as to be refutable only in an argument of ideas.

These sojourns in various corners of the country infused me, somewhat to my surprise on thinking about it, with a great sense of hope. Whatever despair I had come to feel at a waning sense of the real land and the emergence of false geographies—elements of the land being manipulated, for example, to create erroneous but useful patterns in advertising—was dispelled by the depth of a single person's local knowledge, by the serenity that seemed to come with that intelligence. Any harm that might be done by people who cared nothing for the land, to whom it was not innately worthy but only something ultimately for sale, I thought, would one day have to meet this kind of integrity, people with the same dignity and transcendence as the land they occupied. So when I traveled, when I rolled my sleeping bag out on the shores of the Beaufort Sea or in the high pastures of the Absaroka Range in Wyoming, or at the bottom of the Grand Canyon, I absorbed those particular testaments to life, the indigenous color and songbird song, the smell of sunbleached rock,

David Muench photograph

West Valley grasslands, Sangre de Cristo Range, Colorado.

damp earth, and wild honey, with some crude appreciation of the singular magnificence of each of those places. And the reassurance I felt expanded in the knowledge that there were, and would likely always be, people speaking out whenever they felt the dignity of the Earth imperiled in these places.

The promulgation of false geographies, which threatens the fundamental notion of what it means to live somewhere, is a current with a stable and perhaps growing countercurrent. People living in New York City are familiar with the stone basements, the cratonic geology, of that island and have a feeling for birds migrating through in the fall, their sequence and number. They do not find the city alien but human, its attenuated natural history merely different from that of rural Georgia or Kansas. I find the countermeasure, too, among Eskimos who cannot read but who might engage you for days on the subtleties of sea-ice topography. And among men and women who, though they have followed in the footsteps of their parents, have come to the conclusion that they cannot farm or fish or log in the way their ancestors did; the finite boundaries to this sort of wealth have appeared in their lifetime. Or among young men and women who have taken several decades of book-learned agronomy, zoology, silvi- and horticulture, ecology, ethnobotany, and fluvial geomorphology and turned it into a new kind of local

David Muench photograph

Black Rock Desert, Nevada.

knowledge, who have taken up residence in a place and sought, both because of and in spite of their education, to develop a deep intimacy with it. Or they have gone to work, idealistically, for the National Park Service or the fish and wildlife services or for a private institution like The Nature Conservancy. They are people to whom the land is more than politics or economics. These are people for whom the land is alive. It feeds them, directly, and that is how and why they learn its geography.

In the end, then, if one begins among the blue crabs of Chesapeake Bay and wanders for several years, down through the Smoky Mountains and back to the bluegrass hills, along the drainages of the Ohio and into the hill country of Missouri, where in summer a chorus of cicadas might drown out human conversation, then up the Missouri itself, reading on the way the entries of Meriwether Lewis and William Clark and musing on the demise of the plains grizzly and the sturgeon, crosses west into the drainage of the Platte and spends the evenings with Gene Weltfish's *The Lost Universe,* her book about the Pawnee who once thrived there, then drops south to Palo Duro Canyon and the irrigated farms of the Llano Estacado in Texas, turns west across the Sangre de Cristo, southernmost of the Rocky Mountain ranges, and moves north and west up onto the Rocky Mountain ranges, and moves north and west up onto the slickrock mesas of Utah, those browns and

David Muench photograph

Pioneer Lakes, Sierra Nevada, California.

oranges, the ocherous hues reverberating in the deep canyons, then goes north, swinging west to the insular ranges that sit like battleships in the pelagic space of Nevada, camps at the steaming edge of sulphur springs in the Black Rock Desert, where alkaline pans are glazed with a ferocious light, a heat to melt iron, then crosses the northern Sierra Nevada, waist deep in summer snow in the passes, to descend to the valley of the Sacramento, and rises through groves of elephantine redwoods in the Coast Range, to arrive at Cape Mendocino, before Balboa's Pacific, cormorants and gulls, gray whales headed north for Unimak Pass in the Aleutians, the winds crashing down on you, facing the ocean over the blue ocean that gives the scene its true vastness, making this crossing, having been so often astonished at the line and the color of the land, the ingenious lives of its plants and animals, the varieties of its darknesses, the intensity of the stars overhead, you would be ashamed to discover, then, in yourself, any capacity to focus on ravages in the land that left you unsettled. You would have seen so much, breathtaking, startling, and outsize, that you might not be able for a long time to break the spell, the sense, especially finishing your journey in the West, that the land had not been as rearranged or quite as compromised as you had first imagined.

After you had slept some nights on the beach, however, with that finite line of the ocean before you and the land stretching out behind you, the wind first battering then cradling you, you would

Rainbow and coastline, Ecola State Park, Oregon.

be compelled by memory, obligated by your own involvement, to speak of what left you troubled. To find the rivers dammed and shrunken, the soil washed away, the land fenced, a tracery of pipes and wires and roads laid down everywhere, blocking and channeling the movement of water and animals, cutting the eye off repeatedly and confining it—you had expected this. It troubles you no more than your despair over the ruthlessness, the insensitivity, the impetuousness of modern life. What underlies this obvious change, however, is a less noticeable pattern of disruption: acidic lakes, skies empty of birds, fouled beaches, the poisonous slags of industry, the sun burning like a molten coin in ruined air.

It is a tenet of certain ideologies that man is responsible for all that is ugly, that everything nature creates is beautiful. Nature's darkness goes partly unreported, of course, and human brilliance is often perversely ignored. What is true is that man has a power, literally beyond his comprehension, to destroy. The lethality of some of what he manufactures; the incompetence with which he stores it or seeks to dispose of it; the cavalier way in which he employs in his daily living substances that threaten his health; the leniency of the courts in these matters (as though products as well as people enjoyed the protection of the Fifth Amendment); and the treatment of open land, rivers, and the atmosphere as if, in some medieval way, they could still be regarded as disposal sinks of infinite capacity, would make you wonder, standing face to in the wind at Cape Mendocino, if we weren't bent on an errand of madness.

The geographies of North America, the myriad small landscapes that make up the national fabric, are threatened—by ignorance of what makes them unique, by utilitarian attitudes, by failure to include them in the moral universe, and by brutal disregard. A testament of minor voices can clear away an ignorance of any place, can inform us of its special qualities; but no voice, by merely telling a story, can cause the poisonous wastes that saturate some parts of the land to decompose, to evaporate. This responsibility falls ultimately to the national community, a vague and fragile entity to be sure, but one that, in America, can be ferocious in exerting its will.

Geography, the formal way in which we grapple with this areal mystery, is finally knowledge that calls up something in the land we recognize and respond to. It gives us a sense of place and a sense of community. Both are indispensable to a state of well-being, an individual's and a country's.

One afternoon on the Siuslaw River in the Coast Range of Oregon, in January, I hooked a steelhead, a sea-run trout, that told me, through the muscles of my hands and arms and shoulders, something of the nature of the thing I was calling "the Siuslaw River." Years ago I had stood under a pecan tree in Upson County, Georgia, idly eating the nuts, when slowly it occurred to me that these nuts would taste different from pecans growing somewhere up in South Carolina. I didn't need a sharp sense of taste to know this, only to pay attention at a level no one had ever told me was necessary. One November dawn, long before the sun rose, I began a vigil at the Dumont Dunes in the Mojave Desert in California, which I kept until a few minutes after the sun broke the horizon. During that time I named to myself the colors by which the sky changed and by which the sand itself flowed like a rising tide through grays and silvers and blues into yellows, pinks, washed duns, and fallow beiges.

It is through the power of observation, the gifts of eye and ear, of tongue and nose and finger, that a place first rises up in our mind; afterwards it is memory that carries the place, that allows it to grow in depth and complexity. For as long as our records go back, we have held these two things dear, landscape and memory. Each infuses us with a different kind of life. The one feeds us, figuratively and literally. The other protects us from lies and tyranny. To keep landscapes intact and the memory of them, our history in them, alive, seems as imperative a task in modern time as finding the extent to which individual expression can be accommodated, before it threatens to destroy the fabric of society.

If I were now to visit another country, I would ask my local companion, before I saw any museum or library, any factory or fabled town, to walk me in the country of his or her youth, to tell me the names of things and how, traditionally, they have been fitted together in a community. I would ask for the stories, the voice of memory over the land. I would ask to taste the wild nuts and fruits, to see their fishing lures, their bouquets, their fences. I would ask about the history of storms there, the age of the trees, the winter color of the hills. Only then would I ask to see the museums. I would want first the sense of a real place, to know that I was not inhabiting an idea. I would want to know the lay of the land first, the real geography, and take some measure of the love of it in my companion before I stood before the paintings or read works of scholarship. I would want to have something real and remembered against which I might hope to measure their truth.

Live Forever, Vivi River

VIKTOR ASTAFYEV

Of all the vehicles I have ridden in, the helicopter sings the sweetest lullaby. We are not even half an hour out of Tura, the center of the Evenki National District, and one after another our fellow passengers are closing their eyes. Their chins drop down on their chests. Two young Evenkis, wearing jeans and smart jackets, open their books but never turn a page. They doze off, leaning against the sides of the helicopter, huddled together like brothers. Kupets, our old white dog, spends a long time picking out a place for himself in the machine's commodious womb. Finally he plops down on his belly, turning his nose away from the reserve fuel drum. He lies with his tongue hanging out, breathing hard, tossing his head restlessly. His sensitive, delicate nostrils ooze moisture, protecting his keen nose from the gasoline and exhaust fumes.

Our traveling companions, Nikolai, Sabir, and teen-aged Seryozha, cannot hold out for long. They play a listless game of cards, then they slump against the sides of the helicopter in sweet surrender.

Only we city people cannot settle down. After spending the winter and most of the summer in our apartments, we are excited to see our dream of fishing in the pristine vastness of the Evenki District coming true at last. We turn our heads, here, there, jumping from window to window, gazing wide-eyed at the bright green taiga lying between two great rivers, the Yenisey and the Lena. All of the USA could fit here, and part of Canada too.

After visiting the Evenki District for the first time, and then the Gobi Desert in Mongolia, it occurred to me that Europe's crowded humanity has a good stock of land in reserve. There is even room enough here for the Americans, North and South. All we need to do is live in peace on this Earth and channel at least part of our military budgets, at least one small stream of gold, into creative efforts, finding intelligent ways to make these unpopulated expanses our own.

I said "we city people." With me on this trip are my grandson, who also is called Viktor, and Vladimir Alekseevich Zelenov, who is a sculptor and painter from Krasnoyarsk.

I am in the Evenki District for the second time; Vladimir and Viktor, for the first. We are flying towards a river with a wondrous name, Vivi, which nobody has been able to explain to me.

The helicopter hums evenly and peacefully, rocking gently. Passing by under its round iron belly are forests and mountains, streams tangled as the veins on a human arm, and sleepy little lakes on the flat saddles of mountain ridges. From time to time in the bend of a nameless brook or stream, ice gleams like a white noodle. It won't melt now—August is here already. There have been frosts. The ground and water have grown cold and the worst of the mosquito season is past. The little leaves on the scrub willows, the bilberry, and the red currant bushes have withered and begun to sparkle.

An old church by the Volga River.

Not far from here the Tungus meteor exploded. That was back at the beginning of the century, but its mystery remains unsolved; people still argue about it. Was it a meteorite? An interplanetary craft? Might a starship have made a forced landing, then sped away again to other worlds?

Human reason, which wakes out of its habitual sleep only to take fitful action, usually evil or dirty, is still inclined to the view that in all of creation we are alone—certainly the most intelligent of beings. So then, there was no spaceship. A rock fell out of the sky and burned up in the atmosphere, or it plunged so deep into Earth's bowels that we cannot dig it up.

Mankind has always looked for easy answers, for the shortest way to prosperity and happiness, for the solution to every kind of mystery and riddle. The quickest and simplest way to live well, to gain prosperity without going to any trouble, is to pay no heed to anything and to take bread away from your neighbor. If he won't give it to you, crush him, trample him, destroy him. Of course, you will be destroying yourself as well, for war feeds itself and peace does not. Even in the cave of ancient days, the bolder, stronger brother, snatching a bone away from his weaker brother, sentenced himself to death. And the fifteen thousand wars that have taken place on our Earth, the eight billion people who have perished in the fiery whirlwind, this is the execution of that sentence, the terrible curse of Heaven and Earth on the being who used his reason to go against the will of God, the design of nature. Man has defaced himself and has sullied the planet, being unworthy either to inhabit it or to husband it, having no mercy for what lives and grows upon its face. Nature made a tragic mistake in conferring reason on this two-legged being. Now she moans and weeps, racked by spasms, unable to check or set right the deeds of her offspring, who still has not tamed the primordial beast within himself.

In this part of the Evenki District there are no craggy peaks or stone outcroppings. The tops of nearly all the ridges are flat, strewn with bald black

The flood basin of the Oka River.

Evening in Malye Karely town, Karelia.

rocks. On the slopes these same rocks, washed down to their gray flesh, are covered with gray lichen. The cheeks of the mountains and the crests are pocked with enormous funnels and cirques. The snows plunge down into them like frightened rabbits and huddle there forever, never melting. This is the kingdom of rocks and bushes. The eternal winds drive life of every kind into the valleys of the rivers and streams. Only at the height of summer, when the mosquitoes are at their most ferocious, do the reindeer and other beasts, great and small, flee here, seeking refuge in the cold breeze.

We fly and fly above this land. It is huge, endless, little traveled, almost unexplored.

It is only a part, a small piece of the country known as Siberia, a sort of Russian Eldorado, which makes up 29 percent of the Soviet Union, about six-and-a-half million square kilometers. Population density here is lower by factors of ten than in the European part of the Soviet Union. In eastern Siberia, where I write this essay in my native village of Ovsyanka, on the bank of the Yenisey, population density is thirty times lower than on the other side of the Urals, in the west of our country. When Siberia became part of Russia there were practically no Russians living in these gigantic spaces. Most of the population were natives, belonging to thirty-one distinct ethnic groups. Before the Revolution they were called *inorodtsy*—foreign tribes. They numbered just over one million.

Then the great Trans-Siberian Railway was built, stretching tens of thousands of kilometers from Moscow to Vladivostok. It was built, by the way, without any great fuss and without shoddy workmanship, in record time, using primitive tools. Once it was completed, the population of Siberia rose steadily. There had been a little over five million people in 1897; by 1926, thirteen million people were living in Siberia, most of them settlers from the Ukraine, Belorussia, and the poor lands of central Russia.

As roads and transportation networks developed, Siberia began to participate in Russia's trade, producing iron and other metals, timber, coal, oil, and gas for the international market. At present, more than three hundred enterprises in Siberia participate in foreign trade. That is very little, however, for such a country, for such riches. It accounts for only 14 percent of Soviet exports. The rate of growth here is only a little higher than in the country as a whole.

Before the Revolution, Siberia produced more than 360 million pounds of fish each year, or 50 percent of Russia's total catch. Back then, Siberia was first in the world in fur trapping and among the first in gold mining. Butter from Siberia made up 75 percent of Russia's overall butter exports. In 1913, for example, Siberia sold nearly seventy-two thousand tons of the highest quality butter, competing with the big, established producers in Copenhagen, Hamburg, and London, bringing about a decline in prices on the European market. Trade in Siberian butter brought Russia twice as much gold as all of Siberia's mining, a branch of Russia's industry with a long and once-glorious history. Things got so bad that Russian merchants tried to bribe government officials and the railroad authorities in an attempt to keep cheap Siberian bread and butter out of Europe.

Siberia remains a world treasure-house of coal, timber, gas, oil, and peat. Efficiently exploited, it could furnish all of God's green earth with raw materials and fresh drinking water. And Siberia has a well, unique in all the world: Lake Baikal, with its wonder-working waters and singular fauna. The only thing Siberia lacks is a true and zealous husband for its wealth.

The helicopter gives a jolt and turns round sharply. Tilting from side to side, it descends toward a stony spit that projects into a river. The rough water racing around the tip, making a bend like a bird's wing, is three or four hundred meters wide.

The helicopter hovers just above the spit, takes aim, then nests carefully onto the scattered rocks. The pilot shuts down the engine. The blade turns noiselessly overhead for a while, then finally stops, settling into a cross.

"We're here!" cries Nikolai, shaking off sleep. Kupets jumps out as soon as the door is opened and starts sneezing out the acrid gas fumes. Then he lifts his leg against a nearby willow bush. That done, he trots down a path, sniffing and reconnoitering.

We quickly unload our baggage. The helicopter chirrs once more and rises above us. It moves off upriver, above the forests and mountains, until green expanses of earth and blue distances of sky swallow up the jaunty, long-tailed little bug.

The hunter's cabin. It was a separate page in the life of the hunter. He built it himself, with an axe, half underground so it would be warm, so as not to waste wood and the effort of cutting timber. It was low, dark, and damp. He entered by crawling through an opening in the roof, which also served as a smoke hole. There was a stove of piled stones and a sleeping platform of rough-hewn poles. Fir boughs to cover the floor were right at hand. No doors or windows, no lamps or dishes. A pot, an axe, a knife, a rifle, and lots of ammunition—powder, shot, bullets, shells. Everything had to be brought into the taiga and looked after—salt, the dog, rusks, himself, and most important, the ammunition.

The day, short as a sparrow's bill, was spent racing through the taiga. Then the hunter would tumble through the hole into his dugout and get a fire going under the pot. Cursing loudly, coughing, sneezing, wiping back tears from the smoke with blackened, cracked fingers, he would go about his business—a brief rest and a quick meal; then, skin the catch and stretch the pelts out to dry, charge fresh cartridges, knock the ash out of his empty pistols, tap the shiny new cartridges into the charred chambers, pour the fine powder, press in moss wads with a stick, cut firewood, tear off birch bark for kindling.

The kremlin of Tobolsk city, Siberia.

By now the stars would be out. In the bright winter moonlight, the hunter went wearily to a spring that never froze and drew water in his pot. From under the roots of an old tree, he dug up a round birch-bark case and put into it a handful or two of salted burbot roe. There was grayling roe in the case, too, saved up from spring. The burbot were coming to spawn now, in the winter cold, and the hunter caught them in a simple snout-shaped trap woven from willow twigs. After gutting them, he cooked them up in a soup, feeding the heads to the dog and feasting on the raw livers himself—good for your health, especially the eyesight.

In the dead, cold night the hunter sat drinking tea brewed from currant leaves, sometimes with frozen cowberries or cranberries. The two-bucket wooden tub that stood in the corner was already getting low. The hunter's only pleasure, his only joy, was to savor his tea. Crossing himself hurriedly with stiff fingers, he collapsed onto his sleeping platform and fell into a deep, bearlike sleep, wishing that his stone hearth would hold the heat for a while and that his cabin, smelling of sour bark and soot, would not go stone-cold.

Some cabins had elaborate entrances tunneled in under logs. Instead of climbing into them, you crept in lying on your side. In our parts, seasoned hunters sometimes even slept in caves when they could not make it back to their cabins before dark, shuddering through the long night under a mat thrown together from pine branches.

Thank God most people who wear furs have never spent time in the taiga, never seen the elegant, graceful little sable, never had to finish it off after it was snared or wounded in a trap, never undergone the hardships and misfortunes of the taiga. Otherwise the sentimental city-dweller would refuse to wear fur, and the golden industry that has fed the taiga's inhabitants since time immemorial would collapse.

Our roomy cabin on the Vivi is of barked logs, with a slate roof and a planed floor. Inside are a big table and a heavy iron stove. The adjoining bathhouse even has a modern fireplace, a shelf to lie on while you sweat, basins and buckets, wires and lightbulbs. In wintertime, you can turn on the electric motor. The shelves lining the cabin walls hold medical supplies, old magazines, and fishing tackle. Live, hunter. Take a bath. Relax.

The helicopter is the key to it all, the powerful helper, the conqueror of wilderness distances. It can bring everything you need—even things you don't need—to any corner of the taiga.

Today's hunter does not have to charge cartridges; he buys them ready to use. Anyway, most sable hunting is done with traps now. A hunter may put up two or three huts along his "route"—in his territory, that is—so he will not have to return to his base camp after an exhausting day.

What saved the hunter in the old days? What kept him fed? Plenty of animals. The short day and the limited range were enough for him to shoot all he needed. Back in the twenties and thirties a hunter in my native region, if he had a good dog, could take forty or fifty squirrels in a day. Sometimes he would get a sable, too, as a bonus. Then the use of traps came in. But how many traps could a hunter carry in his bag? And the cruel iron traps were too expensive for the country people. They made their own in the old days, our grandfathers' cunning snares for bird and beast: pitfalls, deadfalls, springtraps, pits, nooses. And again, it was work, backbreaking work. The traps had to be rigged, dug up with a shovel, covered over. Good weather or bad, they had to be set and then checked every day. Otherwise mice would eat the catch, or owls, or crows, or free-roaming beasts like the wolverine, fox, or wolf.

Even today the hunter's life, despite modern conveniences, is difficult and dangerous. Nikolai tells us how he once "ran into it" at the mouth of this river with the charming name. Somehow a fire got started in his cabin one night; he had been in bed and didn't have time to dress. He was stranded for five days beside the smoldering ruin, slowly dying of cold and hunger. He is a sturdy fellow, but when they brought him to the hospital he weighed only seventy-seven pounds—like a prisoner from a Nazi concentration camp. Another time he fell through the river ice, and once he was caught by a falling tree. And there have been sicknesses, animal attacks—all kinds of things have happened, have befallen him. But he cannot live without the taiga. The taiga is poison; it is his snare and his freedom, his life and his torment, his work and his rest. He talks about the taiga and his adventures in it easily, without exaggeration or fooling. To work and hunt in the taiga is a tough job, but it is a job he loves, one that satisfies body and soul.

Cemetery of old believers in Archangel'sk region.

Here we are at last, fishing! Fishing is good on the Vivi. Compared with our rivers choked by industry, the Vivi teems with fish. But these fish are choosy, cautious. They bite best in the morning and towards evening.

A squad from a geological expedition had stayed at the cabin to take advantage of the fishing. They left odds and ends of equipment and some bluish spots on the water, took the boat, and moved off upstream, combing the Vivi for the bigger fish. Geologists get the same bad provisions everybody else does in the North these days; without some extras, it would be very rough going indeed. So wherever they go, they fish and hunt in every legal—and more often illegal—way. They have their work to do, too; the field season here is short.

My grandson goes up above the shoals, climbs into the current with his pole, and in short order lands fifteen or so sleek, well-fed graylings. After that, he loses all interest in fishing. He idles along the bank looking for some diversion, or lolls on the sleeping platform in the cabin. There's the generation gap for you. His grandfather, after catching a fingerling in the Yenisey at age five, would have been willing to end his days on a river bank. In slippers full of holes, or sometimes completely barefoot, soles burning on the icy ground, I would go out among the piled-up floes along the river, fix my pole, and sit waiting for a bite. Sometimes my grandmother would find me, legs tucked under trying to stay warm, already blue and shaking, an icicle hanging off my lower lip from my runny nose. She would scold and grumble: "It makes me sick, just sick! Sitting by the bank freezing to death. Someday he really will die. They haven't watched out for the child. It's the evil eye." She would drag me home, continuing in the same vein. I was a lost soul and nothing would come of me. In other words, I would never learn to make money. I would be an eternal proletarian, bumming through the world with my fishing pole and rifle, living from hand to mouth.

Grandmother turned out to be a pretty fair prophet. I never did learn to make money, and I did grow up to be a keen fisherman. Although

The Kama River.

rheumatic since childhood, I want nothing better than to spend my days and nights standing on the lovely bank of a Russian river and, if fate so wills, to take my last, forgetful sleep there.

Sabir came back from the lower shoals with two tench and three big graylings impaled on a stake. Seryozha, Nikolai's son, had caught a black grayling and a tench with his "ship." Volodya's "clunk"—a big foam-rubber float with a cluster of fly-lures fastened to it—pulled in the graylings well. And I, at last, lifted a good grayling out of the water with my rod and pulled him onto the rocks. He fought furiously in the current but suffocated quickly in the shallow water. All he could do was shake his head, trying to spit out the fatal fly, the scarlet flower stuck to his lip.

I caught a golets, too, with my spoon bait. The golets is a northern fish, a close relative of the tench. He looks like a cross between a Taimen salmon, a grayling, and a trout. There is no more beautiful fresh-water fish in our country. And none more full of fight. Once he senses he is caught, the golets struggles furiously for his life. He will leap out of the water, tear back and forth, turn cartwheels, make headlong dashes, lie across the current. Oftentimes he gets away, especially in rapids and shoals.

I hook my fish in a deep, strong shoal. He is lurking behind a rock, waiting for smaller fish to come along, catching himself a real feast. Strong and well fed, he doesn't want to come into the quiet water, towards the bank. He pulls such stunts that I think he will surely get away. When I finally haul him out and toss him onto the rocks, I am shaking from head to toe with excitement. I sit for a long time, watching as that resilient strength slowly wanes, as that beauty burns its last. He is bright as a bird's plumage, with a reddish-orange tail and fins like the petals of Siberian fire-flowers. His sides are covered in spots, spangles, and speckles, with a sharply marked line from gills to tail. He seems all aglow with a furnace-red cast; only the thick-muscled, unsubmissive back is dark and rubbery.

Absolutely everything in this fish was designed by nature for a life of free motion, for clear water, for gluttonous hunting. Its mouth is not large, though, and the teeth are not very sharp. The head is smallish, with a narrow, sloping snout. It is the only one of our northern fishes that can curl itself into a ring on the line. With its powerful muscles it can force open the strongest hand and slip away. It has no scales; the body is covered in a thick, strong skin, with little scalelike bumps that seem to be welded on. In some places it is called the boulder fish because of its strong body, its rounded back and sides, its knack of lying hidden behind a rock and capturing prey without moving more than its head, its ability to wallow in the water through rocky shoals as it ascends rapids to spawn. If necessary, it can even "walk" a little way on grass or wet stones along the bank.

A perfect work of nature! Like any marvel, this fish will not bear captivity, violence, or an alien milieu. He does not just go to sleep; he departs this sublunary world, turning into a dark gray ash that glows but faintly, fading. You bring home a dark-bodied fish like any other, and someone who has never pulled a golets from the water cannot imagine his gay, ardent colors or his fierce fight to live, to get back to the open water, his bright home.

I would like to describe every fish my companions and I catch—and its feisty spirit. Every fish meets its end differently, but none is submissive. Every fish wants to live. It cannot understand death and will not accept it peaceably as we humans do. Wayward, greedy, and full of gab in life, we cower abjectly before death, hoping to the end that, whatever he might do to others, *I* am so meek, so exemplary, so obedient to God and fate that he will not mow *me* down, will pass *me* by, will take pity, will wait a bit.

We catch our share of fish. We even catch some Taimen salmon fingerlings, although nobody gets a big one. The big fish have been taken by Geology and by exalted guests in helicopters. The helicopter pilots, too, are master raiders of the rivers, the taiga, and every other bounty of the land, including the tundra.

And at last my dream comes true. I catch a Taimen with my spoon bait.

The last time I fished for Taimen was—God grant me memory—when? In fifty-eight or so, on a trip down the Chusovaya past the Biser, a grayling stream. Back then the Urals had lots of streams with Taimen, graylings, and many other fish. People lived on the banks of the Chusovaya, the most beautiful river in Europe, and raft after raft, boat after boat passed by with vacationers, fishermen, and campers. Logs floated by, too, gradually but in a fever, with a thundering racket. They kept at it until the land died. Today there is no livelihood to be won in the Urals. Nothing more can be taken out.

Anybody who wants to see the utter bankruptcy caused by the zealous "husbands" of our land should go take a look at the Urals: the bare mountains, the dead rivers, the gigantic, dangerous holes dug into the bowels of the earth,

Birch trees on the banks of the Volga River.

rafted logs, runaways, fallen trees. The tributaries of the Chusovaya were being logged off, one by one. The invasion came right down to its banks, to the water-conservancy zone. In the midfifties one of the local wise men in high places had conceived the notion of pulling out the pines atop the stony cliffs and bluffs along the banks.

I saw the logging, if you can call it that. At that time I worked for a newspaper, the *Chusovaya Worker.* I was "in charge of" forestry and transportation. I saw how, under the pretext of a pressing need to rebuild our economy after the war's devastation—the enemy never sleeps—the ancient, enormously rich land of the Urals was broken, despoiled, murdered, robbed, and clear-cut. Not under which, at great depths, an ocean of hot water bubbles and boils. This last is the only resource today's subjugators of nature have not yet tapped. But tap it they will. They will drown in a scalding inferno themselves, while our ancient land, once mighty, lies silent, stripped, expiring.

The Urals are a vivid example, a bitter reproach to our redoubtable civilization as it enters its second millennium tired, sick, and ruined. We are ashamed to speak any more about the bright future, for the sake of which, supposedly, the mass extirpation of our raw-material resources was undertaken. In the course of a few decades, our blast furnaces have consumed ore deposits meant to last centuries, including Magnitogorsk, the moun-

The peaks of the Main Caucasian Range in the Northern Caucuses.

tain of iron. Coal, oil, and gas resources have been burned up or are burning their last. But the sack, the rape of the Ural forests is a thing beyond all imagining.

In my lifetime I have seen all sorts of things, but I will never be able to forget the logging on the Chusovaya. Winches were erected on the ice. They would take the cable up onto the rocky cliffs, fling a running knot around a tree trunk and drag a tree down. The crown and branches broke, the bark tore, the cold wood splintered. More often than not, the tree got stuck among the rocks. When they did manage to drag something out onto the ice, it was debris—a stump, a mass of roots with no trunk, bearing no resemblance to the proud pine that had grown for a thousand years, clinging to the cliff and at last rearing its green head into the sky. The river's white surface was littered all over with fires, soot, and black chasms where the uneasy waters stirred.

It was not for sentimental or patriotic reasons that the barbarous logging on the Chusovaya was stopped. It was just too expensive, a money-losing operation.

The loggers' crimes concluded with arson. Most of the fires were started by heedless people on a spree. Fires—the eternal misfortune of Russia—finished off the Ural forests. Today the banks of the Chusovaya are desolate. Widely scattered workers' settlements, barely recognizable as the Ural factories of old, are living out their forlorn and wretched days.

In summer the Chusovaya runs dry. In 1988, near the city of Chusovoy, one could walk right across. This was the same river whose high water and fury were described so colorfully by that half-forgotten author, Dmitri Mamin-Sibiryak, back at the turn of the century, in a book called *Soldiers,* named for the region's bluffs and cliffs. Along the whole length of the Chusovaya, the river bottom is strewn with many layers of drowned trees. I am sure that another kind of "logger" will yet return to raise them, to dig them out of the rocky bottom. Need will force this.

I have recalled the Urals in such detail because the Evenki District, too—astronomically distant, unfathomably wild, unthinkably vast—is threatened with disaster. Its main river, the Lower Tunguska—the Gloomy River of the writer/explorer Vyacheslav Shishkov's novel—has been proposed as the site for the world's most powerful hydroelectric station.

At the mouth of the Lower Tunguska, on the Yenisey's high and crumbling right bank, stands one of Siberia's oldest cities—Turukhansk. It arose when the old polar outpost of Mangazeya, on the shore of the Kara Sea between the mouths of two great rivers, the Ob and the Yenisey, was abandoned. For a time the new settlement was called Monastery Village, because of a monastery built on an island opposite the site of what is now Turukhansk. It was also called New Mangazeya.

About 120 kilometers up the Lower Tunguska, amidst great cataracts, the river runs through a stony narrows. The water whirls, turbulent and dark in its restless depth. Bare cliffs stand on either side. An ideal spot for a dam, the engineers decided, promising big savings on construction because of the "advantageous natural conditions."

Once upon a time the same kind of stony passageway, near the Shumikha River, decided the fate of the Yenisey. There, too, the river was narrow, the bottom rocky; the "natural advantages" helped speed a half-baked proposal to confirmation. What good resulted from the building of the Krasnoyarsk Hydroelectric Station, nobody can now remember. But the harm caused by the project—to the city, to the region, to all of Siberia—is enormous and lasting. No kinds of "advantages" or temporary triumphs will compensate. It was projected that thirty square kilometers of the river's surface would remain unfrozen through the winter; it has turned out to be ten times that. Steam rises all winter long, harassing the river and demoralizing the people, especially the million inhabitants of nearby Krasnoyarsk. Every five or six years the station rids itself of "excess" water, bringing disaster. The floods destroy, topple, and carry away everything in their path. In just four days during the summer of 1988, Krasnoyarsk alone suffered more than thirty million rubles' worth of damages.

No one will speculate publicly about the total damages caused by giant power stations in Krasnoyarsk and other cities. It would be awkward, embarrassing. One would have to add in

The Karakumy Desert.

the losses of watermeadows—the region's best land—among many hundreds of kilometers of river, the razing of rich villages and cities, the destruction of forests. By rough estimates, some fifteen million cubic meters of wood still float in the clogged reservoir.

The director of the Krasnoyarsk Hydroelectric Station is named Rastorguev; the local people have nicknamed him, deservedly, Mr. Filch. In looks and manner he resembles Nikita Khrushchev. And it was back in Khrushchev's time that Rastorguev, along with other such movers and shakers, was awarded the title "Hero of Socialist Labor." The brotherhood of the pen he brushes off like flies. "Ah, these scribblers. Always exaggerating! There's only a million and a half cubic meters of wood floating in my reservoir." For Comrade Rastorguev, a million and a half cubic meters of ruined timber is a mere trifle. And the reservoir is "mine," but everything else is "ours." What is his, right down to a ten-kopek meat pie or an expense-account ruble, this vigilant manager knows how to tally, economize, and safeguard. He is no slouch at snatching up bits of the earth's bounty. Until recently, all the local authorities, big and little, did the same. Once I made a trip to the Derbino region, which has the best fishing anywhere in the Krasnoyarsk reservoir. Wherever we stuck our noses in, with our little boat and our meteorologist's launch, we ran into nets. Speed gliders, power boats, and ordinary motorboats raced about, chasing us small-time anglers out. Rastorguev's fishing fleet was replenishing the power station's refrigerator, from which, at the director's command, fish swim off to every corner of the country, especially in the direction of Moscow, to the high-ranking patrons and benefactors of Siberia's subjugators of nature.

Siberia already has 219 artificial reservoirs, and thousands of Mr. Filches are running things, flooding and burning. They are transforming Siberia's forests and other riches into rubbish, into slag heaps. Meanwhile they continue, out of inertia, to boast that such riches are inexhaustible.

But there is nothing left to boast about. By my

Glacial melt at the White Sea.

very rough calculations, the damming of the Yenisey has caused the extinction of thirty-two valuable plant species in the vicinity of my own village of Ovsyanka alone. The stunted plants that remain on the bare, snowless earth, wreathed in cold mists, twist and die under the acid rain from nearby Krasnoyarsk, where the air is unbreathable, especially on windless days.

Last summer the acid rain killed blooming potato plants overnight and left black spots on the cabbage and other vegetables. A name for this vegetable disease was promptly invented, and the press carried warnings: "Burn the tops. If possible, avoid eating the potatoes." A day later nearly all the potatoes had been dug up and stored away in cellars and basements. The people in my village have been eating them, and they are not alone in doing so. The potatoes rot quickly. It can only be hoped that people will not have time to harm themselves greatly by eating the poisoned vegetables. But what will they eat? The state stores continue to offer precious little, and the swaggering traders from Union republics near and distant continue to skin the working people alive at farmers' markets and commercial outlets.

The Krasnoyarsk and Sayan-Shushensk power stations continue to bring countless misfortunes upon Siberia, and especially upon the Krasnoyarsk *krai*. But in the future, Siberia will have to shoulder the main burden of supplying raw materials and fuel for the whole country. By the year 2000, ninety percent of our fuel will come from Siberia. According to the economists' projections, Western Siberia will produce two or three times more oil and gas than will all the rest of the country, and Siberia as a whole will supply 40 percent of our electricity. The Yenisey and its tributaries will have to make room for ten or twelve hydroelectric stations; these stations will turn the Yenisey into one big puddle, just as they have the Volga.

This is how happiness and prosperity are to be provided for future generations. But will they be able to survive, these future generations? I am not certain, and other people who still have a conscience, a sense of responsibility towards the future, are wondering too. They ask, justifiably, to what end we are erecting these industrial giants, and for whom. There are already many parts of the country where it is impossible to live, including the depleted Urals and now Siberia, which is being emptied like a burning house.

Dark fear wells up in the eyes of the Evenkis at the mere mention of the Turukhansk station. And only of the Evenkis? The people of our whole country, and also of neighboring countries, especially Scandinavia, should be on guard. This new project above the Arctic Circle, called once again "great" and "beneficial," could bring calamities a hundred times worse than the accident at Chernobyl. The mania for gigantic power stations, the bewitchment of industrial expansion, savings, and prosperity, has seized our subjugators of nature, especially the hydraulic engineers, with new force.

The Lower Tunguska, the engineers prophesy, will do the work of ten Yeniseys, and the station at Turukhansk, will be ten times more powerful than the ones at Krasnoyarsk and Bratsk. The "benefits" will be transmitted to us over thousands of kilometers and sold for profit abroad—the world's cheapest electric energy. We will flood in radiance the western part of our country, still frightened by the Chernobyl mishap, and while we are at it, light up Old Lady Europe brighter than ever before.

Already they are counting the cost of the kilowatts. Already they are saying that the environment along the Lower Tunguska is of no great worth. The forest offers little variety or potential for production. True, we do not know much yet about the mineral resources, but the vast stores of coal and oil some people expect to find could be exploited even under water, as on the Caspian, at Baku. The local people—there are only ten or twelve thousand—will be settled higher up, in the mountains.

How was that? The Evenki are accustomed to living in the watermeadows along rivers, where there are forests and grazing lands for reindeer, where there are animals, and fish, and berries. They have dwelt thus through the ages. They are used to it. On the cold, windy summits they would simply die. An ancient people would vanish altogether.

The far northern home of the Eskimo.

Well, and so what? More ancient and glorious nations, have perished for the sake of the bright future. "When you cut forests, the chips fly," the Father and Teacher of all Nations used to say. Stalin's motto and his methods of managing the land and promoting progress did not die with him. The flame of those years has dimmed, but there are those alive today who are ready to get down on all fours, to blow on the smoldering coals, to keep blowing until they flame up again, throwing an impassioned glow across the faces of the champions of progress.

The projected super-reservoir on the Lower Tunguska will be some fifteen hundred kilometers in length. The permafrost may be saturated with brine or mineral salts; there may be oil under it, or gas, or other treasures, abundant or not. Nobody knows. But the possibility that the permafrost could melt, releasing salt and oil, is not excluded. Even now the river water at Tura, the center of the Evenki National District, is tea-colored, salty, and basically unfit to drink. What will happen when they make it hot, stagnant, deep, and full of refuse?

Let us give the floor here to people who live in the North, with a filial concern for their native land. Here is a letter from a thinking man, someone who has seen a lot. I will not give his name; I do not want to get him into trouble. Despite *perestroika* and *glasnost*, our petty princes, the local leaders, have not really changed at all. Their words are not to be trusted. They themselves take no stock in what they say; they speak heedlessly, senselessly, hoping for some momentary gain. These local eminences were described as follows back in the fifties:

> Here reigned supreme and swiftly fell
> Our tsars of local fame.
> Church demolition went quite well;
> Shop building, though, was lame.

But, here is what our concerned citizen, a resident of Turukhansk, writes:

I was born in 1941, in the Urals, in the city of Zlatoustye, Chelyabinsk oblast. I lived and worked in the Urals until 1974. In that year, having completed my technical training in night school, I came to work in the North, in Turukhansk. I have lived here ever since. I am a senior geophysical engineer in the Turukhansk exploratory geophysical drilling team. We fly in helicopters to drilling sites three or four hundred kilometers away, coming home only for occasional visits. We look for gas and oil. The dead rivers and streams of the Urals are a painful thing to behold. But you should see what is going on here in Siberia! If we don't save these waters, who will? What will we leave to our descendants? They will curse us for all our "giants"—the world's most powerful—if everything around them is wasteland. Man should be the steward of the land, no matter where he was born or where he lives. If the engineers planning the building of the Turukhansk station would take even one boat trip on our beautiful Tunguska, if they could see its banks, take a look at the Death Cliff where the White Guards shot Bolsheviks and threw them down into the river (that was how the spot received its sinister name), I am sure at least one of them would feel a pang—"What are we doing?"

But there is no way of getting to the people at the top. They are a finger pointing the way. At their slightest motion the eager executives of the next rank down all shout in chorus, "Yes, sir!"

I am convinced that the people at the top are directing the intentional and planned devastation of the Urals and Siberia. Supposing that the Turukhansk station can actually be built, every kilowatt from it will cost several tons of gold. We are hoping to find oil and gas in the Tungus basin, the so-called Tungus syncline. If the entire territory goes under water there is no way of knowing what mineral resources will be lost. In July of this year one of our wells, Moktakonsk One, struck oil. The size of the find has yet to be determined. If an artificial sea is created here, all life will disappear. There will be no fish, no furbearing or other animals, no birds. There will be significant change in the climate as well. The Naginsk graphite mine will also fall within the flood zone. The damage to morale will be simply immeasurable. The native people will lose many ancestral sites. And the camps along the Tunguska, the wood for building, the nut-bearing cedars, all drowned! It is our duty to save the river. No use complaining to our petty princes. For them it is only extra work, extra trouble. Their main concern is not to be fired, not to lose their salaries.

A power station could be built, but not at the expense of nature and people. All the pros and cons of the plan must be given scrupulous consideration, and responsibility should not rest entirely with one agency. Plans must be checked with conservation bodies and should conform to the Law on the Environment.

Now let us hear the opinion of a scientist named Syroechkovsky, who has worked in the Turukhansk area for more than thirty years:

Life has changed, and today we are compelled to give much more consideration to preserving the unique environment of the Yenisey. . . . I believe that building power stations in valleys is inexpedient, not only ecologically but even from the point of view of land management. . . . We have made efforts to stop the building of stations at Osinovka and Sredne-Yeniseysk. . . . At the same time, one could agree to the building of the Turukhansk station . . . but the potential ecological impact has not been sufficiently studied. The waters of the widened Lower Tunguska would cut off the traditional reindeer migration routes, would cause changes in the region's climate, and would affect people's way of life over a large area. Scientists predict that safe nuclear power will be available by the beginning of the next century. Is the Turukhansk station really needed?

This is echoed by the journalist Kamorin:

Hurry, again we're in a hurry. Isn't it time again to let the chips fall where they may? There are at least 50 million cubic meters of commercial timber in the flood zone. No plans whatever have been made for its use. It seems to be cheaper to inundate standing forests, as was done in the Bratsk, Ust-Ilimsk, and Sayan reservoirs. These tremendous losses of lumber shock nobody, so accustomed are we to such enormities.

We should listen to the people, too—to the Evenkis themselves, the most interested segment of the local population. The ethnographers Sagalaev and Gimuev, candidates in historical sciences at the Siberian branch of the USSR Academy of Sciences, have characterized the Evenkis in an article they cannot get published anywhere: "Travelers of the eighteenth century called the Evenkis the 'Frenchmen of the taiga' for their daintiness, their lively minds, their elegance."

On a visit to one settlement in the North, they interviewed an Evenki named Mukto, who together with his brother has won honors for reindeer breeding. Mukto said:

I am very sad to hear that this misfortune will come upon my homeland. The remains of my fathers will be submerged, and I will be far away from them. The work of the Evenki, hunting and reindeer breeding, will vanish. Our distinctive culture will vanish too. First they made us forget our language, our trades. Now they are driving us from our ancient lands. Unless justice triumphs, the Evenki as a people will dissolve among other peoples. In short, we will disappear. I don't want a reservoir to flood my land, the land of my ancestors. . . . I love my village, my river, and of course my home. I can't imagine ever having to leave. No benefits can make up for losing your home. There will be more hatred in people after this.

The Siberian scholars quote the leader of a geological team: "We are going into this project blind!" They write further: "The Lower Tunguska is more than three thousand kilometers long. It is a natural storage battery for people, animals, and plants. Here, over thousands of years, a complex balance of the interests of man and nature has been worked out. It is the only balance possible. The Evenki, as an ethnic unit, cannot continue to exist without reindeer breeding and hunting. Any other way of life would mean their extinction. In the old days the Tungus traders, who bought furs from the native population for next to nothing, were like a curse on the Evenkis."

But what of that? The Tungus traders are gone, aren't they? Nobody is now deceiving the trustful people of the taiga. Nobody is now fleecing them, deciding what should be done with their land and possessions, with no regard for the wishes of this ancient people. Isn't that so?

Passionate discussions are being waged in newspapers and magazines, in conference halls, around tables where friends gather, in offices, in modern houses and traditional native dwellings. Meanwhile, all over the taiga of the Evenki District, the planners are doing their exploratory work. Turukhansk's astoundingly illiterate newspaper *Beacon of the North,* printed a three-part piece, titled "The First Tent," by one of the subjugators of nature, although they forgot to include his name. The author is unmoved by all the outcries and pronouncements, articles and meetings.

A polar bear on the ice field.

The brown bear, master of the taiga.

Storks' nest in Belgorod region.

He writes about the project as something long ago decided. He writes breathlessly, with attempts at lyricism:

The mighty waters of the Lower Tunguska have carved out gorges in the solid rock cliffs with their colossal energy. . . . One of these gorges, one hundred and twenty kilometers distant [an alternative proposal would put the station thirty-six kilometers from the river's mouth], is to become the site of the Turukhansk Hydroelectric Station. The station's power will be without precedent: twenty million kilowatts! At the height of the spring flood, the lower reaches of this river carry something on the order of half a million cubic meters of water per second. . . . This is not a river to be assaulted brashly.

Well, there you have it! They *have* assaulted—assaulted brashly—the Kama, Volga, Don, and Dniepr. They have fettered all the country's more or less notable rivers. They have ruined the Aral Sea and Issyk-Kul, disfigured the Sea of Azov, dealt a crushing, frontal blow to the Gulf of Kara Bogaz. But now we are in a new era, with new songs and new "production" relations. The trouble is, it is hard to put faith in the neatness and efficiency of our dam builders. The Lower Tunguska is exceedingly remote and inaccessible. Human and other resources are lacking. That means the "building project of the century" will cost a mint. And the job might be finished in such a rush, with falsified paperwork concealing shoddy workmanship, that people who have not seen the final stages of building at the Kama hydroelectric station, for example, would have trouble imagining it.

But the Kama station is a sparrow compared to the Turukhansk hawk, whose claws will tear up the entire North. The project could bankrupt us. Just think, for instance, of what it will cost to build two or three thousand miles of railroad from Krasnoyarsk to Lesosibirsk to Turukhansk. Building for the sake of building, a temporary "transportation scheme," as the nameless author of the aforementioned piece evasively calls it. He waxes enthusiastic about the "great economy and efficiency of the new power station."

"Before our eyes, but still hard to believe," as one of our proverbs has it. They promised in the same way that the Baikal-Amur Railway would result in great—indeed, surpassing—economy and efficiency. They wrote songs about it, composed poems. All has fallen silent now. The rails of the Baikal-Amur rust, and the heralds and hymn-singers wait impatiently. What else can they glorify? Where can they look? But the people in the capitals are taking so long getting ready, outfitting themselves for Gloomy River. It seems they will dally forever. Can't we have some glory now? Can't we have some commotion, some praise for daring, heroism, and resourcefulness?

So here is our own homegrown patriot and dam builder, orating on the gray pages of the *Beacon of the North*. He sings shamelessly of "benefits," with not a word about the many misfortunes caused to us and our country by the heroic transformers of our economy and the conquerors of space. Neither the Mongol invasion nor the numerous wars that have raged in the fields of Russia and the Ukraine—not even the ruinous Civil War and the war against the Nazis—have caused such calamities, such losses, as have our "pathfinders" and the wandering hordes of hydraulic engineers and other zealous builders who follow in their wake.

These brazen folk did not appear from nowhere, of course. They are a product of our economic system, a system of self-congratulation and irresponsible planning, of frenzied speechifying that often drowns good sense and intelligent action. Forward, forward, with no thought for the losses, the warnings, the opinions of the people! All for victory! We won't haggle about price.

The engineers have made concessions, have promised to build the dam lower by so-and-so many meters and to make the reservoir a bit smaller. Even so, rumor has it that this insane project has not been confirmed at the top. Not yet! But the "pathfinders" let loose by the building of the Kureyka dam are heading for Tura, expeditions are rustling around in the woods, different commissions are visiting the Evenki District, clever go-getters are circulating among our leaders, and quietly, reasssuringly, the wave rolls forward: "Yes, we will build a power station, but at Sredne-Yeniseysk. We'll build clean. A string of terraces. No damage. Nothing but good for the country, the people, and Siberia."

And once again, in the most beautiful, out-of-the-way spot—at a narrows!

Ah, those blankety-blank narrows! The Creator hid wild gorges in remote, hard-to-reach places. But people found them, wormed their way in!

Man was put in the garden to dress and keep it. Hah! Some keeper! Once again, as so often before, the heavenly chancellery slipped up. Nature made a typo. A two-legged beast was appointed steward of this splendid planet. Surely our Earth is deserving of a more reasonable and polite son, manager, and inhabitant.

We are putting the Earth to death. We plunder it, tear pieces off, foul the seas, rivers, and ploughlands. And we are not alone. Our mindless, unthinking creations crawl over every part of the planet, leaving behind a mute, black trail—burned lands, a darkened sky, murky waters, the

A sable.

corpses of birds and animals, and our own—human—corpses. More and more often these are little corpses, misbegotten amidst the filth of a bloody, drunken frenzy. Our children, our future! The land, the Earth, is already an invalid.

Humanity, you must stop. Put off your pride. Ask yourself before it is too late: Why have you come into this world? To live, or to spend your time on Earth perpetrating atrocities, in evil deeds and impudence? Or does your dim intelligence want a dim, sunless, tainted life and a tainted death?

A certain Terentyev, "engineer and dam builder," sends thick letters to all the newspapers, to writers and journalists, accusing them all of ignorance, backwardness, and obtuseness. Terentyev and his fellow engineers want prosperity and every kind of good thing for us, but we unreasonable, illiterate dolts don't understand, can't understand, or perhaps don't even want to understand.

I know another Terentyev, Andrei, a fitter, who helped to build the Kama, Votkinsk, and Zeya power stations, and one of the others too. He and I "broke into" literature together. We met on a memorable day in 1953—the day Stalin died. It was on that very day that I was moved to take the early morning train for Perm (then called Molotov). A publishing house there had summoned me to look over the proofs of my first book. The cars were of the old-fashioned type, with no dividing walls between corridor and compartments. There were almost no passengers. A bony old woman of devout appearance sat motionless at the little table, staring into space. At Lyamino, the first station out of Chusovoy, a youngish second lieutenant came into the car, and since I hadn't heard the morning news on the radio, I inquired:

"What do they say today?"

"Comrade Stalin has passed away," the lieutenant said quietly.

Evidently the grief on our faces caught the old woman's attention. She blinked once or twice and asked:

"What was it happened now?"

"Comrade Stalin has died, grandmother."

"Lord save us! There'll be famine again!" She began to cross herself over and over.

Perm is a grim, hard-working city. It has seen plenty of death and grief in its time. The mourning flags made it grimmer still. Almost nobody on the streets. Crying in the shops. Crying in the publishing house. Crying in the offices of the Union of Writers, where Klavdia Vasilyevna Rozhdestvenskaya was in charge. The literary gentlemen were crying, old and young; glasses of water were fetched for the literary ladies. A curly-headed young fellow with high cheekbones was doing his best to squeeze out a tear of solidarity but was having little luck.

The funeral meeting was short. One after another those who had wanted to speak waved feebly after their first phrase and staggered back to their seats. They were too grief-stricken.

The curly-headed fellow turned out to be Andrei Terentyev. Even then he was nearly deaf from a concussion. A bachelor, he had an apartment in a wooden house, where he had written his first sketches and a novella titled *The Second Lieutenant.*

There was another fellow with us, a Muscovite, who had just graduated from the Literary Institute. He had been assigned for practical training to a specialized periodical for hydraulic engineers. He also worked, on a volunteer basis, for a literary review published in the Kama region. He was one of those who hold that if two men—let alone two bachelors—sit down together without a bottle between them, they are not really men at all, but some freak of nature.

Alcoholic beverages had been summarily removed from sale until some brighter day. But near the train station a strapping, loud-voiced girl, her jacket stained and torn from handling crates, was still selling "fire extinguishers"—dark bottles of red "port." She had taken more than a nip or two herself. No sad news had yet reached her little booth.

"Port wine for sale! Real good port!" she shouted. "It's going like hotcakes!"

"Quiet down, you damned fool," we said as we loaded a briefcase with bottles. "If you keep up that yapping, they'll put you out of business."

"Who's gonna put me outa business? Show 'em to me! I'll put 'em outa business!" She brandished a bottle, looking fierce.

Being bachelors we had nothing to eat at home, so we went to the cafeteria at the Kama power station. We got some soup, meat patties, a beet salad. We sat talking quietly, a bottle of wine on our table.

"There they are! There!" came a piercing shout. "Drinking wine! The nation is mourning, but they . . . they're celebrating!"

Looking up, we discovered that the cafeteria was now crowded with people. Most of the faces were tear-stained. And a member of the working class was directing this protest towards us. But we refused to heed the hysterial cries that came more and more insistently. Finally a "delegation" came up to our table and announced that if this "outrage" did not cease we would be beaten, and nobody's fault but our own .The astonishing thing was that some of the delegation were staggering drunk themselves. They had been drinking on the sly. Their ire was partly from patriotic indignation but also partly because they couldn't get any more themselves. We were not to be intimidated. We stood shoulder to shoulder and demanded to know who intended to beat us. Come on and try!

An acquaintance of Andrei's came to see what all the fuss was about. She asked us to let the fools be and go home. We spent the rest of the night talking in Andrei's warm, cozy apartment, and we have been friends ever since.

Andrei did not make literature his life. He has remained a worker—his first calling—but he still does some writing, although being completely deaf makes it harder. In Tvardovsky's time he was published in *Novy Mir*, and different publishers have brought out several of his books.

Last summer he turned up in Krasnoyarsk, in a hospital for war veterans. When his course of treatment ended, he could not get a plane back home to the banks of the Zeya. Being deaf, he goes from window to window, shouting at the clerks, thrusting his documents at them. They would bark back: "Don't you raise your voice to us!"

I took him to Yemelyanovo Airport to "appeal," but the authorities had all gone into hiding. The place was packed with delayed passengers. I know several women who work at the airport, and somehow I convinced them to put the invalid on a plane, at least to Irkutsk.

The Lena River in Siberia.

All the time we were together—at my house, on the road, in the airport—my old war buddy and colleague in literature urged me not to write "the whole truth" about the war. It was so shameful, he said, that our children should not know about it.

Andrei is two years my senior and felt the war's full fury. His words were not to be taken lightly. But he did not want me to write about the power stations, either.

"We need them, and the end justifies the means. Besides, we can build clean if we really want to. We built the station on the Zeya clean, without doing any harm." True, he added immediately that the Zeya reservoir is only seventy kilometers long and is well away from farmlands, fields, and cities.

I kept pestering him with a question I had long pondered: Why are our people on opposite sides of the "barricades"? After all, we live in the same country, eat the same bread, and have suffered—continue to suffer—for the same cause.

"As always, the solution to the puzzle is simple," Andrei said with a sigh.

He told me that after the chaotic final weeks of building at the Kama station, the men had received bonuses. The section boss was awarded seven thousand rubles. Andrei, as foreman of a team of fitters, got seventy-five. When he took his money to the boss to be added to "the kitty," the boss informed him that he was a man of principle, a Communist, and did not need tips.

It is not given to us to know how much money Naymushin—the top construction boss—got, or the chief engineer, or the big shots in the head offices. Here, then, is a motivator for dam building—one of the main ones. And if they no longer pay bonuses, that would only mean they have invented something to take their place—"To interest the workers materially," as they put it.

Not long ago I read and jotted down some quotations from Marx. "Nature too is a source of goods, on an equal footing with labor, which is only a manifestation of one of the forces of nature: the human capacity to work" And further: "Under capitalism, nature is only an object to man, a useful thing. It ceases to be recognized as a self-sufficient force, and theoretical understanding of its laws is seen as a tactic aimed at subjugating nature to human needs, whether as goods or as means of production."

We have always been driven by the itch to catch up to and surpass those cursed capitalists. This was particularly true under Khrushchev. Well, now we can dust off our hands. In the barbarous exploitation of nature and our people, we have undoubtedly surpassed the capitalists. In fact, we are so far ahead they will never catch up, although they are trying mightily.

What sunsets there are on the Vivi! Long, tender, spreading. In the evening I sit tiredly on a bench by the cabin, legs aching, looking into the distances beyond the river. A saddle-backed mountain looms far off, rolling gently down to some stream, a tributary of the Vivi. Every tree on the mountain, every leaf, is clearly imprinted against the scarlet, translucent backdrop of the sky. The delicate strip of green dissolving into the sky makes the distant radiance even deeper, quieter.

Nothing disturbs the eternal spaces, the evening quiet. The only sound is a solitary, shy little bird, somewhere in the willows and currant bushes behind the cabin, softly chirping: "Vi-vi. Vi-vi." And so I solve the mystery of "our" river's name.

Kupets has dug himself a hole in the ravine to get away from the mosquitoes. He rolls around in the dirt, brushing the mosquitoes off his muzzle and ears with a paw. Then he shakes himself and yawns sleepily. He stares at me as if to say, "Everybody is asleep. What's keeping you up?"

The tireless seagulls cry, whirling above the water. The white cloud of birds keeps getting thicker, the calls more piercing. The gulls have managed to separate a foolish young merganser from his brothers and sisters as they swim after their mother. He is a fine diver already, but cannot yet fly. Now the gulls will not leave him alone till they have finished him off, pecked him to pieces.

Big, greedy birds like crows and seagulls used to be rare here. Now they are becoming more and more aggressive. It is getting harder to find food in the forests and rivers. Even the bears have become scavengers and pilferers. They eat dead fish at the reservoirs and the cast-off corpses of skinned animals at hunters' camps. They often raid cabins, too. On my first trip, staying in a cabin on the Yaning, one of the Vivi's tributaries, I counted six bears roving the neighborhood. There were many gnawed sable skeletons lying around. The hunters, too, have begun to behave boorishly in the taiga, not to speak of the campers, the exalted guests, and the various expeditions that live and work there for a time.

The evening calms my spirits, and the dying sunset makes me pensive. Gazing at the Vivi, I keep thinking about the fate of Siberia's rivers, the Lena and the Yenisey. There is another river too, the Mana, which in size and beauty could compare with the Chusovaya and many more of our country's lovely mountain rivers. It flows into the Yenisey, after making a sixteen-kilometer loop, about five kilometers above my native village. There is a shoal at a place called Solomennoe, where the river twists like a noose, and beside it is a harbor. It has been there since 1930. That is when they began floating logs down the river. They are doing it still. Everything worth cutting has been cut already; the logs coming down now are like trash. Nowadays the river runs dry in the summers. Because of the labor shortage, men drive bulldozers into the riverbed—sometimes with permission, sometimes on the sly—to push the timber down to the harbor, where it dries out and rots until the water rises in autumn.

They have killed the river, spoiled it, crippled it completely. The animals and birds have almost vanished from its banks; there are no local fish. In spring the fish from the lower reaches of the Yenisey, after crowding past the dam at Krasnoyarsk, come into the Mana to breed. They lay their eggs somewhere, and then the floating logs and power boats break up their pitiful spawns, wash them away and destroy them. Today, catching a gudgeon on the Mana is cause for celebration. Once near Sosnovok I caught a whole bucketful of graylings, with a primitive rod and lure, in a single evening. That was in 1934; I was a boy of ten. It made a feast for our whole glorious family.

What disaster is this? What cataclysm has come upon our Earth? They talk of the "struggle" to keep the rivers, forests, and air pure and sound. What need is there to struggle? We need to be good stewards, to live up to that proud title. That's all. Don't saw off the branch you sit on. Don't inflict injuries on yourself. Put an end to self-extermination, for when you deface nature or sell it to the highest bidder, you are signing your own death warrant.

Night comes at last, cool and starry. The taiga grows dark, merging the distant and the near. The forest stands motionless, monolithic. The seagulls have settled down, and on the mountaintop only two trees can be seen, burning smokelessly in the last faint glow. Down below, the river is gurgling, talking to itself. Soon it must go under the ice to rest until spring, so it wants to say its piece now, splash to its heart's content, live free and easy. This tributary of the Lower Tunguska cannot know that somewhere far, far away, in crowded cities, in clever offices, a death warrant has been made out for it. And everything that swims in it, every green thing that blooms and rustles above it, these things too must fade and die.

"I am the enemy of Heaven, I am the evil of the world. Behold me now, laid at your feet." That was how Lermontov's terrible demon pleaded, having taken human form, before a child of the Earth, his beloved. What should be our plea? At whose feet should we throw ourselves? Shining river, to whom and how should be pray for your salvation and ours?

"Live forever, Vivi River! Songbird, sing the river's song!" As usual when I am out in the woods, away from the frenzy of city life, my heart begins to ferment and my thoughts turn sappy. Something poignant and noble is trying to express itself in a song, but I can't get past the first lines, a rueful, heartfelt refrain. Worry mingles with my affection and sadness, throws me off key.

And finally, as the propeller spins and hums over our heads, the helicopter floats over the mountains and forests. Nothing down below has changed. Everything is just the same: the distances, the mountain passes, the rivers, streams and lakes, the valleys with their ribbons of eternal snow. Over and over again, like an incantation, like a groan from a sick heart, like a lucid prayer from a mind fallen silent in grief, I keep hearing: "Live forever, Vivi River! Vivi River, live forever!"

Art

ELEANOR MUNRO is an art critic and author of, among other books, *Originals: American Women Artists* and *Memoir of a Modernist's Daughter.* Her articles and reviews appear in the national and art press, and she has acted with The Living Theater in New York. A member of PEN, the Authors League, and the American and International Associations of Art Critics, she lives in New York and Cape Code, Massachusetts. She is married and the mother of two sons. At present she is working on fiction.

VIKTOR POTANIN, storyteller and diarist, published his first collection of stories, *The Cranes Have Come,* in 1963. His books include *Give Me a Dove; A Soldier's Heir; Fog on Snow; The Belated Guest; The Jetty; In Foreign Parts; On the Precipice;* and *The Blue Pearl. Above the Cradle,* 1971, introduced the long cycle of *Village Monologues.* Potanin's lyrical collections—*Quiet Water, Memory Will Tell, The Last Horses*—and many of his diaries are especially directed to younger readers, including children. The magazine *Oktyabr* has recently published Potanin's "Letters for My Son: Clouds Can Be White or Blue or Black."

Art in America

ELEANOR MUNRO

Background

A dark streak has run through American art of the past hundred years or so, next to which the art of today may appear to be—but is not—an anomaly. That dark spirit made itself felt even as a number of artists were moving toward a first authentic American vision of the world, that is, one different from the English and Dutch prototypes that had earlier shaped high-style art here. For example, it seems always to have been dusk when the landscape painters of the Luminist and Hudson-River schools arrived at their standing-points before their easels. Even as they watched, the sky was always turning red-gold over the sea or the mountain or river. Such golden light, which takes on added sheen from its juxtaposition with masses of black water or earth, was meant to suggest the reality of a transcendental order, enduring and peaceful. That such immensity of longing for connection with a remote beyond should have been felt by these relative newcomers into a new land, where a civilization was still in its morning, still building, is interesting. Interesting, too, is the fact that a comparable longing would be felt today by a number of American artists who work in the open, now making their art literally out of the stuff of the world, its material substance, its shadows and natural light.

An unmitigated darkness appears in the work of Thomas Eakins, the nineteenth-century genre and portrait painter, whose maladjustment to a genteel middle-class society by which he felt both constrained and grieved infuses his work. Darkness was not something Eakins gravitated to out of affection. Apparently he tried to dispel it by choosing dramatic subjects: an actress in a red gown, for example, or a young concert singer in white satin. But the shadows settled around them, in the folds of their heavy clothing, the lines around their eyes. The darkness was in his own eye; he could not evade it. Darkening skies, melancholy woods, shrouded or evasive faces are painted correlatives to the forests and the parlor populations of American novelists Nathaniel Hawthorne and Henry James. Darkness, of course, was a reality of life before electrification, but an artist's sensitivity to its perceived gradations revealed also his awareness of psychological mood, the characteristically American feeling for the strangeness of human society against a background of wilderness.

Something of the same spirit must have moved the rough solitaries of the early years of this century in America's big cities: Albert Pinkham Ryder in New York, painting moonscapes on scraps of canvas and cigar-box lids; Marsden Hartley, drifting between New York, Paris, Munich, but returning to Maine to paint seascapes ponderous as piled logs. Then there was Joseph Stella in his Brooklyn boardinghouse, painting the ghostly bridge. And, too, the so-called Ash Can School painters, realists who set themselves to depict the city as it looked to them, grubby, poor, but full of personality, sometimes black comedy. Later

Lee Krasner, *Desert Moon,* 1955.

would come Edwin Dickinson, one of America's insufficiently acknowledged masters, whose veils behind veils of ashen perspectives give place to darker figures and their shadows. Edward Hopper, master of the uncanny housescape, belongs among these solemn Americans. So does Georgia O'Keeffe. Though blue skies and poppies express one side of her nature, an equally authentic character suffuses her paintings of a dark-fringed *Black Iris,* her mournful roadside crosses and stripped trees against night skies.

Thomas Eakins, *The Actress,* 1903.

All the same, even during the years of the Great Depression and oncoming war, while anxiety and foreboding grew throughout much of the world, a few European and American artists felt themselves possessed by a new sense of the future, a vision of new possibility for society and art.

Modernism was that new vision. It illuminated the European and American artistic and intellectual frontiers for a few decades until post-World War II political and economic turmoil brought it to an end. Modernism was an aesthetic, an ethic, a political vision, and nearly a metaphysic. Certainly it was a vehicle of faith. The movement began at almost the same time in the first decade of the century in widespread parts of the world—though with a logic one understands in hindsight, among its principal formulators were artists from the country most urgently moving toward revolution at the time: Russia.

One of the symptoms of the movement was irritation with the entrenched status of art taught in most academies of the time and monumentalized in galleries and museums. Research in the sciences had not long since exposed a world of matter invisible to the eye, made up of rays, particles, beams, and other physical and theoretical elements—a "realer" world than the one visible to the naked eye. The question was then asked: could art also be freed from its responsibility to report on the superficial look of the world? Could art, like science, reveal deeper interrelationships between the forms of being? Once artists were liberated from their subservience to the seen world, a wave of inventive energy would sweep all fields, from painting to theater design, music, costume, and book illustration, while Modernist literature and music would follow their own courses.

So Modernism in the arts was a movement of liberation from old problems and solutions. And just as art could engage new conceptual and formal issues, so the teaching of art could become a tool in the development of a new human being and society. Enlightened effort on the part of aestheticians, teachers, and artists could reform the world, its architecture and schools, its arts in all mediums. Such transformations would affect those who create and those who enjoy the arts, and this enlightened populace would formulate new political and ethical structures. Thus the artist, the scholar, and the art-lover could take their places beside the scientist and philosopher where, once upon a time, the priest had stood: in an intuitive relationship to value and truth. As a byproduct of aesthetic theory, the Modernist had an innocently impassioned faith in progress: in the

Georgia O'Keefe, *Black Cross, New Mexico,* 1929.

Arthur Dove, *Thunder Shower,* 1939–40.

power of art to redeem humanity across ideological lines; in the psychological and social value of the free imagination; in the validity of the artist's insight into ethical issues.

These principles of Modernist socio-aesthetics sank into the American mentality and survived here to inspire, in relatively recent times, two important if much-debated museum exhibitions. In 1955, the epochal "The Family of Man" at the Museum of Modern Art presented a photographic panorama of faces, costumes, customs, and rituals from around the world, organized according to sweeping social themes (birth, marriage, death, play, worship, and so forth) which overrode national and cultural differences. Three decades later that same institution mounted a show of African and other tribal artifacts juxtaposed with works of art in the Modernist canon. The submerged agenda of the "Primitivism" show, as of the photographic one, was to argue for the unity of human culture through place and time. Both shows drew large, emotionally engaged audiences but were also attacked by anti-Modernist critics, one for its populism, the other, by a twist of Post-Modern art-politics, for "cultural colonialism."

Back in the first decades of this century, however, when Modernist thinking was first brought to bear on the actual making of art, the result was the abandonment of humanistic imagery in favor of more-or-less purely abstract composition. The new style flowered early in the circle of Aleksandr Rodchenko, Kasimir Malevich, Natalia Goncharova, and others in Russia and quickly spread to artists in Berlin and Paris. Soon a few American painters of Russian origin or traveling in Russia and Europe had come home to show their experiments in the new idiom at the vanguard gallery of photographer-impressario Alfred Stieglitz in New York. The new spirit spread fast. In 1907, Picasso painted *Les Demoiselles d'Avignon;* four years later, Matisse painted his *Red Studio.* The example of these two titanic Modernists would weigh heavily on American artists for some decades, but so would that of Russian Wassily

Larry Rivers, *History of the Russian Revolution*, 1965.

Kandinsky, who by 1913 had painted his masterpiece, the *White Edge*, bought for the Museum of Non-Objective Art in New York by its German-born director, Hilla Rebay. That same year, a debut extravaganza of Modernist art was put before the American public at the Armory Show in New York. The popular response was incredulous shock. A half-century later, the sons and daughters of those first American witnesses to the new art would be bidding into six figures for the least work in the Modernist idiom.

During the years when Soviet culture was being fast-frozen in place by state fiat, the new movement, still impelled by Russian visionaries in exile, spread out and radicalized the avant garde of the West. The Constructivist Vladimir Tatlin's proposed *Monument to the Third International*, commissioned in 1919 by the Soviet government to commemorate the Revolution, was never built at home, but it became an icon of Modernist architecture when its design was published in the West. In fact its spiral ground plan signifying dynamic aspiration was the source of Frank Lloyd Wright's Guggenheim Museum, which replaced the Museum of Non-Objective Art in New York. Meanwhile, Sergei Diaghilev's Ballet Russe, touring the European capitals, attracted Picasso and other artists into collaboration; every now and then one of their epochal productions is re-created on the stage in New York. Apart from that, when the

Reginald Marsh, *Twenty Cent Movie,* 1936.

young American dancer Martha Graham, visiting in Paris, saw a painting by Kandinsky, she is said to have exclaimed, "I will dance like that!" And so, in a sense, she did. American composers like Aaron Copland carried on in comparable directions following Igor Stravinsky and other European innovators: as descriptive imagery was renounced in painting, so traditional melodic line in music was broken up or abandoned; as naturalistic perspective was given up in drawing, so were strict subservience to key and traditional harmonic progression in music.

Once the breakthrough to free formalist invention was made, the rest of the century's art in the West unfolded with momentous logic. In American painting, the process led from small, relatively modest studies in the new idiom by artists like Hartley, Arthur Dove, John Marin, and so on, to larger-scale, dynamic statements around midcentury by Stuart Davis. A culminating expression of Modernist intent in practice and theory would take place in the late 1940s and early 1950s in New York and then, almost immediately, would generate its antithesis, in the aftermath of which we live today.

For a while during the Great Depression, the Federal Art Project of the Work Projects Administration (WPA) gave American artists survival money, encouragement, and experience painting public-spirited murals and otherwise producing a documentary history of the nation from many points of view. Thus in the late 1930s and 1940s, a

Grant Wood, *Fall Plowing*, 1931.

number of antiacademic artists, most of them poor immigrants from Armenia, Greece, Holland, Russia, and so on—as well as a few arrivals from the American Far West—were drawn together in New York into a protomovement devoted to the advancement of art along lines projected by the European Modernists. When World War II broke out, many important European artists, including representatives from the German Bauhaus and Surrealists from Paris, also found refuge here. Then for a few years, bohemian New York in and around Greenwich Village was the refuge of international Modernism.

In fact the essential Modernity of the movement here lay in its international character, though its European root would be forgotten later when it would be touted as the first world-class "American style." In the original loose confederation were the Armenian Arshile Gorky, the German painter-teacher Hans Hofmann, the Dutch Piet Mondrian with his circle of followers, and, coming and going, others like Echaurren Matta, Joan Miró, and Hans Arp. Among younger men were the Dutch Willem de Kooning, the Russian Mark Rothko, Franz Kline from Pittsburgh, Jackson Pollock and Clyfford Still from the West. These men sought inspiration from many Modernist idioms: Russian Constructivism and Non-Objective Abstraction, Parisian Cubism and Surrealism, Italian Futurism and German Expressionism. Beyond these resources, they took language and a sense of their consequence in the history of the world from

Nietzsche. From Freud and Jung they took the principle of the unconscious mind, which can be penetrated by certain maneuvers of art like automatic drawing and free association. Progressively their program clarified: to find a visual language strictly their own which would bypass the then-popular style of American rural realism (promoted by Grant Wood, John Stuart Curry, and Thomas Hart Benton) and would also overleap the European idioms. "To get beyond Picasso" in a new way.

The breakthrough took place after the war's end, when most of the Europeans were gone or on their way home. A stepstone was the translation and publication by Hilla Rebay, in 1946, of Kandinsky's 1911 book, *On the Spiritual in Art*. What Kandinsky proposed as theory would become the working doctrine of the new art: "Color embodies an enormous though unexplored power, which can affect the entire human body as a physical organism . . . color harmony can rest only on the principle of the corresponding vibration of the human soul." The new idiom would be an amalgam of plastic means and the nonspecific emotions and intentions of the artist: the "vibration of [his] soul," one might say. The artists advanced toward this point with a growing sense of collective necessity. Around the year 1947, first Jackson Pollock, then Rothko, Kline, Still, and others left off struggling in the seas of Cubism and Surrealism and went to work directly with pigments poured, brushed, or laid with a palette knife onto the flat field of the canvas. In the same way, sculptors worked directly in open space with molten metal, raw wood, poured plaster, and the like. The procedure was to call forms into being and resolve their interactions as the artist worked.

So Abstract Expressionism, or Action Painting, was a conscious strategy, the deliberate assumption of a program to advance aesthetic experience, to shake up and impress the conservative local art community—next, the world—with the power of the new American vision. The consolidation of the style was heralded by trumpet blasts of rhetoric in the pages of little magazines of the time like *Tiger's Eye*. The tone had already sounded from Russia and elsewhere: "We shall thunder out a new myth upon the world," wrote Vladimir Mayakovsky, the Modernist poet. Rothko echoed: "Only that subject is valid which is tragic and timeless." "I paint the unconscious," said Pollock, and when the German Hans Hofmann chided him for working in the studio out of his head instead of from nature, he grumbled, "I *am* nature." "Let no one underestimate the implications of this work, or its power for life, or for death, if it is misused," said Clyfford Still.

As plastic correlative to these oratorical dramatics, the scale of the art expanded. Early Modernist abstractions had been generally easel-size. Kandinsky's great canvases had already opened up the walls of galleries, but now again the fields of paint enlarged, stretched east, west, and north until the artist had to climb a ladder and work his field like a muralist. Six feet, ten, twenty: these huge works, each with its powerfully idiosyncratic image, each the icon of a man, hold their own on museum walls world-wide today: Pollock's galactic spirals; Kline's gliding gradations of black; Barnett Newman's immensities of red, blue, and black.

And despite the artists' claim that their work engaged universal myth transcending particulars of meaning, *personality* nonetheless infused each man's oeuvre—that is, intention rooted in particulars of individual memory. Pollock worked from memory of furrowed Western prairies and Navajo sand paintings; Rothko, from whatever was locked in his memory of a Russian ghetto and his long transit to the sunset edge of America; Kline, from the dark bridges of Pittsburgh; de Kooning, from memories of Holland, where the sea cuts a constantly moving edge in the land. Rothko said his paintings held the impress of a mind "alone in a moment of utter immobility." Kline spoke about "the awkwardness of 'not-balance'." And de Kooning described his intention "to be both inside and outside . . . no pauses or rests, no in-betweens"; to create "the slipping glimpse." Of his steel figures, the sculptor David Smith said, "I polished them . . . the color of afternoon sun." The language of "light" as it was used by the Abstract Expressionists was a metaphor for

Stuart Davis, *Rapt at Rappaport's*, 1952.

ANY
Stuart Davis
RAPT AT RAPPAPORT'S

Louise Nevelson, *Night Presences*.

the nearly unattainable perfection or "workingness" of a work of art. It still keeps its Platonic aura in some artists' conversation today, a verbal trace of the golden glow in the skies of Luminist paintings of a hundred years ago.

I myself arrived young in New York as the movement was rising out of obscurity into the glare of publicity, and I later wondered why so much violence befell artists so adulated after years of hardship. I think this answer may serve as well as others: what felt to each man like a leap to freedom—variety, spontaneity, the promise of a long future of creative "actions"—turned out to be a closure. The image that had felt so liberating at the moment of its invention later stood in the way of the artist's further growth, in some cases leaving him with no other identity than what his work *had been*. Clyfford Still said of his painting that he'd "forged a solution" to a problem, and what is forged can't be easily bent in other directions. Pollock suffered to find new inspiration in a way of work gone sterile, and Rothko at the end of his life was heard to say, "I could have made *beautiful watercolors* . . . I didn't need to paint *so heavy*."

Also, though these artists had rejected the historic means of visual communication—common imagery, collective symbolism, rational visual structure—they yearned to have their life-experience, which they considered to be prophetic for their age, understood. For men who wanted to be remembered as philosophers, to see themselves instead become the pawns and profiteers of dealers was a source of moral confusion. In some cases, psychic depression followed, and several destroyed themselves. Gorky had died a suicide in 1948; Pollock, age forty-four, killed himself and a companion in a car crash in 1956; Kline died of a heart attack at age fifty-one in 1962; sculptor David Smith died in a speeding truck in 1965. Rothko's

Edward Hopper, *Office in a Small City,* 1953.

last cycle of paintings was steeped in pigmented darkness, and his suicide in 1970 completed this self-obliteration. These Americans were not the first artists to have destroyed themselves in this century of consuming ideologies. Roman Jakobson said, speaking of Mayakovsky, that "during the third decade of this century, those who inspired a generation perished between the ages of thirty and forty, each of them sharing a sense of doom so vivid and sustained that it became unbearable."

There were only a few women in the movement here at first, though Russian and European Modernism had counted many. Those who did manage to survive the combative chauvinism of the New York art world in the 1940s turned out work as dark. Pollock's wife, Lee Krasner, painted several verdantly colorful works after he died, but more representative of her personality were massive dark-umber and white canvases to which she gave titles like *Charred Landscape, Cobalt Night,* and *White Rage.* Louise Nevelson, an immigrant from Russia and passenger on a sea voyage she remembered painfully all her life, made in her seventies a pitch-black wood myth-ship afloat on a black plinth. She titled it *Mrs. N's Palace.* "Black means totality," she once reflected. "It means: *contains all.* . . . We will continue on black because I think if I speak about it every day for the rest of my life, I wouldn't finish what it really means."

For a younger generation of artists, many of them women, Abstract Expressionism was an easier, more flexible doctrine. "Light" came when it was called. The work under their hands stayed open to variations and sometimes to the reintroduction of natural, even figurative imagery. Helen Frankenthaler, Joan Mitchell, Nell Blaine, Mary Frank, all influenced by the elders, continued to work through the 1960s and 1970s when Pop Art was dominant in America. They find themselves at the top of their form today.

To aim for expressive clarity and the inclusive statement, to trust in the relevance of art to life: these were among the illuminations of Modernism in pre-World War II Europe and America into the 1950s. "We tried to understand the world," said literary critic Irving Howe of those years. "We were like scientists, trying so seriously to figure out which way to go," said the artist Robert Motherwell. "We really believed we could save the world," a number of the surviving Modernist artists, architects, musicians, theater people, and writers have recalled. Supported in this trust, many workers in the arts felt their lives take on more than personal meaning. That sense for an ethical mandate by which the success of a life could be measured was another correlative to the old landscapists' golden skies—a darkened vision, but one perhaps not gone forever.

On the other hand, it has to be said that a powerful mainstream style, in this case Abstract Expressionism, dominates its time, suppressing other ways of thinking and working and, in the market-oriented West, draining the coffers of museums and funding institutions. Before long, an antithetical movement would appear in America. But it would surface not out of obscurity, like the 1940s vanguard, but in the full glare of the media. As Pop Artist Robert Indiana would put it later, "The Abstract Expressionists fought and won the bloody battle of the publicity-press pantheon. They did it superbly, and now there is an art-accepting public and a body of collectors and institutions willing to take a risk lest they make another artistic-oversight-of-the-century."

Middleground

It is an axiom in the United States as elsewhere in the democratic West that a nation's artistic life should evolve in a laissez-faire manner independent of government or special interest—that evolution left to itself is a force for social and cultural good. If people are free to develop their ideas and the arts those ideas give rise to, more valuable forms of human enterprise will result.

In the Soviet Union and China, by contrast, it has been axiomatic until recently that the arts be guided by the state to reinforce political right-thinking and social responsibility. On the surface there seems to be a gulf between these two positions. But in fact over the past three decades, since the rise to world prominence of the Abstract Expressionists, the course of American culture has been shaped by a force even more external to aesthetics than political ideology: money. As a result, it is impossible to understand either the look or meaning of American art in the last half of the century—a phenomenon a leading art magazine in 1988 called "The Great Art Explosion—without taking at least a cursory look at the business side of the art world.

In December of 1949 *Art News* magazine—which in those days was capable of not only reviewing every one of the fifty or so shows a month in New York galleries but also including sale prices of works—listed Jackson Pollock's canvases at Betty Parsons Gallery as $150 to $3,000. It took only twenty-four years for the price of one of Pollock's important works, *Blue Poles,* to bring $2 million at auction. And the boom was just beginning. Since 1983, at least twenty-four works by contemporary American artists, among them young turks of the 1960s Pop Art movement—Robert Rauschenberg, Jasper Johns, Roy Lichtenstein, and Ellsworth Kelly—have been sold for more than a million dollars each. In 1988, one of Johns's major works, *False Start,* sold for over $17 million.

Today in New York City alone there are some 700 art galleries, museums, exhibition spaces, and private art dealers; nationwide, there are over 3,500 commercial galleries. In Manhattan, now center of the global art market, European galleries of old-master and modern art have also opened outposts. All these are now jostling for the media coverage on which their income depends, either through sales or, in the case of museums, through fees and contributions by their more than 500 million visitors a year.

In these showplaces, many thousands of professional artists exhibit annually, competing for sales with a couple of hundred American and European superstars like the late Pop Artist Andy Warhol and the German Neo-Expressionist Anselm

Andrew Wyeth, *Adrift*, 1982.

Kiefer. (Top European artists like Kiefer, his late compatriot Joseph Beuys, the Italian Sandro Chia, and so forth, seasonally ride the American money-escalator.) And these, of course, compete for attention (and sometimes sales) with ghosts of art history "rediscovered" or "revaluated" in museum shows, the most impressive of which are called "blockbusters"—enormous events funded by government and multinational corporations.

To contain all this activity, museums across the country are launching multimillion-dollar expansion programs while also enjoying orgies of acquisition of ever more valuable contemporary work, on the argument that museums should be "on the cutting edge" of American culture. The worlds of music, theater, and dance in this country are no less active. The pattern was set in the 1960s, when the historic Metropolitan Opera house in New York was torn down and new space was made available for all the major performing art groups in one big architectural complex: Lincoln Center. Initiative for this grand plan came from the same family that had memorialized itself in the thirties with the awesome Modernist complex of Rockefeller Center at Manhattan's solar plexus. Lincoln Center would be a transitional work in the development of Post-Modern architecture and urban planning. This historically eclectic, more human-scaled idiom is now full-blown in major cities of the States and will reach its apogee in the 1990s with the completion of New York's Battery Park City project on the Hudson River. Lincoln Center and smaller performance spaces around New York now provide over one hundred concerts a week, including four performances of the New York Philharmonic and seven of the Metropolitan

Opera. Since most tickets for Lincoln Center events are priced out of reach save for the relatively privileged, it is well that symphony, ballet, and opera broadcasts on American radio and television reach millions at one coup.

But this activity is only the tip of the iceberg of the American art world today. Each art form in the U.S. rides on a substructure of manufacture and commerce, and all these enterprises are carried along under the press of corporate executives, art advisers, publicity agents, critics, and so forth. By the mid 1970s, enterprises related to the arts were bringing $3 billion into New York City each year. By 1983, the figure was $5.6 billion. In New York City these days,some 117,000 people work at art-related jobs.

Corporate America knows the benefits to itself of this activity. Back in 1966, banker David Rockefeller explained that "involvement in the arts can mean direct and tangible benefits. It can provide a company with extensive publicity and advertising, a brighter public reputation, and an improved corporate image." Since that time American businesses have increased their investments in the arts—by purchase of works and underwriting of high-profile events—from $22 million to $698 million. (One Conceptual Artist, Hans Haacke, has made a career documenting exchanges of influence and profit between corporations, dealers, big collectors, and museums whose imprimatur on works of art and artists assures their rising value.) Compared with these figures, the involvement of the federal government through its twin National Endowments for the Arts and the Humanities seems paltry: in 1988 a budget of $169 million was distributed by the NEA directly to artists and institutions and indirectly through state arts councils and other agencies.

Spearhead to the art boom has been the auction business. The surge began back in 1964 when the then-leading house, Parke Bernet, put on a hugely publicized sale in which Rembrandt's *Aristotle with the Bust of Homer* was sold for an unprecedented $2.3 million to the Metropolitan Museum of Art. Prices obtained each season since in the frenzied horse race of auctions have lifted the Western art world off its feet. In March of 1987, Van Gogh's *Sunflowers* commanded $39.9 million; eight months later, despite the October stock market crash, Van Gogh's *Iris* fetched a world-record price for a single work of art—$53.9 million. While museum directors cry havoc that masterpieces will be beyond their budgets in the future, accessible only to Japanese, Arab, or multinational corporations, the competition for rare objects intensifies. In 1988, Sotheby's held the first-ever auction in Moscow of Russian pre-Revolutionary and Soviet contemporary art. In the last five years Christie's and Sotheby's International have called down almost $2 billion for art purchases.

Ten years ago, the *New York Times* reported that "soaring fees for star musicians are disrupting the concert world." Boom time in the art world is producing comparable results.

Mary Frank, *Natural History*, 1985.

Foreground

Three decades of freedom from the colonialism, so to speak, of Modernist abstraction have seen the rise of an American art world of enormous variety—a democracy (some say anarchy) of radically differing aesthetic principles. To mention only a few of these, there is the surreal-constructivism of Louise Bourgeois; the abstract naturalism of California painter Richard Diebenkorn; the political satire of Leon Golub; the biomorphic expressionism of New York sculptor Nancy Graves; the various feminist idioms of Nancy Spero, May Stevens, and Miriam Schapiro; and the graffiti-influenced art of Keith Haring and Jean Michel Basquiat, the latter recently dead at twenty-seven of a drug overdose.

Conversely, since the Post-Modern art world is an acknowledged marketplace, offering as much junk as any commodity outlet, it should be no surprise to hear a respected art critic describe the scene as "a kind of carnival . . . a very dark age, punctuated sparsely by points of nearly invisible light." Another laments "the commercialization of art, its reduction to a species of cultured entertainment . . . the appalling lack of taste and artistic standards . . . a wholesale rejection of art in favor of a series of carefully calculated gestures that *look like art*."

The virus of what in its full-blown form would be the Post-Modern point of view can be said to have invaded New York in the 1940s in the person of the French Dada artist Marcel Duchamp. Back in 1913, his Cubist *Nude Descending a Staircase* had blasted the complacency of visitors to the Armory Show and made him a celebrity here. From then until his death in 1968, his work-of-the-mind was to mock, undermine, and explode the solemnities of Modernism. By his "Readymades," banal objects mounted and displayed in museums, his Dada constructs with their arch titles, and his irreverence toward the whole matter of making and valuing "art," Duchamp introduced the spirit of Gallic insouciance into a culture that had historically regarded itself with Calvinistic or Old Testament earnestness. Eventually he pretty much gave up making original works of art. As he explained: "Every picture has to exist in the mind before it is put on canvas, and it always loses something when it is turned into paint. I prefer to see my pictures without that muddying." It was not long before his disciple Dada composer John Cage was adding: "The grand thing about the human mind is that it can turn its own tables and see meaninglessness as ultimate meaning."

Alice Neel, *The Family (John Gruen, Jane Wilson, and Julia)*, 1970.

An American advance-guard proselytizer in this spirit was Ad Reinhardt, nominally an Abstract Expressionist, who died in 1967 at fifty-four. If Clyfford Still had said: "Let no man undervalue the implications of this work, or its power for life, or for death, if it is misused," Reinhardt countered with: "Let no man undervalue the implications of this work, or its power for cash, or for bad credit, if it is misused." In the last years of his life, he turned out a series of all-black works with vestigial cruciform images at dead center. Today they hang along with other icons of Abstract Expressionism in museums, swept up in the market along with Duchamp's Readymades.

The first clear signal that Post-Modernism had arrived in New York was sounded in 1953 by the young Texas-born Robert Rauschenberg. He erased a drawing by de Kooning and hung the bit of wreckage as a work by his own hand. In the next years he proceeded to build a career on Duchamp's traces, producing a vast assemblage of *assemblages* of worn-out, discarded materials and objects combined with chaotic, gorgeous passages of paint. In 1955 his friend Jasper Johns produced the work that made him equally famous—an image of the American flag, de-iconized as flag, re-iconized as "art." In 1961 Roy Lichtenstein showed a painting of a peephole in a black wall. Dick Tracy of comic-strip fame had his eye to the hole, peering out at the viewer. The work is called *I Can See The Whole Room! And There's Nobody in It!* The laugh was supposed to be on the public, but some have continued to think the laugh was on that type of art.

Pop Art opposed to Modernism an attitude of ironic *je m' en foutism* in the guise of revolutionary radicalism: the "demolition of bourgeois cultural leadership through an appeal directly to the masses," as one critic put it. For a while the vocabulary of American art would be the *patois* of the streets and media, TV, movies, comic strips, subway graffiti, crime novels. The idiom thrived for about a decade, and a few of its practitioners are still going strong. It is relevant that along these same years occurred the Vietnam War and the serial deaths of the Kennedys and Martin Luther King, Jr. It was a time of psychological and social disorientation throughout the free West. As sculp-

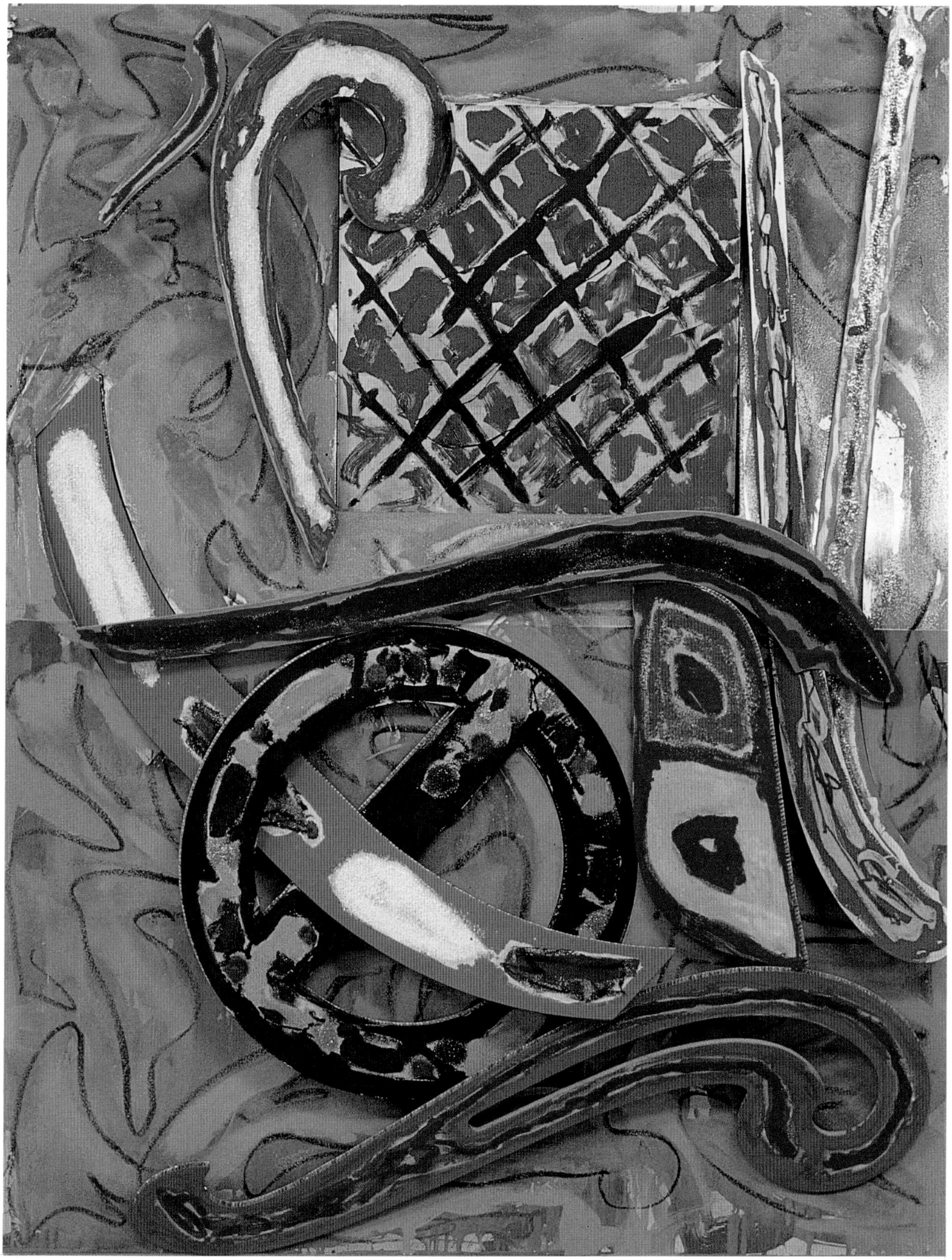

Frank Stella, *Brazilian Merganser,* 1979–80.

tor George Segal would later recall, "moral sense was suspended." (Segal began as a Pop Artist, but his work in plaster, cast from living people, has deepened in mystery and compassion.) The most curious of the Pop Artists was Andy Warhol. He showed his *Campbell Soup Cans* in 1962; not long after came his *Brillo Boxes,* his *Electric Chair* and *Five Deaths* on the subject of a ghastly car accident,

Roy Lichtenstein, *I Can See the Whole Room!,* 1961.

his Marilyns and Ethels and Jackies, and his prison flyers of *Most Wanted Men*—a disconnected drift of visual images that has clogged the Post-Modern consciousness.

After Pop Art, the gates were open. Op Art and Phenomenalism followed; then Minimalism and Conceptualism; more recently Neo-Expressionism, Neo-Geo, and "a return to the figure." Each new idiom has received exegesis by new critics, sometimes in loosely Marxist terms also used in some American art-historical writing today. Still, out of narrow 'isms have come large individuals. Out of Op Art came Frank Stella with his hard-edge field painting. Stella's work has continued to expand in formal density and vibrancy, thanks to the Post-Modern principle of freedom from rigid self-definition. Out of Phenomenalism came the novel neon-light constructs of Dan Flavin and Donald Judd, and, by contrast, Richard Serra's awesome testaments to massed steel. (One of his 32,000 pound, self-balancing constructs toppled in 1988, injuring two people. Serra has had constant trouble trying to fit his monoliths into spaces where people want to breathe and walk.) And Conceptualism has given birth to a number of astute sociopolitical critics, including Jenny Holzer and Barbara Kruger as well as the quixotic Douglas Huebler, who provides for his work a Duchampian rationale: "The world is full of objects, more or less interesting. I do not wish to add any more. I prefer, simply, to state the existence of things in terms of time and/or place."

Inevitably, an anti-Duchampian current has also appeared. After two decades in which Realism and Expressionism were derided as sentimental and embarrassingly subjective, a number of strong artists are working in those styles. Back in 1968 Nancy Graves astonished New York with an exhibition of three utterly realistic, life-sized, stuffed *Camels.* That artist was born into the founding family of a natural history museum full of mounted animals, birds, and other species and phyla. At the time, Graves talked about her work in obscure conceptualist terms, but it came out of her own experience. Now many artists again make open use of remembered experience as at least one source for their work, among them the widely differing, strongly idiosyncratic figurative artists Louise Bourgeois, Eric Fischl, Mary Frank, and Jennifer Bartlett.

In somewhat the same way, many artists today stand in awe of the German Neo-Expressionists Joseph Beuys and Anselm Kiefer. Former Minimalist Robert Morris, for example, has adopted both the giant scale and apocalyptic content of their work, presented with a certain American literalness. His paintings groan in heavily sculptured frames molded with small figures of people, weapons, genitalia—random elements of violence and war—huge baroque structures that hang on the walls like medieval shields.

George Segal, *Walk, Don't Walk,* 1976.

DONT
WALK
WALK

Walter de Maria, *The Lightning Field*, 1977.

Since midcentury, music and theater have developed along parallel lines. John Cage produced his Dadaist constructs in sound and silence; Morton Feldman created what he called Minimalist "washes" of sound (one work was an ode to Rothko's near-black canvases); more recently Steve Reich, Philip Glass, and La Monte Young have composed music in a kinetic Asian mode. One of the original experimental theaters here, The Living Theater of Judith Malina and Julian Beck, which typically in the Modernist 1950s performed plays by Picasso, Gertrude Stein, and Pirandello, in the more politicized 1960s mounted huge theater events in which audiences climbed on stage to join in the activist melee. Robert Wilson's *Einstein on the Beach*, with music by Philip Glass, made a different kind of theatrical history in 1976, one in which hypnotic figures of sound provided background for minimally Expressionist scenarios on a vast, near-empty stage.

Throughout these post-Modern decades, a swell of adulation has followed the younger trio who cut down the Abstract Expressionist old guard back in the fifties. Now, with Warhol gone, the full flow of reverential criticism devolves on Robert Rauschenberg and Jasper Johns. The phenomenon is partly owing to the familiarity of the objects they put together, the readability of their imagery when it appears, and the delicacy, in each case, of their manual work. But there may be another reason for their appeal. These were three (now are two) innocent-looking Protestants from the American hinterland, very different from the shaggy, myth-steeped wildmen of Abstract Expressionism. The younger men presented themselves as cool, even asexual or androgynous. Warhol, "the prodigy, the outsider, the impoverished émigré from Pittsburgh," set the pattern with his changed name, silvery hair, and plasterlike complexion. But all three, by their seemingly artless play with discredited things—beer cans, a stuffed goat, a tire, old newspapers—lightly but ever so lightly exposed the underside of the American scene: a wasteland of material things, worn out, disgraced, and discarded, yet, for all that, perhaps worth something in the eyes of the saints.

As if to put an end to a series of dwindling idioms, along has come the mode recently named "Deconstruction." If the Modernist idiom was heroic, and if Post-Modernism mocked that heroism by playing on peoples' appetite for banal *things*, Deconstruction has drained even that value from the object produced as art. David Salle's enormous canvases provide what a critic has called a "nonnarrative play of detached signifiers." These might typically be a dog's head, a loaf of bread, a badly drawn scenario of sexual abuse: "Salle records a world [writes a critic] so stupefied by the narcotic of its own delusionary gaze that it fails to understand that it has nothing actual in its grasp. Amid seeming abundance, there is no real choice, only a choice of phantasms."

Nancy Holt, *Sun Tunnels*, 1973–76.

Deconstructionist art will disappear, but another mode of art-making has meanwhile appeared which is bound to survive. The first rudimentary Earth Works—an idiom that combines architecture, sculpture, and a new consciousness about the natural environment—were shown in New York galleries in 1967. These were Robert Smithson's Duchampian "Nonsites," bare gatherings of earth, stone, and wood, and Walter de Maria's comparable "Earth Room" filled with loam. If Pop Artists fed off the stuff of the marketplace while mocking it, Smithson, de Maria, and others made use of the *stuff of the world*, treating it neutrally, without contempt or romanticism. From these first experimental pieces, it was but a giant step to Smithson's massive rubble, stone, and water work, *Spiral Jetty*, built directly in the Great Salt Lake, Utah, and de Maria's *Lightning Field*, 400 sharpened steel poles set in a mile-long grid on a New Mexican plateau in the line of seasonal electric storms. Both structures are among the conceptual and visual marvels of the American century. Since Smithson's death in 1973 in a plane crash in the West, a number of women artists, including his wife Nancy Holt, have taken the lead in the movement.

Holt's most striking work is *Sun Tunnels*, four 18-foot-long, 22-ton cement pipes laid down in the form of an open cross in the Great Basin Desert of Utah. The pipes are aligned to the two solstice sunrises and are further perforated in the patterns of star-groups that pass overhead at those seasons.

Maya Ying Lin, *Vietnam Veterans National Memorial*, 1982.

A person standing at the cross-point of these sighting-pipes is centered physically and perhaps also psychologically. For if, as the Post-Modernist accepts, there is no one correct way of looking at the world, there are certain perceptual experiences available to everyone on earth, which can therefore provide a universal order of understanding. One of these experiences is recognition of the earth's place among the sun, moon, and stars. To see sunrise over a point of land on the solstice morning, to greet Orion over the eastern horizon in December: such experiences, the Earth Artist suggests, are good for human beings. By providing a sense of location in the geometry of space, these works stabilize the mind and fill it with wonder. They evoke large questions about the relationship of mind to the inanimate and affirm the historic value of the quest for answers, even if it is endless.

Typically the Earth Artist has retrieved the sense of ethical purpose which Modernism projected. Nancy Holt, for example, is engaged in a public commission to turn a 57-acre plateau of garbage landfill along the New Jersey Turnpike into *Sky Mound*, a park designed both to restore the damaged ground to health and to provide enlightened recreation. Patricia Johanson, another visionary artist, is creating urban parks in Texas and California. Her templates are botanical forms enormously enlarged in cement and stone to provide walking and sitting places along the edges of ponds and the sea.

With Earth Works, one tendency in American culture comes full circle. These artists, like their homesteading forebears, take on the wilderness not to exploit but to husband it. Darkness seen through their eyes is a fact of nature and not the sign of subjective anxiety that it has been for some urban artists. Darkness, viewed objectively, gives way to natural light. A traveler to an Earth Work accepts the Post-Modern challenge: that is, to find from time to time a stable yet not forever fixed position from which to take a sighting on one's own, and then move on.

A common ground, a standing-place for many is provided by the American monument to its dead in the Vietnam War. Designed by artist Maya Ying Lin while she was still in architecture school, it was installed in Washington, D.C., in 1982. It is a work of formal refinement and conceptual power. In its horizontality, its rejection of the verticality of traditional war memorials, it obliterates the myth of Valhalla that served for so long to justify the pain of loss of young people in war. It acknowledges that there is no way to ease the loss or to disentangle the living from the dead. Its black polished surface both proffers the names to be remembered and receives the reflections of the rememberers, so they mingle in the shadow world of memory seemingly just below the stone's surface.

The structure appears to be deeply grounded, even standing in the earth. Its long, low arms reach out and away through grass, rain, snow. It reaches out toward Leningrad.

Monologues for My Son

Viktor Potanin

My village house has gone dark from time and the rains. Sometimes the house seems to heave a sigh, but it's only the poplar outside the window. There is something sad in its rustling. Its leaves have been gone a week already. That means autumn again, rains and fogs. And so it is. Outside a fine rain is falling, as if through a sieve, and the sky has dropped almost to the ground. A bit of poetry comes to mind, something like: "Gray water at flood, gray sky flowing over." That's probably why my street is so completely empty. Even the dogs are hiding under porches. But there's a jackdaw walking on the neighbors' roof. All wet, feathers drooping. A tractor starts chugging somewhere nearby, startling the bird. But after a minute or two the daw gets used to the strange sound, calms down, and starts walking around again, looking for something on the roof. And up above, the rain.

It's really too much for me. If only the snow would come soon, soon.

All my life I have hated this time of year, when autumn has already broken down and winter is still somewhere on the way. Often the gap lasts a week, or even a month, and that month is the saddest, the hardest of all. But, come now. Why should I be suffering—there's a big tiled stove just two steps away from me!

Wassily Kandinsky, *Improvisation.*

So now my stove has come to life, started to hum. The wood is good and dry. I laid it in back in early June. It burns merrily. All I have to do is keep adding a stick or two. That's a job I do with pleasure, and then, with equal pleasure, I sit nearby on a low stool and watch the flames. I watch, and everything in me comes to life, thaws out. I find myself wanting to talk, to be with people. My son seems to sense this. He comes running in from the next room, a bright picture book in his hands. In a year, my Fedya will go to school. He can hardly wait.

"Daddy, who makes up books?"

"Writers."

"What about music?"

"Composers. We call them musicians. . . . "

"And artists draw pictures?"

"Right! How did you guess?"

He doesn't answer, but again his eyes are playful, impatient. He's going to wear me out with his questions. Yes, that's it.

"And the best writers live in our country?"

"Right, Son."

"What about artists?"

"Well, yes, of course! And our musicians are the best. And our actors, too. Soon you'll go to school, and the teachers will tell you about the great culture of our homeland. It's a thousand years old this year."

"Daddy, what do I need culture for?"

"To become good and honest; to fulfill your duty on this earth. . . ." Again I notice his eyes. For some reason they have turned dark, clouded over in vexation. He doesn't understand. But it's too early for him to understand, I tell myself. For him, *culture* is an empty abstraction.

"Daddy, what does *homeland* mean?"

He looks at me keenly, inquisitively. Another second and he will start to cry from impatience. My Fedya doesn't like to be kept waiting. So I hurry:

"Our homeland is, first of all, the people around us. Second, it is our culture . . . that's the soul of our homeland." Once again, it seems, he doesn't understand. So he asks another question:

"Did you have books when you were little?"

"Very few. I waited half a year to read Gaydar's *Military Secret*. That's right, Son; we had to wait for books because there was a war. There weren't enough books to go around. But now things are different. Our country is richer. When you get older, I'll give you books to read. What wonderful things are waiting for you! Pushkin, Tolstoy, Dostoevsky, Chekhov, and Bunin . . . and then there are Aleksandr Blok, Andrei Platonov, Boris Pasternak, and Anna Akhmatova. . . . " Here somebody cuts me off: Enough of your lists! After a moment's thought, my heart is telling me: Your son doesn't need a lot of names, even great ones. Lope de Vega once said, "The only student who does really well is the one who has learned by just one book." When there were not many books, "people knew more, because they learned from less."

The stifled flames knock at the stove's door. Fedya has dozed off in an armchair, probably tired out from asking his questions. They have gotten to me, too, awakening some vague, troubling feeling. It bothers me that our conversation didn't go well. He really will be going off to school in a year. Strangers will start to mold and remake his soul, and I, his father, will have no say in it. But why, why? Can't I teach my own son? I'm a writer, after all. Doesn't that make me a teacher, too?

Twilight has begun outside, but I don't turn on the lights. I like this semidarkness, when the day is dying but still won't surrender. It brings mystery, silence. A huge, endless silence for thousands of kilometers. Only Fedya's breathing interrupts it. The peaceful, even sound is a soothing balm to me.

Darkness gathered outside, and a violet mist filled the room. I was astonished, but more and more poured in until it seemed a living thing. The mist settled on me like a cloud, and I felt my eyes begin to close. Soon my mind grew confused, mixing everything together, dreams and reality. Time itself suddenly became like a soft, endless cloud. I entered it and was lost.

Very soon, though, my eyes opened and I was glad. There before me lay my home town, Utyatskoe, all white and strange. The street where I live was white, too, not the way I knew it. But why? From what? Then I understood. The bird-cherry blossoms! The whole town was flooded with flowering spring trees, and my street, Tobol Street, was flooded too.

Then the moon rose, and the river shone like a huge, long mirror. I saw a boy sitting at the edge of that mirror, not blinking, staring straight ahead. Soon it would be midnight; the moon rose still higher. It was all like some narcotic, the damp smell of the bird-cherry blossoms, the dark hills across the river where the grove was.

The hills stirred and moved as if someone were disturbing them. Suddenly a pillar of flame shot up above the hills, higher and higher. The boy held his breath, fearful, spellbound. The pillar rose up, swaying, and there was some secret in it, a summons. It was no longer a pillar; it was a tall candle. It grew and grew as if it were stretching out and soon would reach the nearest star. What was it? What?

But then the candle sank down, wavering. All that was left was the memory, the fright. At the same moment people started shouting on the opposite bank, calling for the ferryman. A boat pushed off, the oars splashing softly in the spring water. And then. . . . Then my eyes opened. The dream was over. But was it a dream? It had all been just like that, just the same. I was that boy. It was my eyes that had seen the tall candle above the dark hills, like a summons.

The next day the boy picked up his pen and began to write verses, shy, childish, tender, completely disembodied; like that candle of glimmering fire; like the music he had heard not long before at the boarding school where the out-of-town boys stayed. They had just escaped the

Statue of Aleksandr Pushkin outside the Russian Museum, Leningrad.

Leningrad blockade, and they had a phonograph and a whole sackful of records. What was that music? What were the melodies? Maybe it was Glinka, or Tchaikovsky, or maybe Rakhmaninov's famous *All-Night Vigil*, or that sad old song like the wind in the steppe grass. Who could say? And what did it matter when the sounds were so bright and heavenly? They were probably the cause of that bright, marvelous candle—such an improbable image.

The page filled up with verses. From the wall, a painting of Mika Morozov looked down on the boy. The boy didn't know yet that his pet name was Mika. He didn't know the artist either, Valentin Serov. Or even, most important, that it wasn't a painting at all, just a cheap reproduction from some flimsy magazine. What difference did it make though? There was so much sun, warmth, and light in the charming Mika's olive eyes, wide open from happiness, and his shirt was blindingly white, the color of white snow, the color of hope. The boy looked at that snow. And the notebook filled up with verses.

I should tell my son about that boy and his verses. Yes, that would be good—that boy and my Fedya are nearly the same age. Then I'll tell him about Mika Morozov, too, and Serov and Vrubel, and then about Repin and Konstantin Korovin. No, my heart corrects. No. You should really begin with Pushkin. Undoubtedly! Pushkin is our homeland, our culture, our first cradle—and our hope and consolation. Because when the bitter,

Andrei Rubilev, *Trinity.*

hard times come, when life is not sweet at all and even seems in vain, Pushkin's verses are like a prayer, like an incantation, like a shining summons:

> If life should cheat you, do you wrong,
> Hold back your anger, don't be sad!
> Resign yourself when times are bad:
> Glad times in turn must come along.
>
> Our heart's home is the day to come.
> However bleak the present day,
> The moment passes, and is gone.
> We hold as dear what's passed away.

You remember that, and right away things seem better. You feel new strength, an extraordinary uplifting of the spirit. I have felt that, and my son will feel it too. It is certain that he will.

I look over at him and listen to his breathing. It is still peaceful, even. His lips are half open. He has been asleep a long while and is dreaming, of course. I pick him up out of the chair and carry him to his room. Then I go back to my seat and pull in closer to the fire. I throw on a dry log, and the fire blazes up. Cheerful patches of light slide across the walls. But a vague feeling of alarm overtakes me, a sort of obscure expectancy. I find myself wanting living sounds, conversation, but there is nobody around. Only silence. Silence. Like a heavy fluid, thick enough to cut with a knife. It could engulf a person, draining away every desire. I want to escape from it, doze for a little, but sleep just won't come. So then, to find a little diversion at least, I turn once more to my volume of Pushkin. I open it at random and read:

> O empty gift, idle gift,
> Life, why were you given me?
> Or why, by what mysterious fate
> Is death your ordained destiny?

"Why, you ask?" the voice inside me protests. "Well, at least so you can bring up your son, help him choose the right path. So he will turn out good, decent, cultured. Will you have strength enough? Knowledge and culture enough?" my heart asks—but right away, corrects itself: "At least it is possible to teach by example. Whatever you love and venerate, let your son love that too."

In that case, my son, I will begin with Pushkin and the frescoes of Andrei Rublyov. I will tell you about the marvelous music of Glinka and Tchaikovsky, show you the paintings of the famous Peredvizhnik school, and of our modern masters, Aleksandr Shilov, Konstantin Vasilyev, Yuri Raksha, and Ilya Glazunov. I will tell you how a few years ago I had the miraculous good fortune of seeing an exhibition of Viktor Popkov's work at the Tretyakov Gallery. People walked silently, sadly through the rooms, as if they were looking at icons. So it was indeed; a breath of sanctity came from the pictures, a tender, uneasy breath. The air smells the same when you walk into a dark pine forest in spring, or when you bring a bouquet of the year's last mint leaves into a room. The smell reminds you of our mortality, of the approach of bitter, rainy autumn, when the leaves fall from the trees and desires fall away as man prepares to die.

Venetsyanov, *Portrait of a Peasant Woman.*

One of the paintings was even called "Autumn Rains." Pushkin had run out onto the wet, cold porch. On the horizon were autumn, storm clouds, gloom. The same kind of gloom I see out the window now. Provincial, purely Russian, endless in its dreary shadings.

Yes, my son, your father lives a long way from the center of things. We are two thousand kilometers from Moscow. The trip there by train would tire you right out. Even the plane trip would. Yes indeed! We still have such remote corners, such provinces—and such provincial people, too. It's true. There are rotting fences of wattle and boards, and puddles out in the street, and along the fences, withered grass. The conversations in the houses are still the same—weary, faded, aimless, often Moscow gossip that reaches these distant parts almost half a year late. The people are the same, too—tired, beaten down by life, utterly without desires. Somewhat like people and somewhat like dry leaves. Or like tumbleweed, a plant I despise. The wind blows and it tumbles off, not held by the earth, by anything. What's more, in such out-of-the-way places there is usually no theater, no good House of Culture, and the books in the libraries are tattered, from before the war. And amid all this dreariness you will have to live, listening to the ancient music of nature. Listen: how well Nikolai Rubtsov puts it.

> Tall oak. Deep water.
> Shadows lie calmly down beside.
> And silence, as if nothing ever
> Has troubled nature in this spot.
>
> And you plunge the soul, without regret,
> In the mysterious and dear.
> It is overcome with radiant sorrow
> As moonlight overcomes the world.

How exactly right it is: "Overcome with radiant sorrow." I felt the same thing in the Tretyakov that time—that radiant, aching sorrow that came from Viktor Popkov's paintings and literally pursued me. Then I saw the paintings of Konstantin Vasilyev; the pain and sorrow were the same. And in the best paintings of Yuri Raksha, the same spirit again, the same depth.

When you grow up I will tell you about my friendship with a genius, Nikolai Rubtsov. We studied together at the Literary Institute. Several days before his tragic death, I received a telegram from him. Greetings on the New Year, according to the old calendar. The words in the telegram were simple, ordinary. And it asked for something simple, human: Not to forget him. Always to remember. I didn't know then it was a farewell. Other people who were close to him received telegrams of the same kind. Not to forget, always to remember! Five days later the poet was gone. Then every word of that telegram took on a new significance and meaning.

I will tell you, Son, about the splendid Russian writer Viktor Likhonosov. I will show you his books: *Autumn in Taman, In Remembrance, Clear Eyes, Elegy, Happy Moments.* And his letters too. I have several hundred of them. There are so many because we have been friends for two decades now. I watched, Son, as he made his joyful, confident beginning. What word but joy, when Tvardovsky himself opens the door to the great world of literature for you! Joy, when the Moscow newspapers write about you nearly every week and you are just barely past thirty. Joy, when you make long journeys to Russia's sacred places, to the monuments of Russian culture. To Taman, to Konstantinovo, to Trigorskoe and Mikhailovskoe—too many places for a list. Later, many years after, he would write about those unforgettable days and minutes:

> When I was younger I had a great love for Pushkin, Lermontov, Esenin, and the anonymous compilers of the ancient Chronicles. I made trips to pay my respects to them. A writer learns much from paying respects to his predecessors. Visiting their old haunts, their ancestral homes, you find their lives, their destinies. Your love for the classics and for everything belonging to our nation attains the mountain heights. How can I express it? Till the end of my life, the days spent thus will flash for me like summer lightning. But in writing this I have not really conveyed it. There are no words! For me, those journeys meant what Tsarskoe Selo did for Pushkin—excuse the comparison—or what looking at frescoes in Italy did for Russian artists of an earlier time, when the winners of prizes would be sent there for a whole year's study, all expenses paid. But the main thing was the feeling of communion with great poets.

V. Polenov, *Yard in Moscow.*

I have had dreams without which I would be worse than I am.

All the heroes of Likhonosov's tales are united by love and longing for mountain heights of culture, a burning thirst for beauty, and a filial affection for our native land. All of them are wanderers, or more precisely, are pilgrims seeking their dreams and hopes, or still more precisely, their own hearts, the unfathomable mystery.

Dreams and mystery. And right alongside them is life as we live it: grief, joy, meetings, partings, love, anguish. How can it all be brought together, united in a single, moving stream, so that the pages will speak once more with living voices? That is what happened when, after Likhonosov's stories, his novel *When Will We Meet?* appeared. How I dream of you reading it, Son. If only you could grow up faster! It's not just a story, this novel, but a testament, spoken in a voice of piercing strength, astonishingly open and pure. What makes this so is the love in the novel, the suffering, and the central importance, for Likhonosov, of moral concerns. This puts his novel in the best traditions of our classical prose and helps to recreate the spiritual history of an educated man of today, a young man from the provinces, the immemorial source of our culture's most zealous servants.

Modern culture, of course, is one of the novel's leading themes. It is to this theme that the best pages and all the author's most important thoughts are dedicated. In the broad sweep of time and space, the history of our culture becomes a full-fledged character in the work. The author is concerned most of all with man himself—the most immense, the deepest mystery—and with everything in man that is best and most pure. The heartfelt confidences, the mysterious lines of the letters the principal characters write one another, their meetings, their sleepless nights spent in conversation, and the author's own feverish narration—all these make the novel deeply interesting. The pages carry you along; you are truly captivated. Which is hardly surprising, since all the novel's heroes aspire to a single hope: to conquer the big city with their vision and talent.

The big city and the provinces. The concentration of what is spiritually highest, and the little home where you came into the world. Could it be that culture, too, can be big or little, that even people are divided into layers, like some kind of sandwich? No, the author tells us. No. True culture is the same for everybody, and our homeland is the same. There is nothing more precious. All of these grand words and ideas are penetratingly and exactly put in the novel, and they resound with equal force in the reader. They resound with the innermost voice of our homeland. I want you to hear it someday, Son, to hear it and understand that our homeland is great and beautiful, but that your own Utyatskoe is more beautiful and dearer than all the rest.

Yes, our land is great and large, but whatever gifts fate has in store for you, whatever deprivations, my only son, you should always look back to your first home. Let it be like a beacon for you, like hope, like the most cherished prayer said before a long journey. There will be many journeys for you, to the summits of our culture and into yourself. A true book can be a help to you. Remember what the writer said: "I have had dreams without which I would be worse than I am." But what was in those dreams? Longing for a higher good, for the beautiful? Maybe. A new road under the stars, piers, stations, joyful meetings, the warm southern sky above the Taman peninsula? Maybe. Or a sharp needle that pierced the soul, moving it to bare itself? Probably. Yes, probably. Because great art always deals in that sort of revelation.

Isn't Rakhmaninov's music a baring of the soul? Or the great Chaliapin's singing? Or the acting of the incomparable Nikolai Simonov? . . . Yes, Son, my words trail off because my enumeration is only a small drop from the deep wellsprings of Russian culture. I could draw my drop in another place, name other great names, but all the same it would sparkle like a drop of sunlight.

No, I really can't resist. I must digress. There is something I can't get out of my head. A happy memory. Or no, rather a sad memory, because Maria Aleksandrovna Voloshina is no longer in this world.

Back then, though, many years ago in Koktebel, she was still cheerful, full of energy, always telling about her famous husband, Maksimilian Voloshin, about his drawing, his poetry, his love of receiving guests. Once Chaliapin came for a visit. There was a merry supper, wine and conversation, and next thing they knew—no Chaliapin. He had vanished somewhere. An hour passed, or maybe longer, and then they heard his marvelous voice coming from the direction of the sea. He was singing a Russian folk song, his voice rising high, then falling—that glorious voice, the best in Russia at the time. He sang, and they fell silent. They went off towards the magical sounds, and soon they saw the singer himself. He was standing alone on the shore, the waves almost touching his feet. But he saw nothing, heard nothing. He sang, his face shining in the sunset. People were not enough for him, those noisy audiences on every continent. Now he was singing for the sea, the sea alone; and the sea felt him there, understood. Otherwise his face could not have shone so. Soon that voice filled all the vastness of the sea, and there were no more waves, no more seas, only Chaliapin's voice like the voice of God, the voice of fate.

Korovin, *Winter.*

Isn't it the same thing that has happened with Russia's great culture? It has absorbed many sounds, the melodies of many nations, many passions and hopes, and now it seems it will become one with the whole civilized world. That is what great art, a great culture means. When man's soul rises above the sea and merges with the sky, and then reaches still higher, always higher, to where its fetters drop away and all that is left is a sacred flame. Wasn't that what a little boy saw long ago in Utyatskoe? You haven't forgotten, Son? The white light above the hills, the tall candle that rose above the spring river? Maybe it was someone's noble soul rising towards Him.

I'm still sitting here beside my stove, looking into the flames. Outside, night has long since fallen. Silence. The barely audible rustle of rain. A fine accompaniment for writing music, painting pictures, or making poems and immersing oneself in metaphors rustling just as quietly. Or for thinking about one's only son and remembering, remembering. Now my memories are like dreams, as soft and disembodied as a prairie dandelion. But suddenly someone interrupts, stops me, and again I see his eyes and hear that insistent voice:

"And the best artists live in our country?"

Well yes, of course. . . . When you get bigger I will tell you how the famous artist Yuri Raksha once showed me around Paris. He was tireless, drawing constantly, even at night. Once I was lucky enough—and close enough—to see his eyes. You will laugh at that. Well, so what! But I will get the better of you. At that moment the artist was standing twenty meters from the Cathedral of Notre Dame. Standing and simply looking at the cathedral. But his eyes! There was joy in them, and

Vrubel, *Six-Winged Seraphim.*

amazement, and the light of some sad parting. And on top of that, pain. Unbearable pain, anguish. From what? Why? Why was he suffering so? I was utterly perplexed. Maybe he had just remembered something, or was making up his mind about something. While I was still wondering, guessing, he unfolded his portable easel and started to draw. At once his face grew tense, pale. His eyebrows knit together, trembling just the slightest bit. I stood close by and watched him draw. These were only sketches, of course. He was feeling out a theme, an intuition. But his eyes were cold and hard, and soon he no longer noticed what was going on around him. For some reason I kept thinking of some verses by Bulat Okudzhava:

> Mix these colors like passions
>   in your heart, and after,
> Mix these colors and your heart
>   with the sky, and after . . .
> But the main thing is to burn,
>   burn in joy and laughter.
> They may blame you, at the start,
>   but won't forget you, after!

Those lines ran through my head as I watched his eyes, which now saw only the cathedral, the great wonder, with all its endless stone ornaments, stained-glass windows, statues and towers. I watched as his pencil, with a single flourish, gave birth to drawings of all the Bible kings and prophets, outlined in a flash the portals of the Virgin and St. Anne. All this appeared under his small, neatly molded, but steady hand so astoundingly fast that it was like some magician's trick. Or no, not a trick; it was like a photograph being developed. There, on the artist's paper, everything came to life at once, taking on exact form and drawing breath. Yes, breath is the word. The drawings had a life of their own, apart from the artist. A wonder, just like the other.

I was thrilled, looking again and again at the artist, at the drawings. I even tried to ask about something. But he answered very unwillingly, in monosyllables. His face grew tenser, sharper, his eyebrows drew tighter together. I had seen the same determined, single-minded face on the village men in Utyatskoe as they hewed logs for houses, rooted out trees, or cut hay. One sweep of the scythe, one hand set to the plow, and the eyes narrowed, grew stern, as if to tell everybody, to shout for the whole world to hear, "Don't bother me now. Keep away. I'm doing something big now, my great task as a peasant."

Yes, Son, Yuri Raksha was doing his great task too. Although it would be better to use some other word than "task." Like "Passion," with a capital P. In doing so we will restore a higher justice, because Raksha always worked passionately. He was inspired, heedless of everything in the world, even of his terrible, incurable illness. But I will tell about that a little later.

A few days afterwards I visited that immortal cathedral again with Yuri Raksha. There was an organ concert; famous musicians played. I learned they were famous from the advertisements. For once, though, it was the truth. The musicians played splendidly. But to say that is not to say anything. They didn't really play. It was as if they created the music. After hearing them you wanted to cry. Of course, to cry, to dissolve the joy in bitter tears. Otherwise it would be unbearable. In only a few minutes we lived through whole years. Bach followed Schumann, then came Beethoven, and then our music, Russian music.

The cathedral was full of people. Many of them stood; there were no seats left. Lamps were flickering in distant corners, under the dome, but they gave almost no light. And that was good; it was right. You shouldn't listen to great music with bright lights burning. The mystery will disappear; all the mirages and dreams will vanish. That time, everything was as it should be. It was crowded in the cathedral, I repeat, and many people stood packed tightly together. But what is such discomfort in the presence of those sounds! Some of them made you want to grab your head and moan as if in pain; they harrowed the soul. Others, on the contrary, would put the soul at ease. The sound would roll up into a ball and then, as if from some mighty push, soar up and up, soaring off it knew not where. And what was the use of knowing? You were flying alongside it, and all grievances and grief, all doubts and worries were left behind, as if you had just been born, as if the only thing you really wanted, desired, was that this flight should never end. Only the flight? Perhaps the hopes, too.

People were standing all around us. Many were smiling. Yuri Raksha was smiling, too, even though he knew already that he was mortally ill. But music brought hope. With us stood Frenchmen, Americans, Germans, and Englishmen, and all their faces looked alike. Because they all bore the shining stamp of light, of hope, of some sudden relief. And do you know what I thought of, Son? All of us, all people, have been in the same boat for a long time. You could put it another way: All of us have been living for a long time in the same cathedral, under the same dome, under the same brooding heavens. And if somewhere, right now, there is hunger and war, if somewhere nations languish without a breath of freedom, then our soul suffers the same torments. Our world today is made of interconnecting vessels. And it is our culture that has made us this way. Yes, Son, culture is the greatness of our spirit. And if that spirit is alive, our hopes are alive. And knowing that life is unique and unrepeatable, how we should cherish it!

My stove is still burning. I look into the flames and listen to your breathing. You are close by, on

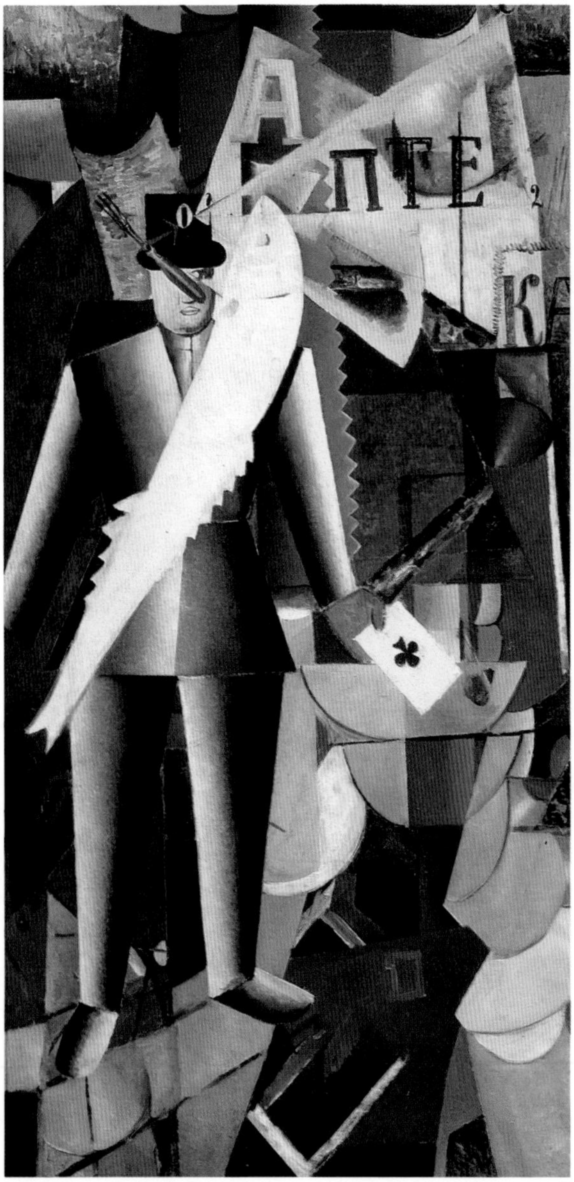

Malevich, *Aviator.*

the other side of a thin wall, and your breathing seems close by, too. And again I fall to musing. Will you, in turn, have the strength to bring up the son you love? Enough culture and knowledge? And, finally, will you have the heart to pass your flame to another? The unlit candle is lit from one that is burning. But excuse me. I digress. I ought to answer your questions:

"Daddy, what do I need culture for?"

"To educate your conscience. To find love inside you, and compassion, for every blade of grass, for everything on the face of the earth. Not long ago, Son, I heard the pianist Mikhail Pletnyov. He came to Kurgan, our regional center, and the town was breathless with excitement. Everyone wanted to get hold of tickets, to be at the concert. I was among the fortunate. The pianist played Rakhmaninov preludes and Skriabin études. He played Tchaikovsky and Shostakovich. The concert went on and on. Encore followed encore. Then it all ended, the hall fell quiet, and soon I was back outside. That was when a strange thing happened. I walked through the city I had known for so long and I didn't recognize anything. Then I got completely lost. Where was I, and what was wrong with me? There were some people coming towards me. They were moving carefully, slowly, as if on slippery ice. I looked at their faces and didn't recognize them. I couldn't understand it at all. Just yesterday they were so gloomy, drawn inward, and today they were all so kind, bright, courteous. Why were complete strangers smiling at me? Probably I seemed different, too. Yes, Son, that is what had happened. On that evening I was changed: I became completely different. By listening often to such music, it is possible to be changed forever. Because the unlit soul is lit from one that is burning.

I understood that again last summer, at the celebration of the one thousandth anniversary of Slavic writing, the one thousandth birthday of Russian culture. I was proud and moved. Everything that is best and most noble in our culture had come together in the ancient city of Novgorod. So many great artists and renowned ensembles! In just a few days I was able to hear the Glinka Choir, the Andreyev Folk Chorus, the Leningrad Seminary Choir, the Bayan Folk Orchestra, and the mu-

Marc Chagall, *Promenade.*

sicians of the Leningrad State Theater. Most wonderful of all, however, was the solemn procession to the center of the city, to the St. Sophia Cathedral. It was a warm spring day; the sky was clear and deep blue. The trees and grasses were in bloom, and the river Volkhov rolled its cold waters mightily along. And high above the Volkhov, above the ancient city, the cathedral stood in majesty. All the space and air and sky around it seemed to be filled with flowers and music.

So it was, indeed. Famous orchestras played; renowned soloists sang; folklore ensembles danced. To crown it all, a choir sang "Glory to the Red Sun" from Borodin's *Prince Igor.* People wept, exchanged congratulations. On what occasion? The thousandth anniversary of Russian culture, the greatness of art, the joy of calling yourself Human. But who were these people? Russians, Bulgarians, Czechs, Germans, Americans. They had gathered from all over the Earth to make a deep bow to our Russian culture. They bowed and swore a silent oath to one another: to work for peace and international understanding, to serve beauty and light!

Sometimes, Son, it seems to me that all of world culture is like a huge necklace of precious stones. Many of the stones are diamonds. And perhaps the biggest diamond of all is our Russian one. Because its faces were cut by Pushkin and Gogol, Dostoevsky and Chekhov, Kachalov and Stanislavsky, Rimsky-Korsakov and Tchaikovsky, Bulgakov and Gorky. And by Pasternak, Nabokov, Chagal, Akhmatova, Mandelshtam, and Brodsky. Grownups in our country are hearing some of these names for the first time. They have been returned to us by *perestroika,* the springtime of our days, the warm winds. Yes, Son, that is how it is. It is autumn outside our windows, but springtime in our country. A mighty time of thaw, of hopes.

What a wonderful word—hopes! And they will come true. It is the law now. Of course, the law, because now all the restrictions are down, all the walls! Now everything is written about, performed, published. Even the arguments about rock music have cooled off a little. All people of intelligence have agreed—everything that shows talent, that bears the true stamp of the heart, should live and flourish. What Pasternak once spoke of has come true:

> I want to get to the very essence
> In everything:
> In work, in searching for the way,
> In the troubles of the heart.

That is what has happened now. We are getting to the essence in everything, dreaming and arguing, turning back to our roots and our prayers. We think about tomorrow, about our children. I think about you, Son, and I worry, because barriers still exist. One of them is the simplicity of our life, its

Exhibition hall at the Hermitage, Leningrad.

After a performance—the Bolshoi Theater, Moscow.

provincialism. It goes without saying! Any American boy can turn on his home computer, can press some barely noticeable button, and the Philadelphia Orchestra comes right into his home, or the voices of famous rock musicians, or Chekhov's *Uncle Vanya*, which has just opened on Broadway.

Here, for the time being, everything is different. We have an old television, Son, and just two channels. How could it be different? We live a long way from Moscow and Leningrad, and although we have fast trains and airplanes, art still reaches us on foot. As in the past, the elite—our famed soloists and ensembles—pass this village by. Probably country folk are considered second-class audiences, or third.

Not so long ago a renowned Moscow quartet performed here in Utyatskoe. The musicians brought a rough, undigested program, as if to say: We'll get our practice here, smooth things out, and then go on that important foreign tour. It is the same with the theaters. A sad affair. Often they present abridged versions, with many of the characters left out altogether. A dismal picture, but how can it be helped? And what about our clubs and discotheques, where everything is decrepit, from the repertoire to the indescribably obsolete equipment? Or our village cinemas, where they are still showing films from before the war? Where are Andrei Tarkovsky and Ingmar Bergman, where are Fellini and Kurosawa?

I could go on with such questions. But I'm not a pessimist, Son. I'm a dreamer. An ordinary dreamer, like all provincials. That is why I want so much for you to get bigger, so that sometime, on a dark, starless night just like this, you can see a brightly shining flame rise high, high above the grove, above the hills. If you can see it, imagine it, it will mean your soul is alive, all your best and brightest feelings—love, goodness, remembrance of what your ancestors accomplished with their talents long ago—and all your dreams and hopes of repeating those deeds. Yes, I mean that—of repeating them! Because I believe, I hope, that some day you too will want to become an artist, or an actor, or a musician like my beloved Mikhail Pletnyov. Or that some day you will take a clean sheet of paper and try to compose a poem like the one by Nikolai Rubtsov, my favorite:

It is bright here inside
From the starry night.
Mother takes the pail
And silently brings water.

In the garden my red flowers
Have faded to the last.
The boat, tied in the shallows,
Will soon be rotted through.

The lacy willow shadow
Dozes on my wall.
Under the tree tomorrow
Will be a busy day.

I will water the flowers
And think about my fate.
Before the starry night returns
I will set the boat to rights.

It's me, Son. I'm sorry, but I'm very worried now. I want to say that I would like to fix up a boat for you, a strong, reliable craft that the wind and

The International Ballet Competition, Moscow. Grand prize winner Galina Stepanenko (USSR) and award winner Michael Shannon (USA) in the pas de deux from *Don Quixote* by L. Minkus.

storms cannot wreck, that cunning and evil fogs cannot lure off course. But I need your help, your goodness, your love.

How splendid they are, the goodness and love in your soul! But why am I so sure, so categorically sure, that these precious feelings are in you? Perhaps, my son, you will not be that way at all. Perhaps you will be an indifferent, ice-cold person. Everything depends on the culture that will uplift and direct you. A noble culture will form an honest, pure character. An abased culture, on the contrary, will create a mediocrity ready to commit any low, antihuman act. It's true. The original meaning of *culture,* after all, is cultivation, nurture. That should not be forgotten.

My stove, it seems, is breathing its last. All the wood is burned, and the night outside is deep and dark. Suddenly I am irresistibly drawn out onto the porch. I get dressed quickly and step outside. At once the sharp cold sets my cheeks burning, as if tens of thousands of barbed, invisible snowflakes are racing through the air, pricking at my hands and face. Another day or two and winter will descend on the land—freezing cold and snowstorms for seven long months! That's what makes these cold, ringing nights. Up in the sky though, is a real cataract of stars. To look at it for long would make you dizzy. Isn't there some breath of life on at least one of those stars? I don't believe there isn't; I never will! Such ideas are invented by people without dreams, without imagination. Do they ever look up at the sky?

What am I going on about?! Drifting off again. It's high time I became a serious, responsible person. I have a son coming up, and I ought to be an example for him. Really, though, how naïve that is—being an example. In five or six years my son may fall into the hands of some Philistine schoolteacher who despises poetry and good theater, and likewise Mozart and Tchaikovsky. And all my efforts of today will crumble into dust, like the philosopher who said he spent his whole life trying to plow the sea.

But maybe in five years we won't have such Philistines in our schools, in our art. And even at the family dinner table we will talk about what is beautiful and noble. Of course it will be so, because of *perestroika.* We are getting used to living a normal, natural life, getting used to being masters of our fate and our desires.

But we are still only getting used to these things. It isn't easy, after all, after suffering through whole decades as if buried in deep snow. It came to be almost the norm for us, a tradition from the darkest days of Stalinism. We had lost faith in spring, in the possibility of change. What few hints there were seemed to be fantasies, fairy tales. But all the same, spring has triumphed, broken through to us. Its first rays have melted the deep drifts, turning them into springs of life, into hopes. We long now to see those hopes fulfilled, those springs swiftly transformed into rivers.

It is not easy, of course. Not only because creativity has lain dormant for so many years but also because we have grown unaccustomed to a clear and simple idea: Any genuine culture is always many-faced, multifaceted. Grown unaccustomed, did I say? No, we have simply forgotten. We even forgot, or tried not to remember, that our own Pushkin, the sun of Russian culture, was not only a genuine Russian but was, first and foremost, "a European, a man of high intellect, of high spiritual needs, who embraced in his consciousness all of Europe's culture and history." That is what Dostoevsky said about him, and we agree.

I stand smiling on the porch—night, silence, and the stars above me—and I think of my son, of Pushkin, of hope. Maybe this is happiness. These days and minutes will pass and never come again. Never. Never. What a sad, heavy word! How I dislike and fear it! Not so long ago, our artistic reactionaries were finding it very much to hand. At every crossroads they shouted, commanded, that never, never should Soviet citizens come into contact with the corrupting culture of the West. Never would we need a new Meyerhold or Shostakovich, a new Zoshchenko or Chagal, and never would our simple, ordinary people open their eyes to them, let alone their souls. So down with all the avant garde, the surrealists, the newfangled Futurists! Let the clear sky of our art never be clouded by storm clouds or icy western winds! And whoever is not with us in this fight is against us! . . . There were even more hysterical speeches, of course, even harsher and more terri-

Scene from Andre Tarkovsky's film, *Sacrifice*, 1986.

ble prohibitions. But there were also people who held on to a unique spirit and character, even in that stifling atmosphere.

Many birds spend their whole lives in overgrown swamps or wild reeds and yet they have plumage of unmatched beauty. But that is nature, and birds are always free. In society, the society of the distant fifties and oppressive seventies, any free-flying soul came under increasing ideological pressure and soon was put outside the law. Enough to recall the example of Pasternak, or the martyr's path Akhmatova was forced to take, that splendid, tragic path.

Of course the crafty overseers of art had their successes too, their victories great and small. No doubt it is a hundred times easier to turn a person into an insensate log than to cultivate a garden in the soul, to plant it with flowers. Any schoolteacher knows that some pupils can never be made into a Mozart or a Skriabin, but every ten-year-old can certainly be molded into an ordinary hard worker who will at least be good for something, someday. No cause for despair. It's not for everybody to pluck stars from the sky.

Ah, my poor, naïve teacher! You yourself came to us out of the years of stagnation, as we now delicately call them. If only you knew how wrong you were in saying, "Not for everybody"! It is exactly the opposite, the other way around. Because each life is unique, unrepeatable. And each person—each person—should set for himself or herself the highest, most longed-for goals. That is the challenge *perestroika* now lays before us.

New people are already coming into the field. Honest people, conscientious people, whose aim is to foster creativity, not carry out orders from on

The USSR State Circus at the opening ceremonies of the 1986 Goodwill Games in Moscow.

high. But the relics of the past, the old stereotypes, are still very much alive. The use of demagoguery is far from forgotten. If my son were a little older, he could draw many curious and challenging facts from the newspapers. Just take the discussion of whether Soviet theater needs the different kinds of actor's studios and youth groups. Only a year ago there were some in our ministries who rejected the idea out of hand. It is hard to manage and supervise such studios, they said. Yes, the familiar phrase, the old syndrome: No getting along without a finger to point the way, a commander. Is it conceivable that the culture of such a vast country could survive without guidance and preformulated recipes?

A few months later, though, and we suddenly discovered that such studios were popping up everywhere, like mushrooms. And in such variety: cooperatives, youth groups, self-financed groups. The studios began to overshadow provincial theaters and orchestras in ticket sales and artistic significance. Because a studio is both a cultural center and a debating society—a university in miniature, if you like.

The furor over the studios has died down now, and new concerns have come to the fore: popular music groups for young people. Every city has dozens of them. They are cropping up in the provincial centers too. It might seem there is no cause for concern or discussion here. After all, it's obvious that popular music, derivative popular music at that, cannot replace Beethoven and Bach.

It would be like replacing Tolstoy with Agatha Christie. To each his own, as they say. To Caesar what is Caesar's, and to God what is God's. But it is equally true and indisputable that our art cannot be for the chosen few, the elite. And our art can be addressed not only to the vast audience of young people but also to intellectuals, thinkers, and poets. It has always been so. It will be so tomorrow and the day after.

Still the arguments continue. Let them. It is a normal, natural process. I could compare it with the years of adolescence and youth, when a person is like new wine. As time passes, the wine clears; only then can it be properly evaluated and registered. That is where we are now. In time, the dispute will end. Real art will remain; talents will grow stronger. And still:

> It's early yet to beat the drums.
> No cause for it, and still,
> I find that now I want to live;
> I wish the same for you.

Again I am thinking of Bulat Okudzhava, a clear and penetrating voice, a little drop of our great culture, like an emerald. Or maybe like that bright blue star there, right above my head. I gaze at it and make a wish. The most secret wish, the greatest wish. Although really, what secret is there? I wish for my son to grow up good and decent, to drink in all the pure and sacred nectar of our culture, never to lose sight of our roots. The star keeps moving toward me. It is so close and clear, it seems I could reach out and touch it. I am even about to try when I hear his voice, as clear and vivid as if he were standing right here.

"Daddy, what does *homeland* mean?"

I answer quietly and carefully, like last time: "Our homeland is, first of all, the people around us. Second, it is our culture. A person can't live without both."

Now the star is right beside me. And again I ask of Someone who is the strongest, the kindest: Let everything come true as the soul has seen it. Whatever is in the soul, after all, is eternal.

Literature

JOYCE CAROL OATES is the author, most recently, of *Because It Is Bitter, and Because It Is My Heart,* a novel and *The Time Traveler,* a collection of poems. She is the Roger S. Berlind Distinguished Professor in the Humanities at Princeton University and has been a member of the Academy-Institute of Arts and Letters since 1978. With her husband Raymond Smith, she edits the *Ontario Review.*

ALEKSANDR MULYARCHIK is an editor and literary critic. He has taught American literature and journalism at Moscow State University, worked for the Committee on Cinematography as an advisor for joint productions with foreign studios, and served as Progress Publisher's editor-in-chief for foreign literature. After many years of working at the Institute of the USA and Canada, he recently joined the Gorky Institute of World Literature in Moscow. He has edited and written prefaces for the first Soviet publication of American writers Thornton Wilder, Nathanael West, Katherine Anne Porter, Joyce Carol Oates, Arthur Hailey, and others. His published works include *the Art of John Steinbeck; The American Novel in the 1920s; Postwar American Novels; The Argument Is about Man: American Literature in the Later Twentieth Century;* and *The Modern Realistic Novel in the USA.*

Jacob Lawrence

American Literary Culture:
A Personal Perspective

JOYCE CAROL OATES

What is the enterprise of literature but the communal flowering of the efforts of individuals, for the most part strangers to one another, as they explore their intensely individual worlds, posit their individual claims, create sequences of linguistic structures to voice their individual propositions concerning the world?—an infinite and seemingly permanent galaxy composed of the finite and perishable? The wellsprings of "creativity" remain inexplicable, but we can consider that their consequences have both a private and a public significance: all art is both personal and autobiographical, and at the same time social, political, historical. The artist is the self-conscious conduit between the world *within* and the world *without,* a sort of Gnostic intermediary giving notice and form to symbols of a humanly universal nature. Society is a living organism ceaselessly defining itself, shifting its boundaries, taking shape from the future no less than from the past; art is the formal record of its inchoate struggles, its dreams, nightmares, and visions. Never has our American literature more clearly embodied these propositions than at the present time, in this final quarter of the twentieth century.

From its beginnings in colonial times, imaginative writing in America has been characterized by thematic, aesthetic, and regional diversity; but in the past twenty years the range and depth of this diversity has dramatically increased. Indeed, for most American writers—certainly for women (both feminist and nonfeminists), for blacks, for Jewish-Americans, for native Americans, for Hispanics, for Chinese-Americans, and other minority groups, including gays and "young" writers (that is, writers in their early twenties)—the present era is by far the most fertile and supportive in our entire history. It may strike a neutral observer as highly ironic, if not perplexing, that so revolutionary a cultural phenomenon has arisen at approximately the same time that the American political climate has become increasingly conservative, if not, in some respects, reactionary; yet more ironic, and perplexing, to consider that there are more than twenty-three million illiterates in the United States . . . a number said to be increasing at an "alarming" rate.

How to account for such paradoxes? How to account for the fact that, each year, fifty thousand books are published in this country . . . of which some, in mass-market paperback, are allowed a life-span as brief as three weeks on the crowded shelves of bookstores? (The logic of the marketplace makes it more economical to pulp books than to store them in warehouses.) How to explain to visitors from other cultures that, though there is no economic egalitarianism in the field of art, the disparity in income between the best-selling literary novelist and the highly regarded but virtually nonselling literary poetic being consid-

Jacob Lawrence *Library Series—Schomburg,* 1987.

erable, there exists nonetheless a social and cultural egalitarianism?—that, from a certain perspective, American literary culture is a living community, a network of mutual support and fructification?

Nancy Crampton photograph

James Baldwin.

It might be argued that such plenitude, so blooming and buzzing a confusion (to use William James's description of the pluralistic universe), cannot fail to suggest a Darwinian struggle of extreme rapacity and cruelty; yet the fact is that never before in our history has the "small press" culture been so healthy, so vigorous, so in a way intransigent. Never before have so many magazines (approximately fifteen hundred) and so many books, both hardcover and soft, been published by the nearly three thousand "small" presses in the country.* The annual anthology *The Pushcart Prize: Best of the Small Presses,* edited by Bill Henderson, is now in its thirteenth year and has become in itself an annual literary event, singling out for inclusion fiction, nonfiction, and poetry from presses as disparate and far-flung as *Antaeus, Paris Review, Hudson Review, Tri-Quarterly, Pipedream Press, Hard Pressed, Holy Cow!, ZYZZYVA.* The familiar complaint that "nobody reads poetry" is surely belied by the fact that a number of prominent poets (John Ashbery, Adrienne Rich, Galway Kinnell, Alan Ginsberg) sell very well, year after year; and that, granted the remarkable quantity of poetry titles issued, not only by small presses but by commercial and university presses, the audience for poetry in the aggregate must be considerable. If the days of the best-selling poet of quality, like Robert Frost, are possibly ended, it is still the case that poets of distinction (among them Philip Levine, Carolyn Kizer, Robert Bly, James Dickey, Maxine Kumin, W. S. Merwin, C. K. Williams, Louise Glück, Rita Dove, Carolyn Forché, Diane Wakoski, Robert Hass, the late Raymond Carver, Tess Gallagher, Ai) have found audiences that buy their books and attend their poetry readings with gratifying enthusiasm. And it is a common observation of our time that, however infrequently the average American reads poetry, it seems that, judging from the quantity of poetry submissions received by presses and magazines, *everyone* is writing it.

In contrast to earlier prevailing theories concerning American literature, even relatively conservative literary historians of the United States

*Many of these presses are partly subsidized by annual grants from the National Endowment for the Arts (NEA) an agency of the United States government. But the NEA exerts no editorial guidance.

Susan Sontag.

Nancy Crampton photograph

have suggested in recent years that each generation is obliged to define the past in its own terms. Since World War II, numerous factors have conjoined not only to fragmentize our society but to vitalize it. The prolonged Cold War—that Manichean drama of projections and counterprojections; the Vietnam War—not generally acknowledged as the longest war in American history (1954–73); the protests against the Vietnam War, which forcibly divided the generations; the civil rights movement; the women's movement; gay liberation: all have permanently shaken our society and have forced new evaluations of American character, "national identity," and definitions of the self. Is there any longer the comforting illusion of a homogeneous America? Can there endure a "typical" portrait of the American writer that is not merely a stereotype?

There is a considerable contrast, for instance, between the 1948 edition and the 1988 edition of the prestigious *Columbia Literary History of the United States,* one of the primary reference books of its sort. (There were no intervening editions between 1948 and 1988, but the new edition is in no way a revising or updating of the old.) Where for Robert E. Spiller and his coeditors forty years ago there was a "unified vision of a national identity"—one that arrogantly or unthinkingly excluded all women and persons of color—for Emory Elliott and his coeditors there is not only no single unifying vision but no desire to discover or invent one. The conscientious literary history of a culture so vast, so complex, so inchoate, so contradictory, indeed so paradoxical as the United States can hope only to present a reasonable compendium of representative viewpoints. Thus, the 1988 edition of the *Columbia Literary History* contains such essays as "Immigrants and Other Americans, 1865–1910," "Mexican-American Literature, 1910–1945," "Women Writers Between the Wars," "The Avant-Garde and Experimental Writing, 1945–1988"—a diversity that would have bewildered, if not offended, earlier generations of academicians. At the present time the "battle of the books" in America continues with much passion on either side: the liberals favor an extension of the canon; the conservatives are convinced that there is but one indissoluble canon. Each side accuses the other of "politicizing" literature; and surely each side is correct? For literature in its public sense is always political.

If we consider American literary culture in the abstract, imagining it, for all its diversity, as an organic whole, we are bound to see that it is expanding at both ends, and not simply in the present. Not all new books being issued from our presses are by "new" or even living writers. Reprints of famous classics continue at a brisk pace, but reprints of "lost" or "neglected" or "suppressed" books more uniquely characterize our time. Where once survey courses in American literature inevitably focused upon a small and unvarying syllabus of writers, most of them male, most of them New Englanders, now students have the option of reading such newly "discovered" writers as Kate Chopin (*The Awakening,* 1899), Zora Neale Hurston (*Their Eyes Were Watching God, 1937),* Jean Toomer (*Cane,* 1923), Anzia Yezierska (*Bread Givers,* 1925), H. D. *(Collected Poems 1912–1944),* Frederick Douglass (*Narrative of the Life of Frederick Douglass, An American Slave,* 1845), Henry Bibb (*Life and Adventures of Henry Bibb,* 1849), Harriet Jacobs (*Incidents in the Life of a Slave Girl: Written by Herself,* 1861), and numerous others. The sentimental "Indian" fiction of James Fenimore Cooper has been replaced by the fiction of native Americans, prominent among them James Welch, Leslie Silko, Gerald Vizenor (whose *Darkness in Saint Louis Bearheart,* 1978, is considered an underground classic by other native Americans), N. Scott Momaday, Louise Erdrich, and Michael Dorris.

Not in opposition to but complementary with the *Norton Anthology of American Literature,* long the staple of university courses, is the *Norton Anthology of Literature by Women,* edited by Sandra Gilbert and Susan Gubar, publication of which, in 1985, aroused a literary controversy that is still raging. The Gilbert and Gubar anthology is notable for introducing to a wide audience such long-forgotten or undervalued writers as Rebecca Harding Davis, whose *Life in the Iron-Mills,* 1861, was a reformist landmark; the virtually unknown Alice James, the witty, sardonic, sharply perceptive invalid sister of Henry and William, who kept a unique diary through the three final years of her life; and Harriet E. Wilson, the first black woman to publish a novel in English and the first Afro-American to publish a novel in the United States: *Our Nig,* 1859. (Harriet Wilson's extraordinary novel received no reviews and was forgotten until the scholar Henry Louis Gates, Jr., reissued it in a facsimile edition in 1983.) Indeed, it is impossible to estimate the degree to which contemporary American fiction and poetry has been revitalized by this extension of the literary canon, for the discovery of predecessors and models is invaluable for young and emerging writers.

Another way in which the concept of "American literature" has been creatively challenged is in terms of "literature" itself: for what after all *is* literature? Exclusively novels, poetry, drama, belles-lettres? Or also diaries, journals, memoirs, biographies, journalism, science fiction, fantasy and horror, detective, mystery, humor, and critical works? Collections of essays by such writers as Lewis Thomas (*The Lives of a Cell*), Joan Didion (*Slouching Towards Bethlehem; The White Album*), and Edward Hoagland (*Heart's Desire*); speculative memoirs like Annie Dillard's *Pilgrim at Tinker Creek;* polemics like Susan Sontag's *Against Interpretation, Illness as Metaphor,* and *On Photography;* fantasy and science fiction by such highly regarded writers as Ursula Le Guin (*The Dispossessed; The Left-Hand of Darkness; The Compass Rose*) and Samuel Delaney (*Dhalgren; Triton;* et al.); the prison journal *In The Belly of the Beast* by Jack Henry Abbott; aesthetic-philosophical tracts by the experimental composer John Cage (*Empty Words*) and William Gass (*On Being Blue*); collages of the nature of Linda Montano's *Art in Everyday Life*: all have revolutionized the definition of "canon." Since the mid-1960s too, the formal boundary between "serious" and "popular" art has been challenged, so that it is not uncommon to see in the midst of mainline literary figures on university syllabi such renegade figures as Raymond Chandler, Dashiell Hammett, Stephen King, and Kathy Acker (the author of "punk" novels). Highly influenced by French literary theorists of the past twenty years—primarily Jacques Derrida, Michel Foucault, and Roland Barthes—contemporary American literary criticism has undergone a series of convulsive changes in the past decade. In consequence, the concept of "interpretation" has been replaced by other more elastic methodologies. What is "meaning" in the context of literary work? Does it reside in the text, or in the reader? Is the text autonomous, or must it be defined in terms of its sociological matrix?

Nancy Crampton photograph

Saul Bellow.

The underlying principle behind these new and, to some, alarmingly iconoclastic theories is cultural relativism: where in the past a direct correlation was posited between text and meaning, now any number of possible meanings may exist, however implausible or mutually exclusive. The tenets of Structuralism and Deconstruction reduce the author to but one interpreter of "his" text. What has been systematically undercut is the dogma of a positive, realist foundation for understanding literature.

Controversial as such radical theories are, and bitterly opposed as they have been by many academicians, most historians concede that the past per se has no existence . . . except, to paraphrase W. H. Auden, as it has been modified in the guts of the living. The evidence examined by the historian cannot yield a single (or singular) past for, of course, *no* past is available to us except as it can be deduced from evidence and presented by the historian, who, in turn, cannot avoid cultural prejudice. Thus, the warring interpretations of the same writers and texts, presented by critics as diverse as Structuralists, Deconstructionists, Marxists, feminists (both "humanist" and "radical"), and New Historicists, each of whom may make some claim for being central to the re-imagining of the American literary canon, yet none of whom has anything like the unilateral dominance of the New Critics of the 1950s or the preceding generations of tradition-bound, biographical-historical critics whose seemingly modest and unexamined project was to present what was "best" in literary culture.

Nancy Crampton photograph

John Cheever.

Naturally, the practicing writer has little need for theory but continues to write and, ideally, to publish and find an audience, without regard for critical methodologies. It is the very nature of language to provoke dissension, since language, or the concept-forming aspect of language, inevitably sets us apart from the world and from ourselves. There is an "I" that exists sheerly as a verbal construct, a subject in a sentence: this "I" is a kind of luminous optic nerve, a radar of sorts, picking up, refining, defining, all that is given. Verbalizing is surely natural to the human species, yet it is just as surely an act of extreme *self*-consciousness, in contradistinction to the self-in-society. For the imaginative writer, the very gift of "imagination" guarantees a consciousness of self that may put him or her actively at odds with society; indeed, it might be argued that the artist's imagination is at least in part the focal point of the ineluctable conflict of wills between the individual and organized society . . . by "organized society" I mean anything from a unit of two persons up through the family, the town, the city, the state, the nation-state. Where all is homogeneity, art plays no role, for art arises only out of conflict. This is so simple a truth it can be overlooked.

For fiction writers who began publishing or who came of literary age in the 1960s (a wonderfully variegated generation-and-a-half that includes E. L. Doctorow, Toni Morrison, Robert Stone, Thomas Pynchon, Robert Coover, Joan Didion, John Gregory Dunne, John Updike, Philip Roth,

Annie Dillard.

Nancy Crampton photograph

Russell Banks, Don DeLillo, Ishmael Reed, Jerome Charyn, Alice Walker, Charles Johnson, Joy Williams, T. Coraghessan Boyle, Marge Piercy, Paul Theroux, the late John Gardner and Raymond Carver, and many others) the seething richness of

Nancy Crampton photograph

John Ashbery.

American society provided us with irresistibly dramatic "historical" material; and individual dissension within society provided numberless aesthetic strategies for expressing that material.

To live, for example, as I did, in Detroit, Michigan, in the 1960s—Detroit, a city billed as both "Automotive Capital of the World" and "Murder City, USA," and the setting of the 1968 riots—was to find myself not only provided with but hardly able to ignore the immediacy of drama, social conflict, tragedy, tragi-comedy . . . the opportunity of realizing firsthand a virtual allegory of American experience. The city of Detroit in its myriad aspects became for me a region of symbolic luminosities: it was itself, of course, uniquely and irreducibly so, but it was also far more—an emblem of American ambition, American delusion, American strife, American hopes, American violence, American dreams-gone-wrong.

Though I was writing and publishing before I came to live in Detroit in 1962, it was only in this city that I conceived of a personal body of literature in which the unique and the emblematic might be conjoined; and the private, the domestic, the idiosyncratic yoked to larger social and political concerns (in such Detroit-set novels as *them* and *Do With Me What You Will,* and such historically focused novels as *Angel of Light, Wonderland,* and *You Must Remember This*). So, too, have such writers as E. L. Doctorow, Robert Coover, Robert Stone, and Russell Banks, among others, realized the complexity of their "political" material by way of individual participatory experience.

For instance, E. L. Doctorow took for his subject the divisive domestic politics of the 1960s, culminating in the persecution and execution of the Rosenbergs, in the novel many readers consider his finest, *The Book of Daniel;* Robert Coover surrealistically reimagined the moral chaos of that era in *The Public Burning*—in which Julius and Ethel Rosenberg are publicly executed, with a narration by Richard Nixon; Don DeLillo in his recent *Libra* reimagined, by way of the Warren Report, the events leading up to and surrounding the assassination of President John F. Kennedy; Robert Stone, Joan Didion, Russell Banks, and others, were analyzing American involvement in Central, Latin, and Carribean American politics years before these politics erupted into tragic headlines.

Norman Mailer's subtitle for his 1968 *The Armies of the Night: History as Novel, the Novel as History,* suggests the relationship between the individual writer and the politics of his time, and, perhaps, the Post-Modernist principle of literary inter-referentiality; Robert Lowell's idiosyncratic sonnet sequence *Notebook* (1969–73) and his other explicitly autobiographical works continue the poet's determination to push beyond the claustrophobic domesticity of confessional verse to the point at which personal history merges dramatically with the history of an era: "Why not say what happened?" the poet asks.

More than three hundred novels have been written on the subject of the Vietnam War, most of them by former combatants and journalists; among the outstanding are Tim O'Brien's *Going After Cacciato,* Stephen Wright's *Meditations in Green,* Larry Heinemann's *Paco's Story,* John Del Vecchio's *The Thirteenth Valley,* Richard Currey's *Fatal Light,* and Susan Fromberg Schaeffer's *Buffalo Afternoon.* (Robert Stone's *Dog Soldiers* is helpfully read as a Vietnam-related novel; Michael Herr's much-acclaimed *Dispatches* is a surreal nonfiction work.) An outstanding dramatist of the war generation is David Rabe, best known for *The Basic Training of Pavlo Hummel;* an outstanding poet, Bruce Wiegel, author of *Song of Napalm.* All these writers employ surrealist and experimental techniques in their work at least intermittently, but the bedrock of their material is a historical and geographical reality. A concern with history seems to be the foundation of America's strongest and most representative work: in many writers, it is catalyst and antagonist in equal measure.

That poetry has undergone remarkable transformations since the early 1960s is partly the consequence of another sort of political upheaval—the women's movement.* In a number of highly influential women poets, the politics of sex and gender merge with the politics of history and become inextricable. Outstanding titles are Adrienne Rich's *The Dream of a Common Language,* and *The Fact of a Doorframe: Poems Selected and New 1950–1984;* Denise Levertov's *Relearning the Alphabet,* and *Candles in Babylon;* Carolyn Kizer's *Yin;* Sharon Olds's *Satan Says,* and *The Dead and the Living;* Carolyn Forché's *The Country Between Us;* Lucille Clifton's *Two-Headed Woman;* Maxine Kumin's *Our Ground Time Here Will Be Brief: New and Selected Poems;* Louise Glück's, *The House on Marshland* and *Descending Figure;* Alicia Ostriker's *The Imaginary Lover;* Josephine Jacobsen's *The Sisters: New and Selected Poems;* and May Swenson's *In Other Words.* This is a revolutionary poetry, very much at odds with the poetry prescribed by T. S. Eliot at midcentury, in which the poet is solemnly advised not to attempt the vernacular, still less to

Nancy Crampton photograph

John Updike.

*One of the most informative books on this subject is Alicia Ostriker's *Stealing the Language: The Emergence of Women's Poetry in America* (Beacon Press, 1986).

Nancy Crampton photograph

Toni Morrison.

celebrate it, but to self-consciously "refine" it in a rejection of the "futility and anarchy" that constitute the history of our time. It is unsurprising that women's poetry is descended by way of Walt Whitman and William Carlos Williams, and not by Way of T. S. Eliot and Wallace Stevens.

It has been remarked that the dominating style of the present is Neo-Realism, and that the self-referential experimental strategies of narration and wordplay of the 1960s and 1970s (as jubilantly practiced by John Barth, William Gass, the late Donald Barthelme, Robert Coover, John Hawkes, Charles Newman, and others) have lost their influence. Partly, this is the result of inevitable change, the necessary conflict of generations; partly, it is the result of concern for social and political issues, which are most effectively explored in that mode of literary narrative called "realistic." (As a writer, I know that all literary modes are conventions, and all are deliberately chosen: whether fabulation, fantasy, allegory, surrealism—or realism. The basic act of writing, the transcribing of words from left to right across a sheet of paper, is a convention.) The political writer who wants not simply to entertain or impress his readers but to instruct, move, inspire, upset, possibly convert them is obliged to appear to represent as faithfully as possible a reality that exists beyond his own invention. Without the illusion—the convention—of authenticity, imaginative literature surrenders a good deal of its power.

Nancy Crampton photograph

Adrienne Rich.

Ours is recognized as a violent society; or, at the very least, a society that openly airs, discusses, and analyzes its violence. A number of American writers of the generation I have been discussing have been charged with "excessive" violence in their work and with a presumably un-American pessimism. The woman writer who ventures into the political or social sphere is often a special target, for [women] writers are perceived as doubly intrusive: as writers, and as women. (I choose to bracket [woman] writer because the writer who is a woman, while perceiving herself as a writer, foremost, and not gender-determined in her art, is nonetheless perceived by others as a woman primarily, and a writer secondarily: thus, [woman] writer. An ontological paradox, for of course there are no [men] writers, only writers—who are men.)

Yet to be possessed by what might be called a tragic sense of life does not mean that one is indifferent to other interpretations, even the comic; there are, in life, happy endings—as often as not. But from a historical perspective it seems more realistic to view the manifold strivings of civilization as essentially tragic in outline, because so frequently bellicose, self-serving, and self-defeating. Within this context one is likely to be more impressed with the fortitude, resilience, and occasional nobility of human beings when, as individuals, they are put to the test; when by accident or design they are in a position to grow into what they are in embryo. Consequently, in tragic art the focus is upon moments of crisis, not harmony; it is in the fissures of happiness that strength of character asserts itself. From this perspective, the tragic view of life may in fact be the most idealistic. And, as Flannery O'Connor once observed, no writer is a pessimist. The very act of writing is an act of hope.

Nancy Crampton photograph

Donald Barthelme.

Postwar American generations differ from previous generations in that we are constantly aware of—indeed, some of our ranks are obsessed by—the possibility of an end: of The End. A generation of children, of which I was one, was baptized into a collective, thus involuntary, sense of mortality in the early 1950s, when atomic bomb drills were routine schoolday exercises under the aegis of the Civil Defense Bureau in Washington, D.C. How like a child's game, the name of this drill: "duck-and-cover"! Like fires, for which fire drills were logical preparations, atomic bomb attacks on America were perceived as not only likely but highly probable. The question was, when? And, who would survive?

Thus, an entire subcategory of mid- and late twentieth-century American literature can be titled the Literature of Paranoia, some of it immensely ambitious, reticulated, and blackly comic: the foremost example being Thomas Pynchon's *Gravity's Rainbow.* The fictions of Robert Coover, Don DeLillo, and John Hawkes also lend themselves temperamentally to this vision. Less ambitious in writerly terms, though no less "nihilistic," are those fictions to which the generic term Minimalist has been given by literary journalists. In part, of course, Minimalism is simply an inevitable response (or reaction) to the increasingly elaborate and self-conscious fictions of an earlier generation; not so much a strategy of defeat as of aesthetic retrenchment and modesty. One senses a vague, even a vacuous Reaganite world beyond the shopping malls, fast-food restaurants, and tract housing of Minimalist fiction, but this world is never explored or even named; it is simply given. The representative Minimalist protagonist is passive, unquestioning, unreflective, and, in some instances, lacking the sort of neurological consciousness one associates with normal human beings. Frequently, the historical present is employed in narration, so that the reader, like the protagonist, moves forward without benefit of retrospection or hindsight. Mary Robison, Bobbie

Ann Mason, and Frederick Barthelme have focused upon Minimalist concerns for the near-at-hand, the domestic, the unexceptional, the unpretentious. Barthelme has become an apologist of sorts for the genre. Other writers frequently associated with Minimalism—Raymond Carver, Tobias Wolff, Richard Ford, Ann Beattie, Amy Hempel—are surely more various, inventive, and lyric than the inadequate term Minimalism suggests. Certainly it is possible to see Carver and Ford as descendants of Ernest Hemingway, whose essentially romantic imagination was so brilliantly served by a seemingly "flat" colloquial prose.

Of new and emerging writers whose names are less known, several would appear to be genuinely gifted, and their early accomplishments are more than routinely "promising." These are Pete Dexter, Carolyn Chute, Mary McGarry Morris, and Pinckney Benedict.

Dexter, the author of two previous novels, has written one of the most powerful novels of recent years in *Paris Trout*, a remarkable portrait of a racist in the context of a largely unexamined racist society: the novel's setting is a small Georgia town after World War II. Carolyn Chute, the author of an acclaimed first novel, *The Beans of Egypt, Maine*, has written a considerably more accomplished, subtle second novel, *Letourneau's Used Auto Parts*, set, like the first, in the mythical Egypt, Maine, in and around the homes (many of them house trailers) of people who live somewhere below the poverty line. But what life in them! what lyricism! what indefatigable human will! It is these men, women, and children who are the "used" parts of American society, but Chute's subtlety is such that the reader, and the reader alone, understands the tragedy of these lives; the plight of the disenfranchised in an increasingly developed country.

Mary McGarry Morris's surrealist *Vanished*, the first novel by this forty-five-year-old writer, is also set somewhere below the poverty line, in rural New England; its plot is both bizarre and strangely plausible, but its great accomplishment is the creation, from within, of the consciousness of a mildly retarded man who is both victim of and participant in a tragic episode of the sort one might find described in a tabloid newspaper. Pinckney Benedict's first book, a collection of short stories titled *Town Smokes*, published when the author was in his early twenties, attests to this young writer's precocious—but not merely precocious—gift for narrative fiction. Set for the most part in rural West Virginia, the stories are told in a poetically vernacular idiom—a seemingly effortless music of a kind, melodic to the ear, however disturbing its content.

Perhaps it is significant that these four remarkable writers have taken for their subjects the lives of apparently marginal Americans; that they are assuredly *not* Minimalists in style or vision; that each is skilled in matters of technique—voice, tone, prose texture, dramatic pacing, structure; that each is obliquely akin to, though not in the shadow of, our greatest "regionalist" William Faulkner; that they are, for all the melodrama and sorrow of their fictions, clearly idealistic, in the mainstream of the American literary tradition.

Indeed, for all the pessimism with which many serious contemporary writers have been charged, it seems self-evident that literature as a vocation, as a life's calling, is invariably an idealistic, even an optimistic enterprise. Some of us write with the hope, admittedly quixotic, of changing the world: yet is not the alteration of a single reader's consciousness, however subtly, an act toward changing the world? To work with the ever-shifting and ever-elusive properties of language is infinitely challenging, and infinitely rewarding. But beyond what one might call the artist's exultation in his or her craft, we have faith that writing is a form of sympathy. Being mimetic, thus bodiless, consisting solely of language, writing demands no displacement or intrusion in the world; it is itself—yet so much more.

We Live and Remember

Aleksandr Mulyarchik

Perestroika in motion, in action. This guideline of Soviet reality in the second half of the eighties presupposes as well a renewal in how we understand our own modern literature and its development through the greater part of the twentieth century. Early in 1988, my colleague Nikolai Anastasyev, a specialist in American literature, told a correspondent from the *Christian Science Monitor:* "In the near future we will have to reconsider our entire conception of Soviet literature." Feliks Kuznetsov, director of the Moscow Institute of World Literature, who is among the leaders of academic scholarship, did not agree with this. He called it too radical, "leading towards subjectivism, towards an impious distortion of historical truth." Speaking on the occasion of the one hundred and twentieth anniversary of the birth of Maksim Gorky, for whom the institution he heads is named, Kuznetsov called not for a reconsideration of the established views but rather for their gradual, thoughtful refinement.

In my view, the disagreement here is rooted not so much in different scholarly positions as in the facts of what publishers are doing these days. In a short space of time a whole series of works, once held up by censorship or removed from circulation right after they were first published, have issued from Soviet presses and become accessible to the reading public. The novels, stories, and tales of Andrei Platonov, Boris Pilnyak, Evgeni Zamyatin, and Boris Pasternak, the poetry of Anna Akhmatova and Nikolai Gumilyov, the verse and prose Vladimir Nabokov wrote as an émigré in Berlin and Paris—all these have added perceptibly to the circle of literary peaks in view, have pushed back the horizons of ordinary readers and specialists alike. Whether to reconsider or to refine is a dilemma still facing us, and unlikely to be decided soon. Nonetheless, anyone who holds dear what has been written in Russian during the twentieth century has already, by and large, arrived at criteria, at reference points, that bring the boundless literary sea within stable shores and sketch out at least the most general contours of the picture that emerges.

I myself have never, even in elementary school, studied Soviet literature in any systematic way. At Moscow University it was not taught to us students specializing in foreign literatures. Evidently they felt we would pick up what we needed out of the air, out of the intellectual atmosphere, which at the end of the fifties was saturated with literary news, disputes, and genuine revelations. That was the time of stormy debates over Vladimir Dudintsev's *Not By Bread Alone,* in which the bitter fate of the inventor Lopatkin was tied up with certain general laws of the Stalinist system. Not long before that Khrushchev, in a speech before a closed session of the Twentieth Party Congress, had plucked back the curtain on the crimes of Stalin and his henchmen. Suddenly it was possi-

Kiprensky, *Portrait of Aleksandr Pushkin.*

ble to write more openly about the negative sides of a society forged by thirty years of dictatorial rule from the Kremlin.

In May of that same year (1956), Aleksandr

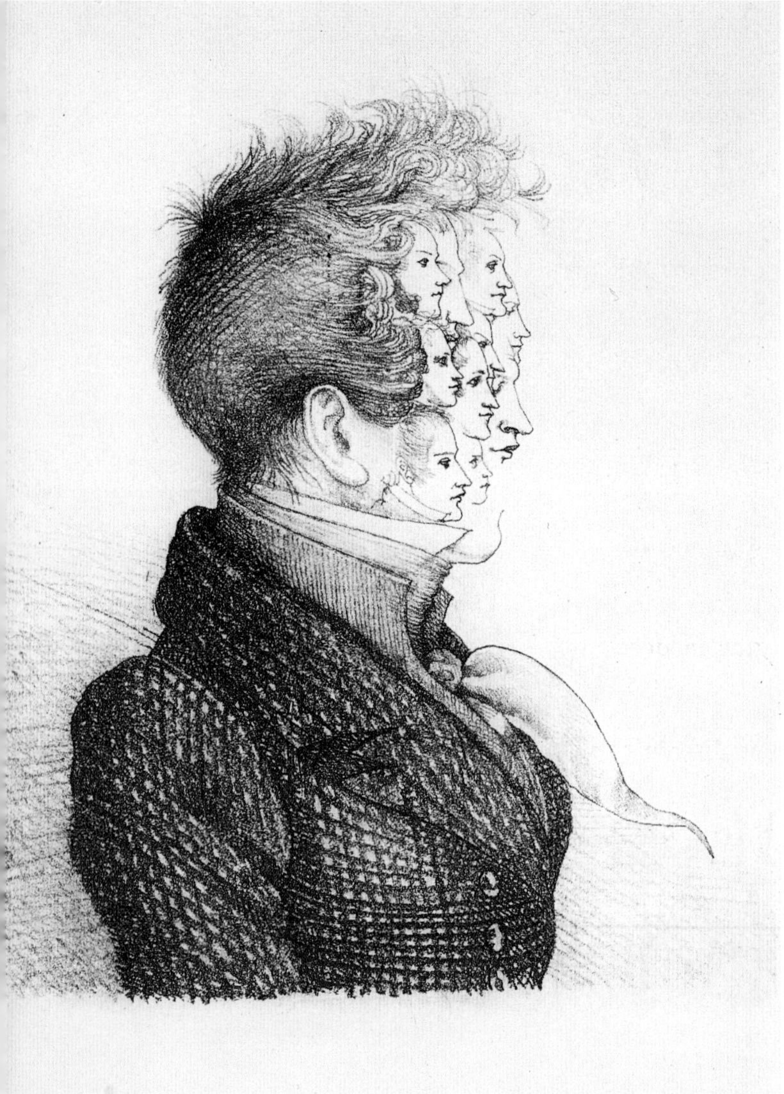

A. Kostin, illustration to *Evgeny Onegin,* in the style of Pushkin's sketches.

Fadeyev, Stalin's trusted deputy in the Union of Writers, shot himself dead. By that time the few prose writers and poets who had survived the repressions had been brought back from the camps and rehabilitated: Lev Razgon, Nikolai Zabolotsky, Yaroslav Smelyakov, Anatoli Zhigulin, and others. Some of them entered literary life quickly. Most needed to get acclimated, especially since the social and political barometer was gradually moving towards "fair." But then came the autumn of 1958. A scandal broke over Boris Pasternak's winning the Nobel Prize for *Doctor Zhivago,* published in the West under circumstances not fully explained. And once again our literary vistas fell under a thick shroud of fog.

The seventy-plus years of Soviet literary history abound in dramatic events like those just mentioned. And in paradoxes, too. One of the sources of our literature, or at any rate the seed that grew into socialist realism—later the officially recognized artistic method—was Gorky's *Mother,* born (like the international workers' holiday celebrated on May Day) in the capitalist United States. Gorky was working on the novel after the collapse of the first Russian revolution in 1905. He went to the United States hoping to make contacts and gather funds to support his social-democrat friends. Let us note, however, that even after the October Revolution had triumphed in Russia, it took quite some time for Gorky's work to become an important reference point for the New Art. For the author of the *Tales of Italy,* written at this time, and the epical, multivolume *Life of Klim Samgin,* unconditional acceptance was still to come. Back in the twenties, writers were insisting on the profoundly proletarian character of the New Art, demanding that the whole legacy of the classics, the "rubbish of the nobles and the bourgeoisie" right down to Pushkin and Lermontov, be "heaved off the ship of modernity."

Their more moderate and, it must be said, far more talented colleagues were in no hurry to throw our common cultural property to the winds. The first group of Soviet prose writers, the Serapion Brothers, which sprang up in Petrograd in 1921, was inspired not by Gorky or Lev Tolstoy, whose experience many would soon call upon, but (as the group's name makes clear) by the German romantic E. T. A. Hoffmann. The group, moreover, is famous mainly for having spawned prose writers such as Konstantin Fedin, Mikhail Zoshchenko, and Veniamin Kaverin, most of whom came to maturity and fame in the late twenties and the thirties. In the period just after the Revolution, prose could not keep up with the rapid march of events. Poetry was much nearer to the forefront of the changes that were touching human souls and, more often than not, wounding them.

Aleksandr Blok's long poem *The Twelve,* written in a single burst of inspiration, is regarded as the first work to embody the whirlwind sweep and tumult of the 1917 Revolution. Twelve Revolutionary soldiers, who are likewise twelve new apostles, put the old order on trial and carry out the sentence, certain of their right to make radical changes. Blok, who arrived at ultimate conviction in his own genius during the memorable days he labored on the poem, was also convinced that revolution was bringing with it renewal and purification. "Listen to the Revolution," he bade his colleagues in the literary workshop. But his three and a half remaining years of life found him utterly becalmed as an artist. He wrote only one poem during that time, and in it he celebrated not the turmoil of revolution, the end of which he never saw clearly, but Russia's age-old culture, or perhaps Russia herself, encoded by Blok in the many-layered meanings of the Pushkin House.

Like Blok, Vladimir Mayakovsky and Sergei Esenin never hesitated in accepting the Revolution. Mayakovsky turned all his "poet's musical strength" not only to singing his Soviet homeland, in which he saw "the springtime of mankind, born in battle," but also to thinking through the weighty problems that loomed ever clearer as the country traveled down the path of socialist construction. During the twenties, Mayakovsky's political voice evolved from the impassioned slogans of posters to biting satires on the inherited and newly acquired foibles of society; from the fairytale play *Mystery-Bouffe,* foretelling swift victory for world revolution, to the caustically skeptic comedies, *The Bedbug* and *The Bathhouse.*

Contrary to Western views, Mayakovsky was not only the poet of political meetings. He also produced sensitive and tender lyric poems. At the beginning of the twenties he wrote the long poem "About This," a projection of his complicated relations with Lili Brik, sister of the writer Elsa Triole. (Triole married the French poet Louis Aragon.) Not long before his death, Mayakovsky was embroiled in another drama of the heart. His suicide in 1930 was brought about in part by his breakup with the "Russian Parisienne" Tatyana Yakovleva. In the twenties Mayakovsky often traveled abroad. His impressions inspired a wealth of writing, including the extensive cycle of "Poems about America," where respect for Americans' vital energy and technological achievements is combined with an assertion of the pride Soviet people felt as they made ready to say a new word in history. As for Tatyana Yakovleva, she married a French aristocrat in the autumn of 1929. Later she gave birth to a daughter who was destined to become the noted writer Francine du Plessix Gray, author of *Days Without End* (1981) and a participant in several recent meetings of Soviet and American literary figures.

Sergei Esenin was also to die by his own hand, in 1925. He had barely reached the age of thirty. Mayakovsky, like the Belgian Émile Verhaeren and the American Carl Sandburg, can be seen as a poet of the modern, more or less cosmopolitan city. Esenin's poetry, by contrast, is inseparable from the singularity of the Russian village. At the same time, Esenin's lyrics spring from a restless, bohemian spirit shared by almost all the world's poets. During his travels with the dancer Isadora Duncan, he too, like Mayakovsky, spent time in the United States. But the visit had no effect on Esenin's work. Esenin's "Russianness" is nearly impossible to render in another language. At least it is hard to catch even a hint of it in the existing translations. Partly for this reason, his reputation outside the Soviet Union does not even come close to the almost universal veneration accorded him in his native land.

During the Civil War and in the first years after it, before strict limitations were imposed on contracts with foreign countries, a good number of writers left for the West. These included Ivan Bunin (who later won the Nobel Prize), Boris Zaytsev, Ivan Shmelev, Mark Aldanov, Marina

Lev Tolstoy.

Tsvetayeva, and the young Vladimir Nabokov. Their work abroad is a separate page—or even chapter—which in our country has only recently come to be seen in the larger context of twentieth-century literature in Russian. True, there have also been examples of the opposite: early return from emigration and active participation in forming new literary forces. This is what happened with Count Aleksei Tolstoy, scion of a renowned aristocratic and literary family, and author of an unfinished historical novel about Peter the Great. Many of Tolstoy's books bear the stamp of Stalinist ideology. Sometimes they distort Russia's distant and not-so-distant past to suit it. Pasternak's *Doctor Zhivago* was in fact written to counterbalance Tolstoy's interpretation of the Revolution's effect on the Russian intelligentsia, as presented in *The Road to Calvary.* Tolstoy's lively imagination and indisputable talent earned popularity for his other works. Among these are the autobiographical *Nikita's Childhood* and *Aelita.* The latter tells about a failed Red revolution on Mars and the tragic love of a Russian engineering genius for a beautiful Martian woman.

In the twenties, Aleksei Tolstoy was regarded for quite a while as one of the "fellow travelers." This implied a certain degree of mistrust on the part of official criticism. Back then a good many of the leading talents of different generations were in the same position. The best known of these were Isaac Babel, Mikhail Bulgakov, and the poets Osip Mandelshtam and Boris Pasternak. Babel, a superb stylist of the school of Chekhov and Maupassant, crafted his words with the same zealous persistence Flaubert had brought to bear on *Madame Bovary.* He won fame for his short stories about the Civil War, telling of the human side instead of painting battle scenes, and also for his colorful sketches of pre-Revolutionary Jewish life. Bulgakov, in contrast to the laconic Babel, wrote a great deal, although many of his manuscripts remained unpublished during his lifetime. So it was with his greatest work, *The Master and Margarita,* which is rightly considered one of the most important books written in Russia during the twentieth century. In almost all of his prose and dramatic works, Bulgakov blended grotesque fantasy with biting satire on everyday life. *The Master and Margarita* does this through the counterpoint of two plot lines: a singular retelling of Christ's ascent to Golgotha, and the incredible events surrounding a visit by Satan and his cronies to the Moscow of Stalin's day.

Our Civil War echoes as loud—if not louder—in Soviet literature as does the American Civil War in American literature. It has found monumental expression in Mikhail Sholokhov's epic, *And Quiet*

Flows the Don. Sholokhov's writing is densely realistic. He makes wide use of blunt Cossack dialect and tries to balance deep psychological penetration with a panoramic view of historical events in all their variety. This contrasts with the lofty, romantic approach of other writers, such as Aleksandr Malyshkin and Nikolai Ostrovsky, to the same material. This romantic vision was also characteristic of certain prose writers who turned to the contemporary scene, trying to make out, through the workaday hubbub and the constant mundane squabbles, the lineaments of the longed-for City on the Hill. It is this ardent faith, easily comparable to the feelings evoked in our time by "We Shall Overcome" (well known in the Soviet Union), that permeates the best books of Yuri Olesha and Ivan Katayev, as well as certain poems by Nikolai Aseyev, Eduard Bagritsky, and Mikhail Svetlov.

A colorful, individualistic diversity had grown up in the twenties. In the decade that followed, it was cut back considerably. The movement towards unification, imposed from above, manifested itself not only in the creation of a single Union of Soviet Writers in 1934 but also in the way the union's members laid maximum emphasis on working out themes connected with the building of socialism. The need for strict adherence to a more rigid political position strained the artistry of even the best books born in the era of the first Five-Year Plans, such as Sholokhov's *Virgin Soil Upturned* and the novels of Ilya Ehrenburg and Valentin Katayev. The satirists were somewhat better off; they took on the task of helping to correct mores at a time when comparatively well-established ethical and ideological values were being radically revised. This was the role assumed by Mikhail Zoshchenko, by Panteleimon Romanov, a prose writer in the tradition of Chekhov, and also by the team of Ilya Ilf and Evgeni Petrov, who authored the novels *The Twelve Chairs* and *The Golden Calf,* as well as *One-Storied America,* a book in many ways still unsurpassed, which records impressions gathered on a trip through the United States by car in 1935.

The sharp break with a mainly peasant social structure, which remained in place until about 1929, found perhaps its greatest chronicler and analyst in Andrei Platonov. Like Knut Hamsun and John Steinbeck, Platonov worked at many different jobs, both white- and blue-collar, before coming to literature. The *Juvenile Sea* and the longer works *Kotlovan* [or *Foundation Pit*] and *Chevengur* embody his reflections on the building of a new Russia and his bitterness at the hasty, ill-conceived, and sometimes downright criminal actions taken by the government at that time. Platonov blends reality with bizarre hyperbole in a style purely his own. Even the most perfect translation has difficulty reproducing it. In the prewar years he grew into a gigantic literary figure, whose true dimensions are only beginning to be understood.

F. Konstantinov, illustration to L. Tolstoy's story, "A Prisoner in the Caucuses."

The official critics had long been sharpening their teeth for Platonov. But by an odd twist of fate he escaped the Stalinist repressions of the late thirties and forties, which by an incomplete accounting carried off to the grave not less than a thousand writers—writers not only in Russian but also in Ukrainian, Georgian, Kazakh, Tadzhik, Armenian, and many other national languages. The literatures of some of the smaller nationalities, such as the Bashkirs, Udmurts, Ossetians, and Altai, then just getting to their feet, were almost snuffed out. At the same time, some whim of the tyrant spared the lives of those, like Pasternak and Akhmatova, whom the press had long since branded "internal émigrés," or who, like certain writers of the older generation—Mikhail Prishvin, Vikenti Veresayev—refused to sacrifice their humanistic principles, even though they did not openly proclaim their opposition.

Soviet literature was fully united in spirit—possibly for the first time—during World War II, as the country gathered together all its strength to defeat Hitler and his allies. With the exception of a few patriotic poems and sketches, these years were not marked by any large achievements. Undoubtedly, though, they fortified writers' sense of a deep bond with their nation and undermined the system of "internal," psychological censorship created by the prewar terror. The hallmarks of this new feeling about the world can be seen in the best books about the war—in Vasili Grossman's *For a Just Cause,* Viktor Nekrasov's *In the Trenches of Stalingrad,* and Aleksandr Tvardovsky's long poem *Vasili Tyorkin.* The last of these presents a truly folkloric image of the Russian soldier, a jokester and master of all trades. In some ways he resembles Yankee Doodle or Davy Crockett, who were born, however, out of completely different circumstances.

The spiritual uplift did not last long. The decade after the war was the most barren in the Soviet period—indeed, in the whole history of literature in Russia. Ironclad aesthetic norms were imposed. A ramified mythology dictated how both the past and present of the existing system, and of the country's relations with the world outside, should be seen. Even real talents were rendered bloodless by all this. The efforts of propagandists created a number of inflated reputations, whose owners (Konstantin Simonov, Pyotr Pavlenko, and the playwright Aleksandr Korneichuk, for example) even gained a certain fame abroad, since it was they who continually represented the Soviet Union at cultural forums of various kinds. The yearly awarding of Stalin Prizes in literature and the other arts established a hierarchy among writers and defined a caste of "untouchables," who could be criticized only with permission from on high. On occasion, albeit seldom, that permission was forthcoming: Even those who had broken all records for servility (Fadeyev, Simonov, Valentin Katayev) could fall into temporary disgrace.

The real turning point in Soviet literature did not come with the publication of Ilya Ehrenburg's *The Thaw* (1954), which is artistically weak, callow, and—like almost everything he wrote—ambiguous. The first herald of the simple human ideals and truths that had been nearly forgotten was Pavel Nilin's *Cruelty* [or *Comrade Venka*], which was to remain his best work. The influence it exerted on people who had been stirred to life by the Twentieth Party Congress was every bit as important as the resounding debates over Dudintsev's *Not By Bread Alone.* Nilin's book was not aimed directly at the present day. (The action unfolds in Siberia at the end of the Civil War.) But it called into question the main principle that had distorted social relations and—as many believe—had hopelessly dislocated the moral guideposts of ordinary people: "Everything is permitted for the sake of The Cause." Of course this Jesuitical logic was not to be set straight overnight. But for the young people of my generation, who grew up in the "Khrushchev decade" that came to an end in the midsixties, *Cruelty* was an important symbol of the advent of an entirely different cultural and spiritual atmosphere.

The latter half of the fifties resurrected a number of works that had long remained unknown. At the same time, young talent was coming forward to refresh and renew the genres and themes our critics traditionally use in talking about literature. Some wrote about the war from personal experience. Among these were Grigori Baklanov, Yuri Bondarev, and, somewhat later, Vyacheslav Kondratiev and the Belorussian Vasili Bykov. Young Prose, which had grown in honesty, was

H. Trofimova, illustration to Radischev's *Journey from Saint Petersburg to Moscow.*

transformed under the pens of Anatoli Gladilin and Vasili Aksyonov. New depths of insight into the position of Soviet workers, engineers, and scientific personnel were plumbed in a cycle of works by Daniil Granin and in Georgi Vladimov's first novel, *Heavy Ore.* In the work of some of these authors you could feel the influence of Western writers—Hemingway, Remarque, Aldington, Kerouac—who were being reread or read for the first time. Meanwhile, the work of subtle lyric artists like Yuri Kazakov and Yuri Nagibin, with their discriminating feel for the riches of the Russian language, was bringing back the tradition of Chekhov and Bunin, which has been so fruitful in this century. The closest analogues in postwar American literature are to be seen in the work of John Cheever and, to a degree, John Updike.

The wealth of names cited in the last paragraph should not surprise. It is but a small part of the rich literary harvest that ripened as the fifties gave way to the sixties. The shifts under way in poetry were no less amazing. As if in an instant, the resplendent plumage of Mikhail Isakovsky and Stepan Shchipachev, the idols of Stalin's time, was cast away. People began to appreciate Leonid Martynov's philosophical themes. Vladimir Lugovskoy and Semyon Kirsanov, outstanding lyric poets who carried the echoes of the twenties down to the present, found a wider circle of admirers. But "stage poetry" was the unquestioned preference of mass audiences in those unforgettable days. It would be simplest to define this as a public-spirited poetry which did not in any way sacrifice the emotional, the personal. Robert

Rozhdestvensky played the leading role here, along with Yevgeni Yevtushenko and Andrei Voznesensky. Even now, in the West, they continue to be thought of as the chief poetic talents of their generation.

In evaluating the last forty years of literature and singling out its most important figures I must, willy-nilly, take on the opinions of my contemporary Joseph Brodsky, recent winner of the Nobel Prize, who is respected in the United States as a leading authority on Soviet literary history. In his

B. Basov, illustration to Dostoevsky's *The Possessed.*

essay "Catastrophes in the Air," included in the collection *Less Than One* (1986) and first presented early in 1984 as a lecture sponsored by the Academy of American Poets at the Guggenheim Museum, Brodsky puts forth a peculiar formulation of postwar literary history in the Soviet Union, which proceeded "with a frequency of roughly two great writers per decade." Brodsky believes that immediately after the war Zoshchenko's work came to hold first place, and that "the fifties started with the rediscovery of Babel." In the Khrushchev period, he continues, the public's attention was divided between Pasternak's *Doctor Zhivago* and the "revival" of Bulgakov. A considerable part of the seventies passed under the sign of Solzhenitsyn. And in conclusion: "At present what is in vogue is so-called village prose, and the name most frequently uttered is that of Valentin Rasputin."

Brodsky thinks that his scheme, far from being a reflection of his personal tastes, is an entirely objective picture, put together, as he says, from the opinions of critics, officialdom, and the creative intelligentsia itself. Now, all these components are easy enough to survey, but once we do so it must be admitted that Brodsky's ideas are in many ways at odds with the facts. The time coordinates are off, and a work's reputation abroad, rather than within the Soviet Union, is more often than not taken as the main criterion for its importance at a given moment.

Let me try to put it in concrete terms. Zoshchenko's name can be associated with the late forties in only one way, having little to do with literature as such. In the summer of 1946 the Central Committee adopted an ill-famed resolution (which, strange to say in these times of democratization and *glasnost,* remained in effect until 1989) which accused an entire literary movement of escapism, the demeaning of socialist reality, and outrages against the cultural values of the Soviet people. The main thrust was directed against Akhmatova's poetry and Zoshchenko's prose. But the truth is that Zoshchenko had already passed his creative peak, which, as I have said, came in the twenties and very early thirties. Over the next fifteen or twenty years Zoshchenko's work traced a downward spiral, whatever the government and press said about him.

So then what characterizes the late Stalin years, including the start of the fifties? I will expand a little on what I said earlier. The important thing was not a "rediscovery of Babel," as Brodsky would have it. (Evidently he forgets that the first posthumous edition of Babel's prose and dramatic works did not appear until the midfifties.) The official sieve of those days sifted very fine, and the Procrustean bed of ideological and aesthetic demands forced many to write cloying books about the "unprecedented successes" of the socialist economy and to resolve, without conflict, whatever minimal hints of social friction might arise. To be fair, we should say that even under those conditions books occasionally, albeit guardedly, raised urgent questions about economic life and public morality. The list here is not long. At the top of it I would put Vasili Azhayev's *Far From Moscow,* about the building of an oil pipeline with prison labor (although this was not said directly in the novel), and Leonid Leonov's *Russian Forest,* where the tangled and swampy wording did not conceal the author's dismay over alarming ecological changes and the simultaneous, catastrophic decline in morals among the Russian intelligentsia, once honored as the preserver and standard of spiritual values.

Chronological and factual slips also crop up in other parts of Brodsky's formula. How can one speak of public interest in *Doctor Zhivago* in the sixties, when, until 1988, this novel was known in Russia only to a handful of dissident-minded men and women of letters? Its influence on our literary and public tastes was insignificant. The same is true, in somewhat lesser degree, of Bulgakov. His masterpiece, *The Master and Margarita,* was published in a somewhat cut version early in 1967; it was then, properly speaking, that his present fame began. On the other side of the coin, widespread interest in Solzhenitsyn dates not from the seventies but from the early sixties, when *One Day in the Life of Ivan Denisovich* and several of his stories were published, with Khrushchev's direct sanction, in the journal *Novy Mir.* For the next ten years or so, Solzhenitsyn waged an uphill battle against the literary establishment and the organs of repression for his right to think, write, and publish independently. After he was thrown out of the country in February of 1974 and deprived of Soviet citizenship, only confused rumors about the work of the Nobel Prize winner (the award was made in 1970) reached his native land.

Brodsky is also mistaken in his concluding assertion, that in the USSR of the mideighties the vogue is for so-called village prose. True, readers are still hearing about Vasili Belov, Evgeni Nosov, and the late Fyodor Abramov. Writers like these worked to keep alive in popular consciousness the moral standards and visible images of village life, long since destroyed by Stalin's policies. But the sad fact is that this movement reached its peak fifteen or twenty years ago. Valentin Rasputin, a

Feodor Dostoevsky.

Siberian novelist whose best known works in the United States are *Farewell to Matyora* and *Live and Remember,* is indeed a leader among the talented and upright literary men and women striving to rebuild the consciousness of their fellow citizens and to resolve social and economic problems. Nonetheless, it is evident that village prose has already passed its glory days, just like America's proletarian novelists of the thirties or black humorists of the sixties.

In our country, the twenty years between Khrushchev's ouster and the mideighties are now usually thought of as a time of stagnation or, worse yet, of slow but steady decline. The stagnation affected every area of life, literature not excluded.

A. Ivanov, *Portrait of Nikolai Gogol.*

Still, it can be said that in the humanities, the realm of Letters and Spirit, our intelligentsia managed to defend a number of strongholds. These gave some hope for the revival of a country that had got stuck on the shoulder of the road. The classics were newly interpreted and commented on by Soviet literary scholars. From them, new generations of readers learned about what Russia had been just a few decades before, about the bleeding sores of the tsarist regime, about the colossal potential that was only just beginning to stir. The publication of the collected works of Dostoevsky and Chekhov played a special role: these writers gave the clearest picture of the era that had brought Russia right up to the Rubicon of its modern history.

Let us remember that Dostoevsky's earliest mature works were written when the icy immobility of the reign of Nicholas the First was giving way before the great reforms that were to transform Russia into a government of laws, putting her in touch with civilized humanity. Dostoevsky died in the winter of 1881, just a few days before Aleksandr the Second, the initiator of those reforms, was assassinated by leftist radicals. Chekhov made his literary debut at the very beginning of the 1880s. It was Chekhov who would paint so vividly the rapid rise of the nation's power over the next twenty-five years, the growth of a cultivated, civilized way of life, and the amassing of an inexhaustible store—as it truly seemed at that time—of cultural treasures. Chekhov died almost on the threshold of the revolutionary upheavals of 1905, which finally made the Russian monarchy agree to let a parliament limit its powers and to respect the civil rights of its subjects. The path marked out by these changes was full of promise. Unfortunately, it was soon to be cut by World War I and its innumerable consequences.

The historical fate of our native land in the twentieth century was of vital concern to writers in the time of stagnation under Brezhnev. For many, it was obvious that the official dogmas, which left no room for independent thought, would have to be revised. Without a doubt the place of honor here belongs to Yuri Trifonov. He was first to point out, in the novel *Impatience,* that the revolutionaries' killing of Aleksandr the Second was a misguided and ruinous act: the tsar was at the point of signing an edict that would have made Russia a constitutional monarchy. Another Trifonov novel, *The Old Man,* weaves an especially tight bond between past and present. Its main hero, an old Bolshevik, thinks back to the Civil War, which left the first and probably deepest scar on the living flesh and collective memory of the multinational Soviet Union soon to be created.

But the most important service performed by Trifonov, who died prematurely in March of 1981, was to show city dwellers, especially Muscovites, a genuine, unretouched image of themselves. The characters of his books are usually people forced by dreary social and economic realities to exchange the spiritual inheritance of Chekhov and

Gorky for some trifle, given in payment for their prudent conformity. The most luminous among them reject this way of all flesh. They try to break through to "another life" (the title of one of Trifonov's novels). They submerge themselves in the past, in mysticism, in pitiful, doomed love affairs. In the end they perish, as fish often do under the ice, right at springtime, because of a lack of oxygen in the water.

Long ago, Russian writers were called to put their conscience at the service of their times. That call never sounded more urgently than in the stultifying and seemingly endless period of stagnation. Many tried to break through the formidable barriers of bureaucratic high-handedness and the resultant crust of public apathy. But only seldom did inborn talent and the conviction that our country faced disaster if writers did not speak out combine to produce noteworthy artistic results. I have already singled out Trifonov and a few practitioners of village prose. And I have noted a handful of works about the war against Fascism which, because it had been won not so much by skill as by numbers, left an indelible, bloody mark on the national consciousness. Many others have tried to express the thoughts and feelings of ordinary people in our time. In my view (and speaking only of Russian-nationality writers), two have succeeded best: Vasili Shukshin and Viktor Astafyev. Shukshin, in his short stories and sketches, captures the material woes and spiritual confusion of yesterday's peasant, unceremoniously thrust out into the cheerless city by the course of economic development. Astafyev's prose evokes the same closeness to Russia's vast hinterland. But it takes on more. Astafyev hopes to provide a vision of how man, nature, and society are linked in the modern world. Sometimes, as in *The Tsar-Fish,* he succeeds.

Up to now I have said almost nothing about Soviet drama. And not without reason. For one thing, it is better to see a play performed than to read it; a play seems not so much a part of literature as of theatrical life. For another, I see too few works since Bulgakov's *Days of the Turbins,* staged in the midtwenties and imbued with the human drama of the Civil War, that would bear comparison with the achievments of prose and poetry.

Nevertheless, there have been some things worthy of note. I will mention Nikolai Erdman's grotesque comedies of daily life in the thirties, *The Mandate* and *The Suicide;* and Evgeni Shvarts's fairy-tale plays, *The Dragon* and *The Naked King,*

Y. Frolov, illustration to Gogol's *Evenings on a Farm near Dikanka.*

which are easily read as modern-day parables. To be ranked with other works of the thaw period is Aleksei Arbuzov's *Irkutsk Story*. Arbuzov was possibly the first postwar Soviet dramatist to resurrect his dead heroes, letting them reconsider the past, much as Thornton Wilder did in *Our Town*. Closer to our own day, the comedies and dramas of Edvard Radzinsky and Mikhail Roshchin stand out among the rest. But the true leader among modern Soviet playwrights, a talent of international dimensions, was the Siberian Aleksandr Vampilov. He died an untimely death, drowned in Lake Baikal in the early 1970s.

Vampilov began as a master of comedy tinged with melancholy lyricism. In *Provincial Anecdotes* he revived certain intonations of Gogol's *Inspector General*; at the same time he partly mastered the lessons of the European theater of the absurd. His most mature works, *Duck Hunting* and *Last Summer in Chulimsk*, for all their surface dependence on Chekhov's theater, are deeply original. They are literally steeped in the atmosphere of the world that gave them birth. What would later be called stagnation oozes from every pore of these perfect artistic creations. But their significance goes far beyond exposé. The existential problem in *Duck Hunting* has to do with friendship and death, love and betrayal. Among the ideas inspiring *Last Summer in Chulimsk*, one can plainly hear Voltaire's undying cry: "We must cultivate our garden."

V. Karasyov, illustration to Saltykov-Schedrin's story, "The Gentlemen of Tashkent."

In naming several masters of earlier generations, I have once again touched on literary influences, a theme that seems to demand additional comment. In "Catastrophes in the Air," Brodsky sees the misfortune of Russian literature in the twentieth century in its inability to emerge from the "long shadow" cast by "the Tol'stoy mountain." Our literature, that is to say, continued to treat reality mimetically, but without the spiritual power and boundless freedom of Lev Tolstoy's genius. This categoric assertion can and should be disputed. There were not many who traveled Tolstoy's road, in the sense of consciously imitating his style, even though criticism in the twenties and thirties, as I have already mentioned, had much to say about the need to make the inheritance of the classics one's own.

Aleksandr Fadeyev's *The Nineteen* [or *The Rout*] should be recognized as the most successful effort in this direction. Fadeyev, one of the main ideologues of the new proletarian art, managed to apply the lessons of Tolstoy's psychology in his descriptions of the vicissitudes of the Civil War in the Far East. But this sort of imitation, sometimes deliberately exaggerated, was not continued as such except in a few minor novels written between the wars by Fyodor Gladkov and Leonid Leonov. In the seventies and eighties, many tried to imitate the sweep of *War and Peace.* There were no visible successes. From time to time Tolstoy's manner creeps into the semijournalistic writings of the same Leonov, and, especially, of Yuri Bondarev. The discrepancy between the fustian trappings and the trivial ideas makes for an almost comic effect.

Where appropriate, I have already pointed out what seem to me obvious cases of modern Western writers influencing Soviet literature. Brodsky takes up this question, too, getting the facts wrong in his usual way. He writes that "in the sixties the best of modern Russian writers were taking their cues from Hemingway, Henrich Böll, Salinger, and, to a lesser extent, from Camus and Sartre." No Russian names are mentioned. Understandably so. With the exception of a few writers of Young Prose, who really were influenced by the prose of J. D. Salinger and the Beatniks, it would be hard to draw any other parallels. Here and there, no doubt, there have been interminglings. In the midsixties it was plain to everyone that Georgi Vladimov, author of *Three Minutes of Silence,* had taken Hemingway as his master. But by then the peak of Hemingway's popularity among our readers had long since passed, and even the belated publication of *For Whom the Bell Tolls* in 1968 could not revive the past enthusiasm.

We are on even less certain ground in talking about the influence of Böll, Camus, and Sartre. Böll was very popular with readers and with theater people: *The Clown* was adapted for the stage and played in many Soviet theaters. In literature proper, though, it is not easy to find traces of Böll's presence. Evidently this is mainly because of a lack of distinction in the German writer. The lights of Sartre and (especially) Camus shone more brightly, of course. But it was not given to them, either, to penetrate the fabric of modern Russian prose. Except for his plays, Sartre has been little translated. Camus, like many twentieth-century thinkers, came to us too late to enter as an organic part into the purview of the literary world. As the Russian proverb has it, a spoon is a valuable thing at dinnertime. It was only at the very end of 1969 that I managed to publish the first more or less representative one-volume collection of Camus's work, including *The Plague, The Stranger,* and *The Fall.* I would like to add that the book became the prototype for a whole series, *Masters of Modern Prose,* in which several twentieth-century classics, hitherto unknown to Soviet readers, made their first appearance.

Anton Chekhov.

Brodsky says that, as far as outside influences go, "the seventies were the decade of Nabokov." To me, this is completely incomprehensible. Until

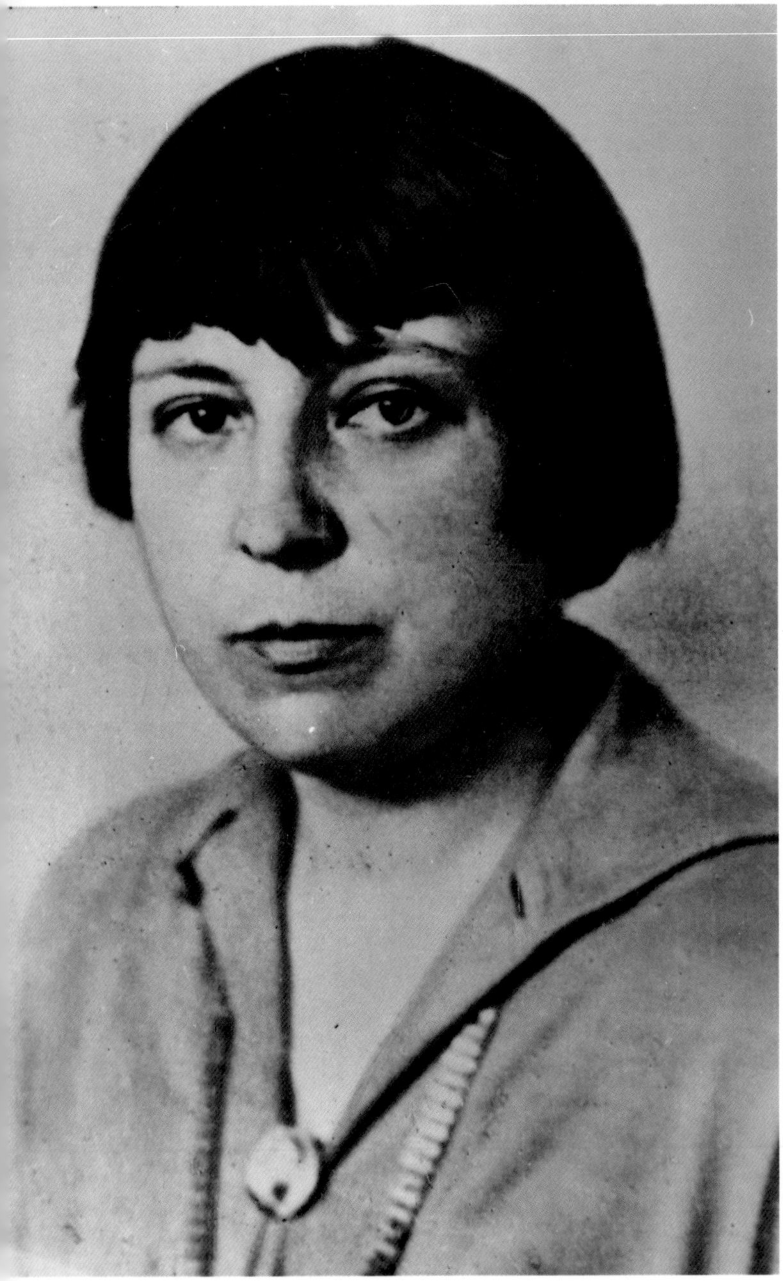

Marina Tsvetayeva.

the end of 1986 practically nothing by Nabokov had been published in the Soviet Union. His books were kept in special repositories and were confiscated at the borders when anybody tried to bring them in. I remember the trouble I had, in February of 1987, convincing customs inspectors at Sheremetyevo International Airport in Moscow to give back *Chorba's Return* and *The Gift,* which I had brought from the United States. I had to point out not only that I had compiled the first large collection of Nabokov's prose and published an article about him in *Literaturnaya Gazeta* but also that *The Defense* had recently been "openly" published in the literary journal *Moskva.* Those events opened the floodgates. In a year or two, nearly everything Nabokov ever wrote in Russian had been published in various periodicals.

In the seventies, and earlier too, Nabokov's work had been read "underground," mostly with interest, at times with passion. "Today an average Russian reader is much smarter than a promising Russian writer," Brodsky correctly notes. The truth of this can be illustrated by attitudes towards Nabokov. Among my colleagues and acquaintances there was considerable interest in Nabokov, mixed with understandable trepidation, back in the middle sixties, when even in the West he was thought of mainly as the author of the scandalous *Lolita.* It appears that Soviet writers, including quite famous ones, knew nothing about Nabokov except that between the two world wars he had published several questionable, supposedly anti-Soviet books under the pseudonym V. Sirin and then had turned up, from out of nowhere, in the United States, where he wrote the odious, "blatantly pornographic" *Lolita.*

In June of 1977, at the first meeting of writers from the United States and the USSR, Yuri Bondarev asked what was the most influential literary force, in a purely artistic sense, then at work in the United States. I remember how shocked some of the Soviet participants were when the Americans (and among them were Robert Lowell, William Styron, and Edward Albee) almost unanimously named Vladimir Nabokov. Just before, at the first working meeting, Bondarev and some others, breathing fire like Cromwell's iron-sided Puritans, had decried the "riotousness" of much of American prose. They hinted at its dangerous proximity to pornography. And suddenly—horror of horrors!—one of the founding fathers of that deplorable trend was practically being put on a pedestal, honored as a genuine artist. As it happened, Nabokov died just a few days later. A decade passed, and with the publication of Andrei Bitov's

Pushkin House and the stories of Tatyana Tolstaya, it became clear that Nabokov's vision and style had in truth put forth shoots that wrapped themselves around the tree of Russian literature. But to claim, as Brodsky does, that Nabokov had returned to his first homeland back in the seventies would be an unjustifiable exaggeration.

Speaking of recent influences on Russian literature, Brodsky adds to Nabokov's name those of Kafka, Borges, and Robert Musil. Here again, it seems to me, he indulges in wishful thinking. The first one-volume collection of Kafka's work in Russian, including *The Trial* and many short stories, was published in 1966. In the decades since, there have been no clear marks of Kafka's influence. Bureaucracy's stubborn vitality in our country and the looming memory of Stalin's lawless repressions would seem to provide an ideal soil for Kafkaism to take root. But only in Boris Yampolsky's novel *A Moscow Street*, written twenty-five years before its posthumous publication in 1988, do we hear a clear echo of *The Trial*. At that, it is hard to say if the echo is intentional. Kafka's monumental novel *The Castle* was published only recently in Russia, in the fierce competition between two literary journals: Leningrad's *Neva* and Moscow's *Inostrannaya Literatura*. And only recently, in the second half of the eighties, have Russian writers and readers had their first serious taste of Musil and Borges. This circumstance alone undermines the claim that Kafka, Musil, and Borges have exerted any perceptible influence on literature in the Soviet Union.

It remains to describe in brief the situation in the period of *perestroika*, or restructuring. Mikhail Gorbachev's policy of *glasnost*, or openness, has found expression first of all in the sphere of literature and art. The critical fervor of the speeches and resolutions at the Twenty-seventh Party Congress and the Nineteenth Party Conference finds its counterpart in the works published as the country turned the corner from stagnation to renewal. There was bitterness and anger over the suffering of our native land, plunged into a grave crisis by the long reign of unshackled bureaucracy. Viktor Astafyev's *Sad Detective Novel* and Valentin Rasputin's *The Fire* overflow with these feelings. There have been grave problems, up to now passed over in silence: drug addiction, alcoholism, spiritual desolation, and, among a certain part of the intelligentsia, the frenzied search for God. These are examined in Chingiz Aytmatov's *The Execution Block*. The beginnings of the permanent decline of the Russian village, going back to forced collectivization in the early thirties, are traced in a

Mikhail Bulgakov.

number of works by Sergei Zalygin, in Vasili Belov's *The Eyes,* and in Boris Mozhayev's *Peasant Men and Women.*

But the lion's share of what attracts every reader's attention in the second half of the eighties is not the product of *perestroika* as such. Rather, it comes from the store of manuscripts that had lain long years without any hope of publication. This is true of the "biggest" work of recent years, Anatoli Rybakov's *Children of the Arbat,* already translated into many languages. The novel is a psychological portrait of Stalin at the time his cult was being formed. The riddle of the dictator's personality, the motives for his crimes, the sufferings of prisoners in the Gulag, the rightness of the historic choice Russia made in the twentieth century—these are the themes of many publications now under way. Beginning in 1989, the writings of Aleksandr Solzhenitsyn are being returned to his native land.

Are there any works of literature directly reflecting the cleansing zeal of *perestroika*? At present they are few, but I can name at least one: Vladimir Orlov's *The Apothecary,* published in 1988 in *Novy Mir,* one of the flagships of *glasnost.* The author became well known after the publication of his previous novel, *Danilov, the Violinist,* over which hovers the shade of E. T. A. Hoffmann, honored by the Serapion brothers almost seventy years before, at the dawn of Soviet literature. The fantastic is present in *The Apothecary,* too, but closely interwoven with reality. This is manifest in the main character, a mysterious and at the same time very earthly enchantress. This "phosphorescent woman," as Mayakovsky would have said, drastically changes the lives of perfectly ordinary Muscovites, my neighbors in Sretenka, in the Meshchanski streets, in Ostankino. She awakens in them the goodness that was reviled and strangled in the years of stagnation. She returns them to their own human nature.

Perestroika is not simply radical reform, not simply restoring good sense to its rightful place. It is inseparable from filling our lives with sensitivity to spiritual values, from the play of imagination liberated by high ideals from glum particularism. It is what guided Russian writers, from Pushkin to Chekhov, in the service of their nation and of all humanity. The best works of Soviet literature are right in line with that tradition.

Boris Pasternak.

Science and Technology

ELTING E. MORISON, recently retired, has been Killian Professor of Humanities Emeritus at the Massachusetts Institute of Technology. He is the author of *Men, Machines, and Modern Times* and *From Know-How to Nowhere,* and editor of the eight-volume *Letters of Theodore Roosevelt.* Now living in New Hampshire in rural and eighteenth-century conditions, he writes occasional articles for *American Heritage* magazine, chairs a committee of the Sloan Foundation Program for the New Liberal Arts, and prepares from time to time a book review for the magazine *Technology and Culture.*

ALLA MELIK-PASHAEVA is a television journalist and a science writer. For several years she hosted her own science program from Central Television, and she contributes science articles to *Izvestia, Nedelya,* and other journals and magazines. With Academician O. Baroyan she co-authored *Lights in the Portrait,* a popular history of microbiology. She has written numerous scripts for science documentaries, and she recently launched a film studio, *Apple,* named for the five legendary apples and representing five principles for children's science films. Currently she is planning a children's "Workshop of Humankind" in the form of books, films, television programs, and videocassettes. The project is called *Period, Period, Comma,* echoing the start of a children's rhyming game for drawing the human figure.

Technology in America

ELTING E. MORISON

One of the things Karl Marx got about right was his sense that the means of production interacted with the character of society. Before his time, blowing wind, falling water, trained horses and, sometimes, slaves were the prime movers in the systems created to supply goods and services. As these sources of energy remained constant for centuries, so the systems they activated stayed much the same—as predictable and limited as the natural causes from which they derived. In such circumstances the people who thought of modifying the structure of society tended to think about new views of truth and beauty and expanded definitions of possible human responses rather than about the redesign of weirs and turbines.

The steam engine changed all that. Twenty-five years after the first steam-powered loom had been put into the little village of Manchester, for instance, the place had become not only a marvel of textile production but also a city of a quarter of a million—a sort of enormous slum. Anyone observing this process could tell that the new means of production would widely alter the character of society.

The nineteenth century spent a great deal of time trying to come to terms with this process in an orderly way. There were many innovative and sometimes improbable experiments. But not surprisingly, the major effort was to find a way to fit all the astounding new goods and services into the received tradition and context of earlier notions of truth, beauty, and human characteristics. That is, the attempt was made to contain all the novel energies, procedures, and things within the confines of the familiar culture. This was a normal approach that, with many stresses and strains, has brought us to where we are now. Necessary perhaps as a transitional process, it is no longer enough.

It is now obvious that the new energy, which two hundred years ago could turn a pastoral hamlet into an industrial city in the twinkling of an eye, has now acquired a mass and velocity that can transform our whole world into a set of technological systems. The question now is how to control the operation of these systems so they will serve our basic needs, our best interests, and our most generous intentions.

The cultural criteria that will enable members of society to manage the condition of things in an enlightened way cannot be derived only from a received set of attitudes; some new cultural imperatives must be invented to meet the modern times.

Since our modern times began—since about the time James Watt thought of the condenser—there have always been a few people in each generation who understood the problem we were facing. Though they used a variety of evidence and put it in different ways, they came to agree on the same point: the means of production must always be

Joseph Stella, *Brooklyn Bridge: Variation on an Old Theme,* 1939.

controlled by the civilizing ends in view. In the pages that follow, I will examine the opinions and evaluations of four men who lived in America at different times; between them they cover all of our national history and therefore present a description of dramatically changing conditions. But in their judgments of what is required to develop a more satisfying life and in their suggestions of how to proceed to achieve it, they arrive at similar conclusions. I hope that their views will continue to be useful to us as we strive and fumble toward the future.

Lars Sellstedt, *The Erie Canal, Buffalo Harbor at foot of Porter Avenue,* 1871.

I will begin with Benjamin Latrobe. Born in England in 1764, Latrobe was educated in that country and in Germany within the Moravian curriculum. He studied biology, chemistry, geology, mathematics through calculus, ancient Greek and Roman history and literature, and modern European history and theology. He could speak and read five (and possibly six) languages. In addition to the method and substance of this formal schooling he also acquired several attractive and interesting skills. For instance, he became "a master in water colors" and an "accomplished musician." As a writer, he was clear, direct, and graceful, whether he was offering a technical report, preparing a scientific paper, or rendering astute perceptions on the state of the society.

In addition to these assets and capacities, Latrobe had his own work to do. In England, he had studied with Samuel Pepys Cockerell, one of the moving spirits in the architectural Greek Revival, and he had worked with John Smeaton, the great designer of the Eddystone Lighthouse. After coming to America in 1775, he became a dominant influence in the building of things in the new land.

It is often said that he found architecture the

polite accomplishment of a few amateurs and left it a solid profession. It has also been said, both then and now, that in the engineering of his time he was first among his colleagues. In sum, he was a builder ready to build anything from a shooting box to a municipal water system, from a canal lock to a private house, from a bank to government office buildings.

In November 1808, a man wrote to him to say that he had looked over the whole field and had decided that Latrobe was the best in the business. He desired, therefore, to join his firm. Latrobe replied that he thought such a letter required a response of "the most perfect candor."

"I believe" said Latrobe, "I am the first who in our own country, has endeavored and partly succeeded to place the profession of Architect and Civil Engineer on that footing of respectability which it occupies in Europe. But I have not so far succeeded as to make it an eligible profession for one who has the education and feeling of a Gentleman, and I regret exceedingly that my own son who is now completing his Studies in St. Mary's College at Baltimore has determined to make it his own."

It is clear enough what Latrobe believed—that designing a municipal water system or building a private house were as much a part of the common social and cultural experience as painting a picture, playing the flute, or conversing with friends on subjects drawn from literature and philosophy. It is also clear that America in 1800 was so busy learning how to build structures that would stand and finding out how to make things work—merely pushing forward the technological—that it had neither time nor inclination to respond to the claims of a gentleman's education and feeling. Probably the passing years would mend this situation.

About forty years later, in 1844, Ralph Waldo Emerson gave a lecture on the subject of "The Young Americans." As our leading philosopher he spent much time speculating on what this country could and should do with its extraordinary resources. He explored everything from the things in the saddle that rode mankind to the transcendental truths that should govern the aspirations of individual men and women. He began his lecture to the Boston Mercantile Library Association with these words: "It is remarkable that our people have their intellectual culture from one country and their Duties from another. This false state of affairs is newly in a way to be corrected.

Benjamin Latrobe.

America is beginning to assert itself in the senses and to the imagination of her children, and Europe is receding to the same degree."

Emerson saw, therefore, an opportunity in America to develop our own scheme of things based on our growing competence, our particular new Duties and our interpretation of a satisfactory life. The place to begin, he thought, was in the search for a sensible and satisfying development of the vast expanses of our land. But to do this properly we needed to acquire new kinds of operating data—examining the character of our mineral riches, giving more attention to scientific agriculture, and studying the arts of architecture and engineering. Even on the East Coast "prudent

Erie Railway Poster, 1874.

men" had begun to realize that such subject matter had a place in a well-planned education.

But something more was required. If we were to apply all the new technical information appropriately, we would have to figure out—using a different sort of data—what kind of a society we wanted to be. What, under our management, the land becomes is "the appointed remedy for whatever is false and fantastic in our culture." Organizing the land and the society in accordance with our newly acquired learning and skill, but more particularly in accordance with our best intentions and highest hopes, Emerson argued, would repair the errors of a scholastic and traditional education and bring us into "fresh relations with men and things." In other words, to take full advantage of the new opportunities it would be necessary to learn how the machinery works, to decide what to use the machinery for, and to devise the means to control the working of the machines in support of the ends in view. Emerson believed we would arrive at a fresh relationship between men and things more by an imaginative interpretation of our own experience than by an undue dependence on the old high culture from abroad.

Ninety years later, social critic Lewis Mumford reported on America in the 1930s. Through technology we had put a lot more things in the saddle, things that were overriding the transcendental promises. "The notion of a complete society, carrying on a complete and symmetrical life, [had] tended to disappear from our minds." This meant that "business, technology, and science not merely occupied their legitimate place but took to themselves all that had hitherto belonged to art, religion, and poetry. Positive knowledge and practical actions, which are indispensable elements in every culture, [had become] the only living sources of our own."

In a striking set of assertions, Mumford posited

our future requirements: we must construct more complete modes of life; we must reconstruct a more vital tissue of ideas and symbols (a culture) to supplant those that have led us into "this sinister world"; and most significant, "in proportion as intelligence [is] dealing more effectively with the instrumentalities of life, it [will become] necessary for the imagination to project more complete and satisfying ends." To reach these desired ends would require nothing less than the conception of "a whole new world."

Today, fifty years later, Samuel Florman has taken it all back to square one. Florman is a civil engineer, and a very good one, with a continuing interest in and concern for the fitting of technology to the broader scheme of things. He brings to his reflections not only a full and varied professional experience but a perspective nourished by graduate studies in literature at Columbia University during the great days of Lionel Trilling, Jacques Barzun, Mark Van Doren, and Douglas Moore. Twenty years ago he wrote the well-known *Engineering and the Liberal Arts: A Technologist's Guide to History, Literature, Philosophy, Art, and Music* (1968). Against this rich background he considers our present condition.

Florman begins with the same anxiety that troubled Latrobe, and he suggests that many of his associates still have little use for "the education and feeling of a gentleman." In his recent book, *The Civilized Engineer* (1987), he indicates that those in his field often consider culture to be "a pose." They like to speak of themselves as "rough" and "tough," as acting "in a construction camp and bar room manner rather than with the deportment that would grace a drawing room."

Closer to the bone, he asserts the "plain truth that most engineers do not read the great books, do not study the history of their nation or any other and are effectively cut off from humanistic, philosophical and civilizing education." From this, he concludes that "in its moment of ascendance engineering [which can now make and do almost everything] is faced with the trivialization of its purpose and the debasement of its practice." What Florman looks for are changes in education and experience that would enable us to build a "culture that weds competence to grace and wisdom to know-how" that has never existed before but that would fit our modern circumstance.

Ralph Waldo Emerson.

These four men collectively have spanned this country's history almost from its beginnings. Each in his time has found a condition of things unlike that of any of the others—a separate stage in the extraordinary development of our physical plant. And each has approached his observations from a somewhat different background and perspective. It is remarkable, therefore, that on certain significant matters they are in agreement. They all say, one way or another, that technological operations should take place in a larger scheme of things—a containing cultural context of some kind. They all indicate that because this is a new world, possessed in its developing technology of a new force, it is therefore necessary to build a new kind of appropriate cultural scheme. And they all suggest

Wright brothers' glider launching, Kitty Hawk, North Carolina, 1902.

that in the building of this scheme, formal education has a dominant part to play.

In the event, none of them has succeeded in making his point. The reasons are understandable. One reason is philosophical and cultural. The scheme we live by is a western culture founded essentially on the ancient Greek view of the world. It is filled with many solid truths and saving graces, but it fosters a peculiar view of work and of the distinction between work done with the head and the hands. In the Greek view, "an art which tended to serve a useful end or practice was probably vile, low, and mercenary." They had small interest in "the mechanical arts" because "they deteriorate the soul." Such attitudes permeated the whole society. Some of the Greek city states, for instance, made it illegal for free men to engage in the mundane activities. The concept went very deep with them. When someone invented a steam engine that might do work, they had no idea of what to use it for and looked upon it, if at all, as a diverting toy.

Plato was the most powerful and convincing spokesman for this point of view. In various ways he drew invidious distinctions between head and hands, making and thinking, doing and speculating. And his views have come down to us, as Benjamin Latrobe discovered when he found that civil engineering was not an attractive calling for those with the education and feeling of a gentleman.

There have also been practical reasons for putting aside the insights of these four observers. During the nineteenth century, our need to investigate the place and meaning of technology in our scheme of things was considerably less than our need to use it to make the vast country habitable and to meet the day-to-day needs of a rapidly growing democratic society, in which one man has as good a claim to what is made as any other. By concentrating on the raw materials and the nuts and bolts of the machinery, the looked-for results came a lot faster than if we had stopped to consider what it all might add up to. And the results were, in fact, astounding.

In the evolution of our textile business we did not stop until we had built the mill with the world's largest capacity; it turned out a mile of fabric a minute. In the organization of our early steel industry we designed our instrumentation and invented a set of procedures that soon made us the world's principal manufacturer of Bessemer steel. In the continued expansion of our railroads we soon had constructed more mileage than anyone else. And so forth.

Along the way we developed certain characteristics or attitudes. We were always more concerned with quantity than quality (the lowest-grade steel used in England was called "American Rail"). We moved invariably toward uniformity in procedure to simplify the process, expand production, and lower costs. Though we received virtually all our basic ideas (in textiles, steel, railways, and electricity) from Europe, we revealed great shrewdness in applying these ideas to fulfill our own requirements. The distinguishing characteristic of our manufacturing was the way we sought to assemble the related parts of a process into an orderly and rational pattern of production; for example, the bringing together of independent installations—mines, blast furnaces, foundries, bloomeries, and rolling mills—into a logical integration for the production of steel. Then, too, in all our technological development there was a governing sense that the customer was almost always everyman—and equal to almost every other man—so the purpose was to satisfy the almost universal need. We went after the Model T, not the Rolls Royce.

What all this is supposed to suggest is that within the scheme of the practical needs of an expanding democratic society, the nature of the means to satisfy those needs has been left to develop, on the whole, as the ingenuity and hardheadness of those directly involved in production have seen fit. And, as noted, the practical results have been gratifying. But there were never many people around who were earnestly seeking the answer to Matthew Arnold's question of what coal, iron, and railroads have to do with sweetness and light. Which was, one way and another, the question that Latrobe, Emerson, Mumford, and Florman kept asking.

Lewis Mumford.

And now our technological resources have reached a point where it ought to be a question of top priority for everybody. We can now make and do practically everything with our machinery. What remains to be found out is how to run the world we have created and what to use it for. I return to Mumford: "In proportion as intelligence [is] dealing more effectively with the instrumentalities of life it [becomes] necessary for the imagination to project more complete and satisfying ends."

Lewis W. Hine photograph

Construction worker, Empire State Building, 1931.

How to do this? How do we consciously build a civilizing culture suitable for framing the life of today? It is a tall order which in time will engage many of our resources and much of our energy. What I hope to do here is to locate a starting point and suggest a few appropriate attitudes. Anyone who has come this far knows that the great obstacle to an inclusive and balanced culture has been the continuing division between being and doing, wisdom and know-how, value and efficiency in operations. The explanation for these divisions has most often been worked out in terms of individual tastes, economic determinism, and persistent class distinction. I would suggest that there is another cause, rarely cited, but crucial to maintaining the division. It is an epistemological explanation embracing the different kinds of knowledge that have been involved. Broadly stated, it is the difference between the useful learning that can be immediately applied to do work and the speculative learning that deals in ideas without attachment to immediate results. As said earlier, the condition for a long time—most of our history—did little to put our situation in jeopardy. Those who searched for the truth as an end in itself did not ordinarily reach findings that interfered with

Thomas Hart Benton, *America Today: City Building*, 1930.

those who were turning stuff out the door; those who turned stuff out the door did not know enough to disturb much the reasonably ordered flow of our existence.

The steam engine and the development in the nineteenth century of more rigorous thinking about the state of Nature changed all that. By the middle of that century William Baron Rogers, founder of the Massachusetts Institute of Technology (MIT), could speak of the dignity and worth of useful knowledge, but nobody paid much attention. In fact, if anyone cares to examine the struggle between knowledge gained for itself and knowledge obtained for use, they could do no better than study the negotiations between Harvard University and MIT that continued over the years in search of common interests and common association. Not sufficient common ground was ever discovered in those negotiations to warrant any kind of joint arrangement.

The situation has now radically changed. What had been through the last half of the nineteenth century and early years of this century a gradual evolution of varied parts of technology became a well-organized and stimulating program of development because of World War II. Radar, sonar,

Aaron Bohrod, *The Big Blow, the Bessemer Process*, 1948.

Loran, jet engines, proximity fuses, the atom bomb, and all the rest of it combined in a convincing demonstration of how new applications of useful learning could create a new kind of world. The war also demonstrated how such knowledge could be rapidly acquired, mobilized, processed, and skillfully applied to achieve predetermined technical ends.

As a result of the change in our body of learning we now have a society that in one particular is different from all its predecessors. We are not only pretty much in charge of all significant operations; we are also responsible for the results. We have the opportunity and obligation to do what Lewis Mumford, fifty years ago, said we must do. We can and must build a safe, sane, and satisfying new world. But, to bring the question posed by Matthew Arnold up to date, how can we fit computers, jet engines, missiles, dialyzers, the colonization of space, spare parts for the body, and nuclear energy into a natural and effective interaction with sweetness and light? How can we put the evolving technological process into a consistently civilizing context?

Ultimately, of course, if our object is to create a new culture and build a new world, it will be necessary to resolve all kinds of conflicting interests and satisfy many different aspirations. In time, if the civilizing process is going to work, everyone—or almost everyone—has to get into the act. But the effort has to begin somewhere. I would start with the universities.

Universities are our oldest, most experienced, and most objective processors of knowledge. They store, acquire, evaluate, and transmit all kinds of information to a varied constituency. They also have some sense of the present novel conditions, because since World War II they have increasingly left the Ivory Tower to engage in the business of the workshop. In fact, nothing so demonstrates that useful knowledge lies at the heart of all recent development in our society than this entanglement of the university with the work that is going forward.

Universities have some defects for the task at hand. From their work with government and business in recent years, they have clearly discovered what William Barton Rogers was talking about one hundred years ago; they have come certainly to understand the great worth, and no doubt something of the dignity, of useful knowledge. And because of this new attitude they have altered their institutional structure, their budgets, and some of their aims to satisfy the demands of the present market. They do not seem, except in presidential rhetoric, to have given much thought to the development of a new relation between the useful knowledge and the timeless truths in their possession.

A second limitation for the task at hand is the fact that universities tend, in compliance with current scholarship, to become large assemblies of small pieces—conglomerates. Given the nature of the departmental structure and the increasing division of all kinds of knowledge, universities are ill equipped to undertake the kind of synthesizing activity that goes into the creation of a civilizing context.

So it must be recognized that everything—well, almost everything—that presently determines the character of these institutions (departmental organization, administrative policy, intellectual training, financial advantage, and the seemingly intractable differences within the body of learning that they hold) will be against such a novel purpose.

How to deal with such resistances and to tap the indispensable resources universities still possess? I suggest a flanking movement. The great tool for discovery in these institutions today is experiment. Use it—without prejudice to other ongoing endeavors—to find out if there is any possible coherence in the body of knowledge with which they are all working. That is, in each university—alongside the labs, agencies, and divisions that are now splitting up information—create a Laboratory for Epistemological Disorders. Assign to it a task of exploring ways to bring together selected bits of the accumulating information (new and old) into larger contexts that make sense (civilizing interpretations). The assumption is this: a society that relies increasingly on knowledge that can be applied to getting things done will have trouble getting *sensible* things done until its body of knowledge is restored to a more sensible order.

Samuel C. Florman.

Charles Sheeler, *Classic Landscape*, 1931.

So how can a Laboratory for Epistemological Disorders achieve the purpose of restoring order? It can take any piece of unfinished business in the society—dialyzers, robots, computers, nuclear waste, missiles, outer space, and so on—and investigate ways and means to put these energies into the satisfying constraints of a civilizing context. That means including in these investigations, as Lewis Mumford indicated, not only the interest and capabilities of business, science, and technology, but the interests of art, religion, and poetry from which people derive insights into the desired civilizing process. And that means that people in this Laboratory must work closely together to bring the elements in the situation into fruitful interaction and connection.

To this end the Laboratory should be staffed by men and women of all appropriate fields who represent the most formidable talents in these fields. They should work together on specific problems of a technological society, seeking through trial, error, and joint endeavor to find out how technological, economic, social, aesthetic, and moral energies can be brought into constructive combination for the orderly and satisfying development of the technological system. That such appropriate connection and interaction between the quantifiable and the qualitative, the measurable and the incommensurable, the operations and the evaluation, has never been achieved before suggests the great difficulties in the process. That the technological is now so powerful as to be able to create any kind of future suggests the necessity for finding and enforcing the kind of future that is safe, interesting, and satisfying. In this whole epistemological exercise I would suggest that the computer has a great part to play. It should serve as the primary instrument of consolidation and synthesis among the several searches conducted by the Laboratories in the different universities.

Here one can do no more than suggest the grand intention for such a Laboratory. But I would add a few concluding remarks. It may be that this is an idea whose time has come—or is at least on its way. Seventy years ago the British philosopher Samuel Alexander said that "the real business" of a university had become "technology," how it works and what, in the best interests of human beings, to use it for. A little later Alfred North Whitehead said we must conduct a search for "that rational coordination of impulses and thoughts" without which life becomes "a mere welter of minor excitements" (like now). And finally, not so long ago, Sir Eric Ashby reported that we had reached a point where "science, technology, sociology and a liberal education are indivisible."

When such counsels prevail, it will be obvious that the place to put all the conflicting impulses and thoughts together is the university. And the findings of a Laboratory on Epistemological Disorders will inevitably in time permeate the whole institution. In that case, the universities will recover two essential functions that they have now let dwindle or have shoved aside.

The first function was described incisively by A. Lawrence Lowell: "One object of a university is to counteract, rather than copy, the defects of the civilization of today."

The other function has a long and honored tradition. Within the university is the college—where undergraduates presumably learn how to deal with the surrounding world; where all the information and ideas generated in the university are brought together into a scheme of things—a civilizing context that presumably produces an informed citizenry. Not much has been done in this area recently, in part because scholarship now

Douglass Crockwell, *Paper Workers*, 1934.

divides things up, in part because universities are more interested in other things, and in part because no one yet has figured out what scheme of things can be constructed out of all the available knowledge to help undergraduates deal with their surroundings.

In a kind of wistful conclusion, it may be said that the dangerous separation of intellectual powers noticed by Latrobe, Emerson, Mumford, and Florman still obtains. It will no doubt continue until universities have found a way to use all the new knowledge at their disposal in satisfaction of their ancient purposes. No other agency in our society can assume this job.

СССР

The Apple of Knowledge

ALLA MELIK-PASHAEVA

"How many apples can you name that have gone down in history?" the man asks me. With his red beard, he might have stepped out of a portrait by Rembrandt. My husband. Not waiting for an answer, he holds up his hand, five fingers spread wide. He bends them in one after another, counting them off with relish:

"The apple in the Garden of Paradise—without it there would be no mankind. The apple of Paris—the cause of the Trojan War. (Do you remember the Iliad? 'Achilles's cursed anger sing, O goddess, that son of Peleus.') Next, the golden apples in the garden of the Hesperides—to obtain them, Heracles had to perform the most famous of his labors, taking the sky onto his shoulders. William Tell's apple—imagine the boy standing motionless, the famous archer taking aim at the apple that sits on his own son's head. What if he misses?! Newton's apple. . . ."

Why does he return so often to the "deeds of bygone days"? What magnetism do those legendary apples hold for the noted physicist Andrei Budker?

A documentary film is being made about Lev Landau. The movie people are interviewing Budker. He says bluntly: "Landau always seemed to me to be the most ordinary, everyday sort of person." The interviewers are dumbstruck. Budker savors their astonishment, waiting just long enough before adding: "The most everyday sort of person, but from a civilization one level above ours here on Earth."

Lift-off of the manned spaceship *Buran*.

The individual is the most interesting thing in science—the same, by the way, as everywhere else.

For me, the "human side" of science—the passions, the characters, the faces—had always been at one remove, viewed as episodes on the editing-room table or framed by a television or movie camera. No matter how wrapped up I got in a film, I always knew it was only a film.

Then suddenly everything was shifted around. For me, science changed from a subject for journalism into the meaning of life itself, the center of all talk around the house. Fate had brought me together with a real scientist.

I saw him joyous and despairing, childlike and wise. I saw his kindness to children and students. I saw his heroic struggle against disease. I saw all of the last eight years of his life.

"If people in different countries, speaking different languages, can say 'Everything is relative,' without stopping to think that that idea derives from the great theory of Albert Einstein, or if they can say 'chain reaction,' understanding it to mean an avalanche of events, without knowing that the formula comes from the discovery of their contemporary, Nikolai Semenov, then that is genuine recognition . . . . Semenov's whole life is a chain reaction of ideas, deeds, events."

With those words, we began a television broadcast commemorating Semenov's ninetieth birthday.

In 1926 Nikolai Semenov invented the science of chemical physics, which made him world famous. In 1931 he founded an institute of chemical physics. Soon a journal called *Chemical Physics* sprang up in America. Thirty years after his discovery of branching chain reactions, Semenov received the Nobel Prize. In his acceptance speech the laureate, breaking with tradition, mentioned every single participant in the work—several dozen names.

Academician Nikolai Vavilov.

On screen is Semenov, reminiscing about the twenties, his first laboratory and first co-workers: "What was it like at the start? We started from nothing, you know. We had to put in a stove and then get it going—it was cold in the building—and fix the water pipe. We carried water in from a hydrant, if it was working; otherwise, we melted snow. It was a good thing when the plumbing didn't freeze. . . . Our scientific work was complicated. But we were in good spirits, you understand, odd though that may seem."

He began in the Leningrad Physico-Technical Institute—"Papa Ioffe's kindergarten." The whole of Soviet physics came out of that institute, you might say, just as the whole of our great literature came out of Gogol's *Overcoat*. At age ninety, Semenov was working on plans for a new scientific center in Russia's non-*chernozem* soil region.

Academician Vitali Goldansky: "If we speak of Russian scientists who have worked at the frontier between physics and chemistry, his name comes third in the series: Lomonosov, Mendeleev, Semenov. You could say that the modern revolution in science and technology began with the chain reaction—the reaction when a nucleus is split—a branching chain reaction, that is. It is a direct continuation of Semenov's work. If we speak of quantum electronics, the avalanche of stimulated radiations is also a branching chain reaction. This is the second part of the revolution in science and technology. Semenov stood beside the revolution's cradle."

Daniil Granin wrote: "The apple plucked from the tree in the Garden foredoomed humanity to eternal torments and the joys of knowledge."

August 6, 1945, found Lieutenant Budker in the Far East, where his unit had been transferred. The news of what had happened in Japan stunned him. But that was not all. It was evidently on that day that he resolved to go into the "atomic problem." In 1946, immediately after his demobilization, Budker began work at the famous Laboratory No. 2 (as the Institute of Atomic Energy was then known), under Igor Kurchatov.

In his thoughts, Budker frequently returns to his teacher: "When I think back to the first years of work on the atomic problem in the USSR, it seems to me we were doing not science, but poetry!

Music! Those years of working every day until two in the morning, without days off or vacations—I remember them now as the brightest, most ecstatic years of my life. I never listened to more music, never read more poetry. We were creating a symphony of joy, of beauty. Every formula was no less beautiful and elegant than a Venetian vase. . . . If Pushkin had lived in our times, he would undoubtedly have been a physicist."

Kurchatov: "The thought of a war with atomic or hydrogen bombs is unbearable." Anatoli Aleksandrov remembers Kurchatov's reaction when the hydrogen bomb was tested: "It's monstrous! God forbid it should be used against people! Such a thing must not be allowed to happen!"

I often heard my husband say that the physicists of his generation—the generation that created nuclear and thermonuclear weapons—owed a debt to humanity. Quite simply, they were duty bound to create a limitless ocean of energy, not for destruction, but for creation.

The idea of restraining plasma with magnetism, on which later projects were based, belongs to Andrei Sakharov and Igor Tamm. Budker conducted his first scientific work, while still an undergraduate, under Tamm's guidance. (The "tamm" has been proposed as a measure of honesty and decency.) He encountered Sakharov in the course of his work, at seminars, and later at meetings of the Academy. He always admired him, both as a physicist and as a man.

When the ideal of a safe thermonuclear reactor was formulated, Kurchatov named four or five theoreticians who must be brought into the work. Budker was among them. From the fall of 1950 onwards, all Budker's thoughts were absorbed by this new problem. He met regularly with Kurchatov, after which he would sit for long hours in silent thought, over pages covered with notations or left entirely blank.

"I was given the job of regulating the planned thermonuclear reactor, of preventing its 'taking off' or going out of control. The job reminds me now of the man who wanted to invent a perpetual-motion machine, so he patented a device to keep it from accelerating endlessly," Budker used to joke.

One sunny summer's day under an apple tree, Kurchatov was writing an article about work on the thermonuclear reactor. He had invited Golovin (his first deputy) and Budker to help him. Budker told him Hegel's story about a sophist who refused to get into the water until he had learned

Academician Sergei Korolyov, founder of the Soviet space program.

to swim. Kurchatov was delighted. They put the joke into the article, and later it became part of Kurchatov's famous lecture at Harwell.

"Whoever wants to go back to the caves and the trees, take one step forward!" If such a summons were issued, I wonder, would there be even one volunteer?

Solar astrophysical observatory in Zelenchuk.

In the sixties, the shortest way to the heart was through the mind. Everybody was interested in science; the pendulum still had a long way to swing. Nowadays, people curse science and blame it for all our misfortunes—economic, political, ecological. But trying to halt the progress of science and technology (which began with the Biblical tillers and herders, or maybe much earlier) is the same as summoning humanity back to the Stone Age.

What about a formula for avoiding disasters, then? In theory, it is well known: Combine science with morality; combine politics with science. "Let your thoughts be kind, and your heart will be wise."

"Kind thoughts, wise heart." That's all there is to the recipe, endlessly simple and endlessly complicated.

Spring 1988. A live Soviet-American television link-up on the problem of cancer. Nancy Reagan appears on my television screen. Cancer has touched her family, too. I know about it from the newspapers. But here she is so close—almost eye to eye, it seems. My father died of cancer. The cup does not pass, not from presidents, not from ordinary citizens.

It is sometimes said that cancer research was in the doldrums during the forties. The problem seemed uncrackable. A new and unexpected approach was needed. It was then that the Soviet researcher Lev Zilber put forth a daring idea: Cancer is a disease of the genes. It is caused by a virus. It embeds itself in a cell's genetic apparatus, making it cancerous.

The idea occurred to Zilber in 1943. The first to hear of it was the director of the prison where Zilber, arrested for a second time, ribs broken during his interrogation, had already served four years of his sentence.

It was an important insight, but nobody believed Zilber. The time had not come. They laughed at him, refuted him, or even thought refutation unnecessary.

I remember well the sultry evening in 1964 when we broadcast live from the Academy of Medical Sciences, to millions of television viewers, a spirited debate on the nature of cancer. Zilber was one of the participants. The audience witnessed an argument that concerns not only the best minds but all of us, our children, our loved ones, mankind as a whole.

"Has anyone ever observed the trace of a virus in a cancerous cell?"—the obligatory, ritual question. The answer, alas, was known both to Zilber and to his opponents.

The search for that trace tormented him. He needed confirmation for his theory.

He looked for the trace of a virus and found certain proteins in tumors that are not present in healthy cells. The consequence was a groundbreaking new method of diagnosing and treating tumors. Zilber became one of the founders of cancer immunology. He had brought new hope.

A student of his named Garri Abelev, together with Yuri Tatarinov, a biochemist from Astrakhan, continued work on a simple and very reliable method of diagnosing liver cancer and certain other malignancies. Today this method is used all over the world.

Zilber was hurrying to finish his most important book, on the viro-genetic theory of cancer. On November 10, 1966, it was finally completed. He wrote on a clean sheet of paper: "I dedicate this, my last book, to my wife, Valeria Petrovna, a true and faithful friend throughout the bright and dark days of my life."

Academician Igor Kurchatov.

Fifteen minutes later, he died. He was just a step away from triumph; he missed it only by a little. Three months later, evidence was found that supported his theory.

Zilber's biography is a real-life drama in three acts, with prologue and epilogue. It represents, in a nutshell, the living history of Soviet microbiology, virology, and oncology from the twenties to the sixties.

It is astonishing how many books we now have that describe gripping and tragic moments in the history of science. There is Daniil Granin's *The Buffalo,* Aleksandr Bek's *A New Assignment,*

Vladimir Dudintsev's *White Raiment,* and Vasili Grossman's *Life and Fate.*

Is this by chance? I think not. To understand something deeply it has to be seen and grasped as a whole—the way a cosmonaut in orbit can see the misfortunes of Earth.

Academician Lev Landau.

One scientist, reflecting about the biosphere, compared it with Gulliver's watch. Do you remember Swift's Lilliputians? They extracted the giant's watch from his pocket and studied it scrupulously. They could perceive the individual details—the hands, the numbers on its face—but they could not get an overall view of the huge mechanism. In the same way, a human being standing on Earth is like a Lilliputian before the biosphere's gigantic face.

Planes and spacecraft, by taking scientists high above the Earth, have given them a completely new outlook. A mathematical model also makes it possible to view a phenomenon as a whole—from above, as it were.

A writer has a special vision, too. He knows how to see big things whole, even if time has not yet moved them far enough away. That is why writers often turn out to be the first historians of science.

I agree completely with Yevgeni Yevtushenko's words:

> Thank God we have literature,
> Russia's best historian.

In science there are many paths; and it is understood that the path others have traveled is not the only good one. Budker was convinced of this. He proposed his own approach to the problem of thermonuclear energy; he invented "magnetic corks"—open traps for the containment of plasma—initiating a whole new line of investigation. Everyone working on the problem was struck by the boldness of his ideas. Later, when the work on nuclear power was declassified, it was learned that the American physicist Robert Post had suggested—at the same time as Budker—a similar system for restraining plasma. Later the device came to be known as the Budker-Post trap.

At one of the seminars, a young man stood up and said: "Calculations show that open traps will not be able to contain hot plasma."

Budker's friends froze in their seats. Knowing his fiery, outspoken temperament, they were expecting an interesting show.

But Budker calmly thanked the young man for his penetrating and well-argued remarks, which he said would give him much to think about. He was pleased to have such youngsters around—talented, impressive, unwilling to take anything on faith. Soon Roald Sagdeev, this twenty-five-year-old critic of Budker, became the leading theoretician of the Budker's new institute. Some years passed, and Sagdeev stepped into the leadership of the Soviet space program.

I really like Isaac Asimov's story, "Profession." In it, if you remember, knowledge is given to

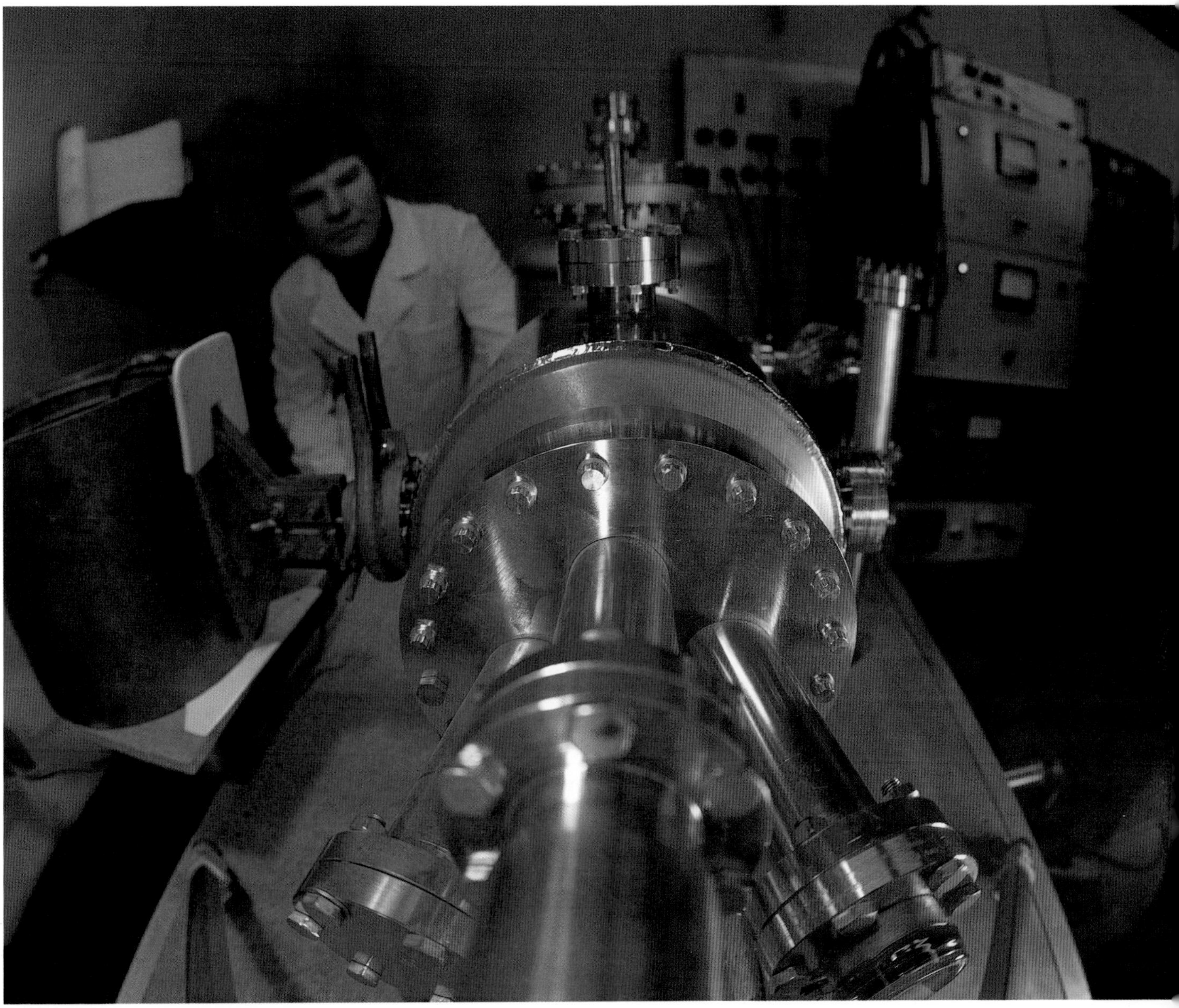

USSR Academy of Sciences Research Institute of Solid State Physics.

students readymade, on tapes and blocks. One "crackpot," though, will not accept the prefabricated truths. And he is the true genius.

Another boy—this one not invented—asked his physics teacher: "If you could run alongside a light wave at the speed of light, would it really seem to be standing still?"

This boy was surprised at something the others, in their indifference, had let slip past their mind's eye. That meant he must be an unusual child. And so he was. The questioning schoolboy was Albert Einstein.

Is it possible to name something that successful scientists have in common? I understand, of course, that each scientist is unlike any other, a "one-of-a-kind" product. But still, I will attempt to construct a homemade typology.

Independent thinking. That above all.

An example?

At a political education course in the winter of

1940, a senior student of physics at Moscow University declared that peace with Hitler's Germany was only temporary, a matter of expedience. (According to the official line, the peace was inviolable, forever.)

Academician Petr Kapitsa.

The teacher turned red in the face. He rushed out of the room, muttering about class enemies raising their heads.

The student was not arrested or even expelled. A miracle. But they did take away his stipend; the teacher insisted on it. So the student unloaded barges. He had a wife and baby to support.

On June 23, immediately after his last examination, the student enlisted as a volunteer. (He had a draft exemption from the factory where he had been assigned work.) Then he put on his uniform and appeared at the university to give the teacher a beating. He did not find him, though. (They say the teacher hid in the women's toilet.) At the end of the war, the young physicist was in the Far East. I have already told you what became of him after that.

On April 15, 1986, Central Television's Channel One carried a program honoring Nikolai Semenov on his ninetieth birthday. (It turned out to be the last broadcast made about him in his lifetime.) Soon afterwards I went to Kiev. I wanted to talk with Sergei Gershenzon, the dean of Soviet biology. I had heard that Gershenzon was the first—before the Americans—to question the ruling dogma of molecular biology on the way genetic material is transferred. Indeed he had, but nobody listened.

I arrived in Kiev on April 26, 1986. The first day of Chernobyl. What had been thought and said about science changed completely then.

Andrei Voznesensky wrote:

> Who is to blame we'll work out later,
> And where the poisoned apple's hid.

The man was already gone. But his shadow was imprinted on a stone. Forever.

That frame from a film about the atom bomb, which she saw in 1953, imprinted itself in Yelena Burlakova's mind. Forever. It was then, as a second-year chemistry student at Moscow University, that she asked herself the eternal question: What can I, personally, do?

She went to the biophysics department, to Professor Tarusov. He was studying how radiation affects living things.

Radiation is like a cannon, shooting live molecules. The resulting fragments, called free radicals, are like the dark forces unleashed during great calamities and disasters. Once released, charged and aggressive, they themselves cripple and destroy biological structures. A chain reaction begins—an avalanche of free radicals. Aggression breeds aggression—radiation sickness, accelerated aging, malignant tumors, birth defects.

It was in 1956 that substances for calming down free radicals were first tested in our country. These substances bond tightly to the radicals—seize them hand and foot, as it were—and render them powerless. Just like wrestlers on the mat.

Burlakova's teacher, Nikolai Emanuel (who had worked closely with Semenov), was in charge of the project. Twenty-seven years later, in 1983, teacher and student received the State Prize of the USSR. But the teacher did not have long to enjoy this belated recognition; he died the following year. Professor Tarusov, who had been called a dreamer, did not live to see himself vindicated; he had died several years before. These three scientists—Tarusov, Emanuel, and Burlakova—had proposed their own, completely new, explanation for radiation damage. They said it was caused by a chain reaction of free radicals.

Could the avalanche of free radicals be stopped *after* the organism had been exposed? After—that was very important. A nuclear attack or an accident at a power plant is not something you expect! They are still working on it; there is still a long way to go.

The last days of April and the beginning of May were magical in Kiev that year. Gardens and parks outdid one another in the freshness and luxuriance of their greenery. The streets were crowded—lots of children.

Afterwards, I learned that since the early fifties there have been twenty-two accidents at nuclear power plants—a big one about once every five years. Chernobyl, unfortunately, became the heavyweight champion.

Why did our country not have even a single institute of radiobiology before Chernobyl? Scientists had raised that question repeatedly.

Perhaps there would not have been such bewilderment, such uncertainty in the face of the disaster. . . .

Dr. Robert Gale, a noted American specialist in bone-marrow transplants, was among the first foreigners to come to the aid of the victims of Chernobyl. An extraordinarily busy man, he nevertheless returned again and again. In particular, he spent many hours with Aleksandr Fridenshtein, who is studying the micro-environment of blood production.

With so many nuclear weapons stockpiled on Earth today, and with so many nuclear power plants in operation, fundamental questions about how blood is produced now involve the interests of all mankind. And therefore the story should be told in more detail.

Academician A. Ioffe.

Blood production and the immune processes can be prompted externally. For this, it is necessary to build a "house" where blood-producing cells can thrive. Location is not so important. Even a seemingly unsuitable spot will do. The house of the blood-producing cells is bone tissue.

In Fridenshtein's laboratory, scientists remove blood-producing builder cells from marrow and produce pure strains of them in test tubes. That makes it easier to observe how they work. These cell strains are then implanted under the skin of an animal, for example, or under the capsule of a kidney, or under the cornea. Of course there is not

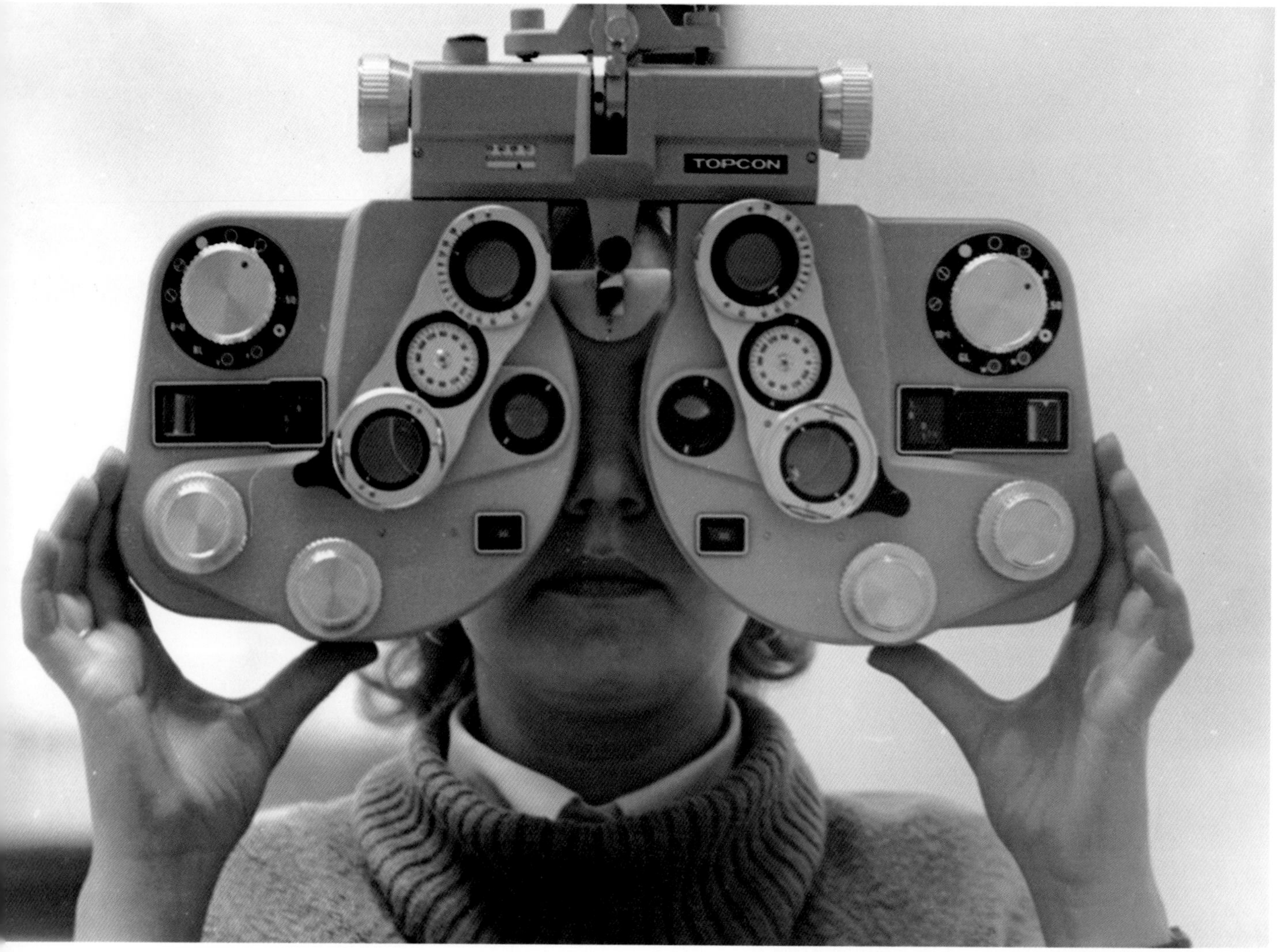

supposed to be any bone in such places, but the transplanted cells quickly form new bone tissue there. The builder cells, having set up in a new house, create the necessary conditions, which scientists call the micro-environment.

I had heard about the micro-environment long ago, from Yelena Luriya, Fridenshtein's wife and closest co-worker. (Fridenshtein's laboratory has been investigating this problem for twenty years.)

St. Petersburg—the turn of the century—the Academy of Military Medicine. A man in a general's uniform strides into a lecture hall. His step is

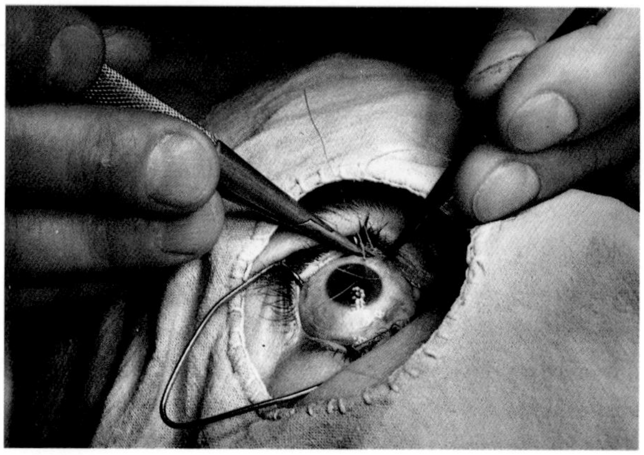

At the Eye Microsurgery Institute, under the direction of S. Fyodorov.

springy, his shoulders straight, his head high. (Yelena tells it as if she had seen everything with her own eyes.) With the elusive gesture of a magician he pulls out his potbellied gold watch and flings it on the table as he crosses the threshold. At the moment when he reaches the blackboard, the watch, after pirouetting dizzily on its side, comes to a dead halt one millimeter from the table's edge.

Professor Aleksandr Maksimov, brilliant general and unsurpassed horseman, was also a virtuoso experimenter, a hard-working scientist, and one of the founders of modern hematology. The idea of a micro-environment for blood-producing cells came originally from him.

In 1922 he went to Chicago, received an endowed professorship, and founded the American school of hematology.

That was how Yelena told it. I had made her acquaintance through her father, Aleksandr Luriya. His American colleagues call Luriya the Beethoven of psychology. His good friend and teacher, Lev Vygotsky, is called the Mozart of psychology. Luriya founded neuropsychology—a new science, born in our country. He also had a literary gift; he wrote easily and vividly. I don't know why he trusted me, when I was just making my journalistic debut, to write the first popular account of his work. He was studying ensembles in the brain responsible for reading, writing, calculating, and speech. These areas are like a mighty and well-rehearsed orchestra, in which every instrument has its part to play. If one of them falls silent, the whole symphony is spoiled.

Unfortunately, the path to knowledge of brain systems serving the higher psychic functions has always lain through their loss, through misfortune and tragedy: wounds, tumors, trauma.

He was tall, light on his feet, always hurrying. I had trouble keeping up. We were almost running down an endlessly long corridor at the Institute of Neurosurgery. Luriya suddenly stopped and opened the door to a ward. We went in.

An emaciated man sat bolt upright in his bed. I will always remember the burning eyes above his pale, sunken cheeks—and his childlike, apologetic smile.

It was Lev Landau.

Why is it that apples are so magical? Could it be that apples are discoveries?

In childhood, we discover the world. (Taking the apple from the tree, Adam and Eve came to know life in a new dimension.)

In youth—love. (The apple of Paris.)

In maturity—responsibility. (Heracles felt its full weight when he took the sky on his shoulders.)

In our own children—the secret of childhood. (William Tell's apple.)

And finally, we discover truth—if, of course,

Academicians N. Amosov and S. Fyodorov.

the luck is there. (The kind of luck Newton had with his apple.)

Having thrown these world-famous fruits into one basket, let's pause to think a bit.

Everybody makes discoveries. But everybody must make his own discoveries for himself.

The stories about apples hold the wisdom of the ages, food for the imagination. But if you want to know the taste, pick an apple and eat it—your own apple.

Budker invented a stabilized, relativistic bundle of electrons—a brightly shining ring, finer than a human hair, suspended in space. He invented a magnetic bottle for the containment of plasma. He also told how it would be possible to produce anti-matter on our planet. But probably his most important discovery—the round table—was an instrument that could turn ordinary people into a

Academician Nikolai Semenov, Nobel prize winner in chemistry, 1956.

most extraordinary creative group.

The "Knights of the Round Table" gathered every day at noon. The average age at the institute was under thirty. Aleksandr Skrinsky, the institute's director, became an academician at thirty-four. The knights were full of high spirits, amiable, with a sense of inner freedom and of their own worth. But the essence was not in form, not in ritual. A creative scientific group must be headed by scientists! Scientists must have the deciding voice.

Discussion at the round table was businesslike but informal, over a cup of coffee. The subject might be a new scientific project, a new employee, the building of living quarters, or the world situation. From time to time bursts of laughter would accompany the witticisms, funny stories, puns, and flights of fancy. There would be passionate controversies; sometimes it would take days to reach an agreement. Doggedly, patiently, they learned to think independently so that they could think as a group. And not a day went by without the propagation of good will, tolerance, and love. People walked into the director's office unannounced, whenever they liked. It was always crowded and noisy, some discussion was constantly under way.

Sketching on a piece of paper Budker explained, "If the administration stands with its face to the director, I don't have to tell you what part will be facing the scientist. But the scientist is the star of the show. In our institute, the whole administrative apparatus, including the director, faces the scientist." He was categorically opposed to letting the institute's administrative staff get too large; paper-pushing could be a terrible and dangerous brake on real work. Science and bureaucracy are incompatible! He even put forward a "proposal" to remove all the bureaucrats from their jobs and send them to a Black Sea resort, at full pay. He was sure the benefits for science, and the savings, would be unprecedented.

Karl Strauch, the noted Harvard physicist, was on his first visit to Novosibirsk. A young man came to pick him up at his hotel. At the institute, the director was already waiting for them. They sat down at the big round table. The director said he would like to begin by giving his personal views on a number of problems in physics. Hearing this, the young man immediately got to his feet. "I've heard all this many times. I'll leave you now and come back in an hour," he announced. And he left, with the director's complete approval.

"Where in the USA, in what laboratory, could something like that happen?" Strauch wondered in amazement. "And this is the USSR! It goes to show the fantastic spirit that has been created at this institute."

The Americans pride themselves on being democratic. Once an American guest in our home (I don't remember just who) remarked: "Ours is the most democratic country in the world. How did the most democratic laboratory in the world end up in Siberia?"

Budker developed one of the four effective models for a creative scientific work group and put it into practice. The other three models belong to Bohr, Kapitsa, and Kurchatov. So says the noted theoretical physicist Yakov Smorodinsky. He was recently asked why the first "Why?" came about. How can the origin of science be explained in simple terms?

"Science is the child of democracy," Smorodinsky answered unhesitatingly. "As soon as the ancient Greeks were able to discuss the laws of government, they began discussing the laws of nature as well."

When Andrei Sakharov was under a cloud, he nonetheless received repeated invitations to come to Novosibirsk, to work in the institute there, to teach in the university.

A hospital intensive-care unit.

The space age began a little later than did the nuclear age. The nuclear age began with the atom bomb; space exploration began with the first sputnik. We were the pioneers. That was only thirty-odd years ago—less than half a lifetime. Today, though, nobody thinks anything of being able to circle the globe in an hour and a half. (It took me that long, using public transportation, to get from one end of Moscow to the other, from the Institute for Space Research to the offices of this book's publisher.)

It was night in our country when the Americans landed on the moon. The control room at Central Television was unusually crowded and quiet. Beside me was the astrophysicist Vladimir Kurt. He had called earlier that day, pleading in an unsteady voice: "I don't care what it takes. This is something I have to see!"

Space is a great teacher. There is nowhere else to learn about prolonged weightlessness or an ultrahigh vacuum. But the main thing, it seems to me, is the new consciousness connected with space. In economic thinking, for example. The costs of experiments in space are on a scale with the national budgets of industrialized countries. That is why our ambitious Vega and Phobos projects have multiple goals. The first Phobos station went into operation in July of 1988. These stations have several important missions; they will study the Sun, interplanetary space, Mars and its satellites, and more.

A Soviet-American expedition to Mars is under discussion. The very idea of such a thing is breathtaking.

It is something else, however, that concerns me most. One wrong line of computer code can result in a complete breakdown on the conveyor of a large factory. One lost comma in a program can delay the launching of a space mission. No need even to mention Chernobyl; the memory is too fresh, too painful.

Complex technology makes demands on humanity. Responsibility, honesty, and decency have ceased to be mere virtues; they are required professional qualifications.

But however high the moral level, a human being is liable to mistakes and slips. He may be tired, or upset over a fight with his wife, or suffering from insomnia. Machines should then come to the rescue, devices that are "idiot-proof." This, by the way, is one of the important lessons of Chernobyl.

One fine summer's day in Novosibirsk, a jet flew under a bridge crossing the Ob River and soared up into the clouds. If the pilot had miscalculated by so much as a centimeter, the great bridge joining the river's banks would have collapsed. Hundreds of the cars that endlessly pass back and forth on it would have been wrecked; buildings would have toppled (the incident occurred downtown); boats on the river would have sunk; many, many people would have perished.

But none of that happened. Stirred by the jet's passage, a wave of river water licked nervously at the bank, wetting the clothing of several bathers. The day was hot and sunny, and the city beaches were as packed with people as a pie filling is with poppy seeds.

The aerial stunt was as masterly as it was dangerous. The pilot, it turned out, had spent years preparing for it—estimating, calculating, checking. He had stood for hours on the bridge, training his eye, noticing details. He had spent time on the beach under the bridge. He had read and studied. He kept asking, "Can I do it?" Until he answered his own question by repeating Chkalov's famous trick.

But he won no glory. He had talent, but he lacked a sense of responsibility towards people.

It is the same in science. How can we trust "daredevils" at the controls?

Roald Sagdeev, chairman of the Committee of Soviet Scientists to Defend Peace Against the Nuclear Threat: "There is much discussion about the militarization and demilitarization of space. The question is highly topical. It is interesting that Andrei Budker, with his vivid imagination and eye towards the future, pointed out back in the sixties that this question could become urgent and vexing. In particular, I remember him saying that even the Moon, in the wrong hands, could become something very close to a military base. He [also] worried that what physicists were doing with accelerators—he made an enormous contribution to that field—could be used for military ends in space. Beam weapons were of special concern; we had many talks about them."

Why is it we return to the famous legends about apples? I put that question to the writer Feliks Krivin.

"At least three of the five apples can be united under a common idea," he answered. "I mean Newton's apple, and the apple of the knowledge of good and evil, and the apple of discord. It could be that the Earth, for us, is all three. It is the apple of earthly gravitation, since there is nowhere for us to go away from our Earth. And sometimes a gravitation towards good goes so far that it becomes a gravitation towards evil, since the apple, like the Earth, is round. It is that gravitation beyond good to evil that turns the apple we share into the apple of discord. Gravitation towards good that turns into evil—that is the story of modern science."

Our tragedy—Chernobyl: "Forbidden Zone."

Scientists know, if anyone does, what nuclear missiles really are. They were the first to see that a new kind of thinking was absolutely necessary.

I talked about that with Stanislav Rodionov. He tested the idea of "magnetic corks," performing classic experiments that are now recounted in every textbook on plasma physics. Today Rodionov is well known as an active member of the International Committee of Scientists for Peace. "If the politicians and generals are not given timely counsel by scientists, they could mess things up. Take for example our whole military policy, which until just recently was based on the principle: 'Do the same thing as the Americans. Even if you can't do it as well, do more.' That leads straight into a trap, and we often fell in.

"The turning point was the question of Star Wars. Right after Reagan's speech, in March of 1983, Soviet scientists organized a committee to

The nuclear power plant at Chernobyl.

give authoritative, expert appraisals of complicated political situations connected with high-tech. It was this committee that suggested an asymmetrical response to the Star Wars program. In the mid-eighties, this became our official policy."

Humanity has always tried to look into the future. Isn't this because the ability to foresee events, to anticipate them in thought—that primordial trait of reason—is built into our genetic makeup? The ancient Greeks made pilgrimages to temples, listened amidst the rustle of the sacred oaks and laurels for the voice of prophecy. In our times the temples (of science) are built from type designs. Communion with the electronic oracle is part of hundreds of people's jobs; the everyday name for it is *programming*.

It seems to me that the main purpose of science, its highest obligation to humanity, lies in foresight and prognosis—especially in our times.

With the aid of computers, scenarios of future events have already been played out in the USA and in our country. (Naturally, they take as their starting points the confusions, hopes, and concerns of today.) An empty Earth plunged in dark and cold—that will be the outcome of the tragedy, even if only a hundredth part of the nuclear stockpiles is used.

"The film is finished. All that remains is to shoot it." That was the favorite saying of a great modern director. God forbid that someone should decide to shoot the scenario entitled *Nuclear Winter.*

But is nuclear danger the only threat to our planet? The ozone layer is already depleted above some regions of the Earth, and harmful emissions into the atmosphere above several cities already exceed the tolerable norm by factors of ten. Already we have witnessed countless natural and climactic disasters. It seems that keeping the Earth from dying because of mankind's everyday activities is immeasurably more complicated than doing away with the threat of nuclear war. The latter is only one part of a danger demanding that we act together, regardless of class or social differences. Science has realized this. That is why our only hope lies in uniting science and politics.

"The first Americans were Siberians!" That is how American newspapermen summarized the findings of the first joint Soviet-American archaeological expedition, which worked at Lake Baikal and on the Aleutian Islands in the early seventies. When the Soviet team returned from America, I interviewed its leader, Academician Aleksei Okladnikov, the renowned historian and archaeologist of Siberia.

The geologists say that Asia and America were united by a so-called Bering land-bridge in at least two periods. It is not impossible that thirty or thirty-five thousand (or perhaps as much as a hundred thousand) years ago, the first discoverers of America crossed over that bridge, following the mammoths and woolly rhinoceroses. America's native peoples—the Indians, Inuit, and Aleuts—are anthropologically similar to the oldest residents of Siberia.

Would the archaeologists confirm this view of the Columbuses of the New World?

Okladnikov recollects: "On the Aleutian Island of Anangula—that means 'whale swimming to the north'—we found no less than twenty-seven Ushkov spear tips (a special type of weapon named after Lake Ushkov, on the Kamchatka Peninsula, where it was first discovered). We were delighted! Here was convincing material evidence of the kinship between two continents. Later a representative from the Aleutian Islands defended the rights of the native population in Congress for two solid hours, using our findings to support his arguments."

I gave an account of this in a piece called "The View from the Bering Bridge" (*Izvestia*). It ended with the reflection that different kinds of bridges ought to be built between the two continents. At the time, though, that seemed an almost unrealizable dream.

In 1965, the first laboratory experiments with colliding beams were done at Novosibirsk and Stanford. The Soviet team was completely "green"; to get the job done they moved to Siberia, far from the supervisors and authorities of the capital. The Americans had to move from California to Alaska.

In 1967, the Siberian physicists were the first in

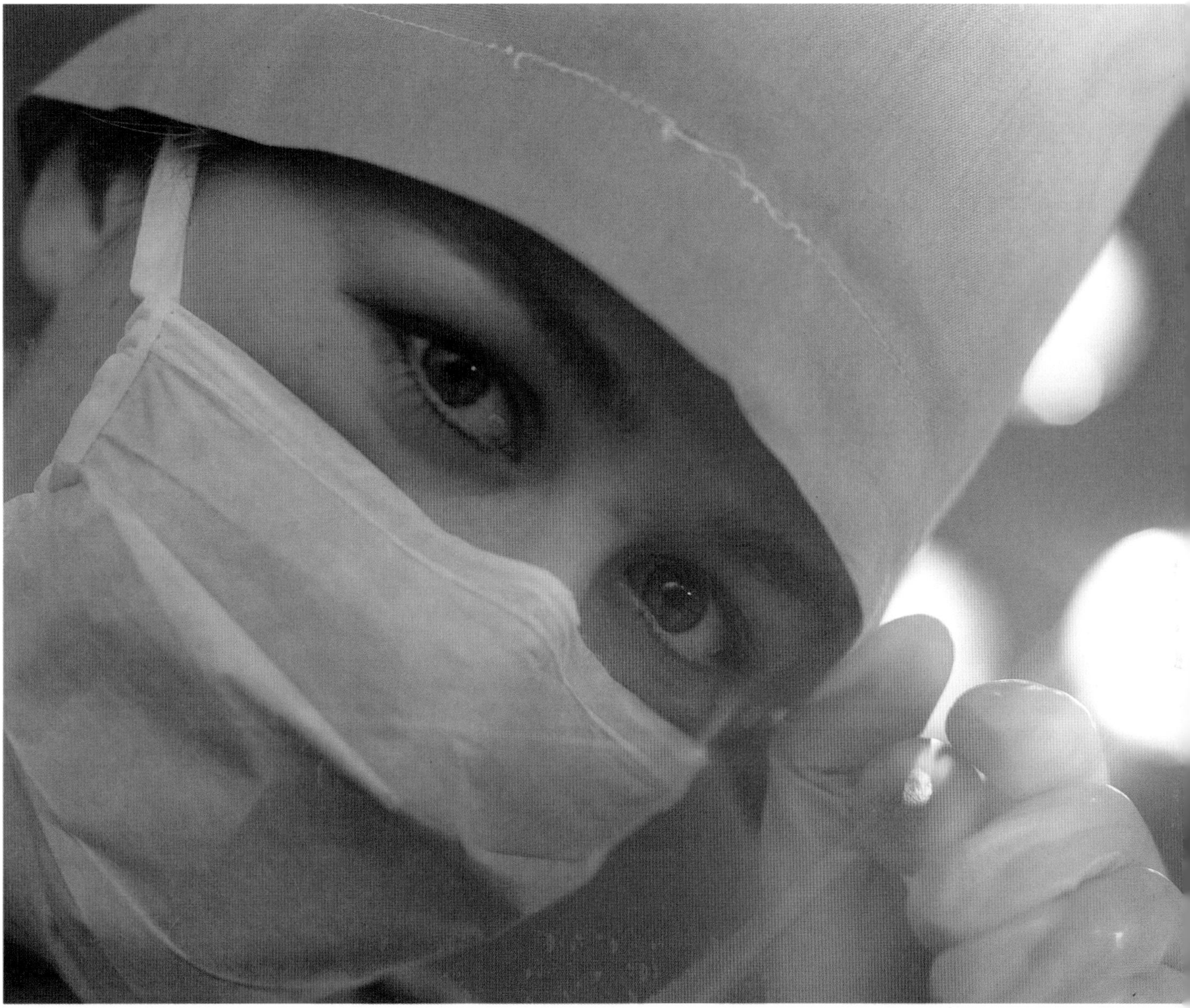

Laser technology—vital to today's medicine.

the world to begin studying the interaction of matter and anti-matter in accelerators with colliding beams. Making beams collide is like having William Tell shoot an arrow from Earth while Robin Hood shoots another from a satellite of Sirius—and having the arrows meet, tip to tip.

Is it because we are playing follow the leader that we lose so often? When loud challenges were being issued to "overtake and surpass" the Americans, the scientists in Novosibirsk put forth a slogan of their own: "Surpass without overtaking!" The only kind of competition they would recognize was the competition of original ideas. Only a new approach could give a chance at victory. After all, the West has many more opportunities for successful experimental work; our technology is at a low level.

Nobel Prize Laureate Burton Richter, director of the Stanford Linear Accelerator Center, has noted that the physics of high energy owes the development of the colliding-beam method to three groups of physicists: the American association in Princeton and Stanford, Budker and his colleagues in Novosibirsk, and the Italian group in Frascati. Richter says the method's success can be judged from the fact that all new ultra-high energy accelerators being built today use colliding beams. These devices are bringing in the lion's share of new knowledge about the properties of matter.

Academician Andrei Budker.

Some American physicists who had never met Budker before were visiting Akademgorodok. Andrei took pleasure in showing them our house in the woods and bragging about the garden he kept himself. Soon I appeared, and Andrei introduced me to our guests, mentioning that until recently I had worked in Moscow as a commentator on Central Television. I quote him on what happened next: "You know, they immediately lost all interest in me [Budker]. Turned their backs on me, even. After all, their conception of a television commentator is somebody who makes presidents!" The recollection always amused him.

He wasn't "jealous" for long. By the time we sat down at the table, he was telling the Americans how once during *News Relay* (a program I anchored in the sixties), Brezhnev, in a long, long close-up that filled the entire screen, had suddenly burst into song in the voice of a popular Bulgarian crooner. "Just a technical foul-up," said Andrei, "But if it had happened in Stalin's time, and not in 1968, I would certainly have been shot as the future husband of the show's anchor, even though I didn't even know her back then!"

In years, Budker was the oldest member of the Novosibirsk team of young physicists. It was recognized by all, however, that he was in spirit the youngest. He would be seventy now, and I often think of the turn his life might have taken if they had suggested he resign as director because of his age.

The old men leave. They leave their positions, it is said, not science. It often turns out, though, that they are leaving life. Among the departed are scientists who worked with Kapitsa, Landau, Kurchatov, Korolev, and Semenov. The true academic spirit was still alive in them. They were dedicated to science itself, not to words about its uninterrupted development. They hated the meddling of administrators and bureaucrats. They were decent, honest. Their code of honor commanded them to be citizens.

Who would have conceived the notion that the Institute of Nuclear Physics, people who look into accelerators—those gigantic microscopes of modern science—should be entrusted with the tiniest motes of creation? That nuclear physicists should concern themselves with protecting grain from pests, working on new ways to bombard cancerous cells, or tackling the problem of sewage treatment? No one. They have undertaken such things themselves.

I think of Aleksandr Yanshin, the world-famed geologist. At age seventy-seven, he ought to be

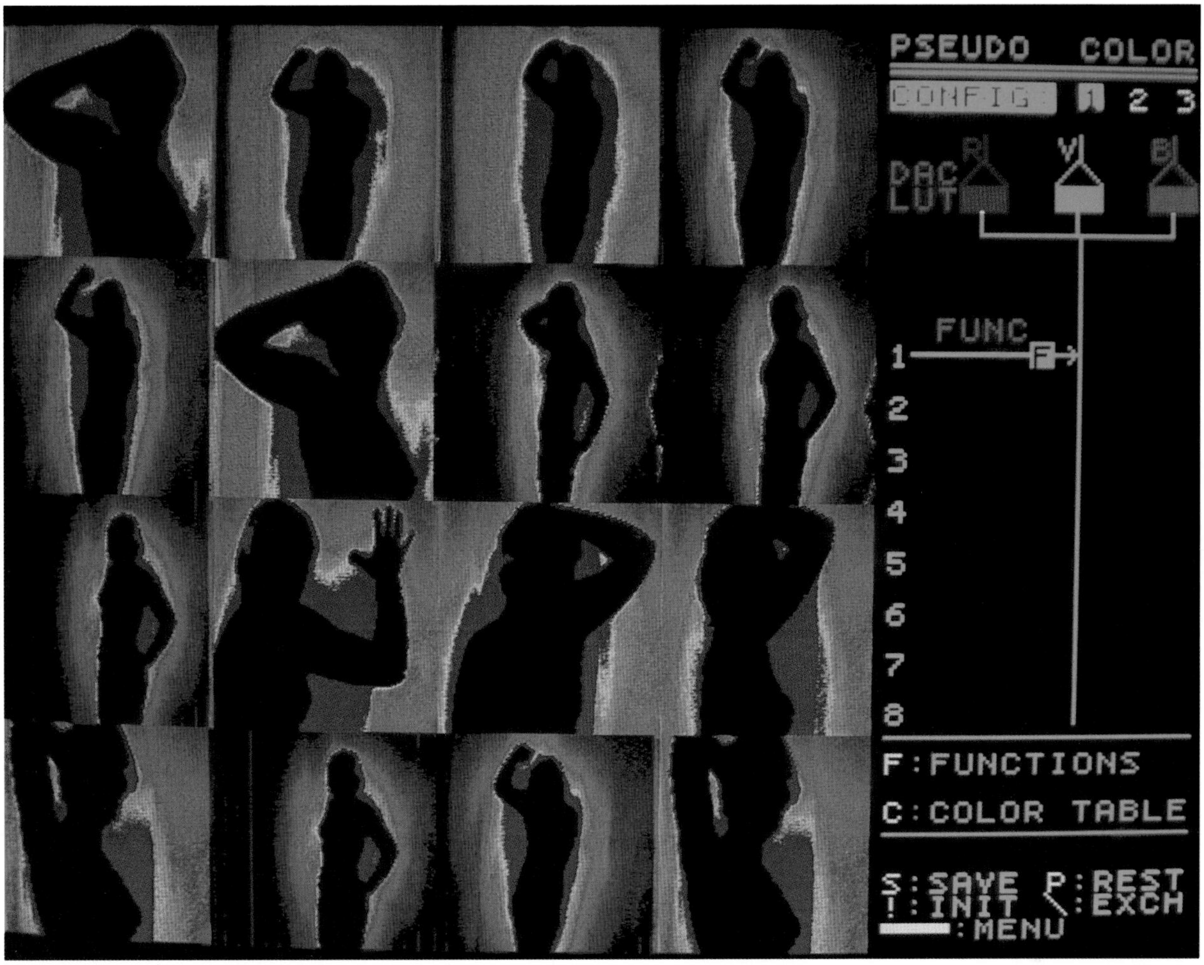

Computer-assisted tomography.

enjoying some peace and quiet, taking pleasure trips, or reading Gumilev, whom he adores. (I believe he has the best collection of editions of that poet.) But no!

The airplane circles and circles above the Aral Sea. The view down below is an absurdism—the only name for it—snow in the middle of summer, ships on the sand. The sea is asking for help, for water. The shoreline has receded tens of kilometers. The water level has dropped twelve meters, leaving salty "snow" and ships on dry land.

Yanshin (the man must be nuclear-powered) has thrown himself into the emergency. He is convinced that the sea can be rescued, if only narrow local interests, routinism, and indifference can be overcome. Once before, he did just that, persuading officials to scrap a major plan to turn northern rivers southwards. Yanshin (working without compensation, for the public good) headed an expert commission made up of ranking scientists. They wrote a detailed, carefully argued letter to the Politburo, explaining why the plan must be stopped. And they won, even though very powerful people and agencies were against them.

So then, let me continue my "typology" of the scientist. The scientist knows how to connect disparate things—things that are far removed from one another, possibly alien in nature. That is important.

Imagine a man from Russia traveling to Poland

in the early sixties and watching, delighted, as Polish teen-agers do the twist. What comes after that? You'll never guess!

Returning home, he launches a campaign: "We must travel to distant villages, to lonely whistle-stops, even to places above the Arctic Circle, in search of children with a talent for science!"

And that is how the school for physics and mathematics in Novosibirsk's Akademgorodok got its start.

To go on, then. A sense of humor is absolutely necessary.

"We know how Kapitsa joked, and Bohr, and Kurchatov. But nobody knows the jokes bad officials play." The aphorism belongs to Yakov Smorodinsky.

Budker meets Sagdeev on the stairs: "Why did you oppress our Russia for three hundred years?" (Sagdeev is a Tatar.)

Sagdeev is never at a loss for words: "Why did you crucify our Christ?"

In every joke there is a portion of joke and a portion of truth. Both men—Tatar and Jew—share the same Russia, and the same faith in it.

During the sixties, some French physicists were visiting Moscow. At the Academy of Sciences, people advised them to go to Novosibirsk and have a look.

"Isn't that where Budker is? No, we absolutely refuse! We hate him!" (They were actually trembling with indignation.)

"You mean to say you know him?"

"No, and we don't want to. It's enough that De Gaulle knows him. We asked De Gaulle for research funds, and he told us: 'I was in Siberia not long ago. There's a man named Budker there. He earns his own research money.' So we got nothing from De Gaulle."

Yes, the first experiments with pay-your-own-way basic research begain in the sixties, in the Novosibirsk institute. Unlike other nuclear physicists, the Novosibirisk team made its own accelerators.

The search for a device for research into matter and anti-matter necessarily leads through intermediate models. Back in the early sixties (when basic research was booming at the institute), the director suggested selling the intermediate models to industry and agriculture and investing the profits in the development of science. That would be to the benefit of all!

He got his way. The institute was allowed to try the experiment.

To produce industrial accelerators, it was necessary to make calls at government offices. Once, Budker found himself in Kosygin's office. The premier was a very busy man, extremely laconic.

"How much money do you need?"

Budker named the sum.

"That's too much. I'll give you half."

"But then we won't be able to keep the commitments we've made to agriculture. . . ."

"What has agriculture to do with accelerators?" Kosygin was genuinely perplexed. Evidently he was certain that talk about economic benefits was pure fluff, a device to get money for science.

"An accelerator in the grain elevator at Odessa, for instance, protects the grain from pests."

Kosygin asked his secretary to connect him with Odessa. No doubt the man on the other end had good things to say about the machine from Siberia. Now Kosygin looked with even more amazement at this academician asking for funds.

Budker then proposed an economic structure that would make it beneficial for science to work hand-in-hand with the economy. The money earned this way in the first few years went to build new laboratories and apartment houses, and there were considerable raises for everyone at the institute. The ugly truth, however, is that this made some of the other directors envious, even hostile. They did their best to "forbid"—or at least limit—the nuclear scientists' initiative and ambition.

When things got really bad, and Budker had no more strength to struggle with the higher-ups, he began to think about organizing a science center in some new place. But he was not just longing to escape the burdens of dogma and prejudice. He saw the new project in larger human terms. Science, production, and a university organized along new lines could inspire the revival of a region, bring the young people back, reawaken in-

Academician Andrei Sakharov.

terest in the land, and aid in intelligent management.

He chose a region with poor soil, at the center of Russia—Smolensk. He hurried off to the writer Sergei Zalygin, his friend: "Sergei Pavlovich, you must go to Smolensk and talk the officials into this. A writer's word counts for more than anybody's!" (Zalygin was one of those who had helped stop the diversion of the northern rivers. He is now editor-in-chief of *Novy Mir.*) Budker worked hard at pushing his project through. He got advice from the best economists and sociologists in the State Planning Commission and the Council of Ministers. He left behind a detailed plan—a program, rather—for creating a new center at Smolensk that would crystalize the experience of the people, their wisdom, historical memory, and culture, around the serious business of modern science, industry, and farming.

Talking once with Tengiz Abuladze, creator of the film *Repentance,* I asked what *perestroika* meant to him. "A return to good sense," was his answer.

Everything that Budker did, or tried to do, was filled with good sense. As a man who had emerged from the people, he could rely on the experience of centuries. Just as in a strong family everything should be decided in common, with no secrets, so Budker knew that life too should be governed by conscience, and the conduct of affairs by good sense. In this way, the individual profits and others benefit. What is this but *glasnost,* democracy, the new economic thinking—everything that today we call *perestroika*? The nuclear scientists at Novosibirsk were doing all this twenty years before the rest of us began talking about it.

The *Buran* returning to the Cosmodrome.

It is a mistake to think that people see the light beginning with some one day, event, or order.

In the twenties, the scientists working at "Papa Ioffe's kindergarten," as the Leningrad Physico-Technical Institute was nicknamed, included Kapitsa, Semenov, Landau, Frenkel, Kurchatov, Aleksandrov, Khariton, Alikhanov, and Zeldovich—more than half of Soviet physics, its brightest minds. And this is only a partial list.

Two unknown young men appeared at the studio of the celebrated Kustodiev. At the time, a portrait of Chaliapin stood on his easel. "Why are you always painting famous people?" they demanded. "Paint our portraits. We will be famous too." Kustodiev laughed and agreed. He painted them together on a single canvas, Nikolai Semenov and Petr Kapitsa.

If someone had the task of giving out legendary apples, the apple of parental love would surely go to Abram Ioffe. Unlike God in the Bible, he forbade his children nothing and did not interfere with them. All he did was help. He helped them to stand up, to take risks. Sometimes his children were struck down by an arrow. He could not save all of them from arrest, from destruction.

People are not the same. Each one is irreplaceable. Talent does not need to be created. It needs to be recognized and allowed to develop freely.

In Kurchatov, Ioffe recognized a genius for organizing scientific work. It was he who recommended the young physicist to head up work on the atomic problem. At the time, many people could not see why Ioffe did so.

Soviet atomic physics was born in the Leningrad Physico-Technical Institute. The interests—scientific and human—of many great physicists coalesced in that work.

Semenov, author of the theory of chain reactions, gave his two best students to the atomic problem: Yuli Khariton and Yakov Zeldovich.

Landau, together with other leading physicists, "worked out" the hydrogen bomb. Landau's life had been saved by Kapitsa. In the spring of 1938, the young physicist was arrested. Risking everything he had, Kapitsa wrote to Stalin and Molotov. In a letter to Beria, he asked that Landau be released on Kapitsa's "personal guarantee." On April 28, 1939, a year to the day after his imprisonment, Landau was released.

Kapitsa was involved in work on the atom bomb from the very beginning. Very soon, however, he found it impossible to tolerate the high-handedness of Lavrenti Beria, the project's curator. He flatly refused to work under "a conductor who could not read the score." The remark became known, and Beria would not pardon it. Kapitsa was separated from the institute, his own child. Still, they didn't dare kill him; he was too important a figure.

Once, as a present, Kapitsa received a Newton apple, along with the appropriate documentation. This was in 1969, in Canada. There is an apple tree there, it seems, directly descended from the legendary tree that dropped its fruit on the head of the genius.

Kapitsa passed the present along to our botanists, so they too could grow a tree from its seed.

I wonder if they succeeded.

It was Kurchatov who shielded Budker from Beria, saving his life. "He is an especially dangerous criminal. But let him live for now. We will still find time to chop off his head." These words of Beria's became known later. Back then, in the early fifties, Budker was "only" denied access to the important work being done on his ideas, some of it his own.

When Beria was shot, certain singularly important files, which he had wanted to keep track of himself, were found in his hidden safe. Among them was Budker's dossier.

Budker often said: "I was hanging by a whisker in Kurchatov's beard."

Not long before his death, Ioffe ceased to be director of the Leningrad Physico-Technical Institute. He was informed in a peculiar way: they boarded up the door leading from his apartment to the director's office.

> A lifetime's just enough to savor
> How bitter the forbidden fruit.

They showed it on television: The French have invented an apple-harvesting machine. Color is included in the robot's program; it picks only the ripe fruit.

Won't even one apple fall onto the head of another Newton?

Sports

GERALD EARLY is associate professor of English and Afro-American Studies at Washington University in St. Louis, Missouri. He received the Whiting Foundation Writer's Award in 1988, and his first book, *Tuxedo Junction: Essays on American Culture*, is being published in 1990 by The Ecco Press. He is currently finishing a study of boxing entitled *The Culture of Bruising: Essays Toward a Definition of Literature, Prizefighting, and Modern American Culture.*

TEYMURAZ MAMALADZE is a journalist and essayist as well as the author of several nonfiction books. A newspaperman for many years, he worked with *Komsomol Pravda* in Moscow, first as special correspondent for Georgia, then as head of the art and literature department. He left the newspaper to return to Tbilisi, where he headed the Telegraph Agency of Georgia. Now back in Moscow, he is an assistant minister in the USSR Ministry of Foreign Affairs. Mamaladze's books include *Tbilisi: Legends and Truths; You, My Vine;* and *Tango Spain*. He is completing a book on soccer entitled *A Ball Autographed by Maradona* and is working on a projected study of Georgian artist Pirosmanishvili. He is a frequent contributor to the magazines *Film Art* and *Smena* and to foreign periodicals.

House of Ruth, House of Robinson: Some Observations on Baseball, Biography, and the American Myth

GERALD EARLY

The most marvelous gift of sports is its faculty for making heroes of underdogs, of lifting the downtrodden up to solid ground.

A. S. Young, *Negro Firsts in Sports* (1963)

For they had much rather see us engaged in those degrading sports, than to see us behaving like intellectual, moral, and accountable beings.

Frederick Douglass, *Narrative of the Life of Frederick Douglass, An American Slave* (1845)

The Ineffable National Pastime; the Expressible National Character

The following tableaus are about baseball, one of the sports I know best, and one that (along with boxing) perhaps defines and reflects the complexities of American culture better than any other. There is little here about the sport itself. The examination is centered on baseball's political, social, and cultural meaning. I leave it to wiser and more scholarly heads than mine to talk about sports as philosophy, as play, as performance, as economic enterprise, or in relation to American history.

It is one of the persistent ironies in our culture that athletic endeavor, such a speechless act, should generate such need for narrative, for language, for story—from the coach's pep talk to the sportswriter's column; from the television sports announcers who describe actions readily seen to sports talk shows and "open lines" that discuss events which, for the most part, are settled on the field of play. What is remarkable about the rise of professional sports in America (beyond the increasingly exacting specialization among athletes themselves) is that the popularity of athletics would not have been possible without the progressive technology of endlessly reproducing discourse about it: newspapers, radio, television, VCRs. The far-reaching varieties of discourse about sports signify not only our commitment to athletics but also our commitment to language as metaexperience; once the athletic event has ended, the discourse about it displaces the event. The event becomes the shadow.

Everyone knows, for instance, that as a young man Ronald Reagan worked as a baseball announcer. He was a very good one, describing games he himself did not see, simply embellishing

Douglas Tilden, *The Baseball Player,* 1888–89.

J. L. Magee, *The Second Great Match Game for the Championship,* 1866.

stark summations he received off a ticker tape. There he sat at the microphone, speaking threads and threads of narrative, shaping drama like a blind Homer. It is fitting that this collective fantasizing should revolve around baseball, which promotes a gamut of fantasies from old-timers' games and daydreamers' camps to card and board games, from professional sports' most publicized All-Star Games to computer match-ups. What Reagan did as a broadcaster is what most rabid baseball fans do; namely, work backward from the facts and statistics and reconstruct the entire narrative structure of ball games, for ball games are insistently and relentlessly narrative. One must not simply *know* baseball; one must *tell* it. Baseball is one of two sports that seek to be an omnipresent—and sometimes ominous—metalanguage. (Boxing is the other.) It is in this maze of fantasy that the hero of Robert Coover's *The Universal Baseball Association, Inc., J. Henry Waugh, Prop.* (1968) finds himself. Our enjoyment of baseball, and of sports generally, is inextricably bound to story, to rhetoric, to conversation, to dialogue, to pure fussing about how the event actually was and how it should be told. The Greeks were right: in a fundamental and timeless way, sports are about our being human, about our being what we are. Only a barbarian would hate sports.

"Sports give people things to talk about other than the inadequacy and unhappiness of their lives," someone once told me. Sports do even more: they give people, specifically men, a language *in* which to talk as well as a language *about* which to prate. Often, sitting in the company of older men during my boyhood, I wondered what would there be to talk about if professional sports did not exist. Discussion and argument were bountiful and eternal about all sorts of questions

The presidential pitch—tossing the first ball at the opening game. President William Howard Taft, 1910.

athletic: how big were Sonny Liston's fists; which was the better local high school basketball team, West Philadelphia or Overbrook; which records did Wilt Chamberlain set at Overbrook High; were the Washington Redskins a racist team; why did the Philadelphia Eagles trade Sonny Jurgenson; who was the better Eagle running back, Timmy Brown or Tom Woodeshick; why could local light-heavyweight Harold Johnson never beat Archie Moore; why could local middleweight Bennie Briscoe never win a title; who was the better center, Bill Russell or Wilt Chamberlain; why was Joey Giardello a pretty good fighter "for a white boy"; who was the better baseball player, Hank Aaron, Willie Mays, or Roberto Clemente; why were the current crop of black ball players (circa the early and middle 1960s) not as good as the old Negro league players; why were current black ball players better than current white ball players; why were old-time Negro league players better than old-time white players; who was the best fighter, Jack Johnson, Sugar Ray Robinson, or Joe Louis?

Around and around the talk went, swirls and eddies, torrents and streams, which, as a youngster, I found both fascinating and enriching, foolish and funny, learned and exhibitionist by turns. "Dammit, nigger, can't you get it through your thick head? Wasn't no way on earth Louis was gonna beat Lil Arthur! Ain't nobody was ever born who was a better defensive fighter than Jack Johnson. Johnson could be hitting you all upside your head and peeling a grape at the same time." "I knows I'm right, man! Josh Gibson got better numbers than Babe Ruth and you can look it up. I got the book at home, man. The book don't lie." "I don't care what nobody say. I *know* that Satchel Paige, in his prime, was a better pitcher than Bob Gibson 'cause I seen 'em both pitch. I know what

President Woodrow Wilson, 1915.

I'm talking about." "It take about five white guys to bring down Jim Brown excepting maybe Sam Huff. You got to give the devil his due there. That Huff is a bad white boy." "How come ain't no colored middle linebackers is what I wants to know. Some colored boys out there be badder than Huff if they give us the chance."

But I was shaken once when, sitting around with the cronies in the local barbershop, one of the guys, Raymond, I think, jumped up and shouted, "Why y'all always sitting around talkin' about these goddam sports? Why don't you talk about something natural that a man is supposed to talk about—like a woman, or a bottle of scotch, or how the world ain't treatin' you right? All this here talking about these jocks and these games ain't natural; it ain't a natural way for one man to talk to another." The fact that the vast majority of athletes experience defeat more commonly than they do victory is why the mystical insistence on unnaturalness is sport's great fascination and great virtue. Alas, the athlete replicates a holistic yet puzzling human experience by giving us the male (and some females) whose vocation and condition are identical. There are two explicit and distinct memories I have of baseball and language.

As a child I remember never discussing baseball with my grandfather, a native of the Bahamas, a short, stern, very black man who, I was told by other family members, was, in his youth, a follower of Marcus Garvey, although I never heard him utter a political word in his life and he has

President Warren G. Harding, 1921.

seemed a particularly accommodating man around whites. I recall one incident I was told several times: during the Depression, in order to feed his quite large family, my grandfather, in desperation, tried to steal some sausages from the local white grocer by stuffing them in his pocket. Such ineptitude made his discovery nearly inevitable. It was painfully embarrassing for him to have to plead his case to the white grocer because my grandfather has always prided himself on being an honest man and on being able to feed his family. The grocer knew my grandfather well and times were hard for everyone, so he did not have him arrested. He simply sent him home. Family members tell the story with a great deal of good-natured humor, although he has never found it funny. I do not recall ever having a real conversation with my grandfather during my entire life, certainly not during my entire childhood. I was too afraid of him.

Yet despite the silence of our relationship he took me to professional baseball games every summer as he was an ardent fan of the sport; in fact, he introduced me to the sport. I remember many a sunny Sunday afternoon (we always seemed to go on a Sunday after church), sitting in Connie Mack Stadium's bleacher section, watching the Philadelphia Phillies play: Johnny Callison making grand catches in right field; Art Mahaffey and his curious windup; Don Demeter fouling balls off his left foot; Dick Stuart, old "Dr. Strangeglove," hitting a homer; the voices of Byrum Saam and Bill

Campbell, the Phillies sports announcers, on radios around the park; Frank Thomas having a racial run-in with Richie (later Dick) Allen; the colorful southpaw Bo Belinsky, who once dated Mamie Van Doren and who, along with pitcher Dean Chance, was, if not one of the playboys of the Western world, certainly one of the most publicized playboys of professional baseball; the less colorful southpaw Dennis Bennet, who never made it; the deadly way Wes Covington cocked his bat before swinging; the two great years Jack Baldshun had as a relief pitcher before being traded away to mediocrity and obscurity.

I hated the Phillies as a boy; virtually every black person I knew felt the same, recalling how the team had treated Jackie Robinson when he first broke into the National League. My grandfather, however, silent and strict-looking, handing out the sandwiches and drinks for our lunch with his usual authority, liked the Phillies a great deal. Perhaps that is why we never spoke to each other about the games. Once, during a twilight double header against the Dodgers (in which Sandy Koufax pitched the first game, winning 6 to 2), he bought me a Phillies yearbook. This was unusual for two reasons: first, we almost never went to night games and, second, he almost never bought anything at the ball park. I had ambivalent feelings about the book; I felt especially treated because my grandfather bought it for me, yet I remember always intensely disliking the *smell* of it. The book always smelled new, even after I had had it for several years. I never read that yearbook; I do not recall even opening it except while standing before my grandfather a few moments after he bought it. I thanked him profusely for buying it. My grandfather bought the book because he knew I liked books about baseball. In fact, I liked them almost more than I liked the game itself.

The books that most readily come to mind from my childhood are Dr. Seuss's *The Cat in the Hat;* L. Frank Baum's *The Wizard of Oz;* Edward Ormondroyd's *David and the Phoenix;* and seemingly miles of juvenile baseball biographies. I would occasionally, if only for the sake of variety, read the biography of an athlete from another sport—the lives of Red Grange, Oscar Robertson, Bobby Hull, A. J. Foyt (if one can consider him an athlete), Benny Leonard, and others. But the baseball biographies were my favorites, and having such books written for young boys was, I suppose, a very profitable market for publishers. Henry Aaron, Willie Mays, Babe Ruth, Lou Gehrig, Joe DiMaggio, Ty Cobb, Walter Johnson, Cy Young, Grover Cleveland Alexander, Felipe Alou, Mickey Mantle—all were presented in ghostwritten, antiseptic volumes that were simply longer versions of articles in *The Sporting News* or *Boys' Life* (Many of the books were autobiographies, but I made no distinction as a boy between self-narrative and reportorial narrative; since all were ghostwritten and all were, in some essential ways, fraudulent works, their core attraction was their *narrativity,* not their authenticity. Or let me say that the books' authenticity was located in something far larger and much more gripping than the normal consideration we give to the nature of biographical writing.) During my boyhood and adolescence, my love for these books was so intense that I once had a fistfight with my friend William Bradshaw over a Warren Spahn biography he had been given. I knew he was not interested in baseball and I wanted him to give the book to me. In fact, I demanded it. He refused to give it to me, so we fought. He, being both stronger and bigger, easily beat me. What is so surprising and dismaying about this in retrospect is that I was very shy and timid as a boy. It is still hard for me to comprehend how I could have been so aggressive about something that did not belong to me.

I learned a certain sort of factual information from these books, the sort of information that a boy who loved baseball would want: year-by-year statistics, career statistics, teams played for, best games played, and the like. But it was not for this information alone that I read these books, information that, after all, was condensed on the back of the baseball cards I sometimes collected. It was the sheer redundancy of the paradigmatic lesson, the comfort of knowing that each player's life was like every other player's, that producing the odd oxymoron of dull, rooted inspiration. You had to work hard to succeed, the books taught incessantly. You had to be single-minded and dedicated. You had to live a pure, clean life. You had to marry your teen-age sweetheart. If you worked

President Calvin Coolidge, 1927.

hard, you would be rewarded sooner or later. The books became better, infinitely more interesting than watching the games themselves in which I could see many of these athletes play. The games began to seem, in my youthful mind, like the end product, although I still enjoyed them a lot. It was far more vital to learn the story of how a man became an athlete. Once he achieved success, his story was finished. There was something like the Ben Franklin father-to-son story in all of this, and something that reminded me, years later, of F. Scott Fitzgerald's Jay Gatsby writing out his day's schedule, as a boy, on the cover of *Hopalong Cassidy.* I did something similar, writing out a schedule for success when I was about thirteen, on the cover of a juvenile biography of Roy Campanella.

It did not occur to me until I taught *The Great Gatsby* and Hemingway's *The Sun Also Rises* in a freshman English class that the connection between sports and literature is central to understanding what sports are and why they exist. On one level, those books are about the very imposture of our national character and our national myth: blacks, Jews, and Catholics as athletes and sportsmen in *The Sun Also Rises;* the fake-yachtsman, fake-polo-player Gatsby, whose name-change resonates with ethnic overtones; the rich, hard, Yale football star. Tom Buchanan, self-centered and racist; the woman's golf pro Jordan Baker, who cheats and feels no responsibility for her reckelessness. These books are the absolute unraveling (unwriting and rewriting) of the American myth through sports. (It is surely no accident that these books were published in the 1920s, the golden age of American professional and amateur sports, both in terms of mass popularity and the production of mass sportswriting in newspapers.)

Obviously, reading those baseball biographies as a child gave me a very usable mythology of male heroism, much more usable than, say, Greek legends or tall tales of the American frontier. The books also provided me with an orientation toward the culture I was to live in as a man, an orientation that was valuable, if not always honest or harmless. Indeed, the true value of the books as cultural orientation may center in the fact that they are dishonest—one must learn, in some ways, to negotiate their simplistic moralizing, which so distorts the real issues of real life. That I never read sports *fiction* as a child is also quite telling: for me, nothing could be made up that was more exciting than the re-creation of a real athletic career. And the re-creation of that young man-career became, over and over, simply the recitation of games, the story of games. We know that sports are an essential part of our cultural history and social fabric, but it is my contention that the sheer narratability of sports, or, at least, our fixation with their narratability, is, whether we are sports fans or not, the incessant reinvention of ourselves as males in relation to our national myth. The meaning of sports biography (and autobiography) is indelibly tied to its narrative dramatization of our national character as a rite of beautiful young manhood.

About two years ago I saw my grandfather while I was revisiting Philadelphia. It has never been easy for us to talk, but I felt very genial, possibly because my children were with me. I remember turning the conversation to baseball, after he had asked me about living in St. Louis. I talked about the Phillies and was in fact eager to show that I still kept up with the game and even with the local team. When I asked him about their chances that year he gave me a curious, almost childlike look, a wan smile, and said, "Oh, I don't know," as if he hardly thought about baseball anymore. I felt momentarily nonplused. But his eyes seemed almost sad at my discomfort as our conversation fell away, almost as if he felt sorry for me, as if, in the calm center of wisdom, he knew, always knew from my childhood and before, what I would only come to know years later: What is there to say about games anyway?

Baseball and the Hollywood Myth

In 1952, Ronald Reagan starred as pitching-great Grover Cleveland Alexander in *The Winning Team.* The movie is one in a series of whitewashed Hollywood biographies—Alexander, for instance, was an alcoholic, an aspect of his life that was never broached in the film—about ball players made in the forties and early fifties: *The Pride of the Yankees* (the Lou Gehrig story, 1942), *The Babe Ruth Story* (1948), *The [Monty] Stratton Story* (1949), *The Jackie Robinson Story* (1950), and *The Pride of St. Louis* (the Dizzy Dean story, 1952). These movies are montages of bathos and incoherence, displaying the kind of shimmering sentimentality that appealed to moviegoers and baseball fans of the day. And Reagan, the former baseball announcer, has always stood in the middle of that cultural muddle.

Most of these films, incidentally, were made at a time when baseball was undergoing changes both from within and without. A post–World War II boom had made it truly the national pastime, and racial integration had radically altered professional ball by enriching the major leagues while simultaneously destroying the Negro leagues. By serving as historical romances, the films undoubtedly permitted both the baseball establishment and society at large to cope with these drastic changes. Even *The Jackie Robinson Story,* with its cameos of a Tom Sawyer boyhood, Washington, D.C., the flag, and the Statue of Liberty, comforted audiences with the reassurance that, after all, the game was still the same.

It goes without saying that these popular films have little to do with the actual biographies of their subjects. Indeed, the lives of these great players are reduced to the insipidity attendant upon a schoolboy morality, a knight-errantry once removed. Here is the Hollywood fantasy, the chivalric code of human sexuality as the life cycle of virginity, monogamy, and, finally, a heroic death without the taint of guilt or sin. But what these films are really about is not morality but morale. They are about the overcoming of adversity which is, after all, the national creed of American life and what passes here for a reasonable facsimile of morality. The films remind the viewer of American individualism, determination, team spirit, fair play, and resourcefulness. In these films, the baseball player is not simply *good,* he is *inventive.*

But getting back to schoolboy morality, there is something insistent in the perennial boyishness that baseball has successful palmed off on the public as a sense of history and tradition; it is this quality that has attracted so many white male intellectuals to the sport: it does not *remind* them of their childhood so much as it *transfixes* it. In that sense, baseball is nothing more than another symbol of the American's quest for eternal innocence. Witness, for example, the 1984 film, *The Natural,* loosely based upon Bernard Malamud's excellent 1952 novel. In the film version, Roy Hobbs ultimately becomes the golden boy who hits the homerun to win the championship instead of the jerk who both sold out and struck out. This revision conflates the celebration of mythical baseball with the celebration of the clichéd Hollywood baseball film.

President Herbert Hoover, 1932.

And these clichéd virtues, celebrated so unabashedly in baseball films, are precisely the virtues that baseball itself wishes to celebrate, not about American life per se, but about itself. Baseball has never been preoccupied with itself as a game; it has been totally preoccupied with itself as a cultural image, a set of signs that indicates an underlying rhetoric of rectitude. This partly explains the excessive use of signs in baseball: the third-base coach sends signs to the runners on

President Franklin D. Roosevelt, 1936.

base and to the batter; the manager sends signs to his coaches and players; the players in the field signal one another about plays; the catcher signals the pitcher while guarding his signs from the view of the batter or the runners on base, because, in this plenitude of silent instruction, one must always be wary of an enemy who is constantly on the prowl to intercept and steal them. Baseball is a game that loves the labyrinths of its own encoding. Baseball has become, in essence, its own Hollywood film.

It has certainly become its own sign whose signification is clear to everyone. The self-evident nature of baseball's simplistic (and largely fictional) integrity has made it an appropriate image to be exploited by presidential candidates. We remember, for instance, Jimmy Carter's regular softball games with the press in Plains, Georgia, when he was candidate in 1976. In the 1988 presidential campaign, staffers for Democratic candidate Michael Dukakis made sure that newspapers across the country ran a picture of him dressed in a baseball uniform (presumably he played Little League) in a blatant appeal to all those Little League, American Legion, sandlot league parents and former players who could recall the sunlit glory of those bygone days. It was also part of the immigrant drama of Americanization which Dukakis tried to reenact, if somewhat clumsily, before blue-collar voters. In her essay, "Insider Baseball," Joan Didion, trailing Dukakis on the campaign beat, describes a ritual Dukakis seemed

President Harry S. Truman, 1951.

particularly to enjoy: donning his glove and playing catch with someone during a campaign stop. I suppose it was meant to conjure the image of both the beginning and the end of *The Natural,* where Robert Redford's character is first the son playing catch with his father, then the father playing catch with his son. Perhaps there was something strikingly Midwestern and homegrown about this ball-catching stuff. But, like Dukakis himself, it never quite caught on with the public. The symbolism just did not work in a campaign where both candidates were searching for some chord-striking image with the desperation of hungry alley cats in quest of food. Dukakis's ball-catching just seemed a dumb stunt. He did not know the Boston Red Sox, as some Boston reporters complained. (He apparently did not know the Boston Celtics, either, virtually a capital offense in basketball-crazy Beantown.) He really did not know baseball. Some Republican presidential candidates have understood baseball much better.

Baseball and Political Autobiography

Nixon at the Bat

Reading Richard Nixon's first book, *Six Crises* (1962), is a bit like walking in an unrelieved twilight. The truths and lies blend so compellingly and compulsively that the book manages to avoid twisting by turns from self-revelation to nonsense and back. The work *is* self-revelation as the nonsensical pathology of self-defense. The "crises"—the Alger Hiss case; the slush fund scandal when he was selected as Eisenhower's running mate in 1952; Eisenhower's heart attack in 1955; Nixon's violent reception when he toured Latin America as vice president in 1958; meeting Khrushchev; and his first campaign for the presidency in 1960 against Kennedy—are really nothing more than a series of Nixon's public victimizations: character "smears" (a word he uses constantly), adversative relationships as the hallmark of character-testing, the endurance of unjustified physical outrage. It is one of the extraordinary ironies of the book that its writer should be so obsessed with character when he seemingly possesses so little of it; and, moreover, that the book should so persistently argue that character (perhaps politics itself) is a profound psychological formation resulting from emotional overload.

President Dwight D. Eisenhower, 1957.

This mentality, I suggest, results from Nixon's absorption of the ethics of sports. Here was a poor, uncoordinated boy who could not play football but who, at Whittier College, as Fawn Brodie writes, "took a vast amount of brutal punishment for four years," trying to make the team. Trying to make the college football team was, in fact, Nixon's first real crisis and his real public victimization. He grew to love football because it possessed what he saw as the real meaning of sport: crisis management and physical endurance. He believed the old saw that sport builds character. That is why he allowed the stuffings to be knocked out of him everyday in the fall for four years during football practice.

Although Nixon makes metaphorical references to a number of sports in *Six Crises,* including boxing, football, track, and gambling (if one can consider gambling a sport; Nixon was a skilled poker player), I find intriguing two specific allusions to baseball, both made in reference to Soviet Premier Nikita Khrushchev, with whom Vice-President Nixon had his famous "Kitchen Debate" in Moscow in 1959.* The premier is characterized as the consummately canny player:

> I even had the benefit of a preview of what I might expect from Khrushchev when Mikoyan and Kozlov, who occupy the next to the top rung on the ladder of the Soviet hierarchy, visited Washington in the period just before I left for Moscow. They threw some pretty fair fast balls and a few curves in the long conversations I had with each of them. But meeting Khrushchev, after talking with them, was like going from minor to major league pitching. He throws a bewildering assortment of stuff—blinding speed, a wicked curve, plus knucklers, spitters, sliders, fork balls—all delivered with a deceptive change of pace. (p. 236)

*It is interesting to note how much Nixon views his life and his "crises" in terms of adversative rhetorical encounters: debates (Kennedy, the Latin American Communists, Khrushchev); cross-examinations (Alger Hiss, the press during the slush fund episode); speeches before hostile audiences and judges (the slush fund speech, the speeches on the Latin American tour, the self-punishment of the entire 1960 campaign).

President John F. Kennedy, 1961.

President Lyndon B. Johnson, 1964.

But Nixon is up for the game:

> This was the moment for which I had been preparing myself for many months. I was on edge with suspense as I entered Khrushchev's office shortly after 10:00. He was toying with a model of Lunik, the satellite which the Russians had shot off toward the moon several months before. It looked like an oversized baseball in Khrushchev's chubby hands. (p. 250)

Obviously, Khrushchev is the pitcher and Nixon the batter, in the most stark and lonely diagram of adversative contest that Nixon can imagine—a baseball game without fielders, without umpires, without teams, simply the repeated existential wonder of confrontation between a pitcher and a batter, each with an instrument that is meant to be the destruction of the other but is also the other's reason for being, for neither instrument has any meaning without the other or apart from the other. It is the perfect analogy to the theory of "the balance of power" and "mutual deterrence." Moreover, because Nixon sees his confrontation with Khrushchev as an individual-within-a-team (or individual-in-an-embracing-ideology) encounter, the baseball analogy is apt, for baseball is the one team sport that perfectly isolates the individual's drama against the background of the team's fate. Football would not have worked, as Nixon knew. Football is the reenactment of the sweep and boredom of war and conquest; baseball is conflict as the mediation of possibilities.

But Khrushchev is no ordinary pitcher. He has an impossible assortment of pitches that no real pitcher has ever possessed. Whoever heard of a knuckle-ball pitcher who could also throw a good fastball? What pitcher ever existed with the blinding speed of Nolan Ryan or Steve Bedrosian or Herb Score and the "junk" pitches of the aging Tommy John or Rick Mahler or Satchel Paige? They are, indeed, nearly mutually exclusive stages in the development and maturation of a big league pitcher. Khrushchev is, in effect, both a youngster and a veteran simultaneously. He is not, in Nixon's mind, simply a pitcher, but a symbol of the implausible perfection of the perverse potentialities of pitching. Khrushchev's skill is not the zenith but the absolute corruption and debasement of pitching. And of course the cagey Khrushchev possesses the illegal spitter, as one would expect: the ultimate subversive man should be master of the subversive pitch. (Fairness, playing by the rules, and the subversion of the rules to win are ever on Nixon's mind. Consider this metaphor from boxing describing one of his encounters with Khrushchev: "I felt like a fighter wearing sixteen-ounce gloves and bound by Marquis of Queensberry rules, up against a bare-knuckle slugger who had gouged, kneed, and kicked. I was not sure whether I had held my own.") It is this utterly impossible array of pitches, all thrown by a pitcher who has uncanny, unnatural control ("change of pace"), that Nixon must face as a batter. No batter has faced a more daunting task, and no batter has succeeded more admirably than Nixon in the face of batting's adverse odds (a pitcher is expected to get a good hitter out 70 percent of the time).

Khrushchev, in Nixon's second allusion, is toying with a model of a Russian satellite in his hands, "like an oversize baseball." Nixon has enlarged the stakes of the game, for the pitcher is seen as a monstrous Soviet leader, a giant who has to be slain. The satellite symbolizes what is at stake: technology, science, indeed, all higher learning as a free human expression. The battle with communism has always been an ideological struggle over who will control not knowledge itself, but the nature of how one knows anything. Nixon's preoccupation is, in fact, with epistemology. Consider that during Nixon's years as vice president and as president he never expressed interest in any body of knowledge or in technical expertise. Nixon is neither philosopher nor intellectual. His sensual being throbs like a star in nova for the visceral reality of mass political manipulation, much like an athlete's for competition.

President Richard M. Nixon, 1973.

Observers are wrong. Reagan was not the first actor as president. Nixon was, because he was the first president since Theodore Roosevelt to think of himself in such purely athletic-turned-moral terms. To be sure, Roosevelt, taking boxing lessons from Mike Donovan and writing about the strenuous life, was more self-consciously the performer, as was John F. Kennedy, who needed to present a robust public figure to hide his poor health. In connection with the Kennedy and Roosevelt myths, both men were president during the peaks in the popularity of football; Roosevelt, when college football was king; Kennedy, when professional football had caught on with the public in a big way. But Nixon was more truly *absorbed* by the power of athletics, by its power as metaphor,

President Gerald Ford, 1976.

or to borrow one scholar's phrase, by "the inseparability of ideals and action." And so the series of confrontations with Khrushchev was, for Nixon, his great moment of truth, his ultimate test of character; it is what the athlete lives for, the proof of his greatness in the challenge of a pressured performance: ". . . the moment for which I had been preparing myself for many months."

It is crucial, in understanding Nixon, to note his singular use of baseball metaphors for his most important confrontation with America's most powerful enemy (as he saw it). He does not invoke an image of baseball as romantic or pastoral. His image of baseball, as with his other sports references, mirrors the frenzy and desperation of the man himself. For those writers who have most promoted the romance of the sport, baseball's pastoral myth conjures up images of harmony and natural bliss. How striking that in the vision of Richard Nixon, baseball becomes the central metaphor for the widest political and philosophical schism that he could imagine.

Bush and the Bush Leagues

Looking Forward, George Bush's 1988 campaign autobiography, written with Victor Gold, reminds the reader of Ring Lardner's *You Know Me Al* (1925), the epistolary novel about a bush league pitcher with a modest career for the Chicago White Sox who thinks himself a great deal more talented than he truly is. But there is an underlying folksy modesty to it all; the brilliant colloquial language makes one unsure how much this young pitcher really knows about himself. Is he a jerk, a fool, an egomaniac, or just a sweet kid?

One asks those questions about Bush as one reads his autobiography, for, although it is not as colloquial as Lardner's novel, it exudes the same folksy modesty, the same plain, unassuming American speech, and the same lack of any real definition of its subject. "Looking forward," the author notes, "reflects [a] philosophy," but of course this is not true. The phrase, taken from the book's epigraph, a statement by Senate Chaplain

President Jimmy Carter, 1979.

Edward Everett Hale, is not remotely connected to a philosophy but rather is the clichéd summation of a bourgeois Christian mood—the sort of maxim or self-motivation jingle that might have been created by Norman Vincent Peale or the Jehovah's Witnesses or the boosters for a university's multimillion fund-raising campaign. It might characterize the attitude of a minor league pitcher who hopes for the big time, or a mediocre politician who hopes to be president.

Bush's book is a story about a self-made man but not a man who is pathologically driven. Though Bush was shot down as a fighter pilot during World War II, he was not dramatically injured as was his Republican rival, Kansas Senator Robert Dole. Bush's heroism seems routine. He is wealthy but he still enjoys backyard barbecues with friends. He started a business that was moderately successful, and his political career has been successfully moderate. That is to say, he has been appointed to a good many important jobs without having to do much to get them other than assure the people who appointed him that he would not do much while he occupied the post. Bush has the type of ambition that reassures his supporters because it does not accompany any particular drive for personal achievement. In this, he is rather like the company man who wishes to experience life as a series of painless promotions that come not because of one's talent but because of one's loyalty. Loyalty is worth a great deal more in politics than mere talent. It is both more durable and more profoundly exacting: it forces the fulfillment of promises and it withstands temptation.

Bush went to Yale, where he majored in economics and earned a Phi Beta Kappa key. He also played baseball there, and this seems as essential as anything he mentions in his book. One can hardly imagine a better way to reacclimate to mythical America after fighting in a war or to reinvest in the hypnotic comfort of the American dream than by going to an Ivy League college and playing baseball. The entire baseball section of the book is sandwiched between two legendary players: Lou Gehrig, Bush's hero, "a great athlete and team leader," "nothing flashy, no hotdogging, the ideal sportsman," who died several years before Bush came to Yale; and Babe Ruth, who visited Yale in 1948 when he was dying of cancer. Bush,

Babe Ruth and George Bush at Yale, 1948.

then captain of the Yale baseball team, met Ruth during a ball field ceremony in which Ruth donated the manuscript of his autobiography.

None of this is without political or autobiographical significance: The passing of Ruth and Gehrig signified the end of an era in the conservative's vision of the American dream, the death of pastoral innocence; after all, 1948 was the year after Jackie Robinson had integrated professional baseball. Inasmuch as conservatism was, for such a long time in this country, an expression of white male privilege, baseball, by this time, was no longer its suitable icon. Conservatism had to reassert its values not through icons and athletic heroes but through a new text. It is not surprising that, in his baseball section, Bush mentions William F. Buckley's *God and Man at Yale* (1951), the book that is credited with regenerating conservative thought in America or at least attaching it to something that was intellectual (Yale) instead of merely sentimental (baseball). Paradoxically, of course, despite the intellectual veneer of its argument and even its continued relevance as a critique of certain aspects of academia and undergraduate education, Buckley's first book is in fact a sentimental work. How seamless American culture is for Bush! Into the vaults goes Ruth's autobiography of a hero of the American dream and out, three years later, comes Buckley's lament that the American dream is no longer taught at Yale.

Bush played first base at Yale and improved from being "good field, no hit" to being "good field, fair hit." Bush quotes an article in the *New Haven Evening Register* that describes him as a "classy first baseman" who happened to be hitting .167, or what a professional ball player would call "a buck and some change." He received some advice about his hitting which in effect told him to be more aggressive at the plate, and he slowly improved as a hitter until by his last game he was hitting .280. Although he admits mild envy of his teammate Frank Quinn, who became a professional ball player, and confesses he would like to say that what took him to Texas was "a fat contract to play professional baseball," one feels fairly sure that Bush did not really want to be a professional player. He would have lost all sense of himself as being a true sportsman, and sport itself would have lost its essentially upper-class appeal for him.

As titans of the American dream, Ruth and Gehrig (though Gehrig went to Columbia) located their mythic power in the fact that they were working-class men. Professional sport for them was upward mobility. Bush's own upward urges could not be satisfied by a professional sports career. Bush had a boyish and typically American worship for his baseball heroes, and Gehrig and Ruth, especially Gehrig, made particularly suitable heroes. Ruth was the orphan boy who made out well

Ronald Reagan and Frank Lovejoy, *The Winning Team,* Warner Bros. Pictures, 1952.

when it was discovered that he could play ball. Because of his outsized sensual appetite and his expansive personality, Ruth was a Rabelaisian boy wonder. Gehrig was more puritanical and driven. Perhaps their nicknames tell the whole story: the Babe for Ruth; Iron Man for Gehrig. Gehrig was the hard-working son of an immigrant, a mother-obsessed boy who was, as baseball historian Donald Honig writes, "the perfect son, the perfect husband, the perfect ball player, the perfect Yankee. . . . one of the game's few inviolable saints." His going to Columbia was part of his upward mobility. His mother wanted very much for him to get a college education, the immigrant parents' dream of a better life for the offspring. And we are reminded in the literature on Gehrig how long a social stretch going to Columbia was. Consider, for example, this passage from Robert Rubin's juvenile biography, *Lou Gehrig: Courageous Star* (1979):

> Lou was not a typical Columbia freshman. Most of his classmates were from well-to-do homes. They dressed smartly and were used to comfortable living. Lou was poor and looked it, going about campus hatless, coatless, his pants and shirt patched and worn. Many of his more fortunate classmates looked down on him because his parents were immigrants who worked at menial jobs. (p. 52)

But, like the typical jock, Gehrig never finished his architecture studies at Columbia, signing a contract with the Yankees after having completed two years. This too is part of the myth, as he supposedly signed to help his parents financially. But George Bush, the son of Prescott Bush, was meant for a different career, which he well understood, and to have become a professional ballplayer himself, if it were possible, would have been out of character.

That Bush omits writing of two crucial instances in his life when he received help from his father, Prescott Bush, Sr., a successful businessman and a United States senator from Connecticut, is not surprising. In fact, it is probably central to understanding not only how and why he is drawn to using Gehrig and Ruth but also the importance of their myth to him as a patrician politician. Omitting to mention his father's help is understandable, since he wishes to present himself as self-made. Moreover, we can see a kind of symmetry between his connecting of Ruth's working-class autobiography to Buckley's privileged, intellectual "education" book, and his use of the myth of Ruth and Gehrig in relation to his own myth as privileged scion of the upper class. Bush wants to bridge a social gulf in America through the image of sports while, paradoxically, not bridging it at all.

The first assistance Prescott Bush provided was a substantial loan so that young Bush could get started in the oil business in Texas. The second was securing for him a key committee appointment when Bush was first elected to Congress in 1966. Yet, despite his admiration of Gehrig and Ruth, Bush does wish to make clear that his father's career is the paradigm for his own. His father attended Yale, fought with the field artillery during World War I, and did not join his own father's firm but went first to St. Louis and then to Tennessee to make his way in business. Finally, he returned to Connecticut to start his political career. It is nearly identical to Bush's own career with the noted exception that Bush did not return to New England. So, after all, it is better to have simply fantasized about a baseball career and thus be like many other boys.

Playing professional baseball is one version of the American dream which in most cases it is better to have dreamed than to have fulfilled. The aspiration has a certain juvenile gentility that transcends class. Indeed, sport is one of the cultural instruments in America that makes class distinction bearable among men and ultimately gives them something to talk about. But the professional sports career, its pursuit, is, finally, nothing more than another class quest for identity and the shape of a career. And that is why Bush would have gone to Texas to enter the oil business without the contract, even if the professionals would have had him (which of course they wouldn't have because he could not hit, and it is easier to teach a good hitter to field than to teach a good fielder to hit). It was time to put away childish things.

But if, with the coming of social integration of the races in the 1950s (or at least an official government policy so stating), baseball could no longer be the same sentimental, childish locus of white conservatism, it did not become something much different. The black player was absorbed, albeit uneasily, into the myth and the tradition.

The Black Athlete in Our Time

Jackie Robinson and Willie Mays

In 1964, at the height of the civil rights movement, Jackie Robinson compiled a book of interviews entitled *Baseball Has Done It,* about the successful integration of the National Pastime. Most of the notable black ball players of the fifties and early sixties were interviewed, including Hank Aaron (who spoke quite absorbingly about James Baldwin), Larry Doby, Roy Campanella, Don Newcombe, Ernie Banks, Elston Howard, and Vic Power. Two prominent black players refused to be interviewed by Robinson: one was Maury Wills, the Los Angeles Dodgers shortstop, who was quoted as saying: "I don't want to be involved in a controversy." This was said by Wills despite the fact that few of the black players had said anything that would have been considered shocking even in 1964. Players such as Banks and Howard, long known as models of self-effacing camaraderie, were positively and broadly accommodating—they tried so hard to be free of the remotest suggestion of complaint that they expressed no political consciousness at all. Perhaps Wills was right, in the end. Controversy *was* in the air, and those who tried the hardest to avoid it were actually confessing that they were drowning in it. Nonetheless, all the players spoke with a certain and earnest blend of honesty and caution, remembering, after all, that they were workingmen in a work world dominated by whites. This meant, in a richly ironic way, that they were precariously perched yet rooted in the twin tradition of both black and white baseball in America.

The other player who did not choose to be interviewed was Willie Mays. His refusal is understandable. Mays's huge and formidable myth—the exuberant Negro man-child, the Nigger Jim of American culture who went cruising with the white American male across the green, flat, achingly mystical expanse of center field in the Polo Grounds and Candlestick Park, locked in some impossibly intricate and gymnastic fox-trot called the pastoral romance, all of which he had so carefully and self-consciously constructed, as he had the myth of his speed by wearing a hat that was too large for him so that it would always come off—was at stake.

I remember as a boy seeing billboards in black neighborhoods with Mays's picture advertising Alaga Syrup. ("Alaga" is a portmanteau word combining the abbreviations of Alabama and Georgia.) "I was raised on Alaga Syrup—*This* Fielder's Choice is Always Alaga's *Real Cane* Flavor," read the sign. I suppose that only blacks used Alaga Syrup, as I never met a white who had ever heard of it and it could only be found in stores in black neighborhoods. A very thick, dark, molasseslike liquid, it was extremely sweet. I consumed gallons of it as a boy, not on pancakes but on biscuits. Many a morning my mother made me and my sisters a breakfast of biscuits which we covered or dipped with Alaga Syrup. At the time I thought these breakfasts to be a huge treat, and I remember eating whole trays of biscuits in a sitting. It was not until I was eighteen or nineteen years old and was told by a "dietetically conscious" Muslim friend that biscuits and syrup was "the breakfast of a sharecropper" that the poverty of my boyhood hit with a wave of shame. What I thought of as the homey ambrosia of my mother's strong, dark hands was nothing more than the malnutrition of degradation made palatable. For many years I could hardly think of biscuits and syrup without feeling ill. Since that day, I have never eaten Alaga Syrup again, although I sometimes think I would like to see a bottle of it. Probably because of his face on the advertisements I saw as a boy, I have always associated Willie Mays with Alaga Syrup, as if his sweetness as an athlete was its sweetness, as if the nausea caused by its memory is precisely the nausea caused by the memory of him.

But it is impossible to talk about Willie Mays without talking about the man he rebuffed, Jackie Robinson. They were the first two black players to enter baseball's Hall of Fame on the basis of their accomplishments in the major leagues, not the

Jackie Robinson, 1947.

Negro leagues, which means they were among the earliest black ball players to achieve an official and eternal fame in American popular culture. They were both American Adams, natural men whose responses to the pastoral myth that engulfed them were disturbing: yet, Robinson hated the prolonged boyhood of professional athletics to the point where he adopted an almost depressive gravity; and Mays reveled in the conviction that eternal boyhood was all life had to offer an athlete. Mays's baseball career was twice as long as Robinson's.

The difference between the two men was akin to the difference between Pap Finn and Jim in *The Adventures of Huckleberry Finn* (1884). Both Pap and Jim were natural men, American Adams; Pap, however, was tormented by his marginality and yearned for status. Jim was satisfied with being outside because it was never his marginality alone that bothered him; Jim never wanted status, simply security. He never thought himself too good for his station in life; he only desired that his humility be respected. The difference between the two men as American Adams is underscored by their responses to codes: Pap was astonished and fearful when he discovered that Huck could read; Jim prided himself on being a master teacher and reader of signs. So Pap became, like Robinson, the most unnatural of natural men, and Jim, like Mays, became the idealization of humanity through nature.

"The only time I recall I ever worked," wrote Mays in his latest autobiography, *Say Hey* (1988), "was the night when I helped a friend of mine wash dishes in a restaurant. I didn't get home until six in the morning. My dad was having breakfast before going to work. He warned me never to come in that late again without telling him or Aunt Sarah." There are two important observations to make about this statement: first, Mays never considered his more than twenty years as a professional ball player to be work or labor. That is not surprising; it is indeed part of his myth as a natural man that he was for so long engaged in a kind of spirited adolescent play. Joe Louis had a similar attitude about his career as a boxer, and one is struck by how much alike Mays and Louis are. Both had very long and successful careers, much longer than the average in their sports; both served in the Armed Forces doing what they did as civilians, performing their sports; they both became greeters in Las Vegas after their athletic careers ended. And they were both celebrated by the white American public in much the same way and for the same reasons: they reminded whites that being a Negro was, in truth, quite a bit of wholesome and boyish fun. Whites were afforded the comfort of enjoying the romance of the unselfconscious black male without feeling burdened by any implications in denigrating him. Mays and Louis were never degraded; they were indulged.

Nothing makes this point clearer, about Mays being indulged, than a second observation about the above quotation. Mays apparently obeyed his father and never stayed out that late again. He also decided to let his family support him in his efforts to become a professional ball player, for his father's prohibition, in effect, made working impossible—the only type of job Mays could have worked as a teen-ager (when this dishwashing incident took place) would have forced him to come home very

Jackie Robinson, 1948.

late at night, since he played sports for most of the afternoon and early evening. Mays's athletic talent was recognized when he was quite young and his family, as he tells us, freed him from the normal duties expected of a black boy who was reared in a working-class black family in the South during the thirties and forties. His uncle did his household chores for him; his aunt gave him ten dollars a week (a considerable sum at the time) for lunch money; and, most important, his father, a Negro league player, taught Mays how to play the game. This last point is especially significant. As Mays writes: "When I was sixteen, in 1947, Jackie Robinson broke into the major leagues. . . . I wouldn't say that Robinson was my idol. My father had always been that."

Robinson broke into white baseball when Mays was at an age susceptible to hero worship. Yet Robinson was never his idol. Robinson could never displace Mays's father. There may have existed between Mays and Robinson jealousy and even dislike, but never any "anxiety of influence." Mays never felt that Robinson was a hero he had to vanquish, because he could not afford to see him as a hero even before they became competitors. Yet, since they played for rival teams, one suspects that their competitive urges were fiercely expressed. Mays, however, had his own father as hero; then he adopted, by his own admission, his white father, manager Leo Durocher, under whom he began his career as a New York Giant. Mays describes Durocher's departure as manager of the Giants after the 1955 season as "my saddest moment in baseball." Elsewhere he writes: "I knew . . . that Leo and I had a relationship that never could be equaled. His departure was a source of regret that stayed with me for the rest of my big-league career." It is also intriguing that Mays married during the off-season between 1955, when Durocher left the Giants, and the start of the 1956 season. As he puts it: "Stickball would be behind me now, along with Leo and the carefree days in Harlem and the ball park." Did he get married because without Leo—or "Mister Leo," as Mays called him, conjuring up uneasy images of overwrought respect and endearing southern courtesy—Mays was really at a loss to find something better to do? The marriage was not successful. But the crucial difference between Mays and Robinson is precisely that: how each man saw the fathers in his life.

Jackie Robinson was high-spirited. He was perhaps known for being very little else once Branch Rickey told him, after two years in the major

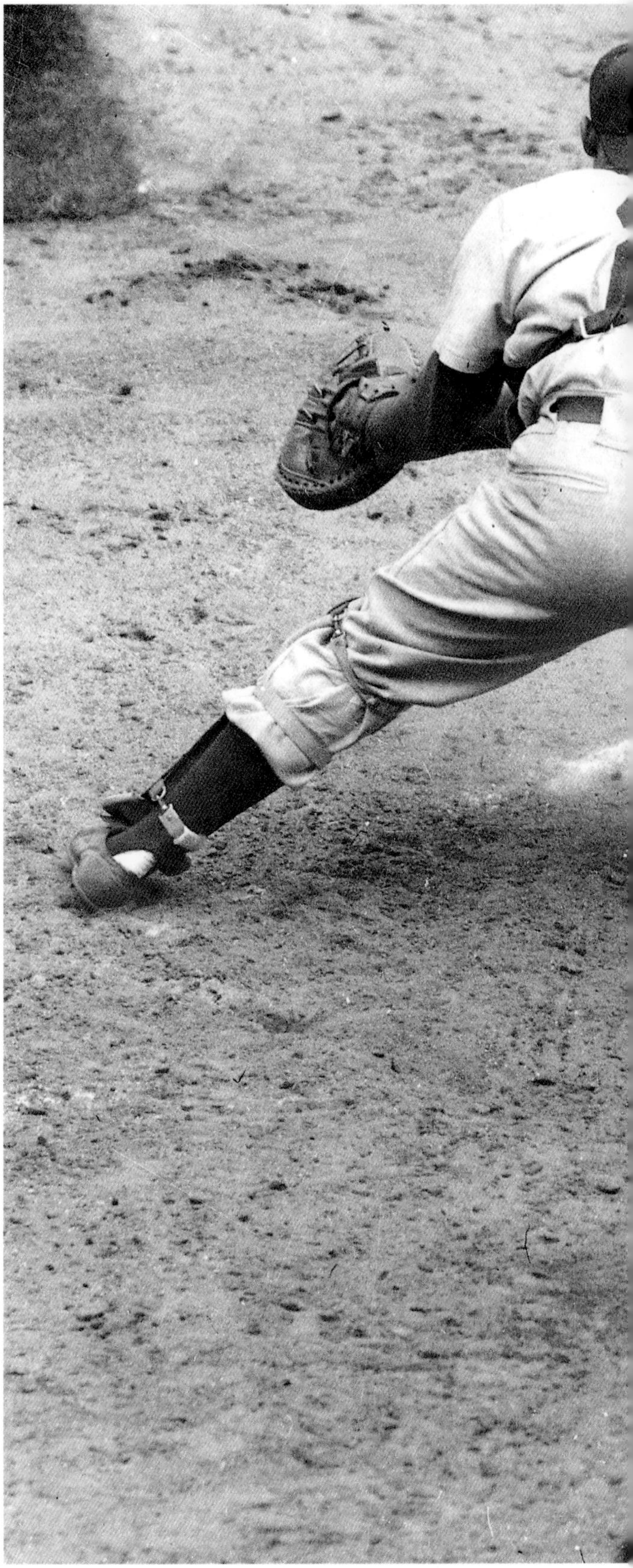

Willie Mays, 1952.

10

leagues, that he was free to be himself. Henry James warned us about people with that quality: "Of course the danger of a high spirit was the danger of inconsistency—the danger of keeping up the flag after the place has surrendered; a sort of behavior so crooked as to be almost a dishonour to the flag." That Robinson was a Republican and a conservative of sorts (he was, after his playing days, a business executive with Chock Full O'Nuts, so his conservatism was of the chamber-of-commerce type), should not be surprising since blacks as a group, especially the middle class, make very good philistines and fairly credible conservatives. There was a great deal of homely appeal in the conservative rhetoric of Booker T. Washington and Elijah Muhammad which is strikingly similar to the current popularity of such "success-ethic" publications as *Black Enterprise* and the speeches of Louis Farrakan (the former singer and dancer, once billed as the Calypso Kid). Perhaps Robinson never forgave himself his Republicanism simply because it was never quite stylish during the civil rights era—he had notable disagreements in his ghosted newspaper column with both Martin Luther King, Jr., and Malcolm X—which may explain why his militancy, while it may have striven unsuccessfully for sincerity, never lacked the vehemence of earnestness. But let us deal with the subject of fathers.

Robinson writes, in *I Never Had It Made* (1972):

> Some of the people who have criticized me have labeled me a black man who has been made by white people. They justify this by stating that I have had three fabulous, white godfathers—Mr. Rickey in baseball, Bill Black in business, and Nelson Rockefeller in politics.
>
> These critics overlook the fact that they are talking about three of the most hardheaded, practical men who ever lived. As capable as all three of these men may be of sentiment, not one of them did what they did out of misplaced emotionalism. Of the three, the closest to me was Mr. Rickey. But even though he was motivated by deep principle to break the barriers in baseball, Mr. Rickey was also a keen businessman. He knew that integrated baseball would be financially rewarding. His shrewd judgment was proven correct. (p. 268)

Robinson's second paragraph seems to beg the question and ultimately ignores the fundamental theme of his autobiography: that Rockefeller, Rickey, and Black were "hardheaded, practical men" scarcely denies the possibility that they possessed some special feelings for Robinson, and it certainly does not speak to the more important issue of what Robinson felt about them. For instance, Robinson writes that the death of Rickey in 1965 "made me feel almost as if I had lost my own father. Branch Rickey, especially after I was no longer in the sports spotlight, treated me like a son." It must not be forgotten that Robinson's book is about lost and found fathers, denied and recognized sons. He tells in the beginning how he feels about his own father:

> To this day I have no idea what became of my father. Later, when I became aware of how much my mother had to endure alone, I could only think of him with bitterness. He, too, may have been a victim of oppression, but he had no right to desert my mother and five children. (p. 16)

Unlike Mays, Robinson was an abandoned son, a son denied, and thus his autobiography becomes a quest for a father. He finds one for each of the major phases of his life: athletic, business, and political. The fact that his fathers are white is all the more fitting as a kind of justice (for it has been the white fathers who have denied the black fathers the right to fatherhood) and a kind of revenge (the inept, uncaring black father must pay for the pain he has caused). The autobiography ends with Robinson's tragic struggles with his own son, Jackie, Jr., who dies in an automobile accident after having fought to overcome drug addiction. The death of that son closes the book and the story possesses, as a result, a powerful symmetry: the dark son who succeeds haunted by the dark father who fails, and the dark father whose success haunts, oppresses, and finally destroys the dark son who fails. In the end, Robinson was obstinate and driven; Mays was driven as well (and often under stress, as his frequent fainting spells indicated), but he was never obstinate. Mays never forced an issue. It is doubtful whether he understood that any issue existed beyond playing the game.

Virtually all of Mays's autobiography is devoted to his career as a ball player; the afterlife is nothing more than a coda. More than half of Robinson's

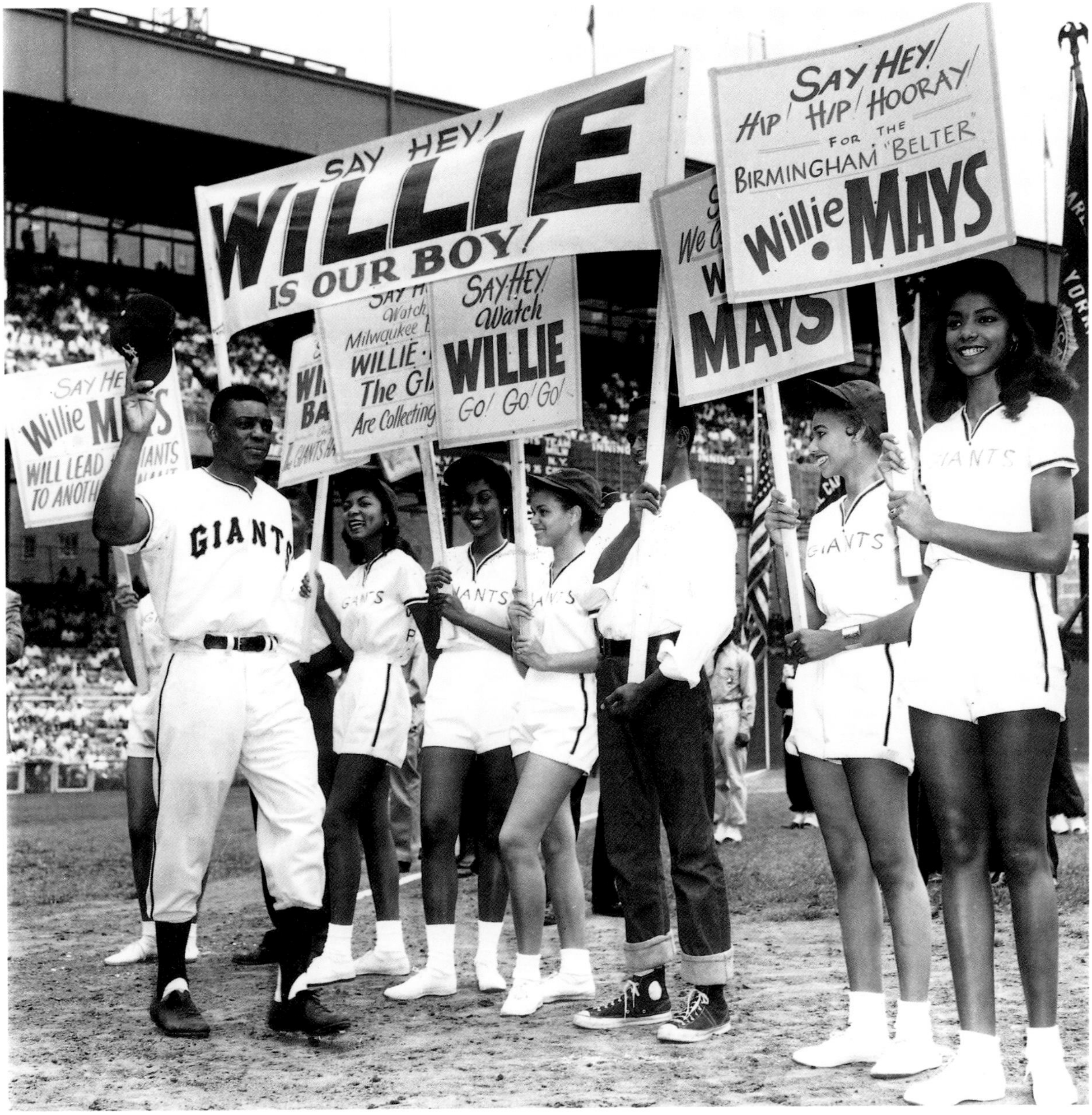

Willie Mays, 1954.

book is about his life after baseball. It is an indication not only of the length of the athletic careers of the two men but also of the shape and meaning of the two careers. Robinson could never really be satisfied by baseball; Mays could be satisfied by nothing else. Robinson describes his life as a series of clashes: as a child in California dealing with the racial taunts of white children; with white opponents while at the University of Southern California; with white officers while in the army; with white players, fans, and hotel and restaurant owners while a ball player; with militants, Uncle Toms, and dishonest white politicians while a businessman and a political aide to New York Governor Nelson Rockefeller. Mays's life is always a resolution: there is no mention of racism in Mays's childhood; he and white children played together; he is not annoyed by the segregated accommodations during his early days as a major league player; army life does not bother him.

Mays and Robinson are in such counterpoise that it is impossible to understand the black athlete as a cultural marvel without also understanding not only the images of self-mythology that are afforded to black men in America but the unique attraction of those images. What does it mean to Robinson and to the rest of us that he was paradoxically the outsized rebel and the symbol of capitulation? What does it mean to Mays that he was not only the pastoral hero but also the symbol of an innocuous black manhood? Is professional athletics in America simultaneously both the triumph and the tragedy of black male ambition, not success without meaning, but success flawed by the very menacing limitations of its meaning? Few have bothered to inquire into what ambition and achievement mean for black men, since black men are usually studied and explained only for their inadequacies and failures. Yet how else is a great athlete to be understood by his culture except as a person consumed by ambition, pursuing a fabulous if narrow excellence, the attainment of which is an achievement that demands nothing more than repetition?

Perhaps the sharp and telling edge of black male ambition is most demonstrably displayed and most intriguingly contemplated in the personality of Frank Robinson (no relation to Jackie Robinson), who is a near contemporary of Mays (starting his minor league career two years after Mays had started playing in the major leagues). It may be instructive to consider, briefly, a black ball player who broke into the major leagues several years after the personalities of Willie Mays and Jackie Robinson had become the stuff of popular culture—which means that in some ways Frank Robinson was influenced by them. Frank Robinson divided his career between two teams, the Cincinnati Reds in the National League and the Baltimore Orioles in the American League. He won the Most Valuable Player Award in both leagues (an incredible feat), was voted into the Hall of Fame after his retirement, and has served, on and off, as one of professional baseball's few black managers. Frank Robinson was one of the most hated players of his era; he played with such manic intensity that he seemed excessively competitive, much like Jackie Robinson. As he writes in his autobiography, *My Life Is Baseball* (1968):

> I have, throughout my career, been called all kinds of names by opposing ballplayers. One guy said I was "deliberately vicious." Another accused me of "trying to maim people." A third said, "I hated his guts when I played against him." Okay, that's their privilege. A lot of this, I think, came because the players didn't know me. To get to know a player, you have to play with him. But that never bothered me. I hate, too. I hate all the fellows around the league who are wearing the other uniform. . . . I don't like so much what's going on in baseball today, this friendliness between opposing players. I think there's altogether too much of it. Say a buddy of yours is playing shortstop for the other side and you're going out to dinner with him after the game. Then, during the game, you're on first base and a ground ball is hit and your buddy is coming across to tag the bag. You're not going to knock him down. You're not going to hit him to break up the double play. You're just going to slide nicely, get up, dust off your pants, and go back to the dugout. (p. 8)

Later he explains why he has not been involved in politics, even when pressure has been applied by black activists for prominent blacks like himself to speak out:

> My life is baseball and I think it deserves all my attention. It's the same even with my leisure. I go to the movies in season, I attend pro and college basketball and football games in the off-season because I love all sports. But I don't have any special interests that I think might distract me from the game. I don't read books. I don't play golf. I don't hunt or fish. I simply don't want to get involved in anything but baseball. (pp. 15–16)
>
> A lot of Negro groups have criticized me for it, because when they call me to lead marches and protests or to make personal appearances I have to tell them no. I sympathize with them, really. They've done a great deal of good; I agree with them on some points and there are some points I disagree with them. But I don't think baseball should be a fight for anything but baseball. (p. 16)

In effect, Frank Robinson combines the personalities of Jackie Robinson and Willie Mays, having the fervent, even overcompensating drive for self-respect and achievement (like Jackie Robinson, Frank Robinson was a fatherless boy whose family moved from the South, Texas in this case, to California) coupled with an almost equally passionate provincialism that expresses itself as a lack of political consciousness (he was the youngest child and, like Mays, was indulged and pampered while growing up).

Some of this can be explained as typical of the working-class male's attitude toward work itself: the tremendous fear of and exaltation over rivalry; hostility towards politics, particularly social-justice causes that smack of overt do-goodism, which always seems tainted with either "making trouble" or effeminacy; and an obsessive anti-intellectualism that prides itself on being masculine. That participation in professional athletics should diminish a man's natural humanizing inclinations toward friendship and civic obligation is troubling (although Robinson's reluctance to have his fame exploited by civil rights organizations is certainly understandable). Moreover, that he should view baseball as a sphere of human activity that is politically neutral, when his very presence is both a political cause and effect, seems the wishful expression of our desire that sport be an image of man beyond politics.

The problem for the black male here—and it is an extremely important one, as athletics provides the only extensive field of survey for analyzing black male ambition in a context where its expression has had an enormous impact on American culture at large—is that while he is preoccupied, obsessed even, in exercising and empowering his manhood, the very nature of athletic endeavor requires that he prolong his adolescence almost in an act of stunting or thwarting his manhood. Frank Robinson's attitudes, his views toward life, are indeed those of an older adolescent male: laughingly bellicose, daringly vain, remarkably close-minded, insistently and uninterestingly self-absorbed. In Frank Robinson, the classic temperamental modes of Willie Mays and Jackie Robinson are flooded by a grandeur of expertise, tuned to a new pitch of passion, but distressingly unresolved, as if a giant potential remains unrealized.

There is an image we all have of Willie Mays and Jackie Robinson, and it is the same image: both are young men running on a baseball field on a bright afternoon, Robinson rounding the bases, Mays in the outfield chasing a fly ball. Their caps fly off; they seem graceful and free. But one must always be aware of the implication that if, in America, a black man is running then he is, to paraphrase a line from an Amiri Baraka poem, being chased by someone or something that hates him. Satchel Paige, the black pitcher whom Jackie Robinson never liked because he seemed so openly an Uncle Tom and whom Willie Mays admired as a "legend," put it best by inadvertently describing the dilemma of the black athlete: Don't look back; something might be gaining on you.

Running for the Turtle

TEYMURAZ MAMALADZE

On August 13, 1988, at the instigation of the publishing house Fizkultura i Sport, I started in a supermarathon. Naturally, I am responsible for the result. The publishing house only decides whether to publish it.

If that should happen, I beg the reader not to judge too harshly the idea of racing through the entire seventy-year history of the Soviet sports movement in thirty pages or so. On such a vast course, the athlete usually sees only the heels of his successful rivals. (That is, unless he manages to break ahead, to join the front runners. I, alas, am no front runner.) Very rarely does he see the whole course from beginning to end, let alone the surrounding landscape. Nevertheless, I will try to provide an overview of the whole route, though I intend to describe mainly my own feelings, running in the segment covered by my own lifetime. I will take in the rest with my side vision, so to speak.

Even a small child in my country would understand why August 13 was chosen for the starting date. Suspecting, however, that in other countries there may be grownups who know nothing of my country and its calendars, I will explain: August 13 is an important Soviet holiday, the All-Union Day of the Physical-Culturalist.

And that term itself needs explaining. The concept of physical culture exists in many countries, but the physical-culturalist per se is found only in ours—at least in this particular form. The term was coined at the time of the Revolution, when divergent ideas were brought together into a new, indivisible whole.

Nowadays no one is surprised when tens of thousands come to the starting line.

It seems I've fallen into the wrong tone. In our country, sport is something to be accompanied by kettledrums. Monumental fogies who have never kicked a ball in their lives preside over our sports movement in poses ripe for memorial marble. Across their medallion faces play many-colored reflections from sporting banners; their mysterious smiles force you to believe in the existence of some noble music only they can hear. From the very beginning—the Spartakiad held in Moscow in 1928 (not to be confused with the Olympic Games held that year in Antwerp)—jaunty music has played on August 13. Brass bands polished like samovars have played medleys of the best Soviet songs, the music by which records are so easily broken and championships so easily won.

I know this from personal experience, and I want to register a complaint. This year, on August 13, the music drowned out other voices.

"It seems we are now crossing over that border zone where statistics are no longer a mirror of events, where everything is determined by tendencies." (*Sovetski Sport*) What is true is true. What is wrong from the standpoint of Russian syntax is absolutely correct from the standpoint of good sense.

"We are ceasing, step by step, to measure the

level of physical culture, as we did earlier, by the number of sporting installations, by the millions in the ranks of its devotees." (*Trud*)

Why are we "ceasing, step by step"?

Well, because "our school-age youngsters are growing weaker, more prone to illness; their weight is increasing while their strength is dwindling." (*Komsomolskaya Pravda*)

The gleaming brass of the bands fades in the rays of *perestroika*. What good are medallion faces and monumental poses when seventy million smokers in our country are racked with precancerous coughs, and when, on any given day, four million citizens are ill? (*Sovetski Sport*) Or when basketballs are no good, and a gymnastics cable is worn out after less than a year's service? (*Komsomolskaya Pravda*) Or when even the Chief Athlete of the Soviet Union—chief not in the sense of best, but in an entirely different, administrative sense—when even he openly admits that to the USA's three million swimming pools we can scarcely muster three thousand?

Well then, shall we sob about all this? Shall the bands croak dirges? Certainly not. If there is anything we desperately need (besides high-tech) it is a sense of humor. Rather than the mysterious smile of dwellers on high, let it be a self-deprecating grin that plays over our bronze lips. For too long, fellow countrymen, we have been too serious, and there is too much evidence that our seriousness has been self-defeating.

Maybe we should laugh at ourselves, so that others—just this once—don't beat us to it. Without belittling the Soviet sports phenomenon (who but a fool would belittle the records of Sergei Bubka, for example?), surely we can laugh at how we adroitly deluded ourselves for so many years. We called dyed-in-the-wool professionals incorrigible amateurs. We counted embryos still forming in the womb among the ranks of rated players and masters of sport, so that, in some republics, the number of manufactured athletes exceeded the total population.

Still, I can't do without some grandstanding. I wasn't brought up that way. *Glasnost* is fine, but those beloved medleys still ring in my ears. My eyes still behold those leaders, each with a Napoleonic hand thrust into the front of his overcoat. So, during the race, if I should happen to raise my voice in song, or shout out the slogan of the moment, or let fall a nostalgic tear, please don't be angry with me. I can't help it. I am a child of my times.

And so, we're off. Look for me at the checkpoints. I'll just take a short detour through my childhood. After that I'll try to get down to serious running.

I turn aside from the course, and here it is—the Veri quarter of Tbilisi, my Yoknapatawpha. If the Veri quarter did not exist it would have been necessary to invent it. But you couldn't invent it any better than it is.

It isn't lightning soccer the children of the quarter play—although given our temperament that would be entirely natural—but multi-storied soccer, which given the ups and downs of our terraces is even more natural.

In the quarter there are upper courtyards and lower, joined by descents and ascents, and when up above an attack is in full blaze, down below the goalies, waiting for the ball, are scutching wool with rods. There are dark alleys in the quarter where even at noontime on a summer day you may meet the shade of some Shasho Vereli (a famous wrestler in old Tbilisi). With an embarrassed cough he will propose a match under the ancient rules of Georgian wrestling.

Don't even think of refusing. The shades of the great wrestling past won't let you by, even if Uncle Gabo opens the way.

Uncle Gabo, bane of my childhood! Keeper of the gates and key at the famed basketball stadium in Kirov Park, Gabo was a ruthless foe to nonpaying interlopers of every stripe, using every known means to hunt them down and punish them.

From which I draw a far-reaching conclusion about the power of autocracy, whether exercised by a watchman at the city's only basketball stadium or by the Generalissimo of the Soviet Union.

A personal monopoly on keys, broom, and rake grows inevitably into tyranny within the confines of a single basketball stadium. The same holds true absolutely within the confines of a single country.

Praise be to you, Gabo, petty stadium generalissimo! You taught a youngster the elements of a great science. And your savage cursing threw into higher relief for him the good-heartedness embodied in the spirit and ways of the Veri quarter.

The things to be found here! And every one of them inimitable, unique.

The maternity hospital where I came into the world. The school where I entered first grade. The ferry from which I dived into the Kura. The park where I kissed a girl for the first time. The registry office where we came to get married, and later to record the birth of our first child. The cemetery where someday they will bury me. Everything is special for me in this quarter. My *genii loci* live here.

I acknowledge the absolute sway exercised over me by the places where I was born and took my first steps, the houses where I lived, the arbor that granted its shade and grapes, the copper faucet to which I pressed my lips in thirst.

Everything that holds absolute power over me is unique. Everything is unique that makes me the way I am.

Even the town crazy man—not the only one, alas—has power over me in the sense that he passed along his quirks. For instance, at fifty I am ready to join the children out behind the church of St. John the Divine, chasing a ball from dawn to dusk. That is, of course, if I have strength enough at fifty to chase a ball from dawn to dusk.

"Enough, enough!"—my mother calls to me from the world beyond—Father Georgi, the priest, had strength enough to do just that in 1942. Just that, but not only that.

Sinful games of our childhood! In them the outcast, the pariah, the untouchable recovered their lost freedom of being. The bullies, the informers, the scum, and the good-for-nothings lost their power over you. With a single blow of the stick, the ball, the knucklebones, you could put them back in their rightful places.

You loved a game because it restored the justice you were deprived of by social circumstances or the harsh dictates of authority. What pleasure to send the ball swooping in, souring the complacent mug on that cur whose father's signature made

Olympic champion gymnast Yelena Shushunova.

one side of the "triangle" when they issued your own father's death warrant! What triumph to knock your opponent's metal-weighted knucklebones out of ring, to make the loathed enemy pay for his crimes!

In rhythmic gymnastics, art and sport are inseparable.

If it is true that a sporting contest is a model of human existence, it is equally true that every form of sport, from the rustic amusement to the sophisticated Olympic event, is a struggle for the triumph of justice, for the restoration of rights to the insulted and oppressed, whether an individual, a people, or a country.

I have turned aside from the course of the supermarathon to touch upon the roots of sport among the people. I owe much to the games of my Yoknapatawpha. Now the time has come to repay my filial debt.

They have faded into the past. Our children do not know them, and we have forgotten them too. Sometimes, pierced by an unexpected recollection, I wonder how they could be revived. Now memory is the only field where their cries can still be heard. And I am seriously thinking about a memorial volume, an encyclopedia of forgotten games.

The letter A, for instance. *Avchaluri.* A bag of corn or beans sent into arching flight with the inner edge of the foot. Who can kick it farther, you or I? The unbroken flights of this prize pouch, filled with the golden nuggets of victory, have been passed down in the genetic code to the soccer stars of our time. If we reflect upon corn and beans—Give us this day our daily bread—it is easy to see what feeds our indomitable urge to win.

I could continue through the entire alphabet. There would be more games than letters. *Lakhti,* for example. A precisely drawn circle becomes a fortress wall. Within it, the defenders stand at the ready. Their goal is to keep the attackers from commandeering their weapons. The weapons are their belts, laid on the ground. It is permitted to snatch them up and lash out at the attackers before they can grab them out from under the defenders and beat them out of the game. The selfsame eternal argument about the relation between defense and offense which in our days has grown so acute.

I could go on forever, reaching out beyond this quarter to every corner of the world. Each nation has always had, always will have, games in which it affirms its first principles of gallantry and justice. And whether or not these particular games

Carite

have survived, it is important for us all that we have carried the flame that burned in each into the universal games of modern times.

This is not nostalgia for the past, but a reminder for the future. Whatever circumstances arise, whatever sort of existence you are forced into, you are invincible so long as you keep these first principles alive in you.

Sometimes the barbell weighs three times as much as the athlete.

I come running out of the former Brick Alley, along the former Olgin Street, towards the former Moscow Gate of our city, once dominated by a tavern. Now it is dominated by a splendid aquatic-sports complex, a silk-weaving factory, and the Square of Heroes. All three sites are specially marked on the map of my adolescence—a triangle of glory and ignominy.

The Square of Heroes was a child of the thirties. The giant building there—a hundred apartments, all conveniences provided—was their child too. In this house on the Square of Heroes there lived, of course, heroes and nothing but. A hundred apartments, a hundred heroes of the time. Some of them (as I understand now) were open heroes, some were secret heroes, and the rest were heroes of one sort or another, or what have you. Some showed their heroism by the light of day, some under the cover of night, and the rest one way or another, or however.

One of their number was clearly a secret hero. He had a most unheroic, but frightening, exterior—a bare, bony skull, the bent back of a laborer in the night trades, a hooked nose, arms outstretched to clasp the handlebars of a mighty Harley-Davidson. A marvelous little spider astride a supercycle. A mechanical centaur of the thirties. Our homegrown rockers of today have never even dreamed of the roars this centaur could produce from his motorized lower parts. A hell of noise, drowning out cries of protest and pleas for mercy.

My Amarcord impels me to regard that figure with heightened, even somewhat morbid attention. There are many reasons. At least three of them lie on the surface of memory. First, I sensed some kind of connection between the little man on the motorcycle and my own fatherlessness. Second, besides being a motorcycle racer, he played soccer at the stadium (which, by the way, was named at that time for Lavrenti Beria). Soccer, to my mind, has more spirituality, more humanity, so to speak, than motorcycle racing. But here too the hero was reputed to have some sort of supernatural, Satanic powers. During a practice, they said, he had kicked the ball from one goal to the other and not only scored but faked out Aleksandr Dorokhov, the famed goalie for Tbilisi's Dinamo.

And finally, the third reason: the centaur, the soccer player, had a daughter.

O Thea! I exchange your real name for this invented one, thereby retaining the right not to change or invent anything else. Having said so much to offend your daughterly feelings, I must add that I loved you. And there is no shame in confessing my love publicly, for my love for you was only a particle of the open and obvious love of our whole nation, since every nation loves its heroes.

Living in the building on the Square of Heroes, you could not be other than a heroine. It is hard to live up to a rank or title that is too grand. You lived up to the title of heroine, Thea. Or rather, it lived up to you, champion of the sidestroke, holder of our republic's record.

"On her left side!" asserted the amorous Raul-Gombesh, winner of regional tournaments in jumping off the number five tram.

"On her right!" countered Boatswain-Chubuk, possessed of an inborn gift for shoving heavy animate objects.

It was all the same to me. From whatever side you looked, the record holder was beautiful as a goddess and, like a goddess, unapproachable.

There are Botticelli women. There are the women of Rubens and Murillo, Goya and Renoir. The personal ideal of a genius embodies the collective ideal of his time. You, Thea, were a woman from the canvases of Aleksandr Deyneka. A woman who ruled over the swimming pool in the Park of Physical-Culturalists, on the Stalin Embankment.

In the film comedies of the day, Soviet madonnas—former cooks and swineherds now metamorphosed into great singers and government figures, active, zestful, and athletic—were breaking records for optimism and success. True, the madonnas I knew were different. They stood in long lines outside prisons. My mother was one of them. But sometimes art is more vivid than life.

When a girl heroine lives in a house of heroes on the Square of Heroes, and a boy non-hero, the son of an enemy of the people, inhabits Brick Alley, no Shakespeare can bring them together. Such a thing was even beyond the bards of my day, who had tucked the Renaissance under their belts and were turning out much more engrossing tragedies.

But when a boy from Brick Alley loves a girl record holder, there is nothing left for him to do but become a record holder himself. That is probably the only thing that could give a modern Montague at least a chance of slipping into the Capulet kitchen.

So the boy enrolled in a school for future record holders. And what difference does it make now whether he became one or not? Something else is much more important now.

A few years back, in the Lenin/Komsomol aquatic-sports complex, I ran into the girl from the Square of Heroes. She was walking along the side of the pool, stopwatch in hand, cheerfully calling out times to a girl swimmer, a perfect image of the girl she herself had been thirty years before. What had been the city's only pool, sparkling like a blue eye from under the bushy green hat of the Park of the Physical-Culturalists, was demolished when they extended the embankment. The Aragvi Restaurant now stands in its place. The Vere River was hidden underground in a pipe, and another pool, incomparably more respectable, was built near the silk-weaving factory.

Wrestling combines both skill and power.

So there she was, walking towards me with a coach's stopwatch in her hand, calling out times for the return lap. She recognized me and smiled. I answered with the same. We recognized each other because we were looking at each other,

Vladislav Trtyak, the Soviet's most popular ice hockey star.

through the changes wrought by time, with the eyes of the past.

"My daughter," she said, having followed my glance. "Does she look like me? She's a record holder too, you see."

"She's just like you. Your copy. Does she do the sidestroke too?" I asked, playing along.

"The breaststroke," she corrected. "The sidestroke isn't used anymore in competition. Didn't you know? You're behind the times."

"Yes, I've lingered too much in the past," I agreed. "I'm up to my ears in it right now."

Sounds came drifting in from the low bank of the Vere. The bells of vanished trams, the skeletal crack of flying knucklebones, the beans clacking like castanets in an *Avchaluri* bag, the creak of gates, the clang of bumper couplings, the clatter of door bolts on freight cars hauling people away to somewhere in Kazakhstan.

The girl champion, daughter of my Thea, was looking at me trustingly, boldly, from out of the malachite water. Gazing into her eyes, wordlessly answering her unasked question, I had a flash of insight. I love my time, my past, without reservation. I love everything about it, the good and the bad, the bright and the gloomy, all the waste and loss in which, bit by bit, I have discovered the person I am today. I have grown, lived, and been formed in it. It is my time; I will have no other. How can I not love it, my time, the time of my friends and family, the time of my country?

When I undertook to write about sport, I brought this feeling with me to the course of my essay. And I will carry it on to the finish line.

The red calico banner fills with wind. It struggles to escape the boyish hands that hold it. "Physical Culture for the Masses!" it says. It is the sail of all my adolescent hopes. I am not the only one to fasten it onto the deck of a life just out of port. I look back to see my friends, acquaintances, neighbors, relatives, co-workers running towards me, catching up. Now we move together in a pack, hearing one another's breathing, and we are no longer a dozen or two, but millions. A vast country is out to run a great race. Its breathing merges with the boom of the surf and the murmur of the pines. Its enthusiasm finds victorious expression in free movement. Above it floats the portrait of the man who sent the people to run this great race. And a slogan banner, red as our hot blood, unfurls and catches the wind like the sail of victory. "Hail to Comrade Stalin, the Best Friend of Soviet Physical-Culturalists!"

Not long before my father's downfall, he took my mother to the Dinamo Stadium in Tbilisi. I don't know if my father was an athlete. But he was a record holder, and a world record holder at that. In the little mining town of Chiatura, which remembers the concession held by Averell Harriman, the American millionaire, my father broke world records as a builder of industrial cableways.

The country was obsessed with records. They were its way of life and its mode of operation.

Scoring a goal—the crowning moment of any game, including handball.

Chkalov the pilot, Stakhanov the coal miner, Vinogradova the weaver, Kupuniya the tea harvester, Nakhangova the diminutive Uzbek cotton picker—thousands and thousands of the famed and the unknown were going beyond the bounds of human capabilities.

The nation of record holders was setting records so as to survive and triumph. "Either we will cover the distance of a hundred years in a single decade, or they will crush us," Stalin once said. The nation of record holders was setting a record such as the world had never known. It was building socialism. By a surpassing exertion of their will and strength, their intellect and soul, the people were bringing their country out of backwardness and placing it among the world giants. And when the war came, this striving for victory—no matter if it seemed impossible, unthinkable—this striving would have its effect. But something else was bound to have its effect, too, even though much later, after my generation had reached maturity.

A record is always an outstanding result, achieved by an outstanding individual. The cowed, the frightened do not set records. The outstanding individual searches out the ideal. Strictly speaking, the record is the ideal towards which the individual strives. For some, it is pushing out into the cosmos; for others, exceeding the tonnage of coal in the plan; for others, performing a difficult ballet step never attempted before on stage; for others, reaching the coldest spot on Earth.

To us the string of records seemed endless, eternal, unceasing. It would go on and on, forever confirming the refrain of our song: "We were born to make fairy tales real. We will master the land and the sea."

One thing I simply cannot understand. How

could our leader and teacher, possessed of such a country and such a people, fail to grasp something so elementary? A theory that makes people into interchangeable parts in a machine is contrary to the practice of the extraordinary, the breaking of records, the expression of our national striving towards a social ideal.

"When our country orders 'Be a hero,' / Then heroes we will be, every one." That order, set to verse in a song epitomizing the command system in a nutshell, dismantled the extraordinary machine that was turning out the best product mankind has ever known: selfless creativity.

But I will save it for later. For now I want to look into the thirties, to that summer day when my father, not yet branded an enemy of the people, brought my mother into the grandstands of the Dinamo Stadium. It was big-time soccer. The mag-

In Olympic and world championship competition, Soviet and American volleyball and basketball players almost always meet as finalists.

INTERNATIONAL
4
CARR
35
14

nificent Basques were playing. There was a war on in Spain, where Fascism was trying out its strength. The Basques were great artists in their sport, but their greatness as warriors surpassed their greatness as soccer sorcerers. They were fighting for the Spanish Republic. *No pasarán*! Fascism will not succeed! Working lads from Bilbao who played soccer like nobody else did at that time had come to the Soviet Union for help.

They got it.

My father was one of the many who contributed what he could to that help. He could have given more, if it weren't for other events that shook the country on the eve of World War II.

Towards the end of that year, my father was arrested. A few months later, he was shot. They simply broke him, like a screw that wouldn't turn under the screwdriver.

I had a legacy from my father: a white soccer ball signed by the great Langara. Later on this object will come to life and will act as one of my tale's heroes.

The family tradition about the match with the Basques is loaded with endearing details. "I had on a dress of crêpe de Chine—it was the height of fashion at the time." My mother used to say that with a smile, not tears. This story, which includes the fashionable fabric of the thirties, refuses to knit together with the epic whose heroine she became.

That epic would make a big book, with many of the chapters written by referees holding stopwatches and tape measures, the recorders of my achievements in the hundred meters and the long jump. As achievements go, mine were laughable. To cite them here would be to demean strong emotions I cannot help having. Although miserable by the standards of today, my seconds and meters finally added up to the result my mother passionately desired for her son. They erased the social inferiority, the shameful brand of fatherlessness.

When my father went to see his countrymen play the Basques, he carried in him a love for the Republicans and a hatred of the Fascists. His was a

Baseball has recently begun to tour the circuit of USSR sports venues.

22

Horse racing—a thrilling spectacle.

complex ideal, cast from the contradictions of the epoch. My mother's ideal was simple: Not only to prevent evil, huge and all-powerful, from crushing a good that was small and helpless, but to allow that good to develop into something huge and all-powerful. People could slight her son wherever and whenever they wanted, hinder him, deprive him, drive him out; but nobody could slight the personification of the formula: "Faster, Higher, Farther." His Excellency the Sporting Result would prevail against the fickleness of social origins.

Armed with the Olympic motto, mother scorned the Olympic canon and entered into a protracted battle, a secret war against Stalin.

She waged it with the support of remarkable allies.

A familiar voice comes flying towards me out of the crowd of runners, and I respond with ringing joy.

"Work, work!" shouts an elderly, balding man. The hand he waves at me is missing one finger. His legs are wiry, and he has the stoop of a distance runner. "Come on, take the lead! You're ahead of the record for this lap! Get out from behind Chubuk's back! Sprint the last lap!"

And the free air of youth pours into my tired lungs. Caught up in unexpected speed, I feel the hand of my first and only coach touching me, sending me forward.

The day he appeared in our schoolyard was not the best in my life. The day before, I had lost my filial inheritance. It was the most banal kind of story. The white soccer ball with the faded signature of the Basque Langara, an object elevated by play and elevating the spirit, fell victim to low passions. It expired under the knife of the thief Tsutsurma.

We were playing out behind the church of St. John the Divine, on a field formed when the gulley was filled with earth excavated for a bomb shelter. St. John the Divine had assigned the cathedral priest, Father Georgi, to help. The church and the bomb shelter did not guarantee our safety. There was an antiaircraft battery too, and the gunners liked soccer. We were playing the battery team. One-eyed Father Georgi was teaching them to sharpshoot goals.

The thief Tsutsurma was squatting on his heels some distance off, playing *zari,* a trivial dice game with nontrivial stakes. The church of St. John the Divine, the bomb shelter, boys playing soccer with a priest and soldiers from an antiaircraft detachment, the thieves of the Veri quarter—and all this on a scrap of land, a few hundred square meters. A model of existence, compressing life and death.

We were winning the match against the gunners. Tsutsurma was losing, and when he had lost everything he had, Black Rat said to him, "Let's play for your life." Tsutsurma wouldn't go along. "Let's play for that ball instead." He knew what he was betting. A reader born at another time than I will never understand what a real soccer ball meant to us. What this ball was for me, you can probably guess.

In the hopelessness of his fatal loss Tsutsurma chose a worthy equivalent of his mortal body. He grabbed the stray ball and plunged his knife into it. The gun-crew commander, Tolik Zhigalin, ran to the gun turret and prepared it for fire over open sights, but Father Georgi stood in the way with arms outspread.

The thieves departed. We remained alone with our grief.

Later Father Georgi would say he had feared for my reason. "Praise the Almighty, something gave you the strength to bear it."

Not something, but someone. And that someone was my running coach, Vitali Ilyich Kadeishvili.

He entered our schoolyard at a hard moment for me. I was trying in vain to pass the test for my BRLD pin.

Probably that abbreviation should be decoded as well, since it too contains a sign of our time. It ought to be explained that a whole hierarchy of heraldic distinctions was conferred on my generation. Among these, the BRLD pin was the longed-for first step.

In a recent television broadcast, the director of a big Moscow stadium deplored the physical

Reindeer racing—the national sport of the northern peoples.

laziness of visitors to his "installation" who ignored his challenge to pass the norms of BRLD. He was talking about voluntarily trying for the pin. For me and my coevals it was obligatory, an obligation coinciding with our aspirations.

A metal relief of a runner breaking through a finish tape with the inscription: "Be Ready for Labor and Defense!" Fastened to the chest, it became the first mark of a young citizen's valor. There was a systematic program for the fitness of the nation's youth, as rigorous as the quota for the smelting of steel. They wanted to temper us like steel. In our first years at school we were taught to throw grenades, fire small-caliber rifles, run obstacle courses, and swim. We competed in races over short and middle distances, in the high and long jumps.

The sails billow with wind.

War against Fascism was inevitable, and the country was preparing for it.

In one song a soccer goalie was compared to a sentry, and the goal he defended, to a border.

Don't draw any hasty conclusions about the militarization of society. No people, no country wishes to lay itself down as a sacrifice. We were making ready for labor and defense in the years of the *Anschluss* and the Franco rebellion, of the Munich Pact and the battle of Khalkhin-Gol. And in the end, the world was saved by boys who had taken the test for their BRLD pins back in school; who had parachuted from towers in parks and from the biplanes of air clubs, for which they received the pin of the Auxiliary for Defense and for Aviation and Chemical Development; who shot at black paper targets and green plywood silhouettes in the hopes of earning the Voroshilov Marksman pin.

Here is a painting by Svarog, *The Writer Maksim Gorky at the Shooting Range.* Authors, world-renowned physicists, unknown housewives, students, and schoolchildren took tests for all kinds of pins. Fastening them to their suit jackets, their plaid cowboy shirts, their ribbed silks and their crepes, they proudly announced: "We are ready!"

It isn't hard to guess that I have no Olympic medal at home in my collection of sporting trophies. But the collections of many Olympic champions in my country contain BRLD pins. In 1952, when Soviet athletes first participated in the Olympic Games and were showered with gold medals, there were many in the world who undertook to learn the secret of this phenomenon.

Here it is, the secret, in the palm of my hand. A five-pointed star with the little silvery figure of a runner, the finish tape breaking across his chest.

The score was running into the millions. From out of their ranks, from the millions of the identical and mutually interchangeable, there advanced the inimitable, the unique. Uniqueness did not fit well with the governmental maxim: "Nobody is irreplaceable!" If the individual is only a cog, who is the motor? But you don't reach new heights by following old theories. And the governmental slogan—"Physical Culture for the Masses!"—was replaced by another: "Mass Participation Plus Mastery." This was the motto of a country that had arrived as a great sporting power. Nobody was fooled by that "plus." Physical culture—sport for the many—had been put in one corner, and surpassing achievement—sport for the few—in another. To Caesar what is Caesar's, and to God what is God's.

Both were centrally planned. The plan worked smoothly; the quantitative factors in the production of BRLD pin-holders and world champions were operating without a hitch. But then a lot of people started to notice that the flame was dying out in the crucible of mass participation, and that the retort of mastery had cracked. In search of an explanation, a lot of people started thinking about what the individual is in sport—a means for achieving victory, or the crown?

Tiny Thumbelina performing the unthinkable elements of Ultra-C on the beam, towheaded giant raising stupefying kilograms of iron on outstretched arms, thinker-athlete straining tendons in the record strides and leaps of the triple jump, good-humored hockey player working with your stick as with an oar on the bark of victory—whose will is it that casts you back into nonbeing once you have done your stint on podiums, in arenas?

And why can't justice towards you ever reach the level of that supreme gratitude your performance arouses in us?

Some day we will ask openly about that. The time will come.

For now, I am standing in a schoolyard, nerving myself for a last attempt. The height is trifling—one meter, thirty centimeters. Everybody has made it but me. Everybody but me has passed the test for the BRLD pin. The physical education teacher, a kindly fellow, loosens the cord between the uprights and tugs it down, encouraging the hapless jumper. Two embarrassments in a row in front of our illustrious guest. It's really too much!

A water sprite.

The guest is not looking at me, though. The reddish brush of his mustache is uplifted, his palm, one finger missing, held to his beetle brows. His narrow squint takes in the crags of the mountain suspended above our school and the paths crisscrossing its bulging, bull-like sides. A week later I would learn where my coach Vitali Ilyich, had been looking. But it would be decades before I knew how he had discerned in me, daunted and dispirited, unable to cross the meter-thirty barrier that day, the sprinter he needed.

"Don't you ever listen to me? Go where I tell

you! What is it you see in that puddle you call Turtle Lake? I told you to run up Udzo mountain and along the Mtatsminda Crest. That's a good hard run. It'll build up your calves and ankles, give you cross-country endurance. And the scenery, the forests and valleys up there! Damn lazybones!"

But sometimes we did go where he told us, with him running out in front, and the running turned gradually into flight, into soaring on outstretched wings above our city with the Kura twisting like a snake in the stifling gray haze, above the blue crest of Ialno with the scattered red scorches of autumn forests, above the fallen roofs of the basilicas where a lonely tree of desire cast its branches towards the uncovered altars, trembling in the wind.

Now I understand it. He set himself the goal of returning us to our various quarters of the city as different people. And in this he succeeded. No, he didn't take away my grief and despair; and the bitter truth about my father still hovered above me. But now my thoughts and feelings were not mine alone. They merged with the unfettered flow of the Vere and the glimmering frescoes of Betani Cathedral, with the blazing snows of the Main Ridge of the Caucasus, with the song of the lark, rising to God knows what height—or rather rising without limit. And because my thoughts and feelings were not mine alone, I grew stronger.

Before teaching us to take a low start and to jump in Khorayn style, to explode towards the finish line and to bear up on the long distances, he showed us, in the way simplest for him, the marvelous world attainable through motion. Running up the crumbling path to the Asuret Fortress, hauling us up its side to the bottomless drop beyond—fly now if you don't want to fall—he was telling us: Here you are, and here is the peak, and there is no other way to unite you with it but for you to go towards it.

And we went. Only a few made it to the very top, but all of us, or nearly all, saw the world from on high. Believe me, at fourteen that is no small thing.

Only later, after all of this, did Vitali our coach pour us drop by drop into the intoxicating bowl of the stadium, raining other joys down on us.

Here, for instance, is a shovel, conferred on me as glory's most reliable instrument.

"Dig," my coach instructed. "Plant the seedling of victory. If you win the start, the finish is yours."

Plant your feet in the pits, propping your outstretched arms against the prickly hardness of the cinder track. Straighten your back and fill your lungs with air. Slump your shoulders in submission to the awaited signal, the pistol shot that strikes off an explosive spark in you.

"You take it through the first stage. Then pass the baton to Guram, just like giving him something in the hall. Guram, take about five meters to speed up to where Temik is, give it all you've got. The baton will nestle into your hand all by itself. Then comes the third stage, and Devi flies around the bend and puts Tolik out in front on the home stretch."

The relay baton, launched into the sky after the finish, descends somersaulting onto the heads of four boys embraced in victory. Removing our cleats and raising them in outstretched arms, we trot on the damp grass, inscribing our limitless joy into the roaring circle of the stadium. We are champions! Perhaps only of a district or a city, but anyone who has experienced moments like this knows that in them he is equal to the greatest athletes.

We are champions, and that means there will be prizes: cotton T-shirts and sneakers, with the rolled-up award certificate thrust inside. They will take us to training camps and give us a little extra food, in the form of ration coupons we are allowed to spend on soft drinks and ice cream. We will see other cities, where we will compete with youngsters like us. Win or lose, we will acquire many new friends, boys and girls. And all this will be a discovery of time, our homeland, and the world.

But that isn't all. You go out to warm up at the same time as Nina Dumbadze, who broke the world record of Gisela Mauermayer. You see her discus sail across the line to a new world record, and being a witness to that miracle makes you

Strength plus grace—body-building gymnastics.

even happier. Before your very eyes Nadezhda Khnykina breaks Galina Turova's long-jump record. The joy of the one and the tears of the other reveal to you the drama of human life, where everything is eternally indivisible. You run in the same heat with Levan Sanadze, and his whirlwind speed marks off for you, hopelessly left behind, the limit you must strive for.

A radiant young Russian, ready for an icy dip.

The space of the stadium allows you to stand together with the strongest and most glorious figures in sport. And the reflection of their glory, falling on you, awakens the hope of better and more. The stadium means equal chances at the starting line for the champion and the novice, and the inequality is measured with the most objective measure this world can possess. Even when the pure liquor of joy is adulterated with deceit and bias, you know that it is an anomaly, a thing done in secret. Real sport is a norm of human integrity, always open to everybody, always the maximum of the individual and the minimum of time. As long as sport remains so, it is eternal.

My idealism about sport was born in the years when Soviet sport was confidently and victoriously emerging onto the world arena, when world and Olympic champions were weaving new rays into the halo of the country that had defeated Fascism. It was a time of building, a time when the world was seeing itself in a new way. One of the paths to that vision was the most constructive kind of international competition—sporting contests.

Enthusiasm is idealism's brother. But everything depends on who interprets the ideal, and how.

One fine day in the fifties we suddenly learned that our country's army sports clubs had been disbanded. Broken up, rather. The national soccer team, many of whose members belonged to the army club, had lost an Olympic match. The supreme commander, irate at this loss (And to whom? The Yugoslavs!), had swept thousands of human destinies out of the arena with a single wave of his hand.

If anything was gnawing away at our sports movement from within, it was this authoritarian high-handedness. The managing apparatus had ossified in bureaucracy. Commands were handed down in place of grass-roots enthusiasm. The athlete was ruthlessly exploited as a machine for setting records.

I am running down a path shaded by acacias on the side of a forest-covered mountain. This is my

A ski race of thousands crowns the Carnival of the North.

last chance to keep my footing on life's track. Yesterday I returned from Moscow, the Olympics. I had gone to Luzhniki Stadium, expecting Viktor Saneev to win the gold a fourth time in the triple jump, and I had brought back a broken heart. Not long before, a noted cardiologist had told me: "You had a serious attack—you know that. It's out of the question for you even to think about running." What? Was I to be left out? The government's new slogan was: "Health Is the Main Record."

"What about jogging—wouldn't that be good therapy?" I ask, hoping secretly the answer will be yes.

"Absolutely not! The strain might be too much, and then . . . "

"So what do I do? Lie down and die?"

"Don't look at it that way. You'll have to follow a diet from now on, and take medication. Slow walking. In time we can think about an operation."

What was my misfortune in comparison with the drama of the retiring Saneev? But as one who has known the joy of struggle and victory, I am his equal. I will not accept defeat prematurely.

A man runs beside me down the path. He wears a blue T-shirt imprinted with a red crawling turtle. The turtle goes slow but lives long. The emblem and the motto belong to the Turtle, a club of walkers and runners. The motto is a mocking challenge to the "speed demons" who race to exhaustion chasing the medal quota.

The emblem, motto, and challenge were invented by the man running beside me in Tbilisi's Vake Park. His name is Dzhumber Khubua. He is a physical education instructor, forty-two-years old, with an incurable enthusiasm for therapeutic running. Besides me, a newcomer, the club he founded now includes about eighty members, ages ten to seventy. Twenty-six have had heart attacks. Three have been champions of Georgia. Eight have won cross-country races in Tbilisi. And not one has had a recurrence of heart trouble since joining the Turtle. Lekso and Tengiz, an engineer and a student, also hold practices. They have their own protégés and their own champions. And if health really is the main record, then Dzhumber, Lekso, and Tengiz are the main record holders, worthy of the title Honored Masters of Sport.

But why talk about titles? Dzhumber doesn't even have a decent pair of running shoes. Robbers broke into his apartment not long ago and carried off everything the least bit valuable. But they turned up their noses at one pair of threadbare shoes, repeatedly patched and glued. These prehistoric relics, labeled as an experimental product from Glavsportprom, are Dzhumber's most prized possession. Deprived of them, he would have nothing to run in. And for him, running is more than a sport. It is life.

Lev Khiterman from the city of Votkinsk, winner of the last Moscow International Peace Marathon, asked that instead of all the prizes he received, he be given a pair of decent running shoes. Incidentally, there is a factory in Votkinsk where until recently they made tactical missiles—a high-tech product, of course. It's no longer a secret. Under the terms of the Soviet-American treaty for the elimination of middle- and short-range missiles, the factory now has a resident American inspection team.

One secret does remain—one that many people are unable to fathom. Why is it that the country that can launch into orbit the Energia, the world's most powerful and advanced carrier-rocket, cannot manufacture sporting equipment that comes up to today's standards? What we produce never trickles down to the ordinary people. Ordinary people, as the new slogan of our sports movement says, are the country's greatest wealth.

I hear the nettled voice of an old-timer: "You are too fed up. Have you forgotten the T-shirt and sneakers for winning the city championship?"

No, I haven't forgotten. I haven't forgotten either, for example, how my friend Vova Chimakadze went about getting himself a pair of cleats. He found the surest path to them—through the heart of a woman. She was a great woman of her time, a holder of world records. And naturally her equipment was first class, imported. But Nina Yakovlevna Dumbadze, like every woman great or ordinary, had an Achilles heel—her son. He was doing poorly in one subject at school, and Vova, having discovered this, got himself appointed as volunteer tutor. The boy became a star pupil, and Vova became the proud possessor of superb English running cleats. He also got into Takhtarov's track and field school, which back then was the very best.

A path like Vova's will hardly do, however, for the millions of men and women for whom exercise, active participation in sports, is a necessary condition for a healthy, happy life.

At the first All-Union Spartakiad in 1928, some of the athletes came barefoot to the starting line. I own a bibliographic rarity, a priceless album of photographs made at the Spartakiad, showing wrestlers facing each other on the mats wearing traditional Central Asian skullcaps and tall fur hats. It wasn't rampant nostalgia that earlier brought to mind the games of the Veri quarter. In those days people came to record-setting sport with a sound background of honest competition in traditional games. Their enthusiasm was ineradicable. It helped them to win. But today, enthusiasm is not enough for victory, whether in elite sport or in the sport of the masses.

Nikolai Ozolin, who triumphed over the other pole vaulters at the 1928 Spartakiad, looked through all the bamboo groves outside the city of Batumi. He personally cut fifty trunks, from which he later selected just one.

Ours is the era of recortane, fiberglass, and composites, of computer models for the optimization of equipment and training. All the poles propping up yesterdays' views of mass physical culture have broken like matches. And the selfless enthusiasm that always helped out, whether in breaking world records or in having everyone earn those universally accessible BRLD pins, has ceased to be a straw that sports authorities can grasp at in their search for champions. Diamonds in the rough there will always be, but their brilliance fades, their carats are fewer, when the soil they come out of is not properly worked.

I will never forget the painful sting the words of a West German coach gave me. My colleague Tengiz Sulkhanishvili asked him what he thought of Soviet soccer.

"It reminds me of your economy," was the answer.

The honorable mentor of Gerd Müller and Franz Beckenbauer was wrong. Say what you will, Soviet soccer is more competitive than our heavy industry. Our teams have beaten the West Germans more than once, which cannot be said of our machine builders or shoemakers. And it isn't simply that nearly all my country's national teams wear Adidas, although Dzhumber Khubua, Lev Khiterman, and millions like them have only rundown tennis shoes. It isn't simply the relation between size and quality of output in group "A" and group "B." When chronic "under-use comes more and more to be the result of under-production," as Soviet scholar Ksenia Myalo has said, it is time to admit that a serious miscalculation has been made somewhere. And of course it will have its effect on sport, too.

Perestroika and *glasnost* have brought into the open all the defects of life in our country. They have affected the sport movement as well. And even though the old bureaucratic thinking and conservatism can still be felt, even though any attempt to shed light on what really ails Soviet sports meets with well-organized resistance from writers the official committees keep in their pockets, we have at last succeeded in making the health of the nation the first priority, in emphasizing that the sport movement must reach out to all. We have at last succeeded in realizing that sport can no longer be oriented towards quantitative development, which leads to an administrative approach just as it does in the economy. We have realized that sport, a democratic mass movement comparable in scale with the peace movement, can no longer be governed by undemocratic methods. It cannot be subject to extreme regimentation, with the accent on the normative and compulsory, the "obligation to follow the rules as given un-

Future champions.

questioningly, without entering into discussion of them."

Paraphrasing what the noted Soviet sociologist Igor Kon has said about systems of morality, we can say that sport should be organized along new

MMMM—The Moscow International Peace Marathon.

lines, in keeping with a higher level of social organization. Mikhail Gorbachev, speaking to the Nineteenth All-Union Party Conference, called reorganizing society the most urgent goal in reforming our country's political structure.

Our country's sport programs are being restructured too, albeit slowly. Without going into the forms that have been tried recently, I would like to express the hope that they will combine the most vital and democratic institutions with the highest degree of individual independence. Only in such a setting, I believe, can real social and athletic creativity find expression.

I am running along a path cut on the side of a mountain by the organizers of the Turtle. I am running in a T-shirt with an emblem applied by their hands. As I run, a doctor, one of the Turtle's enthusiasts, observes me. Tomorrow I will run in a race around the Tbilisi Reservoir, a competition organized by the same informal club. Distance runners from other cities and republics will take part as well, among them champions of Tbilisi and of Georgia. For them the Turtle is an oasis where they can rest from the stifling and numbing bureaucratic desert. For them, I believe, the race is a chance to protest, a chance to refuse and reject everything that chokes off initiative and individuality, everything (again following Igor Kon) that keeps a person from being not a means and condition for effective production, but the highest and final goal of all development. And no matter who wins, victory is ensured for all by such a manifestation of independent initiative.

I am running in a supermarathon, the newly elected president of the Turtle, one of tens of thousands of informal, grass-roots running clubs. I am happy but worried. The democratic initiative of my comrades deserves social and moral support. The club needs equipment and trails; we need the city's consent to hold competitions and its help in providing for traffic safety and food. For the time being, the mixtures we take to keep us going are prepared at home by the members. For the time being, the prizes we award are prizes that Lekso, Dzhumber, and Tengiz buy with their own money. For the time being, we are housed, very reluctantly, at the stadium of Lokomotiv, the club where Khubua works on the coaching staff.

How long can this go on? Happy to have my comrades' trust, I am worried by my obvious inability to push anything through, get hold of anything, organize. There are so many obstacles and barriers in the way. Can it really go on like this forever? No, it can't. There is no way back. The Turtle is moving. It moves slow but lives long. It has lived ten years already, without any kind of support, in an atmosphere of indifference and condescension. It is surviving. And what will happen when all this is behind us and the Turtle is recognized as a socially significant organization? Not the register-book bureaucratic recognition that has nipped more than one popular initiative in the bud, but real recognition, uniting the needs of the individual with the interests of the country. To how many people will the Turtle then restore hope of health, faith in their own strength, joy in movement, and happiness at the very idea of being able to overcome their ills?

All of that will be. For the time being, we are running down a shady path. The run is a sacred ritual of fellow believers; a heartfelt prayer for a better future for our country; a metaphor of movement, forward, forward, with all the speed we can muster.

Speed and the Turtle? But, after all, humor is granted to the strong and intelligent, never to fools.

I am running for the Turtle. It never hurts to smile along the way.

Ways of Life

SCOTT RUSSELL SANDERS teaches literature and intellectual history at Indiana University. He is the author of fourteen books, including *Secrets of the Universe,* a collection of essays that will appear later this year. His previous book of essays, *The Paradise of Bombs,* won the Associated Writing Programs Award for Creative Nonfiction. His novels and stories range from the past in such works as *Bad Man Ballad* and *Wilderness Plots,* through the present in *Fetching the Dead,* to the future in *The Engineer of Beasts* and *The Invisible Company.* His recent awards include fellowships from the National Endowment for the Arts and from the Lilly Endowment. He lives in Bloomington, Indiana, with his wife and two children.

VALERI VINOKUROV is editor-in-chief of the Moscow publishing house Fizkultura i Sport. During his newspaper days he worked with *Sovetski Sport;* he was subsequently literature and art editor for the magazine *Smena.* Vinokurov writes numerous sports articles and literary reviews, and he is the author of several nonfiction books on soccer, including *Steps Toward the Truth.* In addition, with co-author B. Shurdelin, he has written novels and stories on sports themes, including *Your Star and Mine, The Sky above the Field, Whose Sons,* and the story cycle *The Law of Inheritance.*

Living Souls

SCOTT RUSSELL SANDERS

The agent at the Pan Am counter in Indianapolis had to search a long while before he discovered the tomato-red luggage tag marked MOSCOW, USSR. The destination was not a common one for travelers from Indiana. For this particular traveler—an avid reader of Russian literature since high school, a skeptical admirer of Marx, a child of the Cold War—this was a first visit to the Soviet Union. What I knew of that vast and various land had come entirely from television and newspapers and books. What I knew had been refracted through the lenses of my own country, which, in official policy and popular sentiment, had regarded the USSR as a mortal enemy since before my birth.

The tomato-red tag was not affixed until an amiable guard had groped through my suitcase for bombs. "You're clean," he announced. I did not feel clean. I was running with sweat, less from anxiety than from the fierce August heat I had rushed through to arrive at this cautious place. Between here and that other cautious place a third of the way around the earth, my luggage would be searched repeatedly, my papers inspected, my body scanned, as I passed through layer after layer of misgiving.

The Svetenko family near the Kremlin.

The Pan Am Agent, who was the last man wearing a wig I would see before my return to the United States, frowned at my visa, which rendered my name in Cyrillic as СКОТ САНΔЕРС. "I can't make heads or tails of that," he said, returning the document to me with a shrug. I could read the visa, as a result of having studied Russian over the summer, but what I could say in that musical language was less than the babble of a Soviet toddler.

A lusty babble of Russian lilted all around me on the flight from New York to Moscow, the voices of émigrés returning for family visits. "It is our first visit home," a fiftyish woman told me from across the aisle. "Before, we were afraid to return. But now it is a new day."

My seatmates were two Marines, just old enough to buy Bloody Marys from the stewardess, one reading *Newsweek,* the other engrossed in *People,* both wearing earphones over their crew cuts. They were on their way for a tour of six months at the American Embassy in Moscow. Why so brief a stint? "They rotate us through there fast, to keep us from fraternizing," said one Marine. Fraternizing: treating the enemy as though he were a brother. His use of the word brought to mind old photographs of rival soldiers at the front hugging one another during a cease-fire. An elderly woman whose purple tour badge identified her as Bertha paused in the aisle to tell the Marines, "I feel much safer, knowing you boys are going over there with us."

At midnight, Indiana time, I set my watch forward nine hours. I had lost a night. "Now it is a new day," the Russian woman had told me. How new the Soviet day in fact was, and what the human weather promised to be in Moscow, were questions I carried with me across the ocean.

Beyond the passport booths and customs gates and security fences in Moscow's Sheremetyevo International Airport, hundreds of eager faces waited to greet friends and relatives who had arrived on my flight. The man who waited for me was a stranger, husky as a stevedore in his gray pin-striped suit, with a brown flap of hair curling down over his forehead, and quick eyes above a nervous half-smile. Andrei Sergeyevich Svetenko had reason to be nervous. He and his wife had learned only two days earlier that they would be hosting me during my week in Moscow. I could never discover exactly how they and their son had been selected from the city's nearly nine million people as a representative family. Aside from my name and nationality and profession, they knew nothing about me. To open their home and thoughts to an American writer, an outsider who would return to his own country and publish whatever he chose about their lives: that was a brave and perhaps foolhardy act, about which Andrei, as he shook my hand in the lobby, must have been having second thoughts.

Andrei had been led to believe that I spoke Russian, but after our exchange of hellos he knew better. "You must forgive my poor English," he told me in good English, with a robust accent, rich in r's, that gave the words a pleasing weight in the ear. "I have no chance to practice speaking it."

"I understand you perfectly," I told him.

"But wait until I have something difficult to say!"

And so began our week-long dialogue, across two languages and two continents and two ways of life, a dialogue that would stretch Andrei's English and my understanding beyond the limits each of us had imagined.

Outside, the air was cooler by a season than the blistering air I had left in Indiana, more like October than August, and the light on this cloudless day was milder than the insistent corn-ripening sunlight of the Midwest. This gentle northern light shone on buildings and cars and clothes that were the shades of earth, charcoal and gray, buff and cream, making the world appear muted. Along the highway from the airport to the city there were no billboards to disrupt the somber tones, no garish franchises, no neon lights, few traffic signs. Instead there were trees, dark shaggy conifers and white birches that crowded up nearly to the pavement, giving one the sense that the forest was primary, the road secondary. Since childhood, when I had dreamed of making birchbark canoes worthy of Indians, I had loved these white trees with their inky slashes. In Moscow I was to see them everywhere I turned, in parks and playgrounds, on any patch of dirt large enough to support life, ghostly presences, glimmering.

On the drive from the airport, the first landmark Andrei pointed out to me was a monument of crossed black steel girders, an enlargement of the tank barricades from World War II, honoring the spot a few kilometers outside of Moscow where the Nazis were stopped in December 1941. The Soviet name for the prolonged bloodbath, in which some twenty million of her people died, is the Great Patriotic War. I was to see memorials to war and revolution and suffering planted in Moscow almost as thickly as the birches. As we sped past, two newlyweds were posing for photographs at the monument, the bride's white gown like a froth of bubbles against the black steel, the groom as dark as a raven, their smiles uncannily bright against the gloom of memory.

It is a custom in the Soviet Union for newlyweds to visit memorials to those who died in defense of the motherland. On his own wedding day twelve years earlier, Andrei had taken his new bride to lay flowers on the Tomb of the Unknown Soldier, in the shadow of the Kremlin wall. The wall with its many towered gates flashed by our car as he told me this. The bride's name was Marina Nikolayova Filatova, a name she kept intact through marriage. "In our country it is rare for a woman to keep her family name," Andrei said. "But I wanted very much to marry her, so I did not object."

As we approached his apartment block, which

is south of the meandering Moscow River, midway between the second and third ramparts of the ancient city, Andrei began to apologize. The building, like much of the city, like the entire society, was undergoing *perestroika,* reconstruction. Forgive the mess. I was used to mess, I told him, for my family and I had been renovating our old house piecemeal for a dozen years.

"You do the work yourselves?" he asked with surprise.

"Everything except the plumbing."

"Then maybe you can help us with our electricity!" He laughed. Already I could hear that Andrei had a gift for laughter, as others have a gift for storytelling or song.

Instead of a lawn, a thicket of saplings and bushes and weeds surrounded the apartment block. Everywhere in Moscow I was to find the apartments encircled by these young forests that looked at once unkempt and appealingly wild. We picked our way past Queen Anne's lace and chicory and black-eyed Susans, blossoms I was glad to recognize, past heaps of lumber and shattered bricks, past the vigilant eyes of old women on benches, *babushkas* wearing *babushkas,* some of them doubtless widows since the Great Patriotic War, past three locks, and so into a sunny corner flat on the seventh floor.

The woman who had defied convention by keeping her maiden name greeted us at the door. Marina Filatova seemed to possess, as the hollow bones of birds possess, the contradictory qualities of delicacy and strength. A slender woman with a valentine face given to pensive pouts and blazing smiles, elegant in movement, precise in speech, hair in dark brown curls to her shoulders and in bangs over dark shining eyes, she wore a white dress imprinted with red flowers. She was thirty-one, a year younger than Andrei and eleven years younger than myself. During that week she would seem by turns girlish in her idealism and grandmotherly in her wisdom, as Andrei would seem by turns brash and sage. Although Marina pronounced the occasional English word with remarkable clarity, and she understood most of what I said to her, for the present she spoke only in Russian to Andrei, who translated her words into English for me. The language barrier, combined no doubt with her uncertainty about this Yankee guest, gave her the appearance of being shy.

Over dinner they began to sketch for me the outlines of their lives. Andrei is a historian, in charge of the cataloguing department in the Central State Archives for Historical Acts. Marina, a teacher at the Oil and Gas Institute, was on leave from her job while preparing to defend a graduate thesis.

Robert Maksimov photograph

In the Kremlin's Cathedral Square.

"So you're a geologist?" I asked.

My question provoked laughter, followed by an awkward silence. I looked down at my plate, an array of sliced tomatoes, cucumbers, peppers, green peas, black and white bread, with a cheese-topped cutlet at the center, a delight for both eye and tongue, as every one of Marina's dishes would be.

"To tell you the truth," Andrei said at last, "what Marina teaches is the science of communism."

I took this to mean that she kept the young geologists at the Oil and Gas Institute on the straight-and-narrow, that Marina was, in effect, an ideological watchdog for the Party. As with so many other first judgments, this would later come to seem inane, a cartoonish oversimplification.

The dissertation she was preparing to defend

Robert Maksimov photograph

At home in Moscow.

explores the problem of contradictions in Soviet society. Contradictions—as between the citizens and the bureaucracy, or between the workers and the state—were a "problem" because, according to Marx and Lenin, they should have disappeared with the coming of socialism. And yet there the contradictions were, as anyone with eyes could see. Was this an exciting time to study the question, because of *glasnost,* the new openness to debate? Yes, Marina replied, but it was also a time of uncertainty. Who would her examiners be? And how far would they permit her to go?

While Marina explained these matters through Andrei, I sipped my champagne, which, in keeping with Mr. Gorbachev's crusade against drunkenness, was nonalcoholic. "As in your own Prohibition," said Andrei, "some people begin making liquor at home. But even that is difficult, because sugar is rationed." I taught them the meaning of *bootlegger* and *moonshine* and *hooch.*

Their only child, an eight-year-old son named Mikhail, was spending the summer as usual with Marina's father and mother at the parents' *dacha* outside of Moscow. I would meet him on Tuesday. They invariably referred to the boy by his diminutive, Misha, which also happens to be the name for a bear cub, a folk mascot whose place in Soviet culture is akin to that of Mickey Mouse in the United States. In the afternoon, Marina excused herself to go pay Misha a visit.

Andrei and I took a long garrulous walk, down the avenues crowded with Saturday strollers, in and out of neighborhood shops, through the dappled shade of birches and maples in a section of Gorky Park called "The Garden of Un-boredom." To this American eye, accustomed to public eccentricity, the strollers appeared mannerly, restrained, the girls and women linked at the elbows, the boys clasping the hands of grandparents, faces composed, voices playing quietly on private channels.

To any American eye, the shops would have seemed meagerly stocked and drably decorated. On the other hand, because the Soviet economy does not run on the fuel of endless consumption, one is not constantly exhorted there, as one is in the United States, to buy, buy, buy! The sole item universally promoted in the streets and squares and media is the Soviet state, its heroic past and glorious future. One sees this in the slogans that are spelled out in electric letters along the rooflines of buildings, in signs on the hoardings of construction sites, in murals and posters and plaques, in documentaries and newscasts, in war memorials and grandiose statues. The intersection of Lenin Prospect and Kosygin Avenue, near Andrei and Marina's flat, is presided over by a gigantic statue of Cosmonaut Gagarin, the first human to orbit the earth, who is represented not as the compact, intelligent man he actually was, but as a chromium superhero with bulging muscles. Whenever I felt oppressed by this constant promotion of the state, the system, the motherland, I recalled that in an American city there would have been even more urgent, ubiquitous pitches for cigarettes and motorcycles and beer. If the Soviets have made a religion of collective achievement, we have made a religion of private gratification.

My legs were rubbery from jet lag, my head woozy from new impressions. As we walked, Andrei chain-smoked Bulgarian cigarettes ("the taste of cabbage") and commented exuberantly on everything we passed. He perceived the city in four dimensions, three of space and one of time, for behind every building and street name and statue there was a history, which he recounted in fervent detail. Much of the visible past still reflected the rule of Joseph Stalin, whose name Andrei would introduce into our conversation dozens of times that week, always with loathing. According to that quintessential American Henry Ford, "History is bunk." All of Moscow delivers a contrary message, for which my spirited companion was the ideal interpreter: the message that history is inescapable. History is in our bones. To ignore the past is to live as a fool.

Near midnight, after Marina's return from visiting Misha, the three of us took another walk, this time along the river to the enormous gothic tower of Moscow State University. Marina had studied philosophy and the science of communism in that tower, one of seven colossal buildings ordered by Stalin to show that Moscow, like New York, was capable of skyscrapers. From the esplanade in front of the university, in the moonshadow of a tall curving slide used for winter ski-jumping, we gazed across the river at Moscow's web of lights. In the darkess it could have been any great city, half-asleep, half-awake, giving off the ferment of change.

"It is because Marina and I wish to be part of that change, to be in touch with what is happening in our society," said Andrei, "that we joined the Communist Party."

Thus he answered a question I had not asked.

"These days are like the time after the Revolution," said Marina, "when Lenin welcomed debate, disagreement, fresh ideas."

Robert Maksimov photograph

Breakfast with the American visitor.

"Under Stalin, disagreement became a crime," said Andrei. "In the old days, a man thought one thing, dreamed another thing, and spoke something else. Now, we think and dream and say the same thing. What we used to whisper only in our kitchens, we now say on television, in the meeting halls, in the streets."

I woke on Sunday to the grit of truck tires on Kosygin Avenue. Most of those trucks were olive-drab army vehicles, as were most of the bulldozers, earthmovers, shovel loaders, and other heavy equipment I saw in Moscow. This gave to the streets the look of a city under martial law. And yet nearly all the drivers were civilians; the trucks hauled not weapons but cement and bread and steel. Eventually I realized that Soviet army vehicles, whose numbers mount so ominously in the reports delivered by the Pentagon to Congress, take the place of our own municipal fleets, utility company vans, private construction equipment, delivery trucks, and long-distance rigs. Instead of rusting on gravel lots, military equipment is put to use in the constant low-grade war to build and repair the city.

Still, I found the olive-drab tone of the streets disquieting. During a childhood spent mostly in an arsenal, surrounded by soldiers and the machinery of war, I developed an allergy to militarism. Since the framers of our Constitution warned against the danger of standing armies, a suspicion of soldiers has run deep in the American grain, perhaps never deeper than in those of us who came of age during the Vietnam War. In Moscow I encountered a people who view soldiers as heroes, builders, protectors, saviors. This attitude of respect, bordering on reverence, is evident in museums and on television, in the jackets worn by older men decorated with ribbons and medals from the Great Patriotic War, in cemeteries where the tombs of commanders are heaped with flowers, in casual remarks, in the memorials that serve almost as shrines.

However useful it no doubt has been to the pursuit of the Communist dream, the celebration of the military is not an invention of the Soviet era, but rather is a persistent theme in Russian history. Most of the hospitals and churches in Moscow that have survived from tsarist times were built to commemorate a victory—over the French, the Swedes, the Turks, the Finns, the Germans. The list of foes is a long one. For a millennium, the nation centered around Moscow has been invaded from every point of the compass, and has in turn expanded the area of its control in every direction. Over the course of the week, Andrei would speak not only of the struggle against Hitler, but of that against Napoleon in the nineteenth century, the Poles in the seventeenth, the Tatars in the sixteenth, the Mongols in the fourteenth. For him, as for his people, invasion is a present horror kept fresh by the waters of recollection.

On a Sunday morning television show about the Red Army, we saw volunteers cleaning up the radioactive debris from the crippled nuclear reactor at Chernobyl; we heard amputees recalling the war in Afghanistan. As of that week, half the Soviet troops had come home from the war, after 13,000 of their comrades had died and 35,000 had been wounded, and the remaining troops were scheduled to return home within the next year. Andrei reported these numbers with a sigh. When I suggested that his country had made the same mistake in Afghanistan that my country had made in Vietnam, he disagreed firmly, insisting that the Soviet Union had taken sides with the democratic forces, while the United States had backed the reactionaries.

Sunday was to be the most military of my days, as we followed the television show with a walk through Red Square and the Kremlin. "Our history begins here," said Andrei, thumping his shoe on the stones of the square, whose name originally meant not red but beautiful. This place of executions, revolutions, proclamations, and parades recalled for me newscast footage of troops marching and tanks wheeling in formation, missiles drawn on wagons past the faces of enraptured crowds, wizened rulers gazing down from the roof of Lenin's mausoleum. Andrei pointed out to me with satisfaction the burial place near the Kremlin wall to which Stalin, once displayed alongside Lenin in the mausoleum, had been demoted. One of the delegates to the Twenty-Second Party Congress who had voted for the demotion was Mikhail Gorbachev, himself now the central figure presiding over parades, a vigorous rather than a wizened man. Yet the parades these days are no less martial than before.

The Kremlin itself is a fortress, roughly triangular in shape, surrounded by a high crenelated wall. The river still flows along one flank, and in earlier times the other two were protected by a moat. Beyond the moat there were two circular ramparts, which are still visible on the map of Moscow as the paths of ring roads. The word *kremlin* itself originally meant a fortified stronghold. Inside, the tsars built palaces to hold their wealth, barracks for troops, an arsenal for weapons, and cathedrals to capture God. Authority continues to emanate from this place that was built to repel assaults. Entering through one of the twenty towers, Andrei and I shuffled from palace to cathedral to garden in the company of orderly crowds. The only raised voices I heard were American. The only visitors who wandered outside the zebra-striped footpaths, provoking curt whistles and a wave of batons from policemen, were American. I was embarrassed by my own people, as I often am when abroad, and yet I was also growing impatient with Soviet decorum. Where was the play, the zest, the idiosyncracy in their lives?

As we retraced our steps through Red Square, Andrei remarked on a painter who slouched against a windowsill as she worked. Until recently, he said, you would not have seen such unruly behavior, people leaning on buildings! He also mentioned that he had been puzzled to see American young people sitting on the floor of the airport, even lying on the floor, instead of using the chairs. The few times we saw a pedestrian jaywalk, usually across a street that was empty of traffic, Andrei never failed to shake his head at this lawless behavior. I wondered what he would think of the students at my university, the pedestrians in my town, or the children in my house. Would they seem to him slovenly and wayward, or enviably uninhibited?

Although well-mannered themselves, Andrei and Marina viewed this passion for public decorum with a redeeming humor. When we met a skateboarder, one of three I would see in Moscow, Andrei observed that older people strongly disapproved of these reckless contraptions, as they disapproved of break dancing. "But me, I would ride one, if my bones were younger!" It was another sign of the new leniency that police no longer broke up skateboarding tournaments nor chased dancers from the sidewalks. How far this public playfulness would be allowed to go, he could not

Robert Maksimov photograph

At the Central State Archives of Historical Facts.

say. On the Metro one night, Marina laughed at a wall placard, which listed fifty-two rules. "Fifty of them say what you may not do, and only two say what is allowed!" Despite their good humor, I took care not to stand out from the crowd. In walking, in speaking, in handling a fork, in everything I did all week, I was conscious of acting with restraint.

Marina's sense of propriety led us to move on Sunday evening from her and Andrei's flat, where the hot water was mysteriously out, to her parents' flat, which was vacant for the summer. A guest from America must be able to wash. I told her that cold water would do just fine. No, she insisted. Her parents had a couch that opened into a bed, a color television, hot water. We all would be more comfortable there. So we left the three

Robert Maksimov photograph

Reading with father.

worn but meticulously kept rooms, with their parquet floors and papered walls, their glass cases filled with books and china and Misha's war toys, and moved into two larger, better furnished rooms in northwestern Moscow, high in another apartment tower, higher than the derricks that bristled on the Moscow skyline. Here the carpets were plusher, the wallpaper fresher, the stove and refrigerator newer. The glass cases here contained even more books: poetry and novels, science fiction, mysteries, handsome collected editions of works by the great Russian and Soviet writers, along with volumes of cherished foreigners, such as Mark Twain and Jack London. There was indeed a color television in the living room as well as a black-and-white set in the kitchen, and the couch made a comfortable bed. But on Sunday night, at least, there was no hot water. It did not soothe Marina to learn that large sections of Moscow were temporarily without hot water. She was fit to be tied. She promised that in the morning she would heat water herself, on the stove. For tonight I must forgive her, forgive the city, forgive socialism.

Whenever she worked in the kitchen, Marina hummed along to music on the radio or to melodies playing in memory. While frying sausages for Monday's breakfast and heating water for our baths, she was humming a tune from *Jesus Christ, Superstar.* She and Andrei had come to like Western music through listening to cassettes of the Beatles, Rolling Stones, Pink Floyd, and Deep Purple. Now they listened eagerly to such new Soviet groups as Bravo, Aquarium, Kino, Secret, and Nautilus Pompilius, which sing about social problems in the mournful rhythm of ballads or the raucous beat of rock. "It is music not only about teen-age love," Andrei explained, "but about community, about grown people making a world together." For the same reason they cherished the music of their "bards"—singers who speak of crime, prisons, injustice, war, the dark side of the socialist utopia. "Like your own Pete Seeger," said Andrei. "When I was a boy, all the time I listened to British and American pop music. Now, I prefer the bards and classics—Rakhmaninov, Mozart, Grieg!" Before the week was out, I had heard works by all three composers on radios in taxis. One cabbie, who lowered the volume when the news came on, raised it again when he caught the opening measures of Rakhmaninov's second piano concerto. In cars and kitchens, the radio was always on, playing folk music from the more than a hundred ethnic groups of the Soviet Union and from around the world, playing symphonies and arias, big band combos and jazz. Among the few types of music I did not hear in Moscow were country-western and Muzak, both of which I was glad to do without.

The radio at one side of the kitchen table was tuned for my benefit to the English-language version of Radio Moscow, while on the opposite side the television murmured. We ate most of our meals in this cross fire of images and words. As on other days, our conversation over Monday's breakfast lasted two hours, beginning with shaved and sugared carrots at ten and ending with chocolates and coffee at noon. As he grew excited about politics or chess or sports, Andrei would get up and pace, every now and again consulting the tiny Russian-English dictionary he carried in his pocket. More composed, Marina would linger at the table or work at the sink. (She refused to let me clear my dishes, let alone wash them, as I would have done at home.) Lips pursed, she listened to Andrei's English, breaking in with her lilting Russian to correct or embroider on what he said.

Robert Maksimov photograph

Helping mother.

"We need to recover a sense of pride," he declared that morning as he paced, "a sense of having power over our lives. Men do not exploit men here. We have overcome that problem. But we need to recover the spiritual dimension."

What about Marx's claim that consciousness and the realm of spirit were simply reflections of material conditions?

"The two are connected," said Marina, "but our material life will improve only when people feel they are masters of their lives. We must give control back to workers and farmers. We must have real democracy."

In recent months, encouraged by the example of

Raisa Gorbachev, who teaches methods of social inquiry, Marina had interviewed men and women in factories. "They boiled over with emotions. They spoke of their fears, their frustrations, their hopes. For too long they have been silent. For too long no one has asked them what they truly want. I am convinced that we must change not only what they can buy in the stores, but what they feel in their hearts."

This was a constant theme in our talk—the need for a renewal of spirit, soul, heart alongside the economic transformation of Soviet society. In this era of *glasnost* and *perestroika,* when long-suppressed novels and films were appearing, when the media were criticizing the system, when the streets were beginning to buzz with debate, Andrei and Marina sensed all around them the beginnings of a spiritual recovery.

The signs of change were plentiful. Construction of yet another war memorial in Moscow had recently been halted by public outcry against the design. Oil drilling in Siberia had been halted by protests from native peoples concerned about pollution. The often fierce debates from the summer Party Conference had been reprinted verbatim in *Pravda* and broadcast on television, inspiring crowds to gather in Pushkin Park and carry on the debate in open air. The aftermath of the Chernobyl disaster, the explosion of a weapons train, the wreck of the Leningrad-Moscow Express with much loss of life, the failure of a space rendezvous, all were franky discussed on television during my stay, whereas even a year earlier such mishaps would have been concealed in bureaucratic silence. From the Republic of Georgia, where Andrei had once angered a roomful of men by refusing to drink a toast to Stalin, came the broadcast of a puppet show that bitterly and hilariously satirized the Stalinist regime. On Marina's bedside table, the current issue of *Novy Mir,* the journal of the writers' union, lay open to the first installment of *Dr. Zhivago,* the novel that had forced Pasternak into exile a generation earlier. George Orwell's *1984,* long held to be an attack on communism, would appear in the same magazine a few months later.

Another token of the spiritual and cultural renaissance was the screening of films by Andrei Tarkovsky, who had been driven out of the Soviet Union during the Brezhnev era. "We call it the era of stagnation," said Andrei. At a cinema on Monday evening amid a hushed audience we watched Tarkovsky's *Sacrifice.* The original Swedish dialogue was translated by a phlegmatic Russian narrator, making the film incomprehensible to me in two languages. Andrei, too moved to speak during the movie, told me afterwards that it was about a man who cuts himself off from his son, his wife, his home, his work, in fulfillment of a vow he had made when praying that the world be spared a nuclear holocaust. Even in exile, the Soviet artist was brooding on war. When I asked Andrei to translate the line of text that appeared at the end of the film, he gestured that I must wait, and I saw that he was weeping. The last figure on screen was a boy who reminded Andrei and Marina of their own son Misha. The closing text was a message of love addressed to Tarkovsky's son, back in the Soviet Union, whom Tarkovsky would never be allowed to see. "He died in exile, in 1986, the year he made the film," said Andrei. "That is wrong. That is deeply wrong. He was one of our geniuses. He should have been here in his own country, teaching us. Now, at least, we can see his work."

While I savored my dish of cheesecake soaked in gooseberry sauce on Tuesday morning, Andrei rubbed his eyes and complained about having to rise at such a beastly hour. Seven thirty! From the bedroom came the sound of Marina singing. "She is a skylark who likes to go to sleep early and get up early. But me, I am an owl. I prefer to stay up late and sleep even later." Misha was taking after him, becoming an owlet.

We had risen at this hour in order to go visit Misha in the country at his grandparents' *dacha.* A car and a taciturn driver supplied by Fizkultura i Sport publishing house drove us the sixty kilometers west of Moscow. Andrei and Marina had no car of their own, nor would they be able to afford one for another twenty or thirty years, Andrei predicted with a laugh. They asked gingerly if I owned a car. Yes, I told them. And a house? Yes. Did my children have their own rooms? Yes, yes. Were the rooms full of toys? Was my house full of electronic gadgets? Were my closets full of clothes? Too full for my taste and my conscience, I answered. Did all Americans own so much? Not all, but many; perhaps too many for the good of all.

It must have seemed easy for one who owned so much to speak with misgivings about ownership. All week they hinted at a deeper question, without ever quite asking: Did I find their way of life humble by comparison to life in America? Did I find them poor? Had they asked, my answer would have exhausted our shared vocabulary. I would have told them I do not measure the quality of a life by the quantity of possessions. I would have said they live more elegantly, considerately, responsibly with their few things than do many Americans of my acquaintance who own far more. I would have said, quoting Thoreau, that a man is rich in proportion to the number of things he can do without. I would have said that their government, like mine, has lavished far too much wealth on weapons and soldiers, too little on daily needs, too much on public display and too little on private delight. No people in such an abundant land should have to wait in line for bread. No children in such an ingenious land should have to make do with shoddy toys. No archivist, no teacher, should have to spend a month's pay for a suit of clothes. Yes, their lives are harder than the lives of all but the poor in my country, and I do not sentimentalize hardship. I would like to see their stores full of useful and handsome and healthful goods. But I would also like to see our own stores full of such goods. I would not wish on my Soviet friends the acres of plastic, the billboards, the commercials, the highway sleaze, the mass delusion of fashion, the endless borrowing against the future, and the prodigious waste that accompany prosperity in America.

At the village of Aprelyevka we turned from the highway onto a side road that consisted of parallel concrete strips, broken at the joints and half-buried in mud churned up by cows. The cows belonged to a collective farm, across whose pastures the road had been roughly laid. A few morose brown eyes gazed at us from the herd as we lurched by. We also drew stares from a trio of mushroom gatherers clutching lumpy sacks and from an elderly couple who were hauling firewood on the chassis of a baby buggy. Eventually we came to a cluster of about one hundred cottages, encircled by a fence and set off strikingly against the forest of birch and fir. Like all land in the Soviet Union, this belongs to the state, which loaned these few acres to veterans of the Great Patriotic War for the creation of a gardening cooperative. It was evident the cottagers took the word "gardening" seriously, for the 600-square-meter lots had been planted from boundary to boundary with vegetables and fruit trees and flowers. Green and blossoming waves lapped against the foundations, climbed the walls of brick and board, flung tendrils above the fretwork of the eaves onto the peaked metal roofs.

The walkway to Marina's parents' cottage was bordered by red zinnias the size of my palm, scarlet salvia, spiky asters, and nodding sunflowers higher than my head. The cottage itself looked as though it might have sprouted there, for it was made of knotty pine, varnished inside and out so that it gleamed in the sunlight. Our reception was loud and loving, first from Marina's father, Nikolai Ivanovich Filatov, a retired army officer, genial and hearty, with a farmer's tan and a fringe of unruly gray hair; next from Marina's mother, Nina Petrovna Filatova, a retired nurse, gentle, beaming, happily flustered by the arrival of this American; then from Marina's sister, Lena, a large and tranquil woman of thirty-nine, on maternity leave from her job as an engineer; and then, in shy succession, by a trio of grandchildren, eight-year-old Misha and six-year-old Anya and eighteen-month-old Ivan, the latter pair belonging to Lena, all three as blond as cornsilk and as fresh as dawn.

From the look in the children's eyes, I might have descended from a spaceship. I gave Misha the presents my own son Jesse had picked out, bubble gum and baseball cards. Soon young jaws were chewing and small hands were shuffling through glossy photos of pitchers and sluggers.

Mrs. Filatova swept baby Ivan into her arms and crowed to him, "This is a once-in-a-century event, to have such a guest!"

Ivan gazed at me dubiously, then climbed into the stout arms of his grandfather, who cuddled and teased him while showing me around the homemade greenhouses and the garden. The

Robert Maksimov photograph

At the dacha in the Moscow countryside.

black soil spoke exuberantly in carrots, tomatoes, radishes, beets. Climbing beans covered the arbor over the table where we would eat, at the back of the lot near the summer kitchen. Barrels at the corners of the roof caught rain water for the garden. Lush vines hid melons and squash. Anise and dill spiced the air. I took pleasure in the vigor of the place and in the signs of labor. The savory food I had been eating all week had come from this dirt, these hands.

After a while I retired to the porch, hoping to write up some notes. Within moments the grandchildren crept in after me and stood at arm's length, staring. One by one they began speaking to me in Russian, even a few monosyllables from Ivan, then all of them chattered at once, unable to believe that a grownup could not speak their language. Anya in particular kept firing questions, then waiting for answers with hands on hips and lovely saucer face cocked up at me. Misha, a rambunctious towhead wearing a Mickey Mouse shirt, showed me a war scene he had sketched with a burning iron onto a plank, a scene of US and Soviet troops battling Nazis. He pointed to a star on one of the American tanks and then to my chest. Allies. Mrs. Filatova came to shoo the children away, but as soon as she turned her back they materialized again, a circle of inquisitive eyes.

Riding his bike and clambering up trees and rollicking among the cottages with friends, Misha remained elusive all day, so that I had to observe him from a distance. "He is a very good boy," said Andrei, "but he will never be a diplomat. He is too honest. He says just what he thinks. He promises me that he will never, never lie. I say to him this is the important thing, for a man to be honest." At the end of the day, Misha would beg to return with us to Moscow. Marina said no. It was not a good time. He was better off here in the country. In the car going home she would explain to me that some women, such as Lena, were content being mothers only, without jobs, but that other women, including herself, needed a career outside the family.

Far from being elusive, Anya adopted me. Slender like her Aunt Marina, silky hair cut into bangs in front and dangling in a ponytail behind, she wore that day a blue polka-dot dress and white knee socks with red sneakers. When the family went for a saunter through the woods, Anya took my hand and led me gaily forward, only letting go to dash away and pluck a wildflower for me. She kept up a joyful prattle the whole time. Overhearing, Andrei laughed and said that Anya wanted to go back to America with me. Would she like to ride in my suitcase? I asked. Yes, came the reply, that would be fine. By the time we returned to the cottage for dinner, I had a fistful of wildflowers and a heartful of tenderness.

Over dinner, which began with mushrooms and caviar and proceeded through salmon, fish soup, platters of vegetables, chicken, watermelon, and pineapple, the Filatov clan joked and told stories. Sun filtering through the leaf-covered arbor bathed us in a minty light. Although the children were supposed to be eating in the summer kitchen, they kept slipping back to sit with the grownups. Ivan, babbling the universal baby language of "ba!" and "da!" was passed around the table. Anya plumped down beside me and thumbed through a deck of cards, teaching me the names and numbers in Russian, refusing to turn the next card until I had repeated the words to her satisfaction. (Andrei and Marina would later tell me they had feared that Anya, a cheeky little vixen, would act up during my visit, and that, alas, she had. Behavior they regarded as impolite struck me as enchanting.)

Misha teasingly said he would tell Mr. Gorbachev on us, for drinking vodka! Mrs. Filatova drank along with the men, but Lena and Marina stuck with red Georgian wine. After three vodkas, Andrei shrugged and told me he could no longer speak English. Mr. Filatov said that after four vodkas, I would begin speaking Russian. As one who drinks wine seldom and vodka never, I now drank my fourth glass and could barely speak any human language. Fortunately, I did not have to use my legs for a long while, because we sat talking for most of the afternoon. I told them how much I admired their family collective. Now they must have a cow and chickens! A cow, yes, said Mr. Filatov, and we shall put her front end in our

Robert Maksimov photograph

Afternoon conversation.

neighbor's plot, where she can eat, and her rear end in our plot, where we can milk her! Let us do away with nuclear weapons, Andrei proposed. So that I may live here in peace with my beautiful women! Mr. Filatov cried. To understanding between our peoples! To prosperity! To love!

Robert Maksimov photograph

Gifts from America.

As we prepared to leave, Mrs. Filatova solemnly presented me with a bouquet of red zinnias, which I held gratefully all the way back to Moscow, warming myself at their blaze.

Lena called Marina before breakfast on Wednesday to say that all the neighboring cottagers were buzzing about the mysterious visit of the American. They were demanding to know how the Filatovs, out of all the millions of Soviet families, had been chosen for such an honor. Honor? I thought, sitting at the kitchen table in my jeans and ignorance.

"Marina is on the phone all the time," Andrei observed, "to her sister, her mother, her women friends."

"Only a few short calls each day," Marina replied testily after saying good-bye to Lena. "They are necessary for keeping our home. Someone must keep the home!"

There followed a dispute that was playful on the surface but serious underneath—Andrei claiming that Soviet women enjoy full equality with men, Marina insisting that, regardless of laws, women still do all the cooking, shopping, cleaning, washing, and most of the fretting over children. If more of our leaders were women, she claimed, perhaps we would have automatic clothes washers, dishwashers, prepared foods, shorter lines in the shops. If we are to do our work outside the home, we must have more help inside the home, from machines or men.

This was a woman whose colleagues and students at the Oil and Gas Institute were, to a person, male. This was a woman who knew that, the higher she rose, the fewer sisters there would be. This was a woman who kept a volume of Lenin open on the counter while she cooked, snatching moments to read. Washing dishes, a cloth in one hand and a plate in the other, she would speak about communism, capitalism, the Soviet future, not as abstractions but as palpable realities, her eyes alight.

"Marina is more disciplined than I am, more serious," Andrei admitted. "Me, I am drawn to many things, television and sports, the newspapers, mystery stories, long walks. Marina

Robert Maksimov photograph

A family gathering in the country.

works hard. I try to help her. I buy bread. I order food at my work. I don't like to clean plates, but even that I have learned to do."

I asked how she had come to study philosophy. "When I was a teen-ager, many things in our lives I could not understand. There were contradictions between what was said and what I saw around me. So I wanted to find out the truth, to understand economics and society. The task of a philosopher is to explain the world. But first you must understand it yourself. That is why I decided to study philosophy, beginning with the ancient Greeks. I became a teacher in order to share this knowledge with students. I do not want them to imitate *my* ideas, but to think for themselves, to find solutions for our problems. I do not teach propaganda. I teach young people how to think, so that we can

Robert Maksimov photograph

Flowers from the garden.

A father-and-son tennis match.

make a better world, so we can have more beauty in our lives."

"What sort of beauty?" I asked over the omelettes and sliced peppers, above the ruckus of radio and television.

"I want our people to smile," Marina answered. "I want to see them laugh, not only in their homes, but on the streets, in the shops, in the factories. I want to see joy in their faces."

"What would bring joy?"

"Abundance. The certainty of peace. True democracy. Individuals must have the power to influence society. The state must reflect the desires and imagination of ordinary people."

Andrei declared soberly, "Fear must be eliminated from our hearts. Lenin said that in our country the most difficult task is for every man to kill slavery in his soul. And Chekhov said the same before Lenin. It is a very old need for us."

"Only think of Stalin," Marina said.

"It was not simply fear that kept people silent during Stalin's reign of terror," said Andrei. "It was because he declared that his way was Lenin's way. To disagree with him was to go against Lenin, to become an enemy of the people."

"I want Misha to grow up without fear," said Marina. "I want him to study humanities and foreign languages. I want him to travel freely around the world, to enjoy using his mind."

They planned for Misha to join the Young Pioneers at the age of ten ("so that he may learn to be moral, brave, and a true friend," said Andrei), and to join Komsomol, the Communist Youth League, at fourteen ("to learn about the vision of democracy").

"Then will he join the Party?" I asked.

"Misha will decide for himself," Andrei replied. "Marina and I joined in the period of Brezhnev—the time of *zastoy*, stagnation—because that was the only way to become involved in changing society."

"Now there are other ways, other avenues," Marina added.

Andrei said earnestly, "We are very lucky to be alive in this time, when the world is changing around us every day. We are lucky to be young in a time of revolution."

The Soviet Revolution has continued in fits and starts for seven decades, a long time measured against the lifespan of an individual, but a short time measured against the life of Russian civilization. A few months before my visit, the Orthodox church had celebrated the one thousandth anniversary of the arrival of Christianity in Russia. (Andrei made a point of telling me that the festivities had been covered respectfully on television and in the press: another sign of change.) In the years immediately following Red October of 1917, countless churches, monasteries, nunneries, and cathedrals were destroyed, and the destruction continued on through the reigns of Stalin and Khrushchev. Andrei grieved over each loss. As we journeyed through Moscow, he pointed out sites where religious buildings had been razed to make way for a monument, a warehouse, a swimming pool. "Although I am an atheist, I feel our history is bound up in the church. Through all the invasions and wars, the church preserved our manuscripts and art, the life of the spirit."

Despite the losses, enough ornate, onion-domed churches still survive in Moscow to give the city an ecclesiastical air. We never passed one without a comment from Andrei. Outside the gilded church of St. Nikolai, where we stopped Wednesday noon on our way to the archive, he said, "These treasures belong to all of us, believers and unbelievers alike. They speak of our past. We all believe in the spirit inside," he said, thumping his chest, "whether we call that spirit God or by some other name."

The presence of history came through to me powerfully on our tour of the Central State Archives for Historical Acts. Catherine the Great ordered the construction of the building two centuries ago, to store the records of imperial Russia. Our guide was the director, Mikhail Lukichev, dark-haired and intense, quite young at thirty-seven to be a protector of the nation's memory. In his office, lined with bookshelves that reached to a high and shadowy ceiling, Mr. Lukichev showed me with almost religious fervor a number of the most valuable documents, his fingers hovering respectfully above the scrolls and jeweled books and illuminated manuscripts. Then he led me through the five floors of shelves, a maze of history, aisle upon aisle of brown boxes neatly labeled, and I imagined myself inside the convolutions of a brain. It seemed a sluggish yet potent brain, like that of a drowsing giant. In Andrei's department, half a dozen female clerks were laboriously cataloging the millions of documents by hand, writing in ink on stiff cards, without computers. Slow, slow, yet I had a sense in the archives, as everywhere else in Moscow, of a mind recovering from trauma, from partial amnesia, a mind beginning to reclaim its past.

Andrei felt linked to the past by way of his family, about which he told me that evening as we meandered through the old neighborhood called Arbat, vainly searching for a place to eat. Born in Moscow in 1955, an only child, Andrei had lived until the age of ten along with his parents and his maternal grandparents in one room of a three-bedroom apartment. Another pair of families occupied the other two bedrooms. "It was very, very difficult for us, but not unusual in those days." His mother traveled a good deal in connection with her work as a director's assistant for Mosfilm, the state cinema company. His father was an engineer in a factory. Thus Andrei was raised chiefly by his grandparents. The grandfather, a veteran of World War I, the October Revolution, and the Civil War,

Robert Maksimov photograph

The tennis lesson.

told him spellbinding tales of the gory and visionary beginnings of the Soviet Union. While serving his two years in the army as a paratrooper, Andrei was stationed in the northern city of Pskov. The grandfather wrote him a letter about having served there as a soldier himself, half a century earlier, in the war against the Kaiser. He also recounted being jailed under Stalin, losing his army commission, and emerging from prison to an uncertain life of odd jobs. Was the old man bitter? "No, he considered himself lucky to be alive. Many of his comrades died in Stalin's camps. He insisted that the *idea* of communism was just as valid, despite Stalin. He taught me that Stalin was the *deformation* of communism, a turning away from the true path laid out by Lenin."

Andrei had often told these and other family stories to Misha, who pleased him by retelling them to playmates. "Memories must be preserved in people, not only in books and movies. We must not lose history, because it teaches us who we are."

And so a day that began with talk about the Soviet future ended with talk about the past. The ligaments binding the one to the other, visible in the streets and buildings of Moscow, pass invisibly through consciousness. Andrei finished his family chronicle as we strolled by Pushkin Square, where clusters of gesturing men were talking politics. The square had recently become a rallying place for citizens eager to discuss the changes under way in their society. "You see, it is the question on everyone's mind: Where have we come from? Where should we go?"

After feeding me luscious batter-fried eggplant, fresh from her father's garden, Marina asked me Thursday morning how American Communists were viewed in our country.

"As anachronisms, liars, and hacks," I answered. "We see them as robot servants of an alien power."

"It is because, for you, communism still means Stalinism?"

"For many of us."

Andrei turned from the kitchen window, where he always stood while smoking, in deference to Marina's dislike of the habit. He grimaced. "We are still trying to dig out from under Stalin."

Later in the day we toured the graveyard at the Novodevichy Nunnery, where many of the nation's famous and infamous are buried. Bright flowers had been heaped on the somber stones of Chekhov, Mayakovsky, Gogol, on generals and cosmonauts, singers and scientists, film stars and scholars. Khrushchev's angular black and white marker had been designed, at his own request in his will, by the avant-garde sculptor Ernest Neizvestny, whose works Khrushchev had condemned and who had then to choose exile. A solitary rose lay at the foot of the stone. "Few have anything good to say about Khrushchev today," Andrei murmured, "and yet he was the first to speak the truth about Stalin." Hundreds of people shuffled silently through the forested and ferny aisles, laying bouquets, fingering inscriptions, paying their respects to heroes and heroines. I have never known Americans to approach the dead so worshipfully. By far the largest crowd huddled beside the grave of Stalin's wife. Everyone and everything associated with the godlike ruler was still a potent lure. "Even now," Andrei whispered, "many people think back on him as a man of order, one who built up our strength, who made the world respect us."

Family burial plots in less venerated Moscow cemeteries await Andrei and Marina. "We are deep-rooted Muscovites, back several generations," Andrei explained with evident pride, "and so it is right for us to be planted at last in Moscow dirt."

After supper Thursday night we watched a television showing of *Agonia,* a film by Elem Klimov, about the religious fanatic Rasputin and the end of tsarist rule. Made in 1976, the film had been "put on the shelf" because authorities feared that audiences would see parallels between the social paralysis under the last tsar and the paralysis under Brezhnev. Only after Brezhnev's death and Gorbachev's rise to power, marking a dynamic new era, had the film been released. Andrei and Marina sat through it now a second time, never tiring of the steady diet of history.

That evening the radio played a new song, whose lyrics Andrei translated for me: A green

Robert Maksimov photograph

Misha's first day at school.

shoot has broken through the roadway, splitting the stones of the old road, the road of tyranny, and we will never go that way again.

Over coffee and chocolates the next morning we spoke with shared melancholy of the distance that would soon separate us again. "You must not leave!" said Marina. "You must remain with us for another week."

"For a month," said Andrei.

"A year!" said Marina.

"Until you learn Russian!" Andrei boomed his laugh.

The Russian word *nemetz,* like the Greek root of *barbarian,* originally meant anyone whose speech was unintelligible, and thus an outsider, a presumed enemy. Today, *nemetz* means German. As we nibbled our chocolates, a documentary about German atrocities during the Great Patriotic War was playing on television. Strewn bodies, gutted buildings, grieving survivors. Twenty million dead. Perhaps thirty million, according to some estimates. All four of Andrei and Marina's grandfathers had fought in that war. One was killed by the Nazis, another died soon after from wartime trauma. The trauma still ran like a fissure through all our talk, through the streets of Moscow, across the kitchen table. The only memories of suffering I have encountered that rival this one for intensity are those of Jews remembering the Holocaust and of blacks recalling slavery.

The grandiose park on Moscow's north side, called the "Exhibition of the Economic Achievements of the USSR," which we toured on Friday afternoon, celebrates the Soviet present and future. Airplanes, oil derricks, tractors: the heroism of machines. Yet even here I met with reminders of the painful past. Knowing of my interests, Andrei and Marina led me first to the exhibit on space exploration. Amid the towering rockets and intricate satellites, the object that moved me most deeply was the first Sputnik, a mirror-bright sphere about the size of a volleyball, bewhiskered with antennas, the symbol to me since my twelfth year of our power to reach into space. Next Marina showed me the flower pavilion—gladioli, asters, zinnias, begonias, marigolds, all displayed against carpets of moss, feathery ferns, mottled philodendrons. Andrei meanwhile sat on a bench, muttering, "I am not a man of flowers."

Between pavilions, Marina bought us jam-filled doughnuts, orange soda, rolled-up waffles stuffed with cream. On my tongue the sweetness mingled with the bitterness of departure.

Our final stop was at a recently opened exhibit on the nation's history, ranging from medieval Russia to the modern Soviet Union. What struck me about the exhibit, and what captivated throngs of citizens who crowded around the glass cases, were the revelations about Stalin's terror. Case after case documented the lives of the millions who starved in keeping with Stalin's policies, the hundreds of thousands who were imprisoned and murdered, the countless lives broken by his mad whims. Under the title "Erased Names," Stalin-era photographs with faces blacked out were shown next to archival photographs with the faces restored. A history that had been lost from public view was becoming visible; a history known in bedrooms and whispered in kitchens was finally being proclaimed in the open air. Amid the throngs, Andrei and Marina pressed their faces to the glass and, with taut lips, read of their inheritance.

We emerged from the history exhibit into a misty rain that suited our mood. Marina gave one umbrella to Andrei, another to me. When I opened it, she gently took my arm and I felt blessed, as though a bird had settled there. While Andrei stood in line to buy cigarettes, Marina told me in halting but elegantly pronounced English that she hoped one day to write books, books that would illuminate some part of the world for her people. If she worked very hard, and if she were very fortunate, perhaps some day she would become a professor in a university. She tilted her valentine face at me, to see if I thought her dreams too grand. I smiled to show my confidence in her. The rain, the hand on my arm, the brave English, the confession of modest hopes, all together carried me to new depths of sympathy with this woman, her husband, their people.

We took refuge from the rain in an art gallery. Although abstract, surrealist, and expressionist works had recently been put on display in Moscow, after having been officially denounced for seventy years as bourgeois decadence, here all the paintings were conservative landscapes, village scenes, church domes outlined against sunsets. Having neither the space nor the money to carry back a painting, I asked my friends to advise me which of the small prints I should purchase, one I could hang on my wall at home to remember them by. After some deliberation, Andrei settled on a woodcut of workers and soldiers marching before a triumphal arch. "History!" he exclaimed. "The Soviet people!" No, Marina insisted, I should buy the ghostly moonlit scene of a farmhouse and pasture and trees. It reminded her of a childhood spent living in the country with a dear grandmother. "This will make you think of nature and the Russian earth," she said. They disagreed sharply, arguing for their respective visions: city and country, people and soil, human history and timeless nature, crowds and solitude. Both visions were true, so I purchased both prints. I look at the images now as I write, tiny windows onto that immense land.

From the gallery it was only a few steps to the Church of Ivan the Warrior, where we arrived in time for the Friday evening service. Built to commemorate a victory over Sweden in 1709, and thus another sign of the military current that flows through Russian history, the church is a compact jewel box, its varnished icons and gilded ornaments and sumptuous shrines reflecting light from hundreds of votive candles. As we stood in this glow, the church filled with elderly *babushkas,* and then a few young women, then a handful of men, and finally a clutch of children. The old women knelt, pressed fingers and foreheads and lips to the floor, elaborately crossing themselves, then rose on stiff knees to fondle shrines and kiss the golden frames of icons. What did my scientific materialist friends make of this spectacle? "Very beautiful, very strange," Andrei whispered. Without a word, Marina slipped away to light a candle. Returning, she pointed out to me high in the gleaming nave the icon of St. Mikhail, on whose day their son Mikhail was born. The boy had been christened, and so had she.

On the tenth floor of yet another apartment tower, this one built for employees of Mosfilm, we visited Andrei's parents, who fed us roasted duck and exuberant talk on Friday night. Mr. Svetenko was a booming man in his fifties, vigorous, stout, with an Abe Lincoln fringe of beard, and a monkish circle of hair surrounding a polished scalp. A few years older (and by virtue of that the boss of the family, according to Andrei), Mrs. Svetenko was a plump woman with a big laugh, a small voice, and a smile that shone steadily from a face haloed by wispy gray hair.

The television, which burbled at one end of the table like an idiot guest all during supper, drove our conversation. The report of a chess tournament drew cries of dismay and approval from Andrei and his father. "Where are your great American chess players?" Mr. Svetenko demanded of me. News from the Republican convention, where George Bush had just been nominated, provoked a dispute between son and parents concerning the presidential candidates. News from Korea prompted Mr. Svetenko to ask if I thought the United States would win the upcoming Olympic Games. I told him I had no idea. "No idea? You don't care? Our athletes have been *ordered* to win. They must win for the nation!" Every topic was charged with politics, from Nicaragua to Afghanistan, books to medicine, cars to cartoons. Listening, I could hear in the Svetenkos the same passionate engagement with the world that I had found in Andrei and Marina. In all the Soviets I met, there was a degree of political and cultural alertness that I have rarely encountered in Americans, an alertness from a lifetime of battles fought over their land, their cities, their homes, and their ideas.

After supper, I leafed through the family albums, studying photographs of Andrei from his first months up through school, Young Pioneers, Komsomol, the army, his courtship with Marina, their wedding, the birth of Misha. And then, with Misha's baby pictures, the cycle began repeating itself. I thought of waves forming offshore, rising to a crest, then breaking onto the sand, and new waves forming.

When it came time for us to leave, Mr. Svetenko rummaged through his collection of coins and presented me with a 1924 silver ruble, which shows a peasant and a worker set off against a grain field, factory, and rising sun. "Do you know why the date is important?" Mr. Svetenko asked.

"Lenin died that year," I answered.

He slapped me on the back. I had passed a test.

Bidding us goodbye, Mrs. Svetenko lit up with her beatific smile and uttered her favorite English phrases: "Good evening! You are very kind! America is wonderful!"

A knife clattered to the kitchen floor on Saturday morning. Marina laughed. "To drop a knife means a man will visit."

"And here is the man, but he is leaving!" Andrei gestured at me with spread palms, as though handing me a present.

The present they had been handing me all week, even more precious than their company and food and roof, was their trust. I reflected again on how much courage it took for them to accept this foreigner into their home, without any script, without any notion of how I would see their lives, how I would report their beliefs. Andrei told me with amusement of several friends who had been

Robert Maksimov photograph

astonished that he and Marina would expose themselves to such an unknown and potentially dangerous character. "An American! They say what you write may get us in trouble!"

Writing has often brought trouble in the Soviet Union, both for the writers and for those written about. I knew the record only too well. It was encouraging to see that Pasternak, Akhmatova, Bulgakov, and other great writers of the Soviet era had recently been restored from oblivion, that censorship had been relaxed, that journals and newspapers were allowing for sharp differences of opinion. But how far would *glasnost* go? How long would it endure? Would it survive until after my report of Andrei and Marina's lives reached print?

Our last act before leaving the apartment was to sit a few moments in silence. My friends explained that this is a Russian custom, to assure me of a safe journey, a quick return, and a bond between our hearts while we are parted. Joined all week by talk, we were joined at last by silence.

At the airport, the clock forced me to pull away from their hugs. I passed through the first of the many barriers I would have to cross before reaching my own home. When I trusted myself to turn around, blinking at tears, it was too late, for I could not find their faces in the crowd.

On the plane, too numb to write, I leafed unheeding through a newspaper. English looked odd. As we taxied, the birches along the runway slipping by like needles of light against the somber firs, I came to a news item that seemed worth reading. It quoted the chief Soviet cartographer as saying that ever since the Revolution all maps of his country had been distorted for ideological reasons. Villages had been erased, towns and roads had been moved, the location of natural resources had been concealed, borders had been redrawn. Now the new regime was ordering him to draw up a true map. I read of this as we lifted off from Russian soil. Of course no map can be utterly true, since the world is richer than any image we make of it. No history, no record of a week spent with strangers in an alien city, no account of where we are and of how we reached this place can ever be complete. But some maps are more accurate than others, some histories truer. All history is a selective remembering. We are defined as nations and as individuals by what we do not forget.

Parting at the Sheremetyevo International Airport.

Mary Randlett photograph

And in All Our Works

VALERI VINOKUROV

Old man Monty took his guitar out of its case and made himself comfortable in the chair, which stood with its back to the piano in one corner of the living room. Before entertaining us with a few American folk tunes and humorous songs, sung in a creaky voice but with every word clear, he warmed up his gnarly fingers by playing a melody I recognized at once. It was easy to see from the others' reactions this was meant for their visitor from Moscow.

"You know that music, right?" asked Janet, the charming sister of my host, Don Tufts, whose hospitality I had enjoyed for the past nine days. This was my last evening with Don and Pam, and almost all of the huge Tufts-Montgomery clan had gathered to celebrate the birthday of Aubrey Montgomery—old man Monty.

"Yes, it's from the film *Doctor Zhivago.* It was written by Maurice Jarre."

"I didn't know the composer," Janet said. "Is he French? The movie isn't French."

"It was directed by an Englishman, and the Russian was played by an Egyptian. But I think it was made with American money."

"Did you see it in Moscow?"

"No, somewhere abroad."

"And have you read the novel?"

"A long time ago. In Russian, but printed abroad. It has been published in our country, though, just recently, in the magazine *Novy Mir.*"

The people around us were listening in on our conversation now, and Monty was grinning. He had picked the right opening—or rather, the right finale. The evening—warm, cordial, noisy, talkative—was drawing to a close. It seemed my account of the novel's history, of how it came to be published in the homeland of the great poet, was to be my finale. For it, I had to mobilize all the experience communicating in English that I had amassed over the past few days.

The musical coda to the evening, opened by the guest of honor, was continued by the grandchildren. There was classical music and jazz, piano and guitar solos, piano and guitar duets. At the end, before Monty got his presents, everybody sang "Happy Birthday."

When the guests had left and the children had gone upstairs to bed, Don, Pam, and I sat a while longer in the quiet, tidied dining room, as if to review not only that special evening but also my whole stay with them. I would be leaving for the airport early tomorrow, Saturday. But it was not my presence that had made the evening special so much as the gathering of both families. According to Don, it was only rarely that he and Pam had so many of their relatives in the house at one time, for most of them do not live in Seattle.

Awaiting the visitor from Moscow. The second grade class at Stevens School, with Principal Karen Kodama.

Why not follow the trusty old rule of the playwrights who introduce the heroes of their plays right at the start? You shouldn't expect, of course, that what I am going to say about the Tufts family will be dramatic. It's just that one of the first things that struck me about American life is the extraordinary strength of family ties. People always want to stay in touch. Maybe that's why they are constantly trying to help one another in the ups and downs of business and everyday life.

Well then, my friends Don and Pam live in a house of their own and have three children: Sean (eight), Margo (twelve), and Rachael (thirteen). My friends, I said, not my hosts. It does happen, although rarely, that a brief acquaintance, struck up—as this one was—in the course of business, grows into real friendship. There are certain conditions for this, naturally: there must be a meeting of minds, a kinship of spirit and emotions, maybe even of outlook on life. If the reader has patience enough to read through these remarks to the end, and the author has skill enough to show how such a friendship can come into being in just a few days, then this digression will probably prove unnecessary.

Be that as it may, in those last minutes after the departure of the guests, Don, Pam, and I suddenly understood something and confessed it to one another. Rather shyly, I thought. The book would come out, the Goodwill Games would be held in Seattle, but we would never forget our many hours of conversation over the past several days. We would look for chances to meet again, to write letters, to think and worry about one another's children and then grandchildren. When you come down to it, isn't that a higher and more noble goal than even the joint publication of a Soviet-American book, or the holding of American-Soviet games? Isn't that good will in the abiding, original sense of those two beautiful words? A thread, invisible but so strong, stretched over continents and thousands of miles of ocean.

Don is trim, and elegant, a little over forty. He is the youngest of four children. Millie Tufts, his mother, lives not far from Seattle, in Bellevue. Millie lost her husband, the father of her children, more than twenty years ago. He died before reaching sixty, but he had time to help his children get started. Don's eldest sister lives in California with her husband, who virtually owns Cascade Commercial, the company of which Don is president. His other sister, Janet, spent many years with her husband in Europe, but not long ago, after returning to the States, they separated. Janet moved back to Seattle with her spirited, cheerful daughter Susanna, who is black. (Susanna is adopted, but no one in the family ever remembers this. They have thought of her as one of them for a long time.) They lived with Don and Pam for a year, then Janet found work at Boeing. They now live nearby.

Doug, Don's elder brother, is broad shouldered and muscular. The brothers resemble each other in their faces and overall build, but Doug is a superman in comparision with slender Don. It is as if nature gave Doug the same features, but more generously: his face is broader, his cheekbones are more pronounced, his muscles are more prominent, his torso is more powerful. But they are equally affable and easygoing, and both are good listeners. Even in an argument they are obviously trying to meet you halfway, not backing off or giving in, but eager to find something to agree on.

In the kitchen there is a big map of the world. Each morning, before breakfast, little Sean and I would trace the routes from Seattle to Moscow—all across America, the Atlantic, and Europe, or the other way, across the Pacific and all of the USSR. This evening, at the start of Monty's birthday party, Doug had stood in front of that same map, telling me about his two years as a naval officer during the Vietnam War, about veteran's benefits and the compensation he received for his wounded knee. I told him how a few days earlier, at the United Nations headquarters in New York, I had seen the same map of the world, girded, enmeshed with markers, each of which stood for ten rockets. Imagine it—the whole world wrapped in belts of rockets like barbed wire. And every day, prime ministers walk past that map, ministers of foreign affairs, ambassadors from all countries and their advisers. They go past into the conference halls where they conduct their endless discussions about the fate of the planet, and the map, ensnared in barbed wire, is like a silent reproach: Will they ever send somebody to paint over these black symbols of strength, power, and fear?

"If they would let you and me in there," Doug said, laughing, "and ordinary guys like us from every country, we could agree in one day to get rid of the rockets."

But when Doug and I got to talking about whether big countries have the right to interfere—with planes and ships, artillery and infantry—in the affairs of small countries, our discussion lasted under five minutes. We talked about Vietnam and Nicaragua, Afghanistan and Chile, Czechoslovakia and Panama. We mentioned Pinochet and Qaddafi, Bishop and Amin. Essentially, Doug thought it was all right to "send in troops" against regimes that deny fundamental human rights. Examples were Amin and Hitler.

"You don't think Hitler should have been tolerated, do you?" he asked. "Shouldn't he have been overthrown with military force?"

Yes, no one had interfered then; none of the Reich's neighbor countries had prevented the demented Führer from coming to power. It was almost with the silent consent of the countries who later fought against him as the Allies that Hitler seized the Reichstag. Was it for Doug and me to say, now, what should have been done? Could we

Mary Randlett photograph

At the Tufts family home. Pamela Tufts and Valeri Vinokurov.

Mary Randlett photograph

One world—viewing the global map with the sixth grade at Seattle's Meany School.

say, if the politicians and historians cannot?

And who will decide, I asked Doug, which regime is bad and which is good? Your government dislikes Nicaragua but has nothing against Chile. Wouldn't it be better if nobody ever sent their boys in uniform to a foreign land because the regime there seems bad to someone? But our discussion went no further. Doug disregarded my last question as rhetorical. Just then there was a report on television about the plebiscite in Chile. We were both glad Pinochet had been defeated.

Pamela Tufts, born Montgomery, has two brothers, Patrick and Michael. They were born and raised in Washington State, three hundred miles from Seattle, not far from the Blue Mountains, on a farm that still belongs to their father. Old Monty and his wife, Bernice, had traveled those three hundred miles by car, taking turns with the driving, to get to their daughter's for the birthday party.

Patrick is an international pilot for Pan American Airlines. He dreams about visiting Moscow: "It's great that Pan Am and Aeroflot have started working together. They have joint flights already." And Michael was a teacher, but he has recently changed careers. A teacher's pay is not high by American standards these days. Now he and his wife Sandy have a small store. It is probably not easy to take up a new line of work in midlife, but that situation is evidently a common one, nothing out of the ordinary. A lot would depend on a person's general attitude. After all, Don and Pam are vivacious, full of fun and infectious laughter, and both are working in fields far removed from the education they received.

Don went to a liberal-arts college in Massachusetts. As in most American colleges, he was free to choose his courses. So he studied economics, political science, literature, and art. But he ended up at Cascade Commercial, where he became president in 1983. The company is a middleman, so to speak. It buys furniture and equipment for schools and offices from manufacturers in Washington, Oregon, California, and Ohio, and distributes it to retailers around Washington State.

Don understands economics, of course. He was excited and enthusiastic in telling me about his work. He showed me Cascade Commercial's warehouses, its small computer center, and some of the company offices, including his own, with a personal computer. The company is not a big one, judging by numbers of employees or annual income, but no doubt it does a lot of good, distributing inexpensive and comfortable furniture.

Don starts off to work eagerly each morning (during my stay he left the house several times at five or six, and never later than seven-thirty) and he has a lot of interesting things to say about his ideas and plans for expansion. Still, I can easily imagine Don having shaped for himself a totally different career and destiny. I can see him as a politician, a historian, or a literary scholar.

As for Pam, I have not a shadow of a doubt where she gets her strong roots. In the valley near the Blue Mountains—on the walls of the bedroom where they put their guest from Moscow are marvelous landscapes of the parts around there. Wheat fields stretching out of sight; a modest farm house on a green, airy background; silver-blue mountains covered with mixed forest. Pam took music lessons in school and went on to the University of Washington in Seattle. And, I must say, the campus of the University of Washington (35,000 students) made an unforgettable impression on me. So many American novelists have described those campuses, those university towns. You have to see one, though—the buildings for the different departments, the stadium and gymnasiums, the art gallery, the student bookstore—to understand why the graduates continue for the rest of their lives to take pride in their alma mater.

Pam majored in anthropology and literature. Before her marriage, she worked for the government in Washington, D.C. She is proud of her part in developing a plan to improve the American electoral system; among other things, it lowered the voting age to eighteen.

Pam is strong, agile, and athletic. As a student she did a lot of traveling with a pack on her back. On her own, she spent four months in Europe one year, three months in Mexico the following year.

One evening, when the Tufts family had gathered as usual for dinner (the evening meal, I mean, not our midafternoon dinner), and were telling one another about their day, Sean said his teacher had read them a story about Columbus. Margo piped in with the names of the three ships. It seems they study Columbus in sixth grade, too—in more detail, of course. Don went to the living room to get a children's book from a series about travelers. It so captivated Sean that he started his homework right there at the dinner table. Pam and I told the children about the monument to Columbus in Barcelona, and the model of

Mary Randlett photograph

Discussing the pen-pal project with two sixth graders.

his ship in Barcelona Harbor, visited by crowds of tourists.

Don, too, was fond of travel in his younger days. He proposed to Pam at the Grand Canyon, on a rafting trip fifteen years ago. ("I think that traveling in your own country, seeing it and getting to know it, is as interesting as seeing the world, and certainly no less beneficial—maybe more.") At the time, Don was on his way to Paris, where Janet was living with her husband. Pam said yes, and when Don came back, they got married.

Family and children can be key factors in a woman's life. Pam quit her job and left the Capital; or rather she moved back to Seattle. Until comparatively recently, American women did not embark on full-time careers in as great numbers as did young men. But probably all social movements bear fruit sooner or later, and the feminist movement has been no exception. Together with the rising cost of living, which has made a second income important for the material well-being of families, it has brought about a steady increase in the numbers of working women. Pam, with her outgoing temperament, naturally does not want to be just a housewife. Together with two friends, she runs a small boutique—a shop selling fashionable clothing. The profits, for the time being, are modest. It is a start, though, and there are plans and ideas for making it grow. The store is cozy and tastefully decorated; the prices are moderate or slightly higher than average; the clothes are of good quality, many of them handmade. And the shop is near home, right on Capitol Hill, Pam's own neighborhood, where nearly everybody knows everyone else.

Americans have a concept they call "community." The Collins dictionary defines this as "society, a social group." In everyday use, it means first of all a neighborhood. The *Capitol Hill Times,* for example, is a community newspaper serving two neighborhoods, Capitol Hill and First Hill. The word is also used in a second, extended sense to mean a circle of acquaintance. When a family moves to a new city or neighborhood, friends and relatives will ask about their new community, which is to say the people they come into contact with—whether the neighbors are nice, whether there are people they can visit and invite over, whether they can find babysitters. In that sense of the word, Don and Pam live in a wonderful community.

Capitol Hill has a good number of private homes, which means of course that residents are tolerably well off. There is, however, a wide range of incomes. Indeed, prosperity is not the main criterion for a good community. What determines the quality of a community, what makes it good, are common interests, everything we might call a spirit of kinship. In other words, not just the availability of babysitters, but knowing you can talk to your neighbors about art and literature, about politics and problems with the school system, and that they will understand you.

Schools, I should note, play an important part in making a good community. Again and again, as she introduced me to her guests, neighbors, and business partners, Pam would say: Her daughter, or son, is in the same class with Margo, or Rachael, or goes to the same school as Sean.

I think I ought to explain here, in very general terms, how the school system is organized in the United States. I have always thought we know much more about life in America than Americans know about life in our country, and I have found lots of evidence for that. I won't pretend to say just how this situation came about. Maybe it is because for many years we have published contemporary American authors much oftener than Americans have published our contemporaries. (I will say here that things have now changed a bit in that respect.) Or perhaps it's because the image we have of ourselves as lazy and uninquisitive, handed down through the classics of nineteenth-century Russian literature, has long since ceased to hold true. On the contrary, it is my firm conviction that curiosity, or more precisely a love of knowledge, has become one of our national traits.

But Americans, despite their love of travel and the opportunities they have to indulge it, are not inclined to make a deep study of the mores and daily life of other nations. They content themselves with superficial, incidental, tourists' impressions. Although that, too, is changing. Nowadays, when I meet Americans in different countries and on different continents, they ask more questions than ever before—sometimes quite unexpected ones—about every side of life in

Mary Randlett photograph

At *Tess,* their store on Capitol Hill. Pam with partners Jane Ehlert and Cecilia Somerville.

our country. But in Seattle it was clear to me, and my new friends readily admitted it, that we know more about Americans than they know about us.

There was, however, one glaring exception: I knew almost nothing about American schools. Perhaps this was just my personal lack and says nothing about *our* knowledge of American life. At first I was surprised to discover that in the mornings Margo and Rachael left for school by seven-thirty, but Sean, the youngest, would still be deep in the serious business of getting his breakfast at eight. Afterwards we had time to spend half an hour or so journeying on the map. Around nine his friend, the neighbors' daughter, would stop by, and they would race off to school, packs on backs.

In the course of their education, American children attend at least three schools in three different buildings. At age five they can attend kindergarten (equivalent to the oldest group of preschoolers in our system), where they begin their education. Generally they go to school from ages six to eighteen, which is to say they receive twelve years of education. There are minor variations among the states, and even between different regions of one state, but usually those twelve years are divided as follows: elementary school from first grade through fifth, middle school from sixth grade through eighth, and high school from ninth grade through twelfth.

Furthermore, there are public schools and private schools. Private schools, naturally, cost parents much more than the public schools. When

Don and Pam first told me about this, I supposed they had enrolled their children in public schools because the financial burden of three private-school educations would have been too much for them. They agreed with this, by and large, but explained that they would have found a way, were it not for two important circumstances.

In comparing both systems, Don and Pam have concluded that their own children can get a good education in public schools. Not all parents would agree with this, they say, and not all children thrive in public schools. But they are encouraged by their own three children's experiences in the local system. The second consideration is one to which Don and Pam, and many of their friends and neighbors, give great importance: children in some private schools are in a "hot-house" or sheltered environment, whereas in public schools they meet and interact with all classes of society, with all nationalities and races, with native-born Americans and immigrants from Latin America, Asia, Africa, and Europe. (Incidentally, there are special English lessons in the public schools for recent immigrants.)

Mary Randlett photograph

Off to the soccer games. Pam and Don Tufts with Margo and Sean.

To underscore the point that the material well-being of the parents is not the main factor in choosing a school, Pam noted that the owners of a large Seattle race track and stables send their son to the same school as Margo and Rachael. Pam added that some parents may send their children to private schools not so much because they can afford it (some of them have to make real sacrifices) as because they feel they are giving their children good opportunities. Parents who choose private schools feel they are getting a lot for their money. It is a matter requiring thoughtful choice. To conclude this account of the different kinds of schools in Seattle, I will say that there are also parochial elementary, middle, and high schools—the Catholic schools, for example.

Sean's elementary school is housed in a building dating to the last century. The parents are now collecting money, not just for repairs but for some sort of modernization of the handsome old building with its columns and wide wooden staircase. The school is named for Major General Isaac Stevens, governor of the territory that became the state of Washington towards the end of the last century. As I read about Stevens on the memorial plaque, I imagined a typical character from one of those films about soldiers fighting Indians in the Old West. None of those film characters was particularly sympathetic, as you know. I remembered some conversations I had had with Don and Pam, who take an interest in Indian culture. The whole thing made me somehow uneasy.

The middle school the two Tufts girls attend is named for Edmond S. Meany, another nineteenth-century figure, a professor of history at the University of Washington. I think it's better, in any country, to name institutions of learning for scholars and scientists rather than for military men and politicians, towards whom attitudes can change as years go by. And they change, fortunately, in the direction of—well, call it objective justice, or just objectivity. Go ahead and try, for instance, to rename the university in Leningrad or Rostov. You will run into serious resistance.

The elementary school principal, a vital and gracious Japanese woman, was unable to introduce me to Sean's teacher, who was away that morning attending a lecture whose subject says much: How to keep young children away from alcohol and drugs. "It is a very important problem," the principal said, "and we believe we have to think about it now, although it might seem that elementary school is still a little early."

The middle school occupies a modern, or even modernistic, building of red brick. I was introduced to its principal by Pam's friend, Gloria. Gloria is a lively, expansive, genial Philippine woman. She and I had met before, and she had shown me photographs from her trip to Moscow. She is a school counselor and an adviser on sex education, what we might call the psychology of intimate life. Her role is advisory; she does not teach the curricular sex education class. Gloria leads discussions in various classes but usually meets with the students one-on-one. She spends a lot of time at the school, taking part in all the events there, and the students have come to trust her. Gently and quietly, as befits a psychologist, she goes about her skillful and necessary work.

The school's principal is tall, broad-shouldered, handsome, very proud of his excellent, well-run modern school with its computers and fine gymnasium. He is also proud, I think rightfully so, that in this multilingual school (there are English language classes here) friendship reigns. And the discipline here, it seemed to me, is not something stern, hinging on punishment, but a discipline of conscience and commitment. I got a sense of this after the principal and Gloria invited me to attend a lesson in Margo's large sixth-grade class.

Margo's class is taught by a husband-and-wife team. One evening a few days later I visited the same classroom during an open house—what we would call a parents' meeting. The couple talked so vividly to the parents about their children and the fine points of studying each subject (students in this school begin to move to different subject teachers only in seventh grade) that I was fascinated, even though it was hard for me to catch the details. They also told the parents about my recent visit to the class, mostly of course about the children's reaction to meeting a journalist from Moscow.

Mary Randlett photograph

Coach Don in a huddle with Sean and the soccer team.

And so we enter the classroom, unexpected by teachers or students, right in the middle of an English lesson. They react naturally—excitement, smiles, laughter. Somebody jumps up from the back row and moves closer. As I am being introduced I glance at the blackboard, where three sentences have been written as grammar examples. I read the third attentively: "Mikhail Gorbachev is doing everything he can to make his country develop and progress." While I am reading, Gloria is telling the students about the purpose of my visit to Seattle. I turn to look at the teachers, at the class, and ask hesistantly, "Did you know we were coming today?" Smiles, laughter, puzzlement matching my own. How could we have known?! I look back at the board, and at last the husband understands why I am so surprised. "No, of course we had no idea you were coming," he says. And then, with a little smile, "Is it right, what's written up there?" Yes, of course it's right. Of course. You can't even imagine how right it is, I imagine myself telling the class, that we have lived to see the day when, in an American school, in an English class, such a sentence is used as a grammar example. And I think back: When was I in sixth grade? Well, let's see . . . it would have been from September 1952 to May 1953.

The class is in an uproar, everybody talking at once—kids, teachers, guests. Then the teacher asks everyone to settle down and ask the visitor from Moscow some questions. Instantly there is silence. They are all back in their seats, and there is a forest of raised hands. The first question is the only one I can't answer. A black boy asks me to tell about the recent "government meeting" in Moscow. He means the Central Committee plenum. But all I know is what the American newspapers have said; I had been in New York that day. Then, a flood of questions: How did you like New York? What is Moscow like? How is it different from Seattle? Can you buy jeans and running shoes in your country? Why don't people leave Moscow and move to other parts of the country and buy houses of their own, if in Moscow they have to live in big apartment buildings? How are your schools different from ours? Why do you only play soccer, and not American football? Can a person who lives in Siberia move to Moscow?

What an ordeal for someone whose English is not fluent! But the last question is one I can answer in two words: If we write letters to kids in Moscow, will you take them back so we can be pen-pals?

With pleasure!

Seattle is a sister-city to our own Tashkent. (We would say brothers, but for some reason American cities are always feminine gender—sisters.) Many Seattle schoolchildren correspond with children in the Uzbek capital. On the way home Margo says proudly, "But we'll be the first to have pen-pals in Moscow!" I will wind up the subject of schools now. Even as it is, it seems I have got carried away and given it a disproportionate amount of space in these very limited remarks.

And so, I would bring to Moscow letters not only from Margo's class but from Rachel's seventh-grade class, too. In the time it takes for this book to be published and these lines to find readers, our correspondents Margo and Rachel, together with their classmates, will have graduated from the middle school and moved on to high school. Well, no—the sixth-graders will still be in the same school, finishing up. The main thing, though, is that so many letters will continue to make the long journey from Seattle to Moscow; so many unseen and, I hope, strong threads will link our lands across miles and miles of ocean; so many questions will be asked, back and forth, by Soviet and American children; so many new friends will find one another on both sides of the ocean.

At the opening of the Third International Festival of Films by Women Directors, introducing Lana Gogoberidze, the noted Soviet filmmaker, Rosanne Royer, wife of Seattle Mayor Charles Royer, said that some people in the United States laugh—and not always kindly—about Seattle's active ties with the Soviet Union. "They say citizens of Seattle travel to Moscow so often, they must think it's one of our suburbs." I should note that the mayor's wife, born in Yugoslavia, speaks Russian quite well. We talked with her at a reception honoring the festival's opening, and she told us many interesting things about Seattle. I think it is time I introduced this interesting and lovely city, named for an Indian chief who strove to establish peace in the region. I hope what I have told you already makes it clear that Seattle is a most appropriate successor to Moscow in hosting the Goodwill Games.

Seattle is a dynamic port city with skyscrapers downtown. The rest—starting just outside the city center—is what Ilf and Petrov dubbed "one-storied America." One-storied not in the literal sense, of course (even the private houses may have two or three stories), but in the sense that there are no exceptionally tall buildings outside this downtown center. The city itself has half a million inhabitants; taken together with its suburbs, many of whose residents work in Seattle, the figure comes to two million. It is situated on hills, on the banks of Puget Sound, which opens into the Pacific. Snow-capped peaks surround it. Just outside the city, blending into it, are forests. On the other side of its center—farther from Puget Sound—are lakes, which Seattle takes into itself, settling down gracefully and comfortably along their shores.

By a great many social parameters, Seattle is a lucky city. It seems to have all the advantages of American life to a significant degree, and all the disadvantages—well, to a minimal degree. Jobs are plentiful because the city is still growing and developing, and because it has a good many industries (in particular, a huge aircraft industry), farms of different kinds, businesses, and institutions of learning. Unemployment is considerably lower than in the nation as a whole. Many of the problems facing modern civilization in general, and the United States in particular, are being dealt with more successfully here than elsewhere in the country. Racial problems, for instance. People hear on television about racial tensions in the South and East, or they read about them in the press. Some then say: "Maybe if the media would stop blowing up these problems, the country could just get over them, like we have in our state." Naïve, but there is a grain of truth in it. Sensationalism can aggravate problems, instead of helping to solve them. Don's view is steady and forthright: "At night in downtown Seattle, the problems of our youth—alcohol, drugs, alienation, delinquency—are plain to see. The same as in any town in the world, probably."

Seattle's fight for a clean environment began thirty years ago. Back then, the vast and extraordinarily beautiful Lake Washington (crossed by a floating drawbridge) began to show alarming signs of increasing pollution. The state authorities reacted with the indifference characteristic of any bureaucracy. So the citizens of Seattle joined the battle. But while public opinion progressed towards victory, the lake continued to get dirtier. It took ten more years to clean it up. Today Lake Washington is the pride of the city. If you drive with anybody across the bridge, or along the shore of the lake, you are sure to hear about the victorious struggle for the lake. They will stop at the water's edge so you can see for yourself how clean it is. And they won't fail to add: Never expect too much from government and the authorities. We ourselves have to do as much as possible for our city, which means also for ourselves.

Pollution is a constant threat to the ocean beaches, too. Biology students have made this their special concern. They clean up mile after mile of shoreline. Garfield High School students do their own fund raising to take ocean voyages, going even as far as Australia. The University of Washington's biology students are like a detachment of crack troops in the fight to preserve the environment. One often hears about their oceanographic research—together with their professors, of course—and the resultant benefits for this port city's environment.

Mary Randlett photograph

The totem honoring Chief Sealth (Seattle) in the town of Suquamish.

We drive through the city center, down to the water's edge and, after waiting in a line of cars, onto a ferry. We lock the car and take the stairs up to the deck. Our destination is a cottage by the shore of Dabob Bay, on a plot of land that Don's parents bought for a song some thirty years ago. Since then prices have increased tenfold; Don and Pam couldn't dream of buying a place by the bay now. The tiny house, which Don's father built himself shortly before his death, is worth far more to them than what it would sell for. Don's fondest childhood memories are tied to this quiet spot, and his children have been coming here in the summers ever since they were born.

Half an hour on the ferry and an hour's drive—that is the route that lies ahead of us. In fact, you need longer to get there, what with the sights to be taken in along the way. The trip back really does take just an hour and a half. Traveling down the Kitsap Peninsula, we stop to see the Port Madison and Port Gamble Indian reservations. Rural amenities have made an appearance here: there are mini-tractors; mailboxes line the road, bearing the numbers of homes hidden away in the woods. We also stop at a little church to visit the grave of Chief Seattle, and then at an old Indian cemetery with wooden totems.

I think I have already mentioned Don's and Pam's interest in Indian culture. Prints of paintings by Indian artists adorn their living room—some a century old, others modern, stylized. They know the history of the tribes, too, and of the conquest and settlement of these parts.

I had many conversations with these kind people, my hosts and friends. We would talk at the dinner table, in the evenings after the children had gone up to bed, in the car on our numerous outings, at the central city playground where Margo's soccer team played (more later about soccer and its place in the Tufts family's life), in Don's office and in Pam's shop. We talked about everything imaginable. But we seemed to be pulled closest together in spirit when we talked about one of the most inevitable of human themes—history. The history of one's family and kin, of one's country, of the whole Earth, which belongs to all humanity, that huge society in which each of us is a member. I am describing my personal feelings, naturally, but I believe Don and Pam felt something similar, without trying to put it into words—no one had set them such a task.

Now, as I sit at my typewriter, I try to understand why those conversations about history drew us together so. I find different answers. No, not answers—explanations. No, not explanations either. Versions, maybe. Isn't it because the history of the ancient world—of Egypt, Greece, Rome, Babylon, China, Russia, the Mayans and Aztecs—belongs to all the world's nations, and not just to the nations that presently live in one land or another? Or maybe because even in the Middle Ages all of humanity was less numerous than the population of one of today's great nations, so that all people—isn't it so according to the theory of large numbers?—were once closer to one another, despite not having the means of communication we have in the twentieth century? Or could it be much simpler, just a matter of having something in common; namely, the immense interest in history that has sprung up in recent years among Russians and also, as far as I can tell, among Americans?

What about this shared interest, then? The way I see it, right now Russians and Americans are equally keen to learn about the history of our countries over the centuries—the true story, not slanted to please anybody. Hence, among millions of Russians, the eagerness to read Klyuchevsky or Solovyov, and, at the same time, to fill in the blank spots in the recent history of our Communist Party and the Soviet government. That is to say, we seem to need two kinds of historical knowledge: the long-ago and the recent.

And Americans, I think, feel the same sort of eagerness to acquire two kinds of historical knowledge; although, of course, the spans of time involved are not really comparable—the history of the United States encompasses a mere two hundred years.

"Our country doesn't have the deep roots you do in Russia," Pam's brother Patrick said to me. "That's why we are so interested in the countries our ancestors left behind to come to America." Americans really do take pleasure in telling you that one of their grandfathers or great-grandfathers lived in Norway, France, Russia, or Ireland, and that their grandmother or great-grandmother came from England, Italy, Spain, or Poland. Unfortunately I didn't jot down, and so cannot report exactly, which European countries the founders of the present-day Tufts-Montgomery clan came from. I can only recall that among them were Scandinavian countries (Don and Pam visited there as tourists not long ago and spent a few days in Leningrad, as well), and the British Isles, and that Pam's mother, Bernice, told how one of their ancestors had come to America by way of Russia, where he lived for some time. (If, again, memory serves me well. Alas, I didn't write down the details.)

As for the interest in American Indian history and culture, it springs from the natural human desire to know as much as possible about the people who lived here before you, from whom you inherited this lovely land with its natural bounty. And could that desire possibly fail to call forth and foster the desire to preserve nature and the land? Which is one reason why the oddly sonorous, aboriginal Indian names are preserved for regions, towns, plains, and gorges. Which is also why, here and there along the roadsides, you see the Indian totem poles, mythic figures carved in wood—mostly stylized, to be sure, seldom naturalistic.

I would not characterize Don and Pam as actively religious people. They have strong feelings of Christian faith and believe in God, but they do not belong to an organized church. Our discussion of religion in America centered on its historical interest. After all, in Russia and Europe for many centuries it fell to the church to keep the chronicles and annals of human history—both in the literal, material sense and in the figurative.

It is my impression that, typically, Americans are not indifferent to religion. By and large, the United States is a country of many and varied faiths and creeds. It is not coincidence that the words "In God we trust" are stamped on its coins.

"It could hardly have been otherwise," Don says. "Many people came here, from all parts of the world, to escape religious oppression and persecution. And if they refused to conform at home, preferred to cross the ocean instead, then their religion, whatever it was, must have meant a lot in their lives and outlook. So it's easy to see that in the new land, in their new homes, they raised their children in devotion to that religion. But they also remained tolerant of all other faiths. They understood other people who had suffered as they had. We don't have so many religious conflicts in our country, although there are plenty of others. Our ancestors had seen enough religious persecution already."

That kind of thinking, it seems to me, is based on an astounding faith in tradition. And perhaps, it carries within itself the ability to draw the same sort of connection between the living spirit of modern society and the past, which also comes down to us not only through our upbringing but in our genes as well.

Mary Randlett photograph

At the gravesite of Chief Sealth.

Like many of us, Don has such a tight (I might even say grueling) work schedule that he can't find time to organize his books at home. Especially since there are bookshelves in the basement, where I more or less occupied two rooms—a bedroom and a big playroom with a whole wall of books; bookshelves in the first-floor living room; and bookshelves upstairs, where there are three bedrooms for the children and one for the parents. Nevertheless, poking around among these books—and by the way, is there any more interesting pastime in this world?—I did discover a sort of system in the way they are distributed on the different stories of this large but cozy house. Don sometimes says it is "too big," but they feel fortunate to live here with their family. The system, if I can give that name to something that came into being by chance, not by the will of the books' owners, is that the basement playroom holds books Don and Pam read when they were college students, and probably also in the first few years after college, as the publication dates allow me to surmise.

I will give a few titles, grouping them roughly according to subject, but jumping from shelf to shelf: *Politics and Bureaucracy; The Common Market; Communism, Conformism, and Civil Liberties; American Foreign Policy Since 1945. Why Lenin? Why Stalin?* from a series called *Critical Periods in History;* and from the same series, *Lincoln and the First Blow; McKinley, Bryan, and the People; Labor in Crisis: The Steel Strike of 1919;* and *Irish-American Nationalism.* Next to these, not part of the series, are *International Politics Since 1945,* and a thick volume titled *The Bolsheviks,* subtitled *The Intellectual, Personal, and Political History of the Triumph of Communism in Russia,* published by the Harvard University Press in 1965.

I asked Don about the books concerning our country or telling about it directly: "Are the authors hostile towards us, or friendly, or at least trying to be objective?"

"Hard to say, especially since it was a long time ago that I read them. It's probably different in each book. You can be sure, though, that I tried not to read the ones hostile to you. When I was in college, you see, I tried to read as much as I could about the facts, without any interpretation. That's what the professors taught us: Know as much about facts as possible, and look for the explanations yourself. What other way is there to learn how to think independently?"

The living-room shelves hold mostly encyclopedias and books on art, especially painting. This is where *American Impressionism,* which had been presented to me at the university gallery, has found a place. (By this time Don and I have discovered that Impressionism and post-Impressionism are favorites with both of us.) Upstairs, in the hall between the bedrooms, are adventure stories and modern literature: Evelyn Waugh, John Le Carré, Herman Hesse, Norman Mailer (*Why Are We in Vietnam?*), John O'Hara, Arthur Hayley.

And of course on all the shelves, on every storey, the classics. Here my system (invented or discovered?) breaks down. But surely it has to be so: the classics are with us always. So on different shelves I find classics in uniform bindings, like our *Library of World Literature:* Byron, Tennyson, Longfellow, Emerson, Maupassant, and Chekhov. There is a complete Shakespeare, of course, and next to it, *A Hero of Our Time.* From the *Arabian Nights* and Dante; through Franklin, Darwin, and Fielding; to Ibsen, Joyce, and Huxley; and next to these, *War and Peace, The First Circle,* and Stanislavsky's *My Life in Art.*

"What are you reading now?" I ask Don and Pam.

We go upstairs to their bedroom. There are three or four books on each of their night tables. With some embarrassment they admit that both of them usually read several books at once, depending on their mood and how tired they are. Well! And here I have been doing the same all my life, and also feel shy about admitting it. It makes you look scattered, not serious. In my childhood, my father would get after me for "my attitude towards books." Lately, though, I notice him doing the same thing. A lover and respecter of books like him! Is it a sign of our fast-moving times? Has the frantic tempo taken hold of everything, even broken into the intimate sphere of our encounters with books?

Don is reading Le Carré's *A Perfect Spy,* plus a history of the nineteenth century, and *Lonesome Dove,* about cowboys in the Old West. (Pam smiles: "He's a cowboy at heart.") And also two books by Tom Clancy. The latter is very popular in the United States at present. He has written four novels, two of them about how a war could begin between us and the Americans.

"We attacked you of course?" I ask Don.

"You guessed it," he laughs. "I haven't read those books, but I know you're right. These two are about other things."

Back in Moscow I had read (in *Ogonyok*) an interview with Secretary of Defense Frank Carlucci, from which I learned that he reads Tom Clancy. The man who sat next to me on the flight from New York to Seattle was reading Clancy, too. A popular fellow, it seems.(The reader may recall that when we visited Sean's elementary school, his teacher was away. A student teacher was looking after the class. There were no lessons; the kids were drawing. Several boys were drawing combat scenes on separate sheets of paper. Afterwards they glued the sheets together, producing a huge panorama of battle. I couldn't resist asking who was fighting whom. A snub-nosed, freckle-faced boy answered seriously: "We haven't decided yet. But not you and us." He's too young to read Tom Clancy, I guess!)

Pam recently finished reading that same cowboy novel. On her night table now is a novel by Pat Conroy (the story of a young man's coming of age) and a book by Robert Fulghum. I will say a few words about the latter, since the author lives in Seattle. On my very first evening at the Tufts house, a neighbor boy brought by this book, just out, as a present for Pam. Fulghum lived a long life and held many different jobs before he began to write. He calls himself a philosopher, and his title asserts: *All I Really Need to Know I Learned in Kindergarten.* The book is subtitled *Uncommon Thoughts on Common Things.* Pam looks forward to reading the book. She believes education and self-education should be parts of a single process, and she never tires of telling this to her daughters and son.

Busy as they are, Don and Pam spend a lot of time with their children. On weekends they are together from morning to night, although they still have a full timetable. This is determined, first of all, by the schedule of soccer games, which occupies a considerable part of the kitchen wall. The Tufts are a real soccer family; all of them are interested in the game. Don coaches the boys' team that Sean plays on. Pam is a referee for both boys' and girls' games. Margo is the center forward on her team, which by the way is coached by one of the best women soccer players I've seen. Rachael is an excellent player; at the technical competitions she was among the best not only in the Capitol Hill club but in the whole city.

Tacked to the kitchen wall are the rosters of the three teams, the telephone numbers of all the parents, the practice schedules, and a calendar of Saturday and Sunday matches. (Tournaments are in two rounds: at-home games and away.) On a separate list are the games Pam will referee. The children and their parents refer to these schedules no less often than to the school calendar. There are car trips to be made to each practice and then back home, and the whole family likes to turn out for the most important games to root for their team. It couldn't be done without help from the neighbors, to be sure. The parents take turns, depending on who has time, filling up their cars with kids and then dropping them off at their homes after the practices and games. It seemed to me that soccer plays an important part in creating a strong community in Capitol Hill. The clubs are amateur, of course. The minimal dues go almost entirely for the uniforms, which are very handsome. All questions concerning the conduct of practices and competitions are decided democratically, and both parents and children are encouraged to help out.

Mary Randlett photograph

Digging for clams on Dabob Bay.

On Saturday evening, after a full day of soccer (Sean's team won 5 to 1; Rachael's tied 1 to 1; the match Pam refereed ended 0 to 0; Margo's team had an easy practice in preparation for a big game on Sunday), we get into the big car (the "family" car; Don goes to work in a little Peugeot) and head off for the Children's Theater, situated in a large and charming park. The seats are arranged in curving tiers. Children sit up front; parents, in the back.

It no longer surprises me that in the theater—as yesterday evening at the horse races at Longacres—we meet many acquaintances from the community. But today, of course, everybody is with their children. We see a difficult play based on the works of Bel Kaufman. Difficult, in the first place, because of its unusual genre: a satire on school life with a tragic episode—a girl commits suicide when the teachers misunderstand the first stirrings of her heart. In the second place, because of the slang and jargon that fill the dialogue; among the characters are a number of children from poor families. And in the third place, because the play is for grownups as well as youngsters. In the car on the way back, Pam will have a lot to talk over with the children: Did they understand it all? Did they understand it right? Sean had already seen the play, attending it earlier with his school. He didn't understand a lot of it then. Now his mother has explained many things.

When the play is over, the actors come out from behind the curtains, sit down on the edge of the stage, and invite the children to ask them questions. Later, in the car, Margo says the discussion with the actors has helped her to understand. The kids in the audience ask all kinds of questions: about the plot, about the deep feelings of the characters. And also, naturally, the usual question from a youthful audience: Was all this the truth, or was it make-believe? In answer to this last question, the actors say that Bel Kaufman worked as a teacher in New York; many of her writings had to do with the problems of schoolchildren. She wrote about education and relations between parents and children. But the actors also talk about the laws of art, and how sometimes something made up can be the truth, and something that really happened may not have any artistic truth in it.

Mary Randlett photograph

Traveling by ferry on Puget Sound. Two Soviet visitors and their Seattle hosts.

As we were walking back through the park from

the theater, I asked Pam if she knew that Bel Kaufman was the granddaughter of Sholom Aleichem, the great Jewish author who wrote in Hebrew, Yiddish, and Russian. He was born in Russia, where he lived until 1905, and he died in New York in 1916. Pam didn't know about him, although she is familiar with many turn-of-the-century Russian writers. I suddenly remembered having seen Norman Jewisohn's film *The Fiddler on the Roof* several years back; it is based on *Tevye and His Daughters* and other works by Sholom Aleichem.

"Oh! That was a wonderful movie!" Pam exclaimed. "I saw the play, too, but I didn't know that the author was from Russia."

In the car she told Don and the children about this intersection of two literatures in different generations. And although Sholom Aleichem didn't write in English, as his granddaughter does, it is clear that there are no barriers to understanding when the truth is told about the life of a nation. I could see Mikhail Ulyanov in the role of Tevye, and I longed to get back to Moscow quickly.

Nine days in one house—it's like the film *Nine Days in One Year.* But it seems as if an entire lifetime has passed. Or more precisely, into my life a new life has entered, a real life with all its human joys and complications, the life of a warm and loving family. Long after this book appears, long after the Goodwill Games are over, I will still remember my conversations with Don and Pam about the Impressionists, Rembrandt and the Guggenheim Museum, Bach, the Beatles, and Michael Jackson. I will remember showing Janet our Russian alphabet, and her teaching me how to use the enormous atlas. Talking with Margo about the goal she scored and listening to her play "Edelweiss." ("Is it true I play soccer better than the piano?") Watching a home video with Sean, where I see my new friends up in the mountains, skiing with their friends. Spending a Sunday with more of their friends, talking about literary questions (how emigration affects a writer) and political matters (they were trying to choose between Bush and Dukakis). And I will never forget what old Monty told me when we were saying goodbye: "I'm glad that I've lived to see the day that a guest from Moscow is living in my daughter's house, and I can be sure he's a real friend."

On the plane from New York to Moscow I read the *Moscow News*—an issue I didn't have time to read back home and so brought along with me. In an article by the French writer Alain Bosque (a Russian émigré, incidentally), addressed to Soviet readers, I run across these words: "Like the Americans, we tend to think that 'to be is to have.' Citizens of the different Western countries are beginning to feel averaged out, mutually interchangeable. Lying in wait for us are illiteracy, forgetfulness of history, the mechanization of our minds. . . . What you want from us are material goods, visible and palpable things. What we want from you is something invisible, impalpable. The soul, the spirit—it is a simplified concept, difficult to define. You have not lost it."

With hand on heart I can say that I agree fully only with Bosque's concluding phrase. But it is just because we have not lost the soul—and indeed why should we have?—that I cannot agree with the rest of what he says. Of course I won't argue—he has been living in the West his whole life and must know what he is talking about. But, as our proverb says, face to face you cannot see the face. I won't argue, but in principle I disagree even with what he says about us. Do we need friends in the West only for "material goods, things visible and palpable"? Is it only for such things that our souls are open?

I won't argue, but my own experience, which certainly is not as rich as Bosque's, shows something quite different. It shows people always remain people, no matter what goods they have, or how many. Because it is not by bread alone. . . . Because anyone who has preserved his or her soul will certainly include spiritual things in the concept of goods. And as to who puts what first, the material or the spiritual, that depends on the individual, regardless of where one happens to be born or to live. And the soul, the spirit, is not really such a simplified concept. Difficult to define? When we say "a kindred spirit" or "an open soul," aren't these exact definitions? Our souls are open to discover, all around us, kindred souls.

Picture Credits

USA title page: pp. 2–3, photograph © Will Landon. **History:** p. 14, *Abraham Lincoln,* daguerreotype attrib. Christopher S. German (Larry West); p. 16, *Teddy's Rough Riders* (Laurie Platt Winfrey, Inc., New York); p. 17 (Union Pacific Railroad Museum); p. 18, Vail, *Monticello* (Blérancourt Museum); p. 19 (State Historical Society of Wisconsin); p. 20, Homer, *Snap the Whip* (Butler Institute of Art, Youngstown, Ohio); p. 23 (Franklin D. Roosevelt Library); Russell, *Buffalo Hunt No. 39,* Linda Lorenz photo (Amon Carter Museum, Fort Worth); p. 27, Anon., *Washing Gold* (Bradley Smith); p. 28, Culverhouse, *Skating Scene* (J. Clarence Davies Collection, Museum of the City of New York); p. 29, Nat Norman photo (Museum of the City of New York); p. 30, Peale, *Thomas Jefferson* (Independence National Historical Park, Philadelphia). **Geography:** pp. 54, 58, 59, 60, 61, 63, 64, 65, 66, 67, 68, photographs © David Muench 1989; p. 57, Larry Cort, Rainier Mapping. **Art:** p. 98, Krasner, *Desert Moon* (Robert Miller Gallery, New York); p. 100, Eakins, *The Actress* (Philadelphia Museum of Art. Gift of Mrs. Thomas Eakins and Miss Mary Adeline Williams); p. 101, O'Keeffe, *Black Cross* (© The Art Institute of Chicago, Art Institute Purchase Fund, 1943.95); p. 102, Dove, *Thunder Shower,* Linda Lorenz photo (Amon Carter Museum, Fort Worth); p. 103, Rivers, *Russian Revolution,* John Tennant photo (Hirshhorn Museum and Sculpture Garden, Smithsonian Institution. Gift of Joseph H. Hirshhorn Foundation, 1966); p. 104, Marsh, *Twenty Cent Movie* (Whitney Museum of American Art, New York); p. 105, Wood, *Fall Plowing* (Deere & Company Art Collection); p. 107, Davis, *Rapt at Rappaport's,* Marianne Gurley photo (Hirshhorn Museum and Sculpture Garden, Smithsonian Institution. Gift of Joseph H. Hirshhorn Foundation, 1966); p. 108, Nevelson, *Night Presences,* Park Avenue and 92nd Street, New York City; p. 109, Hopper, *Office* (© The Metropolitan Museum of Art, Art Institute Purchase Fund, 1953, 53.183); p. 111, Wyeth, *Adrift* (© Andrew Wyeth, Wyeth Collection, Chadds Ford, Pennsylvania); pp. 112–13, Frank, *Natural History,* Zabriskie Gallery, NY, photo (Betsy and Frank Goodyear); p. 114, Neel, *The Family,* Zindman/Fremont photo (Robert Miller Gallery, New York); p. 115, Stella, *Brazilian Merganser* (M. Knoedler & Co., New York); p. 116, Lichtenstein, *I Can See the Whole Room!* (© Roy Lichtenstein. Leo Castelli Gallery, New York); p. 117, Segal, *Walk, Don't Walk,* Jerry Thompson photo (Plaster, cement, metal, painted wood, and electric light. 104 × 72 × 72 inches. Collection of Whitney Museum of Modern Art. Purchase, with funds from the Louis and Bessie Adler Foundation, Inc.; Seymour M. Klein, President; the Gilman Foundation, Inc.; the Howard and Jean Lipman Foundation, Inc.; and the National Endowment for the Arts. 79.4); p. 118, de Maria, *Lightning Field,* John Cliett photo (© DIA Art Foundation, 1980); p. 119, Holt, *Sun Tunnels* (John Weber Gallery, New York); p. 120, Lin, *Vietnam Veterans National Memorial,* William I. Clark photo (National Park Service, U.S. Department of Interior, Wash., D.C.). **Literature:** p. 146, Lawrence, *Library Series,* Chris Eden photo (Francine Seders Gallery, Seattle); pp. 148, 149, 151, 152, 153, 154, 155, 156, 157, 158, photographs © Nancy Crampton 1989. **Science and Technology:** p. 180, Stella, *The Brooklyn Bridge: Variation on an Old Theme* (1939. Oil on canvas. 70 × 42 inches. Collection of Whitney Museum of American Art. Purchase 42.15); p. 182, Sellstedt, *The Erie Canal* (Albright-Knox Gallery, Buffalo, New York); p. 183, *Benjamin Latrobe* (Office of the Architect of the Capitol, Wash., D.C.); p. 184, *Erie Railway Poster* (Coverdale and Colpitts); p. 185 (Emerson House, Concord, Massachusetts); p. 186 (Photographic Records Office, National Archives, Wash., D.C.); p. 187 (National Film Board, Canada); p. 188, Lewis W. Hine photo (George Eastman House, Rochester, New York); p. 189, Benton, *America Today: City Building* (Equitable Life Assurance Society of the United States); p. 190, Bohrod, *The Big Blow, the Bessemer Process* (National Steel Corp., Pittsburgh, Pennsylvania); p. 191, © Bruce Davidson, Magnum; p. 192, Sheeler, *Classic Landscape* (Mr. and Mrs. Barney A. Ebsworth Foundation); p. 193, Crockwell, *Paper Workers* (National Museum of American Art, Smithsonian Institution, transfer from U.S. Dept. of Labor). **Sports:** p. 220, Tilden, *The Baseball Player* (National Baseball Library, Cooperstown, New York); p. 222, Magee, *The Second Great Match Game* (Yale University Art Gallery, Whitney Collection of Sporting Art); p. 223 (Culver Pictures); pp. 224, 225, 227, 229, 230 (National Baseball Library, Cooperstown, New York); pp. 231, 232, 233 (UPI/Bettmann Newsphotos); p. 234 (National Baseball Library, Cooperstown, New York); pp. 235, 236 (UPI/Bettmann Newsphotos); p. 237 (National Baseball Library, Cooperstown, New York); p. 238, Robert K. Wood photo; p. 239 (Museum of Modern Art, Film Stills Archive); pp. 242, 243, 244–45, 247 (UPI/Bettmann Newsphotos). **Ways of Life:** pp. 302, 305, 306, 307, 309, 310, 311, 313, 315, 317, 318, photographs © Mary Randlett 1990.

Soviet photographers: Dimitri Debabov, Igor Gavrilov, Sergei Kivrin, P. Krivtsov, Aleksandr Makarov, Oleg Makarov, Robert Maksimov, Evgeny Miransky, Vassily Mishin, Aleksandr Pushkarov, Vladimir Raitman, Vladimir Safronov, Vladimir Semyonov, Lev Sherstennikov, Yuri Sokolov, S. Vysotsky, TASS (Telegraph Agency of the Soviet Union), APN (Novosti Press Agency).